CHRIS SCOTT updated this new edi... first staggered up the Pennine Way as a teenager in the mid-1970s, hobbling into Kirk Yetholm with his boots in his hands. Since then he's walked in many of the wilder parts of Britain, the USA, France and Australia.

Among other books, for Trailblazer he's the author of the *Adventure Motorcycling Handbook*, *Sahara Overland* and the forthcoming *Overlanders' Handbook* and *Morocco Overland*.

EDWARD DE LA BILLIÈRE worked on the first edition. He specializes in natural history, conservation, travel and adventure travel stories, writing regularly for *The Daily Telegraph* and *The Independent* as well as various magazines, and freelancing for the BBC's Natural History Unit on Radio 4 and BBC1.

He lives in the Peak District National Park with his wife Pips and their two boys, Barnaby and Toby, and he moonlights as a white-collar crime lawyer in Manchester.

KEITH CARTER is the co-author of the first edition. His interest in the great outdoors was kindled on a school trip to Snowdonia which hooked him for life. Work became what he did between walks and he has since explored almost every corner of the British Isles with occasional forays into France, Austria and the USA.

Writing articles for magazines led him into guidebook writing and he now spends most of his time re-discovering Scotland, cultivating organic vegetables and growing willow. He is the author of *Offa's Dyke Path*, also from Trailblazer.

Pennine Way
First edition: 2004; this second edition: 2008

Publisher
Trailblazer Publications
The Old Manse, Tower Rd, Hindhead, Surrey, GU26 6SU, UK
Fax (+44) 01428-607571; info@trailblazer-guides.com
www.trailblazer-guides.com

British Library Cataloguing in Publication Data
A catalogue record for this book is available from the British Library

ISBN 978-1-905864-02-7

Editor: Anna Jacomb-Hood
Additional research: Lucy Ridout
Proof-reading: Nicky Slade
Layout: Chris Scott and Anna Jacomb-Hood
Illustrations: © Nick Hill (pp53-5)
Photographs (flora): © Bryn Thomas except: C2 middle right,© Edith Schofield;
C2 bottom left and centre © Charlie Loram
Cover photograph: © Chris Scott
All other photographs: © Chris Scott unless otherwise indicated
Cartography: Nick Hill
Index: Chris Scott, Lucy Ridout, Jane Thomas

Warning: hill walking can be dangerous
Please read the notes on when to go (p22-4) and on health and outdoor safety (pp68-70).
Every effort has been made by the author and publisher to ensure that the information
contained herein is as accurate and up to date as possible. However, they are unable
to accept responsibility for any inconvenience, loss or injury sustained by anyone
as a result of the advice and information given in this guide.

Printed on chlorine-free paper by
D2Print (☎ +65-6295 5598), Singapore

Pennine Way

EDALE TO KIRK YETHOLM
planning, places to stay, places to eat,
includes 137 large-scale walking maps
and 235 GPS waypoints

KEITH CARTER
EDWARD DE LA BILLIÈRE

SECOND EDITION RESEARCHED AND UPDATED BY
CHRIS SCOTT

WITH ADDITIONAL MATERIAL BY
DAVE GOODFELLOW, LUCY RIDOUT
TOM READ. PETER STOTT

TRAILBLAZER PUBLICATIONS

Dedications

From Edward: To Pips, who carried the real load
while I was out walking and having fun in the name of work.

From Keith: For Annie

Acknowledgements

From Chris: Thanks to Lucy Ridout, Dave Goodfellow, Tom Read, Peter Stott, Anna Jacomb-Hood and everyone who helped along the way with suggestions and additional information. Thanks also to Julie Francis, David Harrison, Ian Hinks, Ian Molloy, Ian Potts, Chris Sainty, Justin Turner, Rosalyn Vahter and Peter White.

From Edward: It was when I started putting the first edition of this book together that I fully realized how much work goes into keeping the Pennine Way open. It is not just the steward-ship put in by the countless number of farmers over whose land you will walk: there is an army of people who maintain the stiles, the path, the signposts, and even decide on whether a section of the route needs varying. I cannot thank all of them enough for keeping this route going. Additionally the work of the Edale Tourism Association deserves high praise for ensuring your walk can get off to a good start. All of the national parks have been extreme-ly helpful – the Peak District, the Yorkshire Dales and Northumberland – as have the huge number of tourist offices on the route. The Association of National Parks was a great help in aiding my understanding of how these vital national treasures, the parks themselves, came about and fit into the wider community.

Along the route the people I met, asked questions of, and those whose hospitality at B&Bs and pubs I enjoyed, coloured the Pennine Way in rosy glow for me; even though it is as green as Britain gets.

Finally, and most sincerely, I must thank Keith Carter for stepping in to help me out with this project and for his skill, dedication and artistic flair which helped complete the book. And above both of us stands Charlie Loram, whose editorial skill, lawyer-like atten-tion to detail, and passion for all things kind to Mother Earth, led me, and then Keith, along the path to print. Thanks to you all.

From Keith: Thanks to those who helped me complete the first edition, particularly the series editor, Charlie Loram, for his insistence on attention to detail. Also at Trailblazer, thanks to John King, Patricia Major, Anna Jacomb-Hood, Nick Hill for all his work on the maps, and Jane Thomas for the index.

Thanks also to my companions on the trail, to all those who patiently answered my questions along the way, in particular the Bayes family at the Pen-y-ghent Café in Horton-in-Ribblesdale and to Annie, my wife.

A request

The author and publisher have tried to ensure that this guide is as accurate and up to date as possible. Nevertheless things change. If you notice any changes or omissions that should be included in the next edition of this book, please write to Trailblazer (address on p2) or email us at info@trailblazer-guides.com. A free copy of the next edition will be sent to per-sons making a significant contribution.

Updated information will be available on the Internet at
www.trailblazer-guides.com

Front cover: High Cup Nick © Chris Scott

CONTENTS

INTRODUCTION

PART 1: PLANNING YOUR WALK

About the Pennine Way
History 9 – How difficult is the Pennine Way? 9
Route finding 10 – GPS 10 – How long do you need? 12

Practical information for the walker
Accommodation 13 – Information for the foreign visitor 17 – Food and
drink 18 – Money and other services 19 – Walking companies 20

Budgeting 21

When to go
Seasons 22 – Temperature, rainfall and daylight hours 23
Annual events 24

Itineraries 25
Village and town facilities 26 – Suggested itineraries 28 – Highlights 31

What to take
Travelling light 33 – How to carry it 33 – Footwear 34 – Clothes 34
Toiletries 35 – First-aid kit 35 – General items 36 – Sleeping bag 36
Sources of further information 37 – Camping gear 38 – Maps 38

Getting to and from the Pennine Way
National transport 40 – Local transport 41 – Public transport maps 42
Public transport table 44

PART 2: THE ENVIRONMENT AND NATURE

Flora and fauna
Wild flowers, grasses and other plants 47 – Trees, woods and forests 49
Birds 51 – Mammals 56 – Reptiles 58

Conserving the Pennines
Government agencies and schemes 59 – Campaigning and conservation
organizations 62

PART 3: MINIMUM IMPACT WALKING AND OUTDOOR SAFETY

Minimum impact walking
Economic impact 63 – Environmental impact 64 – Access and the right
to roam 66

Outdoor safety
Avoidance of hazards 68 – Weather forecasts 69 – Blisters 69
Hypothermia 69 – Hyperthermia 70 – Sunburn 70

PART 4: ROUTE GUIDE AND MAPS

Using this guide
Trail maps 71

The route guide
Edale 72

Edale to Crowden 74 (Upper Booth 80, Snake Pass 80, Torside 84, Padfield
& Hadfield 84, Crowden 84)

Crowden to Standedge 84 (Standedge 89, Diggle 90)

Standedge to the Calder Valley 92 (Blackstone Edge 94, Mankinholes 94,
Hebden Bridge 99, Blackshaw Head 102)

Calder Valley to Ickornshaw 103 (Colden 103, Widdop 107,
Ponden 108, Stanbury 108, Haworth 110, Ickornshaw 115, Cowling 115)

Ickornshaw to Malham 117 (Lothersdale 117, Thornton-in-Craven 121,
Earby 121, East Marton 121, Gargrave 123, Airton 125, Kirkby
Malham 128, Malham 128)

Malham to Horton-in-Ribblesdale 131 (Horton-in-Ribblesdale 138)

Horton-in-Ribblesdale to Hawes 140 (Hawes 147)

Hawes to Tan Hill 151 (Hardraw 152, Thwaite 158, Muker 158, Keld 158,
Tan Hill 161)

Tan Hill to Middleton-in-Teesdale 163 (Bowes 165, Baldersdale 172,
Lunedale 175, Middleton-in-Teesdale 175)

Middleton-in-Teesdale to Dufton 175 (Holwick 179, High Force 182,
Forest-in-Teesdale 182, Langdon Beck 182, Dufton 188)

Dufton to Alston 192 (Garrigill 200, Alston 201)

Alston to Greenhead 205 (Slaggyford 208, Knarsdale 208, Greenhead 214)

Greenhead to Bellingham 218 (Burnhead 218, Once Brewed 220,
Stonehaugh 224, Hetherington 226, Shitlington Crag 226, Bellingham 228)

Bellingham to Byrness 230 (Byrness 238)

Byrness to Kirk Yetholm 238 (Uswayford 244, Kirk Yetholm 252, Town
Yetholm 253)

MAP KEYS 255

APPENDIX GPS waypoints 256

INDEX 263

INTRODUCTION

Of all the long-distance trails in the British Isles the Pennine Way, 256 miles (412km) along the backbone of northern England, is pre-eminent. The first to be opened as a National Trail, to some it's the best; it's certainly the best known and it's arguably the hardest.

Anyone who completes the Pennine Way will refute the suggestion that it was easy. It isn't. It requires fitness, determination, good humour and adaptability because your walk won't go smoothly all the time. There will be days when you wish you'd never crawled out of bed, but there will be others when you feel invincible, when you can walk all day and arrive at your next stop, raring to go.

The Way takes you through most of the inland habitats of flora and fauna in this country and you'll see a wonderful variety of plant and animal life. You'll start with a testing trudge over the peat moors of the Peak District and continue into the South Pennines past such milestones as Stoodley Pike and Calder Vale. You then move into Brontë country and will pass Top Withens, said to be the Wuthering Heights of Emily's novel.

Your path continues past reservoirs and windswept moorland until Lothersdale, the last former mill town, now a village with an incongruous factory chimney. The bedrock now turns to limestone and you enter the lowlands of the Airedale Gap where a delightful riverside walk leads to Malham. The climbing resumes, up onto Fountains Fell and Pen-y-ghent and then down into Horton-in-Ribblesdale in Three Peaks country, a land of wide skies and magnificent views. Through Swaledale the Way continues, where Hawes and Keld lead to lonely and deserted Baldersdale: the halfway point.

Passing Teesdale's churning waterfalls, the Way then breaches the North Pennines to behold the stunning glaciated chasm of High Cup and thereafter the homely village of Dufton. Here begins the much-dreaded traverse of Cross Fell, at 2930ft/893m the walk's highest point. Gradually descending from the wilds of the North Pennines you reach Hadrian's Wall, archaeologically and historically one of the most evocative places in Britain. Along with High Cup, the walk along the Wall is one of the most outstanding days on the trail.

North of the Wall you enter the vast forests of Wark and Redesdale, eventually reaching the village of Bellingham. One more day to the lonely forest outpost of Byrness is followed by the suitably climactic 27-mile (43km) slog over the Cheviots to the end at Kirk Yetholm.

An unexpected bonus of the walk, particularly for city-based walkers, is the pleasing time-warp effect evoked in some villages; Garrigill being a good example. Here you'll enjoy a kind of Blytonesque rural British apogee: the tranquil village green surrounded by the pub, the post office/shop and a church.

For some the walk changes their lives. Certainly completing the Way proves there's nothing you can't do once you set your mind to it and, however you do it, the Pennine Way stands supreme.

About this book

This guidebook contains all the information you need; the hard work has been done for you so you can plan your trip from home without the usual pile of books, maps, guides and tourist brochures. It includes:

● Guidelines on where to stay; from wild camping to guesthouses
● Walking companies if you want an organized tour
● A number of suggested itineraries for all types of walkers
● Answers to all your questions: when to go, degree of difficulty, what to pack and the approximate cost of the whole walking holiday

When you're all packed and ready to go, there's detailed information to get you to and from the Pennine Way as well as 137 detailed maps (1:20,000) and 10 town plans to help you find your way along it. The route guide section includes:

● Walking times in both directions
● GPS waypoints as a back-up to navigation
● Reviews of accommodation; campsites, hostels, B&Bs and guesthouses
● Cafés, pubs, tea-shops, restaurants, and shops for buying supplies
● Rail, bus and taxi information for all the towns and villages on or near the Way
● Street maps of the main towns
● Historical, cultural and geographical background information

Minimum impact for maximum insight

Nature's peace will flow into you as the sunshine flows into trees. The winds will blow their freshness into you and storms their energy, while cares will drop off like autumn leaves.
John Muir (one of the world's first and most influential environmentalists, born in 1838)

Why is walking in wild and solitary places so satisfying? Partly it is the sheer physical pleasure: sometimes pitting one's strength against the elements and the lie of the land. The beauty and wonder of the natural world and the fresh air restore our sense of proportion and the stresses and distractions of everyday life slip away. Whatever the character of the countryside, walking in it benefits us mentally and physically inducing a sense of well-being, an enrichment of life and an enhanced awareness of what lies around us.

All this the countryside gives us and the least we can do is to safeguard it by supporting rural economies, local businesses, low-impact methods of farming and land-management and by using environmentally sensitive forms of transport – walking, of course, being the best.

In this book there is a detailed and illustrated chapter on the wildlife and conservation of the region and a chapter on minimum impact walking with ideas on how to tread lightly in this fragile environment; by following its principles we can help to preserve our natural heritage for future generations.

About the Pennine Way

HISTORY

In 1935 the journalist Tom Stephenson used the title 'Wanted: A long green trail' for an article. He was the first to suggest a public trail along the backbone of England, the Pennines, ending just over the Scottish border.

His quest was taken up by many and over the years new rights of way were created until eventually one long chain of 256 miles (412km) was established from Edale in Derbyshire to Kirk Yetholm in Scotland. It officially opened as the Pennine Way in 1965,

Who'd begrudge this slab causeway across sodden Black Hill?

making it the first official long-distance footpath in Britain. In its early days the Pennine Way was hard-going because a substantial part of the route crossed water-logged bogs which made sodden feet a guarantee at some stage. Today walkers never get wet as often as 20 years ago because of the Herculean efforts that have been made to lay a trail of reclaimed stone slabs. Most welcome these, others scorn them. They are but an example of how the face of the British countryside has changed, and will continue to change, over the relatively short time that this route has been open.

HOW DIFFICULT IS THE PENNINE WAY?

If attempted in a single continuous slog, the Pennine Way is tough. Although only a few days might be really challenging, walking daily for at least a fortnight come rain or shine will take it out of you. The weather can whip in unchallenged from the west coast and leave you drenched or even frozen. Without GPS, navigation is sometimes tricky, especially for those unfamiliar with map reading. Half the Pennine Way is on open moorland and one quarter on rough grazing; only a tenth passes through forest, woodland or along riverbanks.

This level of difficulty is what gives the Pennine Way its kudos. You'll end most days feeling the strain but ideally will recover overnight, and once the aches subside you'll be able to bask in the glory of your achievement.

If attempted in a single continuous slog, the Pennine Way is tough.

Do not be put off. Although the walk is not as popular as it used to be and fewer than 4000 people attempt the trek annually, overall the **gradients** are pretty tame; it's the duration that does you in. There are 178 miles (286km) on gentle slopes of less than five degrees, 20 miles (32km) on slopes of ten to fifteen degrees, and only 3¹/₂ miles (6km) on steep slopes of more than fifteen degrees. All in all this totals 40,000ft/12,000m of ascent but if you can both read a map and comfortably walk at least 12 miles (19km) in a day you should manage it; just don't expect every day to be a walk in the park.

ROUTE FINDING

Winding your way through villages and farmyards and out over open moorland, navigation along the Pennine Way can – depending not insignificantly on your route-finding experience – be notoriously tricky.

There are plenty of photogenic wooden signposts along the route (as pictured left), but there are also plenty of places where you'll be left guessing. Fortunately, on some open moorlands, the presence of slabbed causeways not only make for easy going across the mire but also act as an easy-to-follow trail, even in zero visibility. Nevertheless, there are enough places on the Pennine Way, both in the valleys and on unslabbed moors, where poor visibility could leave you helpless. In such conditions, if you've lost track of your position, the traditional map and compass are of little use. With the absence of visible landmarks to correlate with a map, at best you can guess your position and head off cross-country on a bearing hopefully leading to a recognizable track or road. In some conditions such actions can be a recipe for a hill-walking disaster.

GPS
I never carried a compass, preferring to rely on a good sense of direction... I never bothered to understand how a compass works or what it is supposed to do... To me a compass is a gadget, and I don't get on well with gadgets of any sort. **A Wainwright**

While modern Wainwrights will scoff, more open-minded walkers will accept GPS technology as an inexpensive, well-established if non-essential navigational aid. To cut a long story short, within a minute of being turned on and with a clear view of the sky, GPS receivers will establish your position and altitude in a variety of formats including the British OS grid system (see p38), anywhere on earth to an accuracy of within a few metres.

One thing must be understood however: **treating GPS as a replacement for maps, a compass and common sense is a big mistake**. Although current units are robust, it only takes the batteries to go flat or some electronic mal-

PLANNING YOUR WALK

function to leave you in the dark. GPS is merely a **navigational aid or back-up** to conventional route finding and, in almost all cases, is best used in conjuction with a paper map. All a GPS does is stop you exacerbating navigational errors or save you time in correcting them.

Using GPS with this book is *an option*. Without it you could find yourself staggering around mist-clad moors all night, or ambling confidently down the wrong path. With it you can reliably establish your position, or quickly find out how far and in what direction it is to a known point on the trail.

Using GPS with this book

It's anticipated you won't tramp along day after day, ticking off the book's waypoints as you pass them because the route description and maps are more than adequate most of the time. Only when you're **unsure of your position** or which way to go might you feel the need to turn on the unit for a quick affirmation.

Most of the book's maps feature numbered waypoints from Edale to Kirk Yetholm. These correlate to the list on pp256-62 which gives the longitude/latitude position in a decimal minute format as well as a description. You'll find more waypoints on bleak moorland sections such as Cross Fell, where a walk can degenerate into a prolonged stumble through thick mist. Typically the end or start of a slabbed section is also marked, as well as cairns and other significant landmarks or turnings. In towns and villages waypoints are less common but in places can still be useful to pin down an unsigned turn down an alleyway, for example.

You can either manually key the nearest presumed waypoint from the list in this book into your unit as and when the need arises. Or, much less laboriously and with less margin for keystroke error, download the complete list for free as a GPS-readable file (but not the descriptions) from the Trailblazer website. You'll need the right cable and adequate memory in your unit (typically the ability to store 500 waypoints or more). This file, as well as instructions on how to interpret an OS grid reference, can be found at: 🖳 **www.trailblazer-guides.com/books/pennine way/GPS**.

You'll soon discover that it's possible to buy state-of-the-art **digital mapping** to import into a GPS unit with sufficient storage capacity. Advanced GPS users may like this option but it has to be said it's about as useful as

Some days are clearly better than others.

internet on a mobile phone. Reliability and battery/charging issues aside, the pocket-sized receiver you'll typically use will have a screen far too small to give you the 'big picture' and currently the cost of this digital mapping will exceed a set of easy-to-use OS paper maps which, while bulky, are always preferable.

It's worth repeating that 98.2% of the people who've ever walked the Pennine Way did so without GPS so there's no need to rush out and buy one. Your spending priorities ought to be on good waterproofs and a sturdy pair of boots. However, all those thousands will have had their frustrating moments of navigational uncertainty and reliable technology now exists to reduce mistakes. Correctly using this book's GPS waypoints will get you back on track and dozing in front of the pub fireplace or tucked up in bed all the sooner.

HOW LONG DO YOU NEED?

It's no surprise: the slower you go the more you'll take in and get out of the Pennine Way, if for no other reason than you're not continually preoccupied by aching limbs and attaining your next destination. Nevertheless some stages along are simply not shortenable without resorting to the flexibility of wild camping (see p14) and for many, time is money; not all of us can afford to dally. The Pennine Way record stands at an absurd if impressive $3\frac{1}{2}$ days; most mortals average 17 days over the walk, and even then not without some gnashing of teeth. On this schedule there'll be some long days of well over 20 miles (32km), but at least one rest day. Anything less, even a couple of days, can be really pushing your luck and is best left to fit walkers or second attempts when you know the lie of the land and how to pace yourself.

... most mortals average 17 days over the walk

Doing the walk in several stages

While most walkers set out to do the Pennine Way in as short a time as possible, they include those who fail early or wage an increasingly miserable battle of mind over matter. Doing it in a single stage you get the weather and conditions you're given. There is no time to nurse injuries, exhaustion or low moods as, especially if you've booked accommodation, you must always press on.

My recollection of doing the Pennine Way in the 1970s was much like this: a gruelling march from hostel to booked hostel. Thirty years after my first walk, this update was undertaken in four four-day stages (partly because of the amount of research required). At this pace I found the combined 16-day walk never came close to being a chore. Within reason I was also able to pick good spells of weather while also avoiding crowded weekends with their need to book accommodation. Each four-day morsel was anticipated with pleasure rather than dreaded, as some days had been in my teens.

Although I had no choice this time round and a part of me still itches to bang it out in one go, I feel sure I got more out of doing the walk in stages and met as many doing it like this as those taking it on in one fell swoop.

Before you plan anything read the comments from Pennine Way walkers in the boxes on p25, p29, p30 and p32.

Practical information for the walker

ACCOMMODATION

Places to stay are numerous and well spaced along most of the Pennine Way, allowing for a modest flexibility in your schedule. Apart from in the high season (mid-summer), it's not necessary to **book** bunkhouses, hostels and B&Bs weeks ahead but doing so a few days in advance adds to peace of mind (see box below.

Unless you take the hardcore camping option, accommodation adds up to the **biggest expense** of your walk, and because you can have a fortnight in Thailand for the same money as a fortnight's B&Bing on the Pennine Way, the trail is less popular than it used to be. As a result many B&B owners, often in important villages, are throwing in the towel; Thornton-in-Craven in 2006 was a good example. In that same year the drastic YHA hostel closures proved to be less of a disaster than anticipated, with many hostels taken on by new independent owners. In reality, at the time of writing, only two hostels have not reopened (see p16).

❏ **Should you book your accommodation in advance?**

When walking the Pennine Way it's advisable to have your night's accommodation booked by the time you set off in the morning. Although it may compromise your spontaneity, most daily stages are pretty clear cut and booking enables you to enjoy the walk (or suffer its torments) knowing you have a secure bed come nightfall.

That said, there's a certain amount of hysteria regarding the booking of accommodation, some insisting you start booking at least six months in advance. Whilst it's true that the earlier you book the more chance you'll have of getting precisely the accommodation you want, booking so far in advance does leave you vulnerable to changing circumstances.

In my experience, the situation is not as bad as some suggest, at least not outside the high season (by 'high season' I mean the summer period coinciding with the long school holidays in the UK – from the middle of July to the first week of September). Outside this period, and particularly in April/May or September, as long as you're flexible and willing to take what's offered you should get away with booking just a few nights in advance, or indeed often just the night before. Indeed for this update walked in May and June I never booked accommodation and only got caught out in Alston and Greenhead of all places and had to get a taxi to a distant B&B. The exceptions to this rule are **weekends** and places where accommodation is limited.

If you're planning on staying in **youth hostels** the same applies though do be careful when travelling out of high season as many hostels close for a couple of days each week and shut altogether from November to Easter. Once again, it's well worth booking at least one night before, and well before that if it's a weekend or the summer holidays, to make sure the hostel isn't fully booked or shut.

If you have to **cancel** do try and telephone your hosts; it saves a lot of worry and allows them to provide a bed for someone else.

PLANNING YOUR WALK

Campsites

Campsites along the Way range from a sloping field shared with livestock and a basic toilet, to offer-it-all caravan parks with widescreen DVDs to rent. Short of wild camping, this is by far the cheapest option at generally around £5 per person although in these crowded British Isles, for a walker **campsites** might not be considered the best of all worlds. You lack the freedom and exhilaration of sleeping out in the wilds (see below) and the negligible sound proofing of close-packed tents means a rowdy group can ruin your evening.

... consider combining camping with the convenience of eating in local cafés and pubs.

Furthermore, many 'campsites' these days are actually caravan parks with just a small patch of grass allocated for the dwindling numbers of backpackers. You end up in the corner of what feels like a grassy car park surrounded by static, sat-dished caravans occupied by weekenders. You'll spend little money of course, but the only real advantage over wild camping is a perceived sense of security, the ablutions block and a pub meal down the road. Compared to B&Bing, your rucksack will of course be heavier and the rub is that the price you pay for good quality lightweight gear (4-6kgs for a tent, mat and bag) would pay for a week of B&Bs.

However, as long as you can avoid packed campsites, autonomy in sleeping arrangements lightens the load in other ways; there's no need to book accommodation, you can change your plans as you go and so treat yourself to something more comfy whenever it's available.

As you'll typically be in or near a village or town, carrying **cooking gear and food** is not really necessary; the Pennine Way may be tough but it's not remote. Consider making life easier for yourself by combining inexpensive camping with the convenience of eating in local cafés and pubs.

Wild camping (see also box p28)

The Scots have a more enlightened attitude but the official line in England and Wales is that sleeping wherever you like is not allowed **unless you have the permission of the landowner**. Acquiring this permission is in most cases totally impractical and will doubtless be negative but, up to a point, in the hills wild camping is generally **tolerated on the uncultivated open fells** beyond the last farm wall or fence and well away from any livestock.

And so it should be; if walking along England's backbone is a great adventure, in good weather how much better can it be to watch the sun set and rise in some of these wild places? Indeed, if you're attempting the walk in less than a fortnight, some nights in the wild will be your only option. Whether you have to or you want to, the chance to spend the night out in the Pennine wilderness cannot fail to make your experience all the more memorable.

The key to this activity is **discretion and respect**.
● Camp late or out of sight (use green tents or bivi bags) and leave early
● Camp in very small groups; two tents maximum
● Never make open fires

● Bury or pack out your toilet waste (see p65-6)

● Leave no trace of your passing

If you get spotted by the landowner, as long as you clearly look like a walker in transit he probably won't shoot you, but if he asks you to move on, you must comply. Bedding down late and leaving early should avoid the chances of such a confrontation.

As for **eating**, as suggested opposite, eliminate the paraphernalia and chores involved with cooking. Eat

Maybe not every night, but this is the way to really enjoy the Pennines.
© Geoff Crowder

locally then walk on to your pitch with a back-up of ready-to-eat foods. Try and plan your camp spot so that you can get to a café within an hour or two of setting off next day.

In the Pennines one wild camping black spot is the **Kinder Scout**; the first day out of Edale. Because of the high peat fire risk during very dry and always busy summers it's not unknown for rangers to set out of an evening to harry wild campers. Spare the hassle and save your wild nights until you're over the Snake Pass, if not the A62. Ever busy **Hadrian's Wall** is also a place you'd want to camp discreetly or just keep going; head for the Wark Forest instead.

Camping barns, bunkhouses and hostels

Basic stone barns to always crowded, booked and busy hostels await you and it's possible to stay in this type of accommodation on almost every night of your walk, so keeping your expenses to a minimum.

Apart from this good value, their other appeal is the ease of **meeting fellow walkers** and having the time to get to know them, rather than a transient 'ow do' on the trail. This bonhomie can get tested when the kitchen resembles Dresden circa 1945 or a snorer gets into their stride (earplugs are a must), but you get what you pay for.

The simplest and cheapest of all are **camping barns** (£4-5 per person) which, at a minimum, provide a roof over your head, a sleeping platform on which to lay your bag and mat, a cooking area for your stove and a toilet. You'll need to bring full camping gear apart from a tent but some barns also provide hot water, showers, cooking facilities and a wood-burning stove.

Bunkhouses (£6-13) are independent hostels in all but name; they are sometimes part of the YHA but not always. They are equipped with bunkbeds, full cooking facilities, showers and a drying room. Most assume you will have your own sleeping bag with you, although it's often possible to hire bedding for the night. A few even provide breakfast and an evening meal.

Accommodation is usually in bunk-bedded same-sex rooms and there's always a self-catering kitchen. In addition, a good-value three-course evening meal costing £10 and a packed lunch (about £5) are available at some places.

PLANNING YOUR WALK

To stay at a **YHA hostel** you need to be a member of the **YHA** (☎ 0870-770 8868, 🖳 www.yha.org.uk, or join at any hostel). Annual membership costs £9.95 for under-26s or £15.95 for over 26s (which includes under 18s travelling with you). You can either book accommodation online through the YHA website or by phone. If booking less than a week in advance phone the hostel direct.

Including Kirk Yetholm in Scotland, there are 14 **YHA hostels** along or close to the Pennine Way, a few still owned by the YHA, the smaller ones now independently owned or bought and leased back by local councils, but all still bookable via the YHA under its 'Enterprise' scheme. Their size and facilities vary from simple cottages, as at Mankinholes or Byrness, to purpose-built buildings like Hawes or Malham, or former country houses turned into activity centres where uncorked kids drugged by the country air bounce off the walls; Edale YH springs to mind. Prices range from £12 to £15 including breakfast.

Of the other former YHAs which were dropped during the big sell-off in 2006, Keld has new owners, Baldersdale is no longer a hostel, and in 2007 Bellingham (see p228) re-opened on a new site.

Bed and breakfast

B&Bs are a British institution, although not always for the right reasons. For anyone unfamiliar with the concept, you get a bedroom in someone's home along with in most cases the legendary cooked Full English Breakfast the following morning. The main advantage on the Pennine Way is you can travel light, sleep well and start the day with a good feed. At the more rural places, or those with friendly owners, you also gain an insight into how the locals live.

British B&Bs in popular or seaside locations can be notorious for both jamming in beds and crumby facilities; it has to be said B&Bs along the Pennine Way are of a much higher standard. Tacky or fussy joints with 'polite' notices on all surfaces are far outnumbered by well-kept town establishments, unpretentious old farmhouses or characterful country homes with enthusiastic owners.

What to expect Any B&B depending on Pennine Way custom can be considered 'walker friendly' and arriving looking like a drowned rat is expected. Some places have drying facilities and understand that you may well want to do nothing more than collapse.

An **en suite** room attracts a premium although often this can be just for a cramped shower cubicle squeezed in next to a loo. So don't automatically turn your nose up at a bathroom across the corridor which is often more spacious with a deep, inviting bath just waiting for you to turn the taps on and ease away the aches with a long hot soak.

Single rooms are usually poky 'box' rooms and are rarely offered. **Twin** rooms have two single beds while a **double** is supposed to have one double bed. **Family** rooms sleep three or more. Some B&Bs offer an **evening meal**, particularly if there is no pub or restaurant nearby. Check what the procedure is when you book. Many will do a **packed lunch**, too; ask the night before.

Rates B&B prices are usually quoted on a per person per night basis and range from a very rare £18 for a room with a shared bathroom up to £50 or more per person for a very comfortable room with private bathroom and all mod cons. Most places listed in this guide are around £30.

Be warned that if you're staying on your own most places will charge you a **single person's supplement** of between £5 and £10 if only a twin or double are available – some even charge you for a double and, unless you pay for two people, many won't accept bookings from solo travellers for double or twin

---

❏ **Information for foreign visitors**

● **Currency** The British pound (£) comes in notes of £100, £50 (both rarely seen or used), £20, £10, £5 and coins of £2 and £1. The pound is divided into 100 pence (usually referred to as 'p') which comes in silver coins of 50p, 20p 10p and 5p and copper coins of 2p and 1p.

● **Rates of exchange** Available from 🖥 www.xe.com/ucc, among other places.

● **Tipping** is not expected as it is in the US, but is welcome at around 10%.

● **Business hours** Most **shops** and main **post offices** are open at least from Monday to Friday 9am-5pm and Saturday 9am-12.30pm. Many choose longer hours and some open on Sundays as well, while some village shops may close early one day during the week. **Banks** have a variety of opening hours from as early as 9am to as late as 5.30pm. As a rule of thumb most are open from at least 10am to 4pm Monday to Friday, but in small places they may only be open for, say, three half days per week.

● **Pub** opening hours have become more flexible lately so each pub may be different. However, it's likely that most pubs on the Pennine route will continue traditional opening hours from 11am to 11pm with some still closing in the afternoon.

● **Holiday periods** Most businesses in England shut on the **national (Bank) holidays**: New Year's Day (January 1st), Good Friday and Easter Monday (March/April), the first and last Monday in May, the last Monday in August, Christmas Day and Boxing Day (December 25th and 26th). **School holiday** periods are generally as follows: a one-week break late October, two weeks around Christmas and the New Year, a week mid-February, two weeks around Easter, and from late July to early September.

● **Weights and measures** In September 2007 the European Commission announced they would no longer attempt to ban the pint or the mile: so milk can continue to be sold in pints, as can beer in pubs, and road distances will still be given in miles. Most food is now sold in metric weights (g and kg) but the imperial weights of pounds (lb) and ounces (oz) can also be displayed.

● **Telephones** The international access code for Britain is +44, followed by the area code minus the first 0, and then the number. It's cheaper to ring at weekends and after 6pm and before 8am on weekdays. If your overseas **mobile phone** (cell phone) does not work in the UK due to band issues, basic models can be bought new from £25 without a SIM card, after which a 'no strings' pay-as-you-go tariff will be most convenient in the short term.

● **Emergency services** For police, ambulance, fire and mountain rescue dial ☎ 999.

● **Travel/medical insurance** The European Health Insurance Card (EHIC) entitles EU nationals (on production of the EHIC card) to necessary medical treatment under the UK's National Health Service while on a temporary visit here. However, this is not a substitute for proper medical cover on your travel insurance for unforeseen bills and for getting you home should that be necessary. Also consider cover for loss and theft of personal belongings, especially if you are camping or staying in hostels, as there will be times when you'll have to leave your luggage unattended.

● **British Summer Time (BST)** BST starts the last Sunday in March, ie the clocks go forward one hour, and ends the last Sunday in October ie the clocks go back one hour.

rooms at **weekends** as they can usually be sure to fill them with two people. Owners change their prices at a moment's notice in response to the number of visitors, so use the prices in this book as a rough guide. In the low season (September to March) prices may come down to some extent.

Guesthouses, hotels, pubs and inns

Guesthouses are hotel-like B&Bs. They're generally slightly more expensive (£30-40 per person) but can offer more space, an evening meal and a comfortable lounge for guests.

Pubs and inns often turn their hand to mid-range B&B accommodation in country areas and although these businesses are less personal; you may find the anonymity preferable. They can be good fun if you plan to get hammered at the bar, but not such fun if you're worn out and trying to sleep within sound of the same rowdy bar. In this case it's best to ask to see the room first or specifically ask for a quiet room.

Hotels cost around £60-120 for the room, usually inclusive of breakfast. Some are fantastic places with great character and worth the treat – but more likely they are places you're forced to go to when all the cheaper alternatives are full.

FOOD AND DRINK

Drinking water

Even in our day-to-day lives most of us are usually under hydrated. On the trail it's now widely accepted that an adequate intake of water is essential to your well being. What is adequate will depend on the individual but a person of average height and build needs between **two and four litres a day**.

Filling up at Hern Clough, just before Bleaklow, on a hot day out of Edale.

These days many walkers use a plastic water bag (eg a Camelbak) which often slots into a purpose-built sleeve in their pack. The drinking tube enables you to effortlessly sip on demand without breaking your stride. This system is by far the best way to ensure you drink regularly and frequently, but because the unseen bladder can run out (or may not be big enough on a hot day) carry a **500ml bottle as a back up**.

On longer days over wild country you'll need **extra water** so look out for opportunities for refills: farmsteads will often oblige. There are days, however, when taps are in short supply and you have to resort to natural sources. Many people are squeamish about using such water – the 'dead sheep upstream' is a commonly invoked scenario. The fact is, on the **high fells** away from livestock, agricultural run-off and former mine workings, water is as pure as it gets in the UK. Using these sources can **reduce your water payload** or give yourself a good drink (or even a cooling wash) without cutting into your own supplies.

What is safe is really just a matter of using your common sense and intu-

... a person of average height and build needs between two and four litres of water a day

ition. The higher the source or the faster the river the better; avoid slow-moving or stagnant sources although sipping from transient rockpools filled by recent rains is fine. If you still have visions of a rotting ewe's eye staring at you just upstream, use one of the many compact, pump-action **water filters** (tablets are too slow). Near running water wild campers in particular should employ the toilet guidelines given on pp65-6.

Note that whatever the adverts imply, beer is not a thirst-quenching substitute for water, while tea and coffee are diuretics which shoot through the body. Along with food to help absorb it, **fresh water** is best, its loss minimized by a **hat** and backed up by a handful of rehydration sachets, such as Dioralyte (see p35).

Buying camping supplies

With a bit of planning ahead there are enough shops to allow self-sufficient campers to buy supplies along the way. All the known shops are listed in Part 4. The longest you should need to carry food for is **two days**. Hours can be irregular in village shops although camp stoves, gas canisters or meths are usually available in general stores. Coleman Fuel is not so widely found.

Pubs

Pennine pubs are a great place to unwind and, apart from the few towns with restaurants, are often your only choice for a meal. With Britain's long overdue food revolution continuing apace, pubs have also been forced to become more than drinking dens. Places where your meal flips from freezer to microwave to plate are thankfully in decline. Despite the name, **bar meals** can be eaten at a regular table and at best have a home-

A Lamb Henry and chips at the Stag in Dufton. God save the Queen!

cooked appeal which won't find you staring bleakly at an artfully carved radish entwined around a lone prawn. All menus include some token vegetarian options and, if there is a traditional Pennine Way dish it must be **Lamb Henry**, found on menus from Edale to Dufton and beyond. How better to recharge your stomach than with a quivering shank of Pennine lamb slathered in gravy, two veg and of course a pint of Black Sheep. It makes the walk worth walking.

MONEY AND OTHER SERVICES

Cash and a couple of cards are the best means of paying your way on the walk. Don't expect an **ATM** in every village but remember that many shops now have ATMs or offer 'cashback' when you buy something. It's also worth knowing that most accommodation places including B&Bs will take **cheques** from a British bank. **Travellers' cheques** are of limited use on the Pennine Way.

While there may not be **banks** or ATMs in every village, several **Post Offices** now allow cash withdrawals with a debit card and PIN number, or a chequebook and debit card. However, as the era of the country post office is in decline check with the Post Office Helpline (☎ 08457-223344) that the post offices en route are still open. Post offices also provide a useful **Poste Restante** service (see box p25 and 🖥 www.royalmail.com). Where they exist, special mention is made in Part 4 of **other services** such as **outdoor gear shops**, **laundrettes**, **pharmacies**, **medical centres** and **tourist information centres**.

WALKING COMPANIES

If you prefer the planning and baggage carrying done for you, or like the company of other walkers as well as an experienced guide, the **walking companies** below will be of interest to you. Packages usually include meals, accommodation, transport arrangements, minibus back-up and baggage transfer.

Baggage-forwarding services also serve independent walkers, collecting and delivering your gear to your next accommodation by late afternoon; all you need on the hill is a daypack with essentials. The cost is around £6.50 a day and you can book collection for any stage you need it. Don't overlook the ethical and ecological issues of such services: a fleet of half-empty vans trundling around the Dales doesn't do much for your hitherto pristine carbon footprint. Recognize that **taking too much** is a very common mistake. For those not camping or intent on carrying the complete works of Dostoyevsky in hardback, it's hard to see how you'd need more than 10kg of gear.

● **Brigantes Walking Holidays** (☎ 01729-830463, 🖥 www.brigantesenglish walks.com) Self-guided holidays, accommodation booking and baggage collection along the entire route as well as car storage near Edale.
● **Discovery Travel** (☎ 01904-632226, 🖥 www.discoverytravel.co.uk) Offers a comprehensive range of walking holidays for the Pennine Way and other footpaths. They have a 21-day self-guided holiday or three one-week holidays, with B&Bs and baggage forwarding.
● **Footpath Holidays** (☎ 01985-840049, 🖥 www.footpath-holidays.com) Runs guided tours of the Pennine Way in wisely broken up six-day stages of around 80 miles with accommodation in one town which you return to nightly (the southern section is based in Hebden Bridge, the central in Hawes; the northern section is based in Hexham).
● **Sherpa Van Project** (accommodation ☎ 01609-883731; baggage ☎ 01748-826917, 🖥 www.thepennineway.co.uk) Sherpa does not offer the walk as such but operates an accommodation-booking service as well as baggage collection from Malham northwards; they also have an online forum.
● **UK Exploratory** (☎ 01942-826270, 🖥 www.ukexploratory.co.uk) A well-selected 6-day/85-mile self-guided holiday from Edale to Malham (£380; single supplement £60) and a 7-day/106-mile holiday from Malham to Alston (£420; single supplement £80). They also offer a baggage-transfer service.

Budgeting

Compared to its neighbours England is no longer a cheap place to go travelling. Your trip budget depends on the level of comfort you're prepared to lavish upon yourself – and, up to a point, how fast you can walk! Obviously the least expensive scenario would be walking flat out on the fast pace schedule in the itinerary boxes on pp28-30, wild camping every night and and living off wild roots, berries and roadkill. At the other extreme you could avail yourself of a fully guided tour being collected nightly by minibus to your cosy hotel.

Even if you may think that spending opportunities are rather limited along the Pennine Way, the tendency among many walkers is to budget over optimistically.

Your budget depends on comfort levels ... and up to a point, how fast you can walk!

ACCOMMODATION STYLES

Camping
You can get by on less than £5 per person per day if you wild camp and cook all your own food; if visiting a campsite add another fiver. Most walkers would find it tough to live this frugally and know that part of the fun is the odd shower, pint and a Full English every now and then, in which case £10-12 per day would be more realistic.

Bunkhouses and hostels
You can't always cook your own food in hostels/bunkhouses so costs can rise: £18-23 per day will allow you to have the occasional meal out and enjoy a few local brews. If you plan on being fed most nights, add another £6-9.

B&Bs
B&B rates per person can range from £20 to £50 or more a night but of course you get a good feed to set you up for the day. On top of that add £10-15 to cover a packed lunch and a pub meal in the evening. You'll soon find doing the walk at a relaxed three-week pace could put your budget into four figures.

OTHER EXPENSES

Think carefully about how you're going to **get to Edale** – fairly straightforward – **and back from Kirk Yetholm** – more convoluted. If using trains, buy a flexible ticket well in advance to gain a reasonable fare. Incidental expenses can add up: pub lunches, soft drinks or beer, taxis to take you to a distant pub or back onto the trail in the morning. This does not include finding out that some vital item of your equipment has been left at home or is not performing well. Add another fiver a day to cover such eventualities.

When to go

Wildflower meadows above
Gargrave in early June.

SEASONS

The **main walking season** in England is from Easter (March/April) through to October; in terms of weather and the lack of crowds the best months in which to do the walk are **May, June** and **September**.

With rising temperatures – but excepting the monsoon-like weather of 2007 – the Pennine's once-sodden reputation is becoming less reliable.

Spring

The month of **April** is one of the most unpredictable for walkers. The weather can be warm and sunny, though blustery days with showers are more typical; there might be snow still lying on the hills. On the plus side, the land is just waking up to spring, there won't be many other walkers about but there will be plenty of wild flowers and the bird song will be at its best.

May and **June** are a great time for walking the Pennine Way; the school holidays and associated mayhem are weeks away and all you'll meet are fellow walkers. Temperatures are not too warm, the weather is as dry and clear as can be expected, wild flowers are out in their full glory and the daylight will outlast your stamina. Make the most of it.

Summer

July and **August** herald the arrival of the tourist hordes. Places such as Haworth, Malham and the Dales become leisure battlezones at weekends, tiny villages are congested with traffic and accommodation gets booked out. But, as always in England, there's still a good chance of at least some rain during this time.

Pinhaw Beacon in May – there may be
trouble ahead.

Autumn

A slower pace of life returns as schooling resumes. Late **September** and early **October** see stunning colours in the woods and on the hills. You're less likely to meet other walkers, but more likely to encounter rain and strong winds. Temperatures remain mild.

Winter

Late **October** and **early November** reliably bring up a crop of glorious crisp clear days, but winter is on its way. The days shorten, the temperature drops noticeably and with it many B&Bs, campsites and even shops close.

You need to be pretty hardy to walk between late **November** and mid-**March**. True, some days might be bright and sunny, and snow can add a magical element to the hills, but you are far more likely to be walking through driving rain and sleet, accommodation is what you can get and the short days are a problem on longer stages.

TEMPERATURE, RAINFALL AND DAYLIGHT HOURS

These days the Pennines are certainly less wet than their reputation suggests and if you pick your time of year you can minimize your chances of spending days encased in a rustling cagoule.

Just don't expect your plan to be foolproof. If there's one thing you can plan on with the English weather it is unpredictability. The tables on the right can only provide a guide.

If walking in autumn, winter and early spring, you must take account of how far you can walk in the **available daylight**. It's not possible to cover the same distance you can in mid-summer.

The table on the right gives the sunrise and sunset times for the middle of each month at Hawes, a town about halfway along the Pennine Way which gives a reasonably accurate picture for daylight for the whole trail.

Depending on the weather you can get a further 30-45 minutes of usable twilight after sunset. By this time you should be nearly done anyway, following a clear path to a village bathed in warm lamplight.

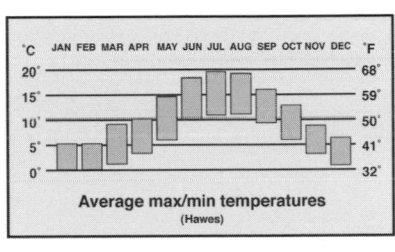

Average max/min temperatures
(Hawes)

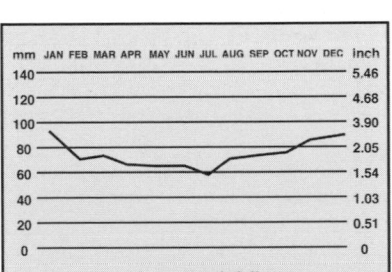

Average rainfall
(Hawes)

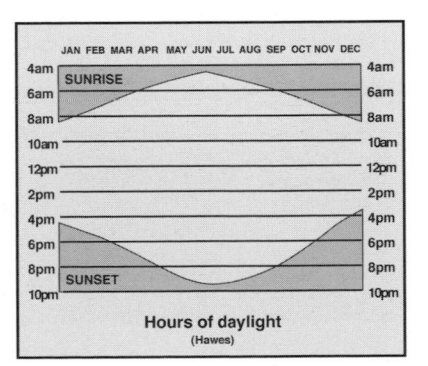

Hours of daylight
(Hawes)

❏ Annual events along the Pennine Way

- **Edale Country Day** (🖳 www.edalecountryday.org.uk) Jazz, wacky races, wood turning, sheep shearing, bands and maypole dancing; held mid-June.
- **Hebden Bridge Arts Festival** (🖳 www.hebdenbridge.co.uk/festival) Music, comedy, drama, talks and exhibitions held in the first half of July.
- **Thornton-in-Craven Village Fête**. (🖳 www.thorntonincraven.co.uk) Early July.
- **Gargrave Show** (🖳 www.gargraveshow.org.uk) Well over a century old, an agricultural show featuring prize cattle, fell racing and sheep dog trials; mid-August.
- **Malham** (🖳 www.malhamdale.com/events.htm) Several summer events from the kiddy-oriented Safari in late June to late August's agricultural show.
- **Three Peaks Challenge** (🖳 www.threepeaksrace.org.uk, see box p140; held on the last Sunday in April), Horton-in-Ribblesdale.
- **Hawes Gala** (🖳 www.yorkshiredales.org) A Saturday in late June as well as Craft Fairs most summer weekends and several Yorkshire Dales National Park events.
- **The Hardraw Brass-band Contest** (🖳 www.greendragonhardraw.com) Running since 1884 in the grounds of the Green Dragon Inn; second Sunday in September.
- **Swaledale Arts Festival** (🖳 www.swaledale-festival.org.uk) Brass bands, jazz and various art events; held over two weeks from May.
- **Bowes Show** (🖳 www.bowesshow.org.uk) Farming show in early September.
- **Middleton-in-Teesdale Carnival** (🖳 www.middleton-carnival.co.uk) Carnival Queens, Scarecrow Trails and much more; held last Saturday in July.
- **Dufton Show** Agricultural show and sheepdog trials; last Saturday in August.
- **Twice Brewed Roman Wall Show** Shepherds show on a Saturday in mid-June.
- **Bellingham Show** (🖳 www.bellinghamshow.com) Last Saturday in August.
- **Yetholm Festival Week** (🖳 www.yetholmonline.org.uk) Second week in June climaxing with Trolley Dolly Jean's duck race.

❏ Walking with dogs

Dogs are a pleasure to walk with providing they are well behaved and are fit. They must be under control at all times and kept on the lead when near livestock. You may know that your dog doesn't chase sheep but farmers don't. You'll be walking through many conservation areas so you must also carefully control your dog when there are nesting birds or fledglings around; they make tasty meals for a dog, and even if chased and not caught they can sometimes die later.

Be sure your dog is up to the task; it's not unknown for dog walkers to have to end their Pennine walk early because their pet has injured or exhausted itself. Accommodation too can be a chore; you will of course have to identify dog-friendly places in advance.

Itineraries

All walkers are individuals. Some like to cover large distances as quickly as possible, others like to stroll along and stop frequently. (Indeed this natural variation in pace is what causes most friction in groups.) You may want to walk the Pennine Way all in one go, tackle it over a series of weekends, or use the trail for linear day walks; the choice is yours. To accommodate these differences this book has not been divided up into rigid daily stages, though many will use it that way. Instead, it's been designed to make it easy for you to plan your own optimal itinerary.

The **planning map** (see inside back cover) and **table of village/ town facilities** (see pp26-7) summarize the essential information. Alternatively, have a look at the **suggested itineraries** (pp28-30) and choose your preferred type of accommodation and pace. There are also suggestions (see pp31-2) for those who want to experience the best of the trail over a day or a weekend. The **public transport maps** and service table (pp42-6) will also be useful.

Having made a rough plan, turn to **Part 4**, where you will find summaries of the route; full descriptions of the accommodation, suggestions for where to eat and information about other services in each village and town; as well as the detailed trail maps.

Most people walk the Pennine Way **south to north**. There are practical reasons for this; the prevailing south-westerly wind and rain are behind you, as is the sun. Head north–south if you want a better face tan! The maps in Part 4 give timings for both directions and, as route finding instructions are on the maps rather than in blocks of text, it ought to be straightforward using this guide back to front.

> **Most walk south to north; the prevailing south-westerly wind and rain are behind you, as is the sun.**

❏ **The next time I do the Pennine Way...**

... I will endeavour to allow more time in the day to lounge around and watch the world go by. Previously I'd sometimes reached my destination by 2pm, regardless of the time in hand. I should have spent longer at viewpoints, village centres and points of interest and simply arrived later.

I'll definitely take more photos by carrying my camera around my neck or in a pocket; it was amazing how few photos I took with the camera in my rucksack. I'll also make more journal entries during and at the end of each day. Over time the brain muddles the facts and a more permanent record of my trip would be perfect.

I'll definitely research the villages along the way for fêtes, village days or festivals. I just missed two on my route and both sounded spectacular.

I'll also make use of the Post Office's 'Poste Restante' service to allow maps, clean clothes, guidebooks etc to be picked up along the way.

And I will definitely not leave a pair of shorts drying on the line at the Tan Hill Inn after a few too many the night before.   **Dave Goodfellow**

VILLAGE AND

Place name (Places in brackets are a short walk off the Pennine Way)	Distance from previous place approx miles/km	Cash Machine/ ATM (in bank, shop or post office)	Post Office	Tourist Information Centre (TIC) Point (TIP)
Edale/Nether Booth	Start	✔	✔	✔
Upper Booth	2 (3)			
Torside, (Padfield & Hadfield)				
Crowden	14 (23)			
Standedge	11 (18)			
(Diggle)				
Mankinholes	10 (16)			
Hebden Bridge	4 (6)	✔	✔	✔
Blackshaw Head	1 (2)			
Colden	1 (2)			
Ponden & Stanbury	10 (16)			
(Haworth)		✔	✔	✔
Ickornshaw & Cowling	4 (6)	✔	✔	
Lothersdale	2 (3)			
(Earby)		✔		
East Marton	5.5 (8)			
Gargrave	2.5 (4)	✔	✔	
Airton	3.5 (6)			
Kirkby Malham	1.5 (2)			
Malham	1 (2)	✔		✔
Horton-in-Ribblesdale	15 (24)		✔	✔
Hawes	14 (23)	✔	✔	✔
Hardraw	1.5 (2)			
Thwaite	8 (13)			
(Muker)				
Keld	3 (5)			
Tan Hill	4 (6)			
(Bowes)		✔		
Baldersdale	10 (16)			
Lunedale	3 (5)			
Middleton-in-Teesdale	3.5 (6)	✔	✔	✔
Holwick	2.5 (4)			
High Force	2.5 (4)			
Forest-in-T'dale/Langdon Beck	3.5 (6)		✔	
Dufton	12 (19)			
Garrigill	16 (26)		✔	
Alston	4 (6)	✔	✔	✔
Slaggyford & Knarsdale	6 (10)			
Greenhead	11 (18)			
Burnhead	4 (6)			
Once Brewed	7 (11)			✔
(Stonehaugh)				
Hetherington	9.5 (15)			
Bellingham	3 (5)	✔	✔	✔
Byrness	15 (24)			
(Uswayford)				
Kirk Yetholm/Town Yetholm	27 (43)		✔	
TOTAL DISTANCE	256 miles (412km)			

TOWN FACILITIES

Restaurant/ Café/pub ✔ = one; ✔✔= two ✔✔✔= 3 +	Food Store	Campsite	Hostels YHA/ H (IndHostel)/ CB (Camping Barn) B (Bunkhouse)	B&B-style accommodation ✔ = one; ✔✔= two ✔✔✔= 3+	Place name (Places in brackets are a short walk off the Pennine Way)
✔✔✔	✔	✔	YHA, CB, B	✔✔✔	**Edale/Nether Booth**
		✔	CB		**Upper Booth**
✔			B	✔✔✔	**Torside, (Padfield & Hadfield)**
		✔	YHA		**Crowden**
✔✔✔		✔		✔✔	**Standedge**
				✔✔✔	**(Diggle)**
✔		✔	YHA	✔	**Mankinholes**
✔✔✔	✔			✔✔✔	**Hebden Bridge**
		✔		✔	**Blackshaw Head**
✔	✔	✔			**Colden**
✔✔✔	✔		YHA	✔✔✔	**(Haworth)**
✔	✔			✔✔	**Ponden & Stanbury**
✔✔	✔	✔		✔✔	**Ickornshaw & Cowling**
✔					**Lothersdale**
✔✔✔	✔		YHA		**(Earby)**
✔✔		✔		✔	**East Marton**
✔✔✔	✔	✔		✔✔	**Gargrave**
			H	✔	**Airton**
✔				✔	**Kirkby Malham**
✔✔✔	✔	✔	YHA, B	✔✔✔	**Malham**
✔✔✔	✔	✔	B	✔✔	**Horton-in-Ribblesdale**
✔✔✔	✔	✔	YHA	✔✔✔	**Hawes**
✔		✔		✔✔	**Hardraw**
✔	✔			✔	**Thwaite**
✔✔		✔		✔✔	**(Muker)**
	✔	✔		✔✔	**Keld**
✔		✔		✔	**Tan Hill**
✔	✔	✔		✔	**(Bowes)**
				✔	**Baldersdale**
		✔		✔	**Lunedale**
✔✔✔	✔	✔	B	✔✔✔	**Middleton-in-Teesdale**
✔		✔	B	✔	**Holwick**
✔				✔	**High Force**
✔			YHA	✔✔	**Forest-in-T'dale/Langdon Beck**
✔		✔	YHA	✔✔✔	**Dufton**
✔	✔	✔		✔✔✔	**Garrigill**
✔✔✔	✔	✔	YHA, B	✔✔✔	**Alston**
✔		✔		✔✔	**Slaggyford & Knarsdale**
✔✔		✔	YHA, CB	✔✔✔	**Greenhead**
✔				✔	**Burnhead**
✔		✔	YHA, B	✔✔✔	**Once Brewed**
		✔			**(Stonehaugh)**
				✔	**Hetherington**
✔✔✔	✔	✔	B	✔✔✔	**Bellingham**
		✔	YHA	✔	**Byrness**
				✔	**(Uswayford)**
✔	✔		YHA	✔✔✔	**Kirk Yetholm/Town Yetholm**

PLANNING YOUR WALK

WILD CAMPING* AND CAMPSITES (▲)

Night	Relaxed pace Place	Approx Distance miles (km)	Medium pace Place	Approx Distance miles (km)	Fast pace Place	Approx Distance miles (km)
0	Edale		Edale		Edale	
1	Crowden ▲	16 (26)	Crowden ▲	16 (26)	Black Hill	20 (32)
2	Standedge ▲	11 (18)	Blackstone Edge	15 (24)	Blackshaw*	20 (32)
3	Withens Moor	10 (16)	Walshaw Reservoir	17 (27)	Pinhaw	20 (32)
4	Withins Height	14 (26)	Pinhaw Beacon	13 (21)	Fountains Fell	20 (32)
5	East Marton ▲	13.5 (22)	Fountains Fell	20 (32)	Hawes ▲	21 (34)
6	Fountains Fell	15 (24)	Dodd Fell	17 (24)	Sleightholme	20 (32)
7	Old Ing Moor	12 (19)	Keld ▲	16 (23)	Middleton	20.5 (33)
8	Gt Shunner Fell	14 (23)	(Rest day)		Rail wagon	19 (31)
9	Tan Hill Inn ▲	11.5 (18)	Deepdale Beck	12 (19)	Greg's Hut	23.5 (38)
10	Deepdale Beck	7.5 (12)	Rail wagon	15 (24)	Glencune Burn	24.5 (39)
11	Middleton ▲	9 (15)	High Cup Nick	10 (16)	Wark Forest	18 (30)
12	Rest day	0	Greg's Hut	13.5 (22)	Byrness Hill	23 (24)
12	High Cup	16 (26)	Alston ▲	11.5 (18)	Kirk Yetholm	25 (40)
13	Greg's Hut	13.5 (22)	Glencune Burn	14 (23)		
14	Alston ▲	11.5 (18)	Wark Forest	15 (24)		
15	Glencune Burn	14 (23)	Deer Play	15 (24)		
16	Wark Forest	15 (24)	Coquet Head	15 (24)		
17	Deer Play	15 (24)	Kirk Yetholm	19 (31)		
18	Byrness Hill	11.5 (23)				
19	Windy Gyle	12 (19)				
20	Kirk Yetholm	12 (19)				

20 nights	**17 nights**	**12 nights**
Average 12.8 miles/day	**Average 15 miles/day**	**Average 21.3 miles/day**

* Wild camping obviously allows overnighting where you please. Where possible the approximate locations of wild camps have been proposed on the fells, ie where discrete and unobtrusive stays are most easily made. Most places have also been chosen for their scenic appeal, the vicinity of Glencune Burn being a notable but unavoidable exception. On other days the ideal distance – be it 'relaxed' or 'fast' – puts you so near a town it's simpler to stay on a campsite or even at a B&B. In Kirk Yetholm B&Bs are the only option unless you camp out around White Law on the alternative route, a couple of miles from the end.

The flexibility of wild camping enables greater daily distances to be covered which is why the three proposed itineraries above are a little faster than the accommodated options given overleaf.

PLANNING YOUR WALK

STAYING IN HOSTELS, BUNKHOUSES AND CAMPING BARNS

Night	Relaxed pace Place	Approx Distance miles (km)	Medium pace Place	Approx Distance miles (km)	Fast pace Place	Approx Distance miles (km)
0	Edale		Edale		Edale	
1	Crowden	16 (26)	Crowden	16 (26)	Crowden	16 (26)
2	Standedge*	11 (18)	Standedge*	11 (18)	Mankinholes	21 (34)
3	Mankinholes	10 (16)	Mankinholes	10 (16)	Ick & Cowling*	20 (32)
4	Haworth§	15 (24)	Ick & Cowling*	20 (32)	Malham	16 (26)
5	Earby•	9 (14)	Malham	16 (26)	Horton-in-Rib	15 (24)
6	Malham	12 (19)	Horton-in-Rib	15 (24)	Keld	26.5 (43)
7	Horton-in-Rib-	15 (24)	Hawes	14 (23)	Middleton-in-T	20.5 (33)
8	Hawes	14 (23)	(Rest day)		Dufton	20.5 (33)
9	(Rest day)		Keld	12.5 (20)	Alston	20 (32)
10	Keld	12.5 (20)	Baldersdale*	14 (23)	Greenhead	17 (27)
11	Bowes*	12.5 (20)	Langdon Beck	15 (24)	Bellingham	21.5 (35)
12	Middleton-in-T	15 (24)	Dufton	12 (19)	Byrness	15 (24)
13	Langdon Beck	9 (14)	Alston	20 (32)	Kirk Yetholm	27 (43)
14	Dufton	12 (19)	Greenhead	17 (27)		
15	Garrigill*	16 (26)	Once Brewed	7 (11)		
16	Knarsdale*	10 (16)	Bellingham	14.5 (23)		
17	Greenhead	11 (18)	Byrness	15 (24)		
18	Once Brewed	7 (11)	Kirk Yetholm	27 (43)		
19	Bellingham	14.5 (23)				
20	Byrness	15 (24)				
21	Uswayford*•	12 (19)				
22	Kirk Yetholm	15 (24)				

22 nights Av 12 miles/day   **18 nights Av 14.2 m/d**   **13 nights Av 19.6 m/d**

No hostel/bunkhouse/barn; stay in B&B   §*3.5 miles (6km) off-route therefore +3.5 miles each way*   •*1.5 miles (2km) off-route therefore +1.5 miles each way*

❏ The next time I do the Pennine Way...

... I'll pick the long but uncrowded days of early summer again. Knowing some good spots now, if the weather's good I'll pace myself to wild camp most nights, but to save the hassle of cooking I'll eat meals in the towns and pubs. Thanks to the 16-hour days I'll be able to walk slowly from early morning into the dusk, and still have regular rests or even a siesta while keeping on target. I'd also make more use of the natural springs and other potable water sources to reduce the amount of water carried.

The hill camping will greatly enhance the wilderness experience, with towns only passed through by day rather than slept in overnight. Although I will probably regret it, instead of an expensive lightweight tent I'll just use a flysheet, either as a groundsheet on fine nights or pegged out and kept up with walking poles. (I may also make an effort to get into using walking poles by day.)

I wouldn't expect to wild camp all the time and every third or fourth day (or if the weather's crap) I'd check into a B&B, bunkhouse or whatever for a wash and a proper night's sleep and a full English breakfast (FEB).   **Chris Scott**

PLANNING YOUR WALK

STAYING IN B&Bs

Night	Relaxed pace Place	Approx Distance miles (km)	Medium pace Place	Approx Distance miles (km)	Fast pace Place	Approx Distance miles (km)
0	Edale		Edale		Edale	
1	Torside	15 (24)	Torside	15 (24	Torside	15 (24)
2	Standedge	12 (19)	Standedge	12 (19)	Mankinholes	22 (35)
3	Hebden Bridge	14 (23)	Hebden Bridge	14 (23)	Ponden	17 (27)
4	Ponden	12 (19)	Ickornshaw	16 (26)	Malham	22.5 (36)
5	Earby*•	13 (21)	Malham	16 (26)	Horton-in-Rib-	15 (24)
6	Malham	11 (18)	Horton-in-Rib-	15 (24)	Keld	26.5 (43)
7	Horton-in-Rib-	15 (24)	Hawes	14 (23)	Middleton-in-T	20.5 (33)
8	Hawes	14 (23)	(Rest day)		Dufton	20.5 (33)
9	(Rest day)		Keld	12.5 (20)	Alston	20 (32)
10	Keld	12.5 (20)	Lunedale	17 (27)	Greenhead	17 (27)
11	Lunedale	17 (27)	Langdon Beck	12 (19)	Bellingham	21.5 (35)
12	Langdon Beck	12 (19)	Dufton	12 (19)	Byrness	15 (24)
13	Dufton	12 (19)	Alston	20 (32)	Kirk Yetholm	27 (43)
14	Garrigill	16 (26)	Greenhead	17 (27)		
15	Knarsdale	10 (16)	Once Brewed	7 (11)		
16	Greenhead	11 (18)	Bellingham	14.5 (23)		
17	Once Brewed	7 (11)	Byrness	15 (24)		
18	Bellingham	14.5 (23)	Kirk Yetholm	27 (43)		
19	Byrness	15 (24)				
20	Uswayford•	12 (19)				
21	Kirk Yetholm	15 (24)				

21 nights Av 12 miles/day   **18 nights Av 14.2 m/d**   **13 nights Av 19.6 m/d**

* No B&B; stay at hostel   • 1.5 miles (2km) off-route therefore +1.5 miles each way

❏ The next time I do the Pennine Way...

... I'd change little from the first. I'd walk south to north, facing the more demanding terrain towards the northern end. I'd take 20 days again, giving time to relax between shower and dinner each evening. Having a couple of days under ten miles in the final week provided encouragement, while staying at Uswayford made the Cheviots a fine two-day traverse. I'd again use youth hostels, B&Bs and baggage forwarding, and dine at some fine hostelries along the way. I'd again use Bridgedale socks and liners, and two walking poles, train in advance and use whey protein daily to aid muscle recovery. But I'd make an earlier start on the first day and this time get a quality ruck-sack. I'd navigate more carefully off Bleaklow summit. I might slip a bottle of real ale into my luggage for that first night at Crowden YH, which is nowhere near a booz-er although I would take more parental responsibility in moderating the consumption of Brenda's superb homemade sherry trifle at Ponden House. I'd never again try to squeeze my wet clothes into a packed-out YH drying room but hang them out in the dormitory. And I would never again drink keg bitter after consecutive days of real ale.

Tom Read

❏ **HIGHLIGHTS**

The best day and weekend (two-day) walks

One great way of experiencing the Pennine Way without burning yourself out is to do it in a series of days or weekends that take in a section at a time, not necessarily consecutively. Over a period of time it would be quite possible to complete the entire route this way. Another advantage is to walk only the best sections, leaving the intermediate dross to the end-to-enders.

The following are some suggestions for linear walks intended to get the most out of the time available. Getting back to the start is not always straightforward but by using bus and train timetables, taxi firms and some ingenuity it's possible.

Day walks

● **Edale to Kinder Downfall via Upper Booth, Jacob's Ladder and Kinder Low** (see pp74-8) There and back is a popular walk of 10 miles (16km) which gives a true taste of the Dark Peak and the groughs and edges of the Kinder Plateau. The area gives a fine feeling of wilderness yet is not very far at any time from civilization.

● **Thornton-in-Craven to Malham via East Marton and the Leeds–Liverpool Canal** (see pp117-31) 10 miles (16km) of easy, low-level walking initially through meadows and fields, then on the canal towpath before visiting Gargrave. Beyond Gargrave you follow a lovely riverside path along the River Aire via Airton and Kirkby Malham to arrive at Malham where, if time allows, a visit to the Cove is a must.

● **Malham to Horton-in-Ribblesdale via Fountains Fell and Pen-y-ghent** (see pp131-40) A 15-mile (24km) walk which is one of the best day walks as you surmount the Cove and follow the dry gorge behind it to the Tarn and beyond. You soon rise out of farmland to gradually surmount Fountains Fell where you drop down again in time to take the stiffer trek up Pen-y-ghent followed by the long, long descent to the lovely village of Horton.

● **Middleton-in-Teesdale to Langdon Beck** (see pp177-83) This low-level walk of 9 miles (14km) follows the banks of the River Tees, an area rich in wild flowers and birds offering constant variety and many diversions. The falls of Low Force and High Force are passed, the latter in spate is an awesome sight. By crossing the footbridge at Holwick Head, a visit to High Force Hotel can be made for lunch or a pint and a night in the remote hamlet of Langdon Beck is a treat.

● **Dufton to Garrigill over Cross Fell** (see pp192-200) This one needs an early start so perhaps stay in Dufton the night before. It is 16 miles (26km) to Garrigill and the weather over Cross Fell is likely to be unpredictable so go well prepared. There's a mountain refuge hut just below the summit (Greg's Hut) where shelter can be sought if necessary. Then there's a long foot-numbing walk down the miners' track to the quaint village of Garrigill.

● **Greenhead to Once Brewed** (see pp216-21) This walk is a great introduction to Hadrian's Wall following the ramparts themselves as they swoop and soar along Whin Sill. It's 7 miles (11km) and will only take a morning. Thirlwall Castle can also be visited, a later fortification than the Romans yet built using stone from the Wall itself.

● **Kirk Yetholm to The Schil and back** (see pp253-249 and vv) This 10-mile (16km) walk follows the high-level alternative route southwards, returning by the low-level route via Old Halterburnhead (ruin) and the road along the Halter Burn. It visits White Law and Steer Rig before topping out on The Schil (1985ft/605m). In good weather you should have fine views and if you've done the Kinder Scout day described above, all that remains is the 240-odd miles in between. *(contd overleaf)*

Weekend (two-day) walks (*continued from p31*)

● **Edale to Standedge** (see pp74-91) This 27-mile (43km) walk takes in the Kinder Scout, Bleaklow and Black Hill massifs and offers a chance to experience the true meaning of the name 'Dark Peak' or 'peat' for short. A night at Crowden hostel, or a Torside B&B, comes as a welcome break in the route, much of it mercifully slabbed to ensure you keep your boots dry and your spirits high.

● **Thornton-in-Craven to Horton-in-Ribblesdale** (see pp117-40) A 25-mile (40km) route following a pleasant and then outstanding section of the Way, taking in the best of the limestone country. After the lovely riverside walk along the meandering River Aire you arrive in Malham. On day two you have some climbing to do over Fountains Fell, then up to the windy heights of Pen-y-ghent to end an exhilarating weekend at Horton and a train home.

● **Hawes to Tan Hill** (see pp151-61) This 16½-mile (27km) walk could be done in a day but what's the rush? Plan an overnight stop in the tiny hamlet of Thwaite, perhaps taking advantage of a mini-break at the charming *Kearton Country Hotel*. Tan Hill could be reached for a late lunch on the second day, allowing the rest of the day to call a taxi to take you down into Kirkby Stephen where there's a train station. The walking is superb and includes Great Shunner Fell and a lovely stretch high above the Swale.

● **Middleton-in-Teesdale to Alston** (see pp177-205) Fancy a stiff training walk incorporating the crème-de-la-crème of the North Pennines? Then this 40-mile (64km) stretch will give you something to get your teeth into. Up to High Force is tame, but beyond the wild moors move in, ending at the glorious amphitheatre of High Cup. After a night in quiet Dufton it's a tougher trek up over Cross Fell followed by the truly interminable tramp along the Corpse Road down to Garrigill (consider overnighting here, it's much nicer than Alston, five tiresome miles away). Once completed the lure of the Pennine Way will be all but irresistible!

● **Byrness to Kirk Yetholm** (see pp238-53) This easy weekender explores the heart of The Cheviots – and overnighting at one of the bothies is great fun if the weather is on your side; or there's always Uswayford Farm. The full 27-mile (43km) crossing follows the Border fence, switching from England into Scotland and back again. Luckily most of the boggy upland sections are slabbed for your walking and route-finding pleasure. As you arrive at Kirk Yetholm you can only imagine what it must feel like to have come all the way up from Edale.

❏ **The next time I do the Pennine Way...**

... will be in 2013, marking 50 years since my first south–north odyssey.

Next time I shall take my time, and that will be a first! I'll book all my accommodation in advance, ensuring a framework of low daily mileages. I'll gratefully stop and stare – and even divert from the trail – wherever the fancy takes me. If the weather hits me hard, I'll be able to pass my spare hours in the occasional pub and tearoom. I'll carry only what I need for the day: baggage transport rules OK, so I'll have a wardrobe of clean clothes to wear in the evenings, books to read, and enough money to eat and sup well.

Next time won't be remotely like the first time, and it will be the last time, bookending a fascinating and fulfilling series of treks along this inspiring trail. **Peter Stott**

(**Opposite**) **Top**: Greg's Hut (see p196), the bothy near the summit of Cross Fell. **Bottom**: First steps: starting out from the Old Nag's Head (see p74) in Edale. (Photos © Chris Scott).

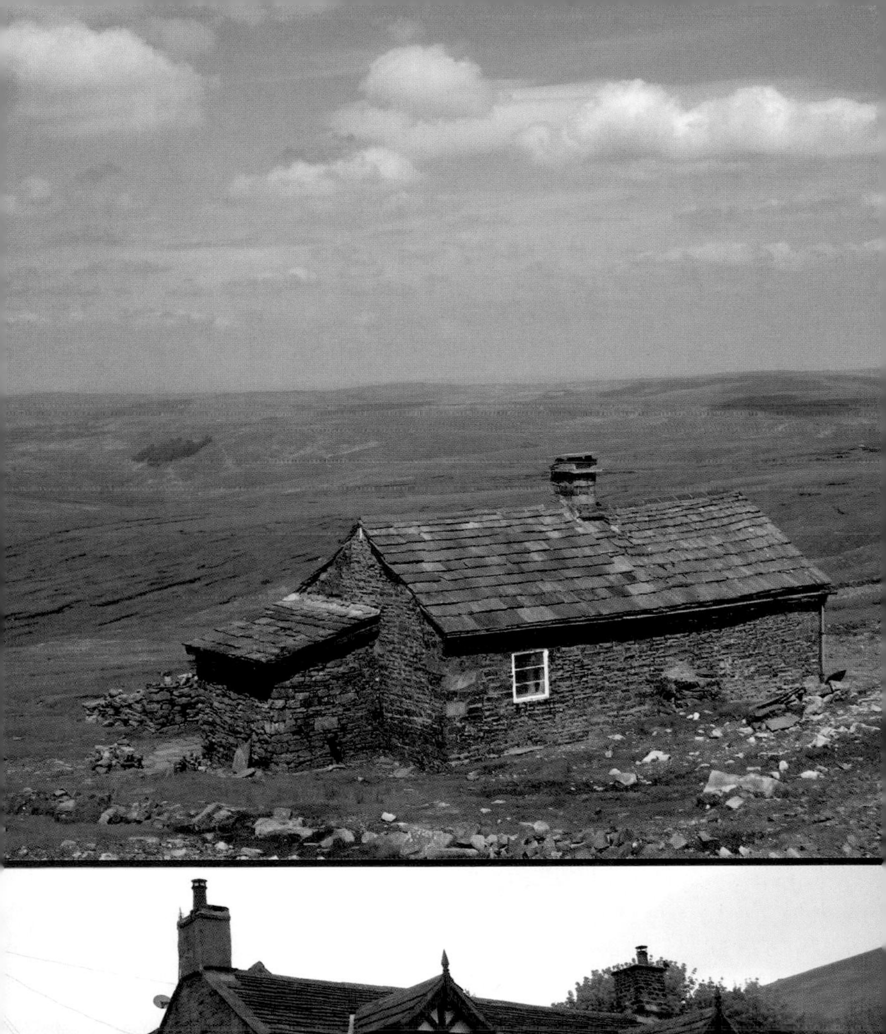

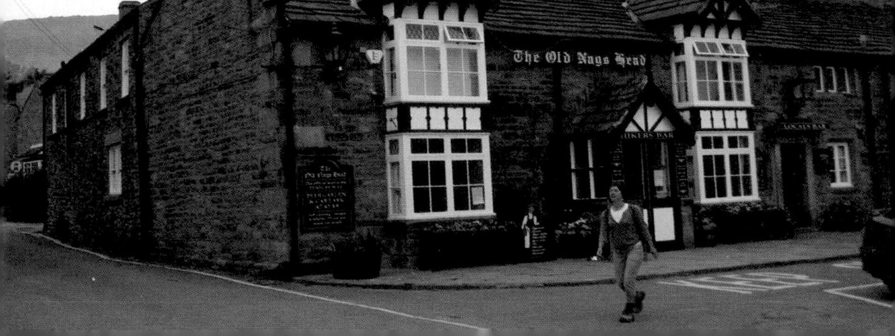
The Old Nags Head

What to take

Not ending up schlepping over the fells like an overloaded mule with a migraine takes experience and some measure of discipline. **Taking too much** is a mistake made by first-time travellers of all types, an understandable response to not knowing what to expect and not wanting to be caught short. The post office in Hebden even has a special counter for Pennine walkers sending stuff home.

By UK standards the Pennine Way is a long walk but it's not an expedition into the unknown. Experienced independent hill walkers trim their gear down to the essentials because they've learned that an unnecessarily heavy pack can exacerbate injuries and put excess strain on their already hard-pressed feet. Note that if you need to buy all the gear listed, keep an eye for the ever-frequent online **sales** and at outdoor gear shops; time it right and you could get it all half price.

TRAVELLING LIGHT

Organized tours apart, baggage-forward-ing services are tempting for walkers but partially miss the point of long-distance walking: the satisfaction of striking out from Edale knowing that you're carrying with you everything you need to get to Kirk Yetholm. However, if you've chosen to carry it all you must be ruthless in your packing choices.

An ultralight camping set-up in a 35-litre pack. The walking sticks act as tent poles.

HOW TO CARRY IT

Today's **rucksacks** are hi-tech affairs that make load-carrying as tolerable as can be expected. Don't get hung up on anti-sweat features; unless you use a wheel-barrow your back will always sweat. It's better to ensure there is thick padding and a **good range of adjustment**. In addition to hip belts, use an unelasticated **cross-chest strap** to keep the pack snug; it makes a real difference.

If camping you'll need a pack of at least 60-litres' capacity. Staying in hostels 40 litres should be ample, and for those eating out and staying in B&Bs a 20- to 30-litre pack should suffice; you could even get away with a daypack.

Although many rucksacks claim to be waterproof, use a strong plastic **bin liner**. It's also handy to **compartmentalize** the contents into bags so you know what is where. Take **plastic bags** for wet things, rubbish etc; they're always useful. Finally, pack the most frequently used things so they are readily accessible.

(Opposite) Top: The glaciated valley known as High Cup (see p188) is one of the most impressive sights on the walk. **Bottom**:High Force (see p181). (Photos © Chris Scott).

FOOTWEAR

Boots

Not surprisingly on a walk of around half a million steps, choosing a good pair of boots is vital. Scrimp on other gear if you must, but not on boots. Expect to spend at least £100 on quality three-season items which are light, breathable and waterproof and have ankle support and the key feature – flexible but thick **soles** to insulate your own pulverized soles as you limp down the stony Corpse Road off Cross Fell. With modern fabric boots **breaking in** is a thing of the past but arriving in Edale with new unworn boots is unwise – try them out beforehand with a full pack over a weekend.

An old and trusted pair of boots can be transformed with shock-absorbing after-market **insoles**. Some are thermally moulded to your foot in the shop but the less expensive examples are also well worth the investment even if the need for replacement by the end of the walk is likely. If you get bad blisters refer to p69 for blister-avoidance strategies.

Although not essential, it's a treat to have **alternative footwear** when not on the trail to give your feet a break or let boots dry. Sport sandals or flip-flops are all suitable as long as they're light.

Socks

As with all outdoor gear, the humble sock has not escaped the technological revolution (with prices to match). But to paraphrase L'Oréal, 'your feet are worth it' so invest in two pairs designed for walking. Although cushioning is desirable, avoid anything too thick which will reduce stability. A correctly sized boot with an anatomically shaped insole gives a sure-footed feel. As well as the obvious olfactory benefits, frequent washing will maintain the socks' springiness.

> ... to paraphrase L'Oréal, 'your feet are worth it' so invest in two pairs designed for walking

CLOTHES

Tops

The proven system of **layering** is still a good principle to follow. A quick-drying synthetic or a less-odiferous merino-wool **base layer** transports sweat away from your skin; the mid-layer(s), typically a **fleece** or woollen jumper, keep(s) you warm; and when needed, an outer 'shell' or **jacket** protects you from the wind and rain.

Maintaining a comfortable temperature in all conditions is essential; this means not **overheating** just as much as the more obvious effects of **wind chill**. Both can prematurely tire you. Trudging out of the Calder Valley on a warm day will have you down to your base layer, but any exposed and prolonged descent or rest on an unsheltered summit with the blowing wind will soon chill you. Although tedious, the smart walker is forever fiddling with zips and managing their layers and headwear to maintain an optimal level of comfort.

Avoid cotton; as well as being slow to dry, when soaked it saps away body heat but not the moisture – and you'll be wet from sweat if not rain. Take a change of **base layers** (including underwear), a **fleece** suited to the season, and the best **waterproof** you can afford. **Soft shells** are an alternative to walking in rustling nylon waterproofs when it's windy but not raining.

It's useful to have a **spare set of dry clothing** so you're able to get changed should you arrive chilled at your destination, but choosing **quick-drying clothes** and washing them reduces your load. Once indoors your body heat can quickly dry out a synthetic fleece and nylon leggings. However, always make sure you have a **dry base layer** in case you or someone you're with goes down with hypothermia (see p69). This is why a quality waterproof is important.

Leg wear

Your legs are doing all the work and don't generally get cold so your trousers can be light which will also mean quick-drying. Although they lack useful pockets, many walkers find leg-hugging cycling polyester **leggings** very comfortable (eg Ron Hill Tracksters). Poly-cotton or microfibre trousers are excellent. Denim jeans are cotton; a disaster when wet.

If the weather's good, **shorts** are very agreeable to walk in, leaving a light pair of trousers clean for the evenings. On the other hand **waterproof trousers** would only suit people who really feel the cold; most others will find them unnecessary and awkward to put on and wear – quick drying legwear is better. As the worst of the peat bogs are tamed by slabs, **gaiters** are not needed.

Headwear and other clothing

Your head is both exposed to the sun and loses most of your body heat so carry a woolly beany for warmth and a peaked cap for UV protection; a bandana makes a good back up. Between them they'll conserve body heat or reduce the chances of dehydration. **Gloves** are a good idea in wintry conditions (carry a spare pair in winter).

> **... have two hats: a woolly beany for warmth and a peaked cap for UV protection**

TOILETRIES

Besides **toothpaste** and a brush, **liquid soap** can also be used for shaving and washing clothes, although a ziplock bag of **detergent** is better if you're laundering regularly. Carry **toilet paper** and a lightweight **trowel** to bury the results out on the fells (see p65-6).

Less obvious items include **ear plugs**, **sun screen**, **moisturiser** and, particularly if camping, **insect repellent** and a **water purification system**.

FIRST-AID KIT

Apart from aching limbs your most likely ailments will be blisters so a first-aid kit can be tiny. **Ibuprofen** helps numb pain although rest of course is the cure. 'Moleskin', 'Compeed', or 'Second Skin' all treat blisters. An **elastic knee support** is a good precaution for a weak knee. A few sachets of Dioralyte or Rehydrat powders will quickly remedy mineral loss through sweating. Also consider taking a small selection of different-sized **sterile dressings** for wounds.

GENERAL ITEMS
Essential
Carry a **compass** and know how to use it with a map; also take a **whistle** (see p68) and a **mobile phone** for emergencies; a **water pouch** (at least two litres); a **headtorch** with spare batteries; **emergency snacks** which your body can quickly convert into energy; a **penknife, watch, plastic bags, safety pins** and **scissors**.

Useful
If you're not carrying a proper bivi bag or tent a compact foil **space blanket** is a good idea in the cooler seasons. Many would list a **camera** as essential but it's liberating to travel without one once in a while – instead take a **notebook** in which to record your memories; a reading **book** will help you enjoy mid-summer wild camps and a **vacuum flask** is great for carrying hot drinks in cooler seasons. Studies have shown that nothing improves a hilltop view on a chilly day like a cup of hot tea or soup. Also consider taking **sunglasses**, **binoculars** and **walking poles** (see box below).

SLEEPING BAG

If you're camping or planning to stay in camping barns you'll need a sleeping bag. Some bunkhouses offer bedding but you'll keep your costs down if you don't have to hire it. All youth hostels provide bedding and insist you use it.

A **two-season bag** will do for indoor use, but if you can afford it or anticipate outdoor use, go warmer. The choice over a **synthetic or down** filling is a debate without end. Year by year less expensive synthetic-filled bags (typically under £100) approach down's enviable qualities of good compressability while expanding or 'lofting' fully once unpacked to create maximum warmth. But get a down bag wet (always a risk in the UK) and it clogs up and loses all its thermal qualities; and washing down bags takes half a day at the laundrette.

❑ **Walking poles; must have or don't need?**
I decided to find out and, turning back just in time from splashing out £90 on some Leki Super Makalus, I bought a similarly sprung pair for £15 off eBay.

The first thing serious walkers must know is that one pole is as useful as one boot. You'll often see 'leisure walkers' along tow paths and the like using single poles as walking sticks but on the hill **you need two** if you want them to work for you.

The most effective application was found to be on long steady ascents such as Great Shunner or Fountains Fell. Here, as long as you could maintain your rhythm, they had a positive aerobic value, adapting your arms into 'forelegs' to bear some weight and propel you forward faster than normal, though of course using more energy. After a good day of uphill poling you'll notice some soreness in your chest muscles.

Only on the very steepest, slipperiest downhills, like that off Kinder Scout, might poles be an aid to steadying yourself. At any other time or on the flat they're a hindrance. Do you collapse them and tuck them away or carry them? I never got fully into them because my pack was fairly light and I was content to slog unpoled up most hills. With a heavy pack or on a fast end-to-end schedule, making the effort to get acclimatized to walking poles would be worthwhile.

❏ SOURCES OF FURTHER INFORMATION
Trail information
Pennine Way National Trail (🖳 www.nationaltrail.co.uk/PennineWay) The website provides an up-to-date accommodation guide as well as FAQs and even GPS waypoints.

The two main **online** sources of chat covering the Pennine Way are: 🖳 **www .coast2coast.co.uk/ubb/cgi-bin/Ultimate.cgi** which has its own Pennine Way forum and 🖳 **www.ramblers.co.uk/forum** which covers walking in Britain. A thorough scan over the previous months' postings on the former forum is bound to come up with some useful nuggets of information.

National parks and tourist information centres along the Pennine Way
The Pennine Way goes through the Peak District, Yorkshire Dales and Northumberland **national parks**; see box p60 for contact details.

Most **tourist information centres** (TICs) are open daily from Easter to September/October, and thereafter more limited days/hours, often weekends only. Unless you're stuck for accommodation or have a specific query, they're of little use to an organized walker once underway. Some TICs are also national park centres.
Edale (☎ 01433-670207, 🖳 edale@peakdistrict.gov.uk); **Hebden Bridge** (☎ 01422-843831, 🖳 www.hebdenbridge.co.uk); **Haworth** (☎ 01535-642329, 🖳 www.visit brontecountry.com); **Malham** (☎ 01969-652380, 🖳 malham@yorkshiredales.org .uk); **Horton-in-Ribblesdale** (☎ 01729-860333, 🖳 Horton@ytbtic.co.uk); **Hawes** (☎ 01969-666210, 🖳 hawes@yorkshiredales.org.uk); **Middleton-in-Teesdale** (☎ 01833-641001, 🖳 tic@middletonplus.myzen.co.uk); **Alston** (☎ 01434-382244, 🖳 alston.tic @eden.gov.uk), **Once Brewed** (☎ 01434-344396, 🖳 tic.oncebrewed@nnpa.org.uk); **Bellingham** (☎ 01434-220616, 🖳 bellinghamtic@btconnect.com).

Organizations for walkers
● **Backpackers Club** (🖳 www.backpackersclub.co.uk) For people interested in light-weight camping. Members receive a quarterly magazine, access to a comprehensive information service (including a library), discounts on maps (see p38) and a farm-pitch directory. Membership is £12 per year, family £15, under 18s and over 65s £7.
● **The Long Distance Walkers' Association** (🖳 www.ldwa.org.uk) For anyone keen on long-distance walking. They publish a *Long Distance Walkers Handbook* and a jour nal (quarterly). Membership costs £13 per year, or £19.50 for families.
● **The Ramblers' Association**, (☎ 020-7339 8500, 🖳 www.ramblers.org.uk). Long-established charity promoting walking in Britain with discussion forums (see above). Annual membership is £24, joint/family membership is £32.

Some books
● *Laughs Along the Pennine Way,* Pete Bog (Cicerone, 1987; OP) A collection of hit-and-miss cartoons, some of which will have you chuckling with recollection.
● *The Pennine Way,* Tony Hopkins (Zymurgy, 2005) Medium-format picture book with good background text but spoiled by the occasional less-than-crisp shot.
● *Aerial Britain – The Pennine Way* (2006, DVD 53 mins) A great idea – flying along the Way – made unwatchable by poor encoding from the original early '90s VHS. Not every mile is covered and the narration wasn't written by a walker which makes you wonder who this DVD is for, farmers looking for lost sheep?
● *British Wildlife* (Collins Wild Guide, 2005) Includes birds, wild flowers, trees, insects, wild animals, butterflies and moths but is not entirely comprehensive.
● *Birdwatcher's Pocket Field Guide*, Mark Golley (New Holland, 2003)
● *Birds*, Peter Holden (Collins Wild Guide 2004)
● *Complete British Wild Flowers*, P Sterry (Collins, 2006) User friendly tome.

CAMPING GEAR

If committed to the exposure of wild camping you'll need a **tent** you can rely on; light but able to withstand the rain and wind. At campsites you may just get away with a £7 tent from Argos. Otherwise, a good one-man item suited to the wilds can cost less than £100 and weigh just 1.5kg, with a sub-2kg two-man example costing around £220.

An inflatable **sleeping mat** is worth many times its weight. As for **cooking**, is it really worth the bother on the Pennine Way; the extra weight and hassle is only viable when shared by a group of three or more.

MAPS

The hand-drawn maps in this book cover the trail at a scale of 1:20,000 but are in a strip only two miles wide. In some places, particularly on high moors where navigation points are scant, a proper **topographical map and a compass** could be of great use. But, as mentioned on p11, when the mist comes down and all landmarks disappear, a **GPS** *used with a map* comes into its own.

In Britain the **Ordnance Survey** (🖳 www.ordsvy.gov.uk) series is peerless. Their orange 1:25,000-scale 'Explorer' features pin-sharp cartography and detail that makes navigation a doddle. From south to north nine sheets cover the Pennine Way: **1** *The Peak District – Dark Peak area;* **21** *South Pennines*; **2** *Yorkshire Dales – Southern & Western areas*; **30** *Yorkshire Dales Northern & Central Areas*; **31** *North Pennines – Teesdale & Weardale*; **19** *Howgill Fells & Upper Eden Valley*; **5** *The English Lakes – North Eastern area*; **43** *Hadrian's Wall*; **42** *Keilder Water and Forest*; **16** *The Cheviot Hills*.

Packing such a stack of maps, especially the bulky laminated weatherproof versions, is a chore. Walkers either post them ahead or mark the Way and trim off the flab with a pair of scissors. Alternatively, members of the **Ramblers' Association** (see box p37) can borrow these maps for up to six weeks at 50p per map from their library and members of the **Backpackers Club** (see box p37) can buy OS maps at a significant discount through their map service.

❑ **Talking the talk**

Although we all speak English after a fashion, the finely honed ear will perceive at least **five** distinct accents along the Pennine Way, each with its own regional expressions, with greetings being most evident to the walker. These will be most noticeable in deeply rural areas, particularly among agricultural workers who may sound unintelligible to an unacclimatized foreigner.

From the High Peak of northern Derbyshire ('*ahyallrait*?') you'll flit between the cultural frontier of erstwhile county rivals, Yorkshire and Lancashire, who both share a curt '*ow do*?'. Then, as you leave the Dales another invisible boundary is crossed and the accent takes on the distinctive 'Geordie' tones of County Durham and Northumberland ('*allreet*?') before your final linguistic watershed over the Cheviots into Scotland where a barely discernible nod means you've a new friend for life.

❏ **Online satellite imagery**

More for inspiration and planning than navigation on the trail, free online satellite mapping like Google Maps (🖳 maps.google.co.uk) helps bring your surroundings alive. And it's made all the more impressive with basic free software packages such as Google Earth (🖳 earth.google.com) or NASA World Wind (🖳 worldwind.arc.nasa .gov; PC only). This 'Earth browsing' software allows you to effortlessly zoom in and steer from 25,000km out in space to a few metres above the tip of Stoodley Pike monument. Once there you can then tilt the projection and glide off along the Pennine Way at your preferred altitude, tracing the exact course of the trail which is usually clearly visible.

In fact you could do a lot worse than export this book's GPS waypoints (see p11) as a KML file, open it up in Google Earth and press 'play'. You can then sit back and let the software 'fly' you from waypoint to waypoint from Edale all the way to Kirk Yetholm. It's no exaggeration to say the experience will blow your mind!

OS Explorers are the ultimate Pennine maps but there are two handy map series which give the big picture during planning and work fine on the trail as a back up to this book's maps. Both use 50-years-old out-of-copyright OS maps as bases and then add or update contemporary information (although you may still spot the odd long out-of-date detail).

Footprint Maps (🖳 www.footprintmaps.co.uk) produces a compact set of two double-sided sheets: *Pennine Way Part 1 – South: Edale – Teesdale* and *Part 2; Teesdale – Kirk Yetholm* (both 2005) printed on waterproof paper. Each 60cm x 40cm sheet has 16 panels at around 1:50,000 scale. With a commentary of recommended daily stages, incremental mileages from 1 to 255 and an uncluttered design, their only drawback is the lack of a grid to work with GPS.

Harvey Maps (🖳 www.harveymaps.co.uk) produce a similar set of maps: three waterproof sheets covering *Edale to Horton*, *Horton to Greenhead* and *Greenhead to Kirk Yetholm* (all 2005) in a series of north-oriented strip panels at a scale of 1:40,000 and with similar information. The panels cover a broader area each side of the path but being one-sided like an OS can be a bit cumbersome in windy conditions although crucially they include the OS grid to work with GPS.

Getting to and from the Pennine Way

Travelling to the start of the Pennine Way by public transport makes sense. There's no need to trouble anyone for a lift or worry about your vehicle while walking, there are no logistical headaches about how to return to your car when you've finished the walk and it's obviously a big step towards minimizing your ecological footprint. Quite apart from that, you'll simply feel your holiday has begun the moment you step out of your front door, rather than when you've slammed the car door behind you.

❑ Getting to Britain

● **By air** There are plenty of cheap flights from around the world to London's airports: Heathrow, Gatwick, Luton, London City and Stansted. However, Manchester and Edinburgh airports are the closest to the start and finish points of the Pennine Way. There are also airports at Newcastle and Leeds.

● **From Europe by train** Eurostar (🖥 www.eurostar.com) operates a high-speed passenger service via the Channel Tunnel between a number of cities in Europe (particularly Paris and Brussels) and London (St Pancras International). St Pancras is located between King's Cross and Euston stations from where trains operate to the north; these stations also have connections to the London Underground. For more information about rail services from Europe contact Rail Europe (🖥 www.rail europe.com) or Railteam (🖥 www.railteam.eu).

● **From Europe by bus** Eurolines (🖥 www.eurolines.co.uk) have a huge network of long-distance bus services connecting over 500 cities in 25 European countries to London. Check carefully, however: often, once such expenses as food for the journey are taken into consideration, it does not work out that much cheaper than taking a flight, particularly when compared to the fares on some of the budget airlines.

● **From Europe by car** P&O Ferries (🖥 www.poferries.com) and Norfolk Line (🖥 www.norfolkline-ferries.co.uk) are just two of the many ferry operators from Europe. The main routes are between all the major North Sea and Channel ports of mainland Europe and the ports on Britain's eastern and southern coasts. Direct Ferries (🖥 www.directferries.co.uk) lists all the main operators/routes and sells discounted tickets.

Eurotunnel (🖥 www.eurotunnel.com) operates the shuttle train service for vehicles via the Channel Tunnel between Calais and Folkestone taking one hour between the motorway in France and the motorway in Britain.

NATIONAL TRANSPORT

Manchester and **Sheffield** can both be used as gateways to the start of the Pennine Way being only 30-45 minutes from Edale by train, the most convenient way to get there. At the northern end of the walk **Berwick-upon-Tweed** is the main transport hub, reached from Kirk Yetholm in about four hours by changing buses at Kelso.

By rail

Manchester and Sheffield are served by frequent trains from the rest of Britain, and Berwick-upon-Tweed is on the east-coast mainline between London, Newcastle and Edinburgh. There are stations on the Pennine Way at Edale, Hebden Bridge, Gargrave and Horton-in-Ribblesdale. Other useful stations with good bus services linking them to various parts of the Way include Huddersfield, Skipton, Penrith, Darlington, Haltwhistle and Hexham. The main rail operators are Northern, GNER, Virgin and Trans-Pennine Express. Megatrain (🖥 www.megatrain.com/uk) also serves Manchester, Leeds and Berwick-upon-Tweed.

National Rail Enquiries (☎ 0845-748 4950, 24hrs, 🖥 www.nationalrail .co.uk) will be able to give you the timetable and fare information for rail travel in the whole of Britain. Tickets can be bought by phone or online through the relevant rail operator (see box p46) or online at 🖥 www.trainline.com or 🖥 www.qjump.co.uk. It's worth planning ahead, at least two weeks, as it's the only way to save a considerable amount of money. It helps to be as flexible as possible and don't forget that most discounted tickets carry some restrictions; check what they are before you buy your ticket. Travel on a Friday may be more expensive than on other days of the week.

For a comprehensive list of taxi companies operating from railway stations contact Train Taxi (☎ 01733-237037, 🖥 www.traintaxi.co.uk).

By coach

National Express (☎ 0870-580 8080, lines open 8am-8pm daily; 🖥 www .nationalexpress.com) is the principal coach (long-distance bus) operator in Britain. There are services from most towns in England and Wales to a number of towns and cities on or near the route including: Manchester, Sheffield, Crowden, Keighley, Skipton, Otterburn, Byrness and Berwick-upon-Tweed (see box p45). **Megabus** (🖥 www.megabus.com/uk) also serves Manchester and Berwick-upon-Tweed and fares start from £1 plus a 50p booking fee.

Travel by coach is usually cheaper than by train but takes longer. Advance bookings carry discounts so be sure to book at least a week ahead. If you don't mind an uncomfortable night there are overnight services on some routes.

By car

Both Edale and Kirk Yetholm are easily reached using the motorway and A-road network from the rest of Britain. Unless you're just out for a day walk however, you'd be better leaving the car at home as there is nowhere safe to leave a vehicle unattended for a long period.

LOCAL TRANSPORT

Getting to and from most parts of the Pennine Way is relatively simple due to the public transport network including trains, coaches and local bus services. This opens up the potential for linear walks from an hour to several days without the nuisance of parking and getting back to your car.

The **public transport map** on pp42-3 gives an overview of routes which are of particular use to walkers and the table on pp44-6 lists the operators (and their contact details), the route details and the approximate frequency of services in both directions.

If the operator details prove unsatisfactory contact **Traveline** (☎ 0870-608 2608, 7am-9pm, 🖥 www.traveline.org.uk) or **Public Transport Information** (🖥 www.pti.org.uk), both of which have timetable information for the whole of the UK. Local timetables can also be picked up from tourist information centres along the Way.

Note that many services in rural areas operate on a **Hail and Ride** basis ie the driver will stop to set passengers down or pick them up as long as it is safe to do so.

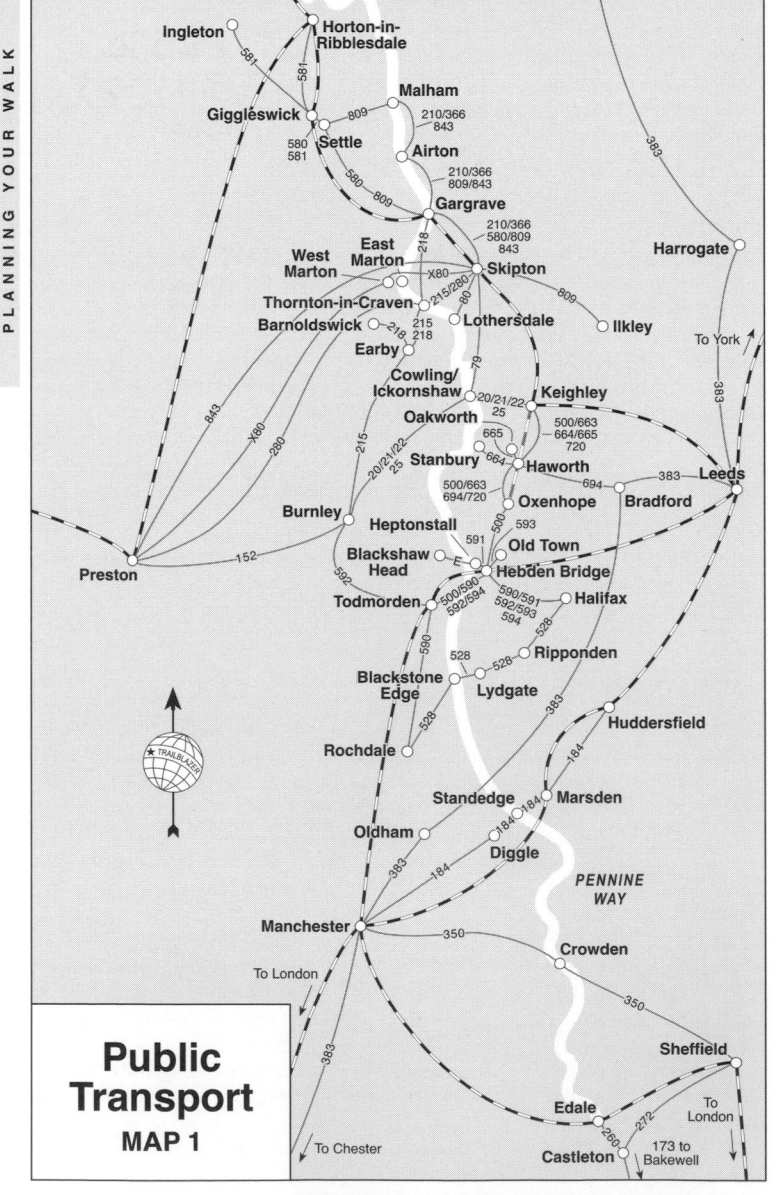

Public Transport

MAP 1

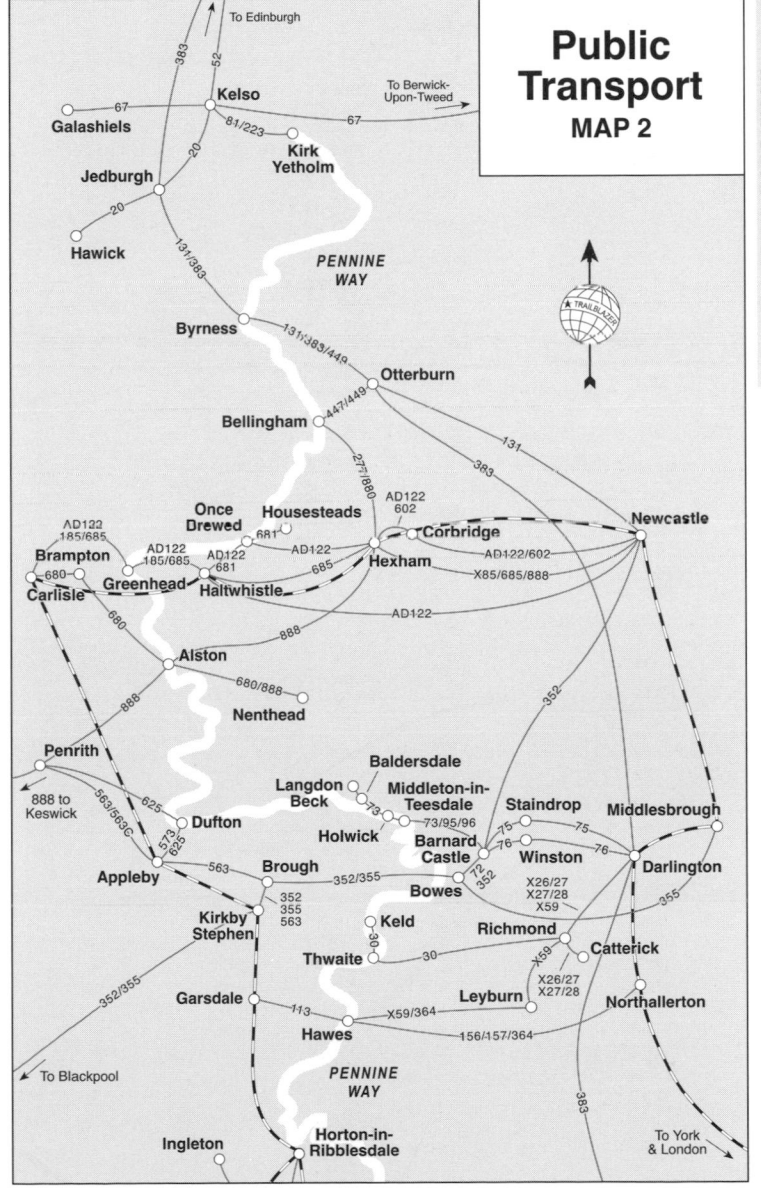

Public Transport MAP 2

PLANNING YOUR WALK

PUBLIC TRANSPORT SERVICES
Bus services
Alston Road Garage (☎ 01833-640213)
73   Langdon Beck to Middleton-in-Teesdale, Mon-Sat 3/day plus 1/day if pre-
     booked or requested to driver + Wed 2/day to/from Barnard Castle. If pre-
     booked the service will also go to Forest-in-Teesdale, Holwick, Lunedale
     & Baldersdale; contact the company for details.

Arriva (💻 www.arrivabus.co.uk)
X26/27/X27/28   Catterick to Darlington via Richmond, daily 2-3/hr
75   Darlington to Barnard Castle via Staindrop, daily 1/hr
76   Darlington to Barnard Castle via Winston, Mon-Sat 1/hr
95/96 Barnard Castle to Middleton-in-Teesdale, Mon-Sat 1/hr, Sun 4/day
602 Newcastle to Hexham via Corbridge, Mon-Sat 2/hr, Sun 1/hr
685 Newcastle to Carlisle via Hexham, Haltwhistle & Greenhead, Mon-Sat
     12/day, Hexham to Carlisle via Haltwhistle & Greenhead Sun 4/day
X85 Newcastle to Hexham Sun 1/hr (four of which connect with the Sunday 685
     services see above)
X59 Darlington to Hawes via Richmond & Leyburn, Mon-Fri 1/day

Burnley & Pendle (☎ 01282-427778, 💻 www.burnleyandpendle.co.uk)
20/21/22 Keighley to Burnley via Cowling, Mon-Sat 1/hr, Sun 6/day
25   Burnley to Keighley via Cowling, Mon-Sat 1/hr, Sun 6/day
152 Preston to Burnley, Mon-Sat 2/hr, Sun 1/hr

Central Coaches (☎ 01325-300604)
72   Barnard Castle to Bowes, Mon-Sat 3/day (+1/day term-time Mon-Fri)

Classic Coaches (☎ 01207-282288, 💻 www.classic-coaches.co.uk)
352 Newcastle to Blackpool via Barnard Castle, Bowes, Brough & Kirkby Stephen,
     May-Nov & Xmas & Easter fortnights 1/day, rest of year Fri-Mon 1/day
355 Middlesborough to Blackpool via Bowes, Brough & Kirkby Stephen, May-
     Nov Fri-Mon 1/day

Dales & District (☎ 01677-425203, 💻 www.dalesanddistrict.co.uk)
156/157 Northallerton to Hawes, Mon-Sat 8/day, Sun 4/day

First (💻 www.firstgroup.com/bustravel.php)
184 Huddersfield to Manchester via Marsden, Standedge & Diggle, Mon-Sat
     1/hr, Sun 5/day
500 Keighley to Todmorden via Haworth, Oxenhope & Hebden Bridge, daily 4/day
     plus 1/day Keighley to Todmorden
528 Halifax to Rochdale via Ripponden, Lydgate & Littleborough/Blackstone
     Edge, daily 1/hr
590 Halifax to Rochdale via Hebden Bridge & Todmorden, daily 1/hr
591 Halifax to Heptonstall via Hebden Bridge, Mon-Sat 1/hr
592 Halifax to Burnley via Hebden Bridge & Todmorden, daily 1/hr
593 Halifax to Old Town via Hebden Bridge, Mon-Sat 1/hr
594 Halifax to Todmorden via Hebden Bridge, Mon-Sat 2/hr, Halifax to Hebden
     Bridge, Easter to Sep Sun 4/day

Grand Prix Coaches (☎ 01768-341328)
563 Penrith to Kirkby Stephen via Appleby & Brough, Mon-Sat 6/day

Hadrian's Wall Bus Service (🖥 www.hadrians-wall.org.uk)
AD122 Carlisle to Hexham via Greenhead, Haltwhistle & Once Brewed, Apr-Oct
daily 5/day + Haltwhistle to Newcastle via Once Brewed Apr-Oct daily 2/day
681 Haltwhistle to Housesteads via Once Brewed, Mon-Sat 2/day
185 Carlisle to Haltwhistle via Crosby-on-Eden, Brampton, Gilsland, Longbyre,
Greenhead & Walltown, Mon-Sat 2/day + 1/day from Housesteads via Once
Brewed (operated by Stacey's of Carlisle)

Harrogate District Little Red Bus (☎ 01423 526655, 🖥 www.littleredbus.co.uk)
30/30A Keld to Richmond via Thwaite, Muker (Farmer's Arms), and Reeth, Mon-
Sat 2/day; and Reeth to Richmond Mon-Sat 6/day
113 Hawes to Garsdale, Mon-Sat 5/day

Hulleys of Baslow (☎ 01246-582246, 🖥 www.hulleys-of-baslow.co.uk)
260 Castleton to Edale, Sun & Bank Hol Mon only 6/day
173 Castleton to Bakewell, daily 3/day
272 Sheffield to Castleton, Mon-Sat 3/day plus 9/day operated by First Mainline

Jacksons of Silsden (☎ 01535-652376, 🖥 www.dalesbus.org)
809 Settle to Malham circular route (Malham Tarn Shuttle), Sat, Sun & bank hols
5/day, April-Oct (1/day starts in Ilkley and goes via Skipton & Gargrave to
Settle and 1/day continues from Settle to Ilkley via Gargrave and Skipton)

K&B Travel (☎ 01768-865446)
563C Penrith to Appleby, daily 2/day (see also Grand Prix Coaches opposite)

Keighley & District (☎ 01535-603284, 🖥 www.keighleyanddistrict.co.uk)
79 Skipton to Cowling, Mon-Sat 2/day
80 Skipton to Lothersdale, Mon-Sat 1-2/day
663/5 Keighley to Oxenhope (663)/Oakworth (665) via Haworth, daily 1/hr
664 Keighley to Stanbury via Haworth, Mon-Sat 1/hr
694 Bradford to Oxenhope via Haworth, Mon-Fri 1/day
720 Keighley to Oxenhope via Haworth, Mon-Sat 1/hr

Kirkby Lonsdale Coach Hire (☎ 01524-733831)
581 Ingleton to Horton-in-Ribblesdale via Giggleswick & Settle, Mon-Sat 3/day

Munro's of Jedburgh (☎ 01835-862253, 🖥 www.munrosofjedburgh.co.uk)
20 Kelso to Hawick via Jedburgh, Mon-Sat 6/day
67 Galashiels to Berwick via Kelso, Mon-Sat 6-7/day, Kelso to Berwick Sun
3/day, Kelso to Galashiels Sun 2/day
81 Kelso to Kirk Yetholm circular route, Mon-Sat 7/day
131 Newcastle to Jedburgh via Otterburn & Byrness, Mon-Sat 1/day
223 Kelso to Kirk Yetholm circular route, Sun 3/day

National Express (☎ 08705-808080, 🖥 www.nationalexpress.com)
350 Manchester to Sheffield via Crowden, daily 3/day
383 Chester to Edinburgh via Otterburn, Byrness & Jedburgh, 1/day

Pennine Motor Services (☎ 01756-795515, 🖥 www.dalesbus.org)
215 Burnley to Skipton via Earby & Thornton-in-Craven, Mon-Sat 1/hr, Sun 7/day
218 Barnoldswick to Gargrave via Earby & Thornton-in-Craven, Mon-Fri 1/day
580 Skipton to Giggleswick via Gargrave & Settle, Mon-Fri 1/hr, Sat 6/day
(cont'd overleaf)

Bus services *(continued from p45)*
Robinson's (☎ 01768-351424)/**Morris Minor Mini Coaches** (☎ 01768-352772)
573   Appleby circular route including Dufton, Fri 2/day
625   Penrith to Appleby via Dufton, Tue & Sat 1/day
680   Carlisle to Alston via Brampton, Mon-Sat 2/day + 1-2/day during term-time

Royal Mail Postbus (☎ 08457-740740, 🖳 www.postbus.royalmail.com)
366   Skipton to Malham via Gargrave and Airton, Mon-Fri 2/day
277   Hexham to Acomb via Bellingham, Mon-Fri 3/day, Sat 1/day
364   Leyburn to Northallerton via Hawes, Mon-Sat 1/day plus Northallerton to
      Hawes circular route Mon-Fri 3/day

Snaiths Travel (☎ 01830-520609)
447   Otterburn to Bellingham, Mon-Fri 1/day term-time only
449   Byrness to Bellingham via Otterburn, Mon-Fri 1/day year-round

Stagecoach (🖳 www.stagecoachbus.co.uk)
210   Skipton to Malham via Gargrave & Airton Sat 3/day
680   Carlisle to Nenthead via Brampton & Alston, Mon-Sat 2/day plus Sat 1/day
843   Preston to Malham via Skipton, Gargrave & Airton, Sat 1/day

Lancashire United (☎ 0845 272 7272, 🖳 www.lancashireunited.co.uk)
X80 Skipton to Preston via West Marton, Mon-Sat 4/day Sun 2/day

Tyne Valley Coaches (☎ 01434-602217) with **Tyne Blue Line** (☎ 01661-832333)
880   Hexham to Bellingham, Apr-Oct Mon-Sat 7-8/day

Tyrer Tours (☎ 01282-611123, 🖳 www.tyrertours.com)
X80 Skipton to Preston via West Marton, Mon-Sat 4/day (see also Stagecoach)
280   Skipton to Preston via Thornton-in-Craven, Mon-Sat 6/day

Wright Brothers' Coaches (☎ 01434-381200, 🖳 www.cumbria.gov.uk)
680   Carlisle to Nenthead via Brampton & Alston, Mon-Fri termtime 1/day plus
      1/day Brampton to Nenthead (see also Stagecoach)
888   Newcastle to Nenthead via Hexham & Alston, Mon-Sat 1/day plus Newcastle
      to Keswick via Hexham, Alston & Penrith, Jun-Sep daily 1-2/day

Wymetro (☎ 0113-245 7676, 🖳 www.wymetro.com)
E   Hebden Bridge circular route via Mytholm and Blackshaw Head

Rail services
DalesRail (🖳 www.dalesrail.com)
● Blackpool to Carlisle via Preston, Horton-in-Ribblesdale, Garsdale, Kirkby
Stephen & Appleby, Apr/May to Sep Sun 1/day plus 1/day Preston to Carlisle

Keighley & Worth Valley Railway (☎ 01535-645214, 🖳 www.kwvr.co.uk)
● Keighley to Oxenhope via Haworth, Sep-June weekends & bank holidays only 5-
11/day; July & Aug daily 5-11/day

Northern Rail (🖳 www.northernrail.org)
● Manchester to Sheffield via Edale, Mon-Fri 8/day, Sat1/hr, Sun 8/day
● Manchester to Huddersfield via Marsden, Mon-Sat 1/hr, Sun 7/day
● Leeds to Manchester via Hebden Bridge & Todmorden, Mon-Sat 2/hr, Sun 1/hr
● Leeds to Carlisle via Keighley, Skipton, Gargrave, Giggleswick, Horton-in-
Ribblesdale, Kirkby Stephen & Appleby, Mon-Sat 5-6/day, Sun 4/day
● Newcastle to Carlisle via Hexham, Haltwhistle & Greenhead, daily1/hr

Trans Pennine Express (🖳 www.tpexpress.com)
● Manchester to Newcastle via Leeds, York, Northallerton, Darlington &
Middlesborough, Mon-Sat 1/hr, Sun 8/day

PART 2: THE ENVIRONMENT AND NATURE

For such a small place Great Britain has an extraordinarily wide range of habitats. They include orchid-strewn grasslands, woodland, heathland, moorland and mountains as well as coastal and freshwater areas.

What follows is a brief description of some of the many plants and animals you may encounter so you can understand what their business is as they scuttle, fly or run past you, or if a plant simply bows its head in the breeze as you walk by. Just as it's good to have some background knowledge before visiting a new country, so it is with the glories of the countryside.

The countryside is a community; the birds, animals and insects have evolved to be able to exploit different food sources so they are not in competition with each other. Please try and fit into this community by taking note of the points made in the following chapter on minimum impact walking.

Conservation issues are also explored in this chapter on the premise that to really learn about a place you need to know more than just the names of all the plants and animals in it. It is just as important to understand the interactions going on between them and man's relationship with this ecological balance.

Flora and fauna

WILD FLOWERS, GRASSES AND OTHER PLANTS

Many grasses, wild flowers, heather, mosses and liverworts (lichen-type plant with liver-shaped leaves) owe their continued existence to man's land management; global warming notwithstanding, if left to its own devices much of the land would return to the natural state of temperate regions: the woodland of 10,000 years ago.

Rare breeds of livestock are often excellent grazers for rough grassland because they are hardier so do not have to be fed extra food that will then over fertilize the ground. They also seem to be more selective in what they eat, and taste better too.

❏ **Why are flowers the colour they are?**
The vast majority of British wild flowers range in colour from yellow to magenta and do not have red in them. The poppy is the most notable exception. This is because they are largely insect pollinated as opposed to being pollinated by birds. Birds see reds best, insects see yellow to magenta best.

Spring and early summer is the best time to see wild flowers. You may be amazed by how many are edible. Some examples are given below, but seek expert identification before trying any as some plants are poisonous.

Intensive agriculture took its toll on the wild flower population in the same way that it did on the birds and mammals. The flowers are making a comeback but it is illegal to pick many types of flowers now and the picking of most others is discouraged; it is always illegal without the landowners' permission, no matter what the type. Cut flowers only die, after all. It is much better to leave them to reseed and spread and hopefully magnify your or someone else's enjoyment another year.

Bogs and wet areas

Look out for **cotton grass** (a type of sedge), **deer-grass**, **cloudberry** (a dwarf blackberry with a light orange berry when ripe that can be used as a substitute for any fruit used in puddings and jams) and the insect-eating **sundew**. Drier areas of peat may be home to **crowberry** (a source of vitamin C) and **bilberry** (see below).

Peat itself is the ages-old remains of vegetation, including **sphagnum mosses**. This type of moss is now rare, but may be found in 'flushes' where water seeps out between gritstone and shale. Also look out for **bog asphodel**, **marsh thistle** and **marsh pennywort**.

Woodlands

Not much grows in coniferous plantations because the dense canopy prevents light getting in. But in oak woodlands the floor is often covered with interesting plants such as **bilberries**, whose small, round black fruit is ripe for picking from July to September and is much tastier than the more widely commercially sold American variety. It's recommended in jams, jellies, stews and cheesecake. Bilberry pie is known in Yorkshire as 'mucky-mouth pie', for reasons you can work out, and is eaten at funerals. Moorland **Cowberry** (also used in jams),

---

❑ Orchids

These highly prized plants, the occasional object of professional thefts, are often thought to grow only in tropical places. They come from one of the largest families in the world and their range is in fact widespread, right up to the Arctic Circle in some places. In Britain over 40 types grow wild and you'd be unlucky not to see any on the Pennine Way, especially in quarries and on hillsides. The **Lady's-slipper**, first discovered in Ingleborough in 1640; the **narrow-lipped helleborine**, which grows in Northumberland and the **frog orchid** are just some you may come across. The **early-purple orchid** (see photo opposite) is made into a drink called Saloop, which was popular before coffee became the staple.

Although they have a tendency to grow on other plants, orchids are not parasites, as many believe; they simply use them for support. They are distinctive as having one petal being longer than the other two and many growers say they're no more difficult to grow at home than many other houseplants. With their flowers being generally spectacular and the wonderful strong scent they're well worth the effort.

Foxglove
Digitalis purpurea

Meadow Cranesbill
Geranium pratense

Water Avens
Geum rivale

Common Vetch
Vicia sativa

Heartsease (Wild Pansy)
Viola tricolor

Germander Speedwell
Veronica chamaedrys

Early Purple Orchid
Orchis mascula

Violet
Viola riviniana

Red Campion
Silene dioica

Spear Thistle
Cirsium vulgare

Common Knapweed
Centaurea nigra

Common Fumitory
Fumaria officinalis

Bell Heather
Erica cinerea

Heather (Ling)
Calluna vulgaris

Blackthorn
Prunus spinosa

Devil's-bit Scabious
Succisa pratensis

Harebell
Campanula rotundifolia

Bluebell
Endymion non-scriptus

Cowslip
Primula veris

Marsh Marigold (Kingcup)
Caltha palustris

Meadow Buttercup
Ranunculis acris

Ox-eye Daisy
Leucanthemum vulgare

Tormentil
Potentilla erecta

Birdsfoot-trefoil
Lotus corniculatus

Dandelion
Taraxacum officinale

Common Ragwort
Senecio jacobaea

Primrose
Primula vulgaris

Rosebay Willowherb
Epilobium angustifolium

Rowan tree
Sorbus aucuparia

Gorse
Ulex europaeus

Lousewort
Pedicularis sylvatica

Herb-Robert
Geranium robertianum

Scarlet Pimpernel
Anagallis arvensis

Hemp-nettle
Galeopsis speciosa

Ransoms (Wild Garlic)
Allium ursinum

Yarrow
Achillea millefolium

wavy hair grass and **woodrush** are other species you may see. Other shrubs to look out for include **guelder rose** and **bird cherry**.

Higher areas

Much of the high land is peaty and many types of grass turn brown in winter. Those present include **matgrass**, **heath rush**, **bent**, **fescues** and **wavy hair grass**. Flowers include **tormentil** and **harebell**.

Heather is the main plant of higher areas and is carefully farmed for grouse. It is burnt in strips over the winter to ensure new growth as a food supply for the birds. It has many uses, including as a tea and flavouring beer, and makes a very comfortable mattress on a warm, sunny afternoon. When it flowers around August time, the moors can turn purple. **Bracken, gorse** and **tufted hair grass** are all signs that the land is not being intensively managed.

Lower areas

These places are where you'll see the most flowers, whose fresh and bright colours give the area an inspiring glitter, particularly if you have just descended from the browns and greens of the higher, peaty areas.

On valley sides used for grazing you may see **self heal**, **cowslips** (used to make wine and vinegar), **bloody cranesbill** and **mountain pansy**. **Hawthorn** seeds dropped by birds sprout up energetically and determinedly but are cropped back by sheep and fires. This is a good thing; these shrubs can grow to 8 metres (26ft) and would try to take over the hillsides to the detriment of the rich grasslands. They do, however, have a variety of uses: the young leaves are known as 'bread and cheese' because they used to be such a staple part of a diet; the flowers make a delicious drink and when combined with the fruit make a cure for insomnia. **Rushes** indicate poor drainage. Also look out for **bird's eye primrose**, **white clover** and the grasses such as **crested dog's tail** and **bent**.

TREES, WOODS AND FORESTS

Woods are part of our natural heritage as reflected in our folklore, Little Red Riding Hood and Robin Hood for example, and also in our history with the hunting grounds of Henry VIII and his subsequent felling of the New Forest to construct the fleets that led to Britannia 'ruling the waves'. To the west of Edale, at the start of the walk, is the small town of Chapel-en-le-Frith. Translated, its name

THE ENVIRONMENT AND NATURE

❏ **Fungi, micro-organisms and invertebrates**

In the soil below your feet and under the yellow leaves of autumn are millions, possibly billions, of organisms beavering away at recycling anything that has had its day and fallen to decay. One gram of woodland soil contains an estimated 4-5,000 species of bacteria. Almost all of them are unknown to science and the vitally important role they play in maintaining the natural balance of our ecosystems is only just beginning to be appreciated. Many scientists now believe these organisms actually run the earth. Research into them is at an early stage but as one American academic put it, 'As we walk across leaf litter we are like Godzilla walking over New York City.'

> ## ❏ The Forestry Commission
> The Forestry Commission is the governmental body in charge of Britain's forests. It states its mission to be 'To protect and expand Britain's forests and woodlands and increase their value to society and the environment'. It manages 800,000 hectares of woodland throughout Britain, and although it was largely responsible for encouraging the vast numbers of acres of coniferous woodland, it is now a driving force behind diversification of tree species in woodlands.

means 'chapel in the forest' because it used to be a small clearing in an enormous forest that stretched to Edale and beyond.

Ten thousand years ago as Europe emerged from the Ice Age but before man started to exert his influence on the landscape, 90% of the country was wooded. In 1086 when William the Conqueror ordered a survey it had declined to 15% and it then shrank to 4% by the 1870s. Today, less than 9% of England is wooded with an estimated 1.3 billion trees. What these figures disguise is that a huge proportion of the tree cover today, as opposed to 900 years ago or even 100 years ago, is made up of plantations of conifers (see box above).

It is hoped that by 2020 woodland will cover 20% of England and that a large proportion will be made up of indigenous species, such as oak. Despite this progress England will still be one of the least-wooded countries in Europe where the average wood cover is 36%.

Oak and broadleaf woodlands
The number of **oak** trees has increased by 20% in 20 years. They are now the commonest species in England. There are two native species: the **common** and the **sessile**. Sessile woodlands are generally remnants of the woodland of William the Conqueror's time and before. Broadleaf woods, that is deciduous (annual leaf-shedders) hardwood, including **beech**, **sycamore**, **birch**, **poplar** and **sweet chestnut**, have grown by 36% since 1980. However, they still only account for 1% of the Yorkshire Dales National Park.

In areas of poorer soil you will also see 'pioneer' species such as **rowan**, **silver birch**, **downy birch** and the much rarer **aspen**. In a natural environment

The wooded vale of Ickornshaw.

these improve the soil for longer-lasting species such as oak.

Coniferous woodland
The full extent of the demise of our native woodlands was not fully comprehended until the Second World War when politicians realized we had an inadequate strategic reserve of timber. The immediate response was to plant fast growing low-management trees such as the North American **Sitka spruce** across the agriculturally unvi-

able land of the British uplands. The mass-planting continued apace into the 1970s and '80s with big grants and tax breaks available to landowners and wealthy investors.

You can see the result of this 'blanket planting' in the northern Pennines; acres of same-age trees with such a dense canopy that nothing grows beneath. As with all monocultures pests easily build up and have to be controlled with chemicals. The deep ploughing damages soil structure and also leads to a higher incidence of flash floods as drainage patterns are altered. It's also been found that acid rain gets trapped in the trees and is released into the streams during a downpour killing young fish and invertebrates.

What's more, the end product from this environmentally damaging land-use is a low-grade timber used mainly for paper, a waste of a valuable raw material. Perversely and misleadingly this is often advertised as 'paper from sustainable forestry'. There are now efforts under way to replant felled coniferous timber with a wider range of species and the number of conifer plantations has fallen by 7% in the past 20 years. These new woodlands are not only planted for timber, but also promote recreation, tourism and are good for wildlife.

BIRDS

One thing you will see a lot of on your walk is birds and the best way of identifying birds is through their song. Each species sings a different tune, and not just for your pleasure. It is their way of letting others know that their territory is still occupied and not up for grabs, as well as a mating signal. The dawn chorus is such a cacophony because most avian fatalities take place at night, so when they wake and are still alive they have to let opportunist home-hunters know it. They also have a call, or alarm, which is different again from the song.

Birds evolved from reptiles. Their feathers are made from keratin, as are reptile scales. Feathers give birds their shape, warmth, distinctive colour, waterproofing and the ability to fly. All birds moult at least once a year.

A bird's beak is an extension of its upper jaw. It is used for nest building, eating, preening and as a weapon and has evolved to suit individual needs. A wading bird, for instance, will have a probing beak of a length to suit its feeding ground, whether it be mud, sand or shallow water. Different types of waders can therefore feed in the same area without competing. Because its brain is suspended by quasi-ligaments a woodpecker can bang its bill against wood in a way that would leave other birds and most humans brain-damaged.

Birds' feet have evolved to particular tasks too. Perching birds use a tendon along the back of their legs that tightens the toes as the leg is bent. This keeps it on the perch as it sleeps. Feet have different coverings too, being either feathers or bristles, scales or leathery skin. Owls can turn their outer toe backwards to help them grasp branches and their prey.

Claws help with this too, and they have also evolved to perform different tasks. Birds of prey tend to have stronger, curved talons; short, strong blunt claws are good for scratching the ground; the heron has adapted a comb-like claw for preening.

THE ENVIRONMENT AND NATURE

Some birds, such as the swallow, perform incredible annual migrations, navigating thousands of miles to exactly the same nest they occupied the previous summer. Recent research suggests that some birds ingest their own organs to keep themselves fuelled for the flight. Swifts are believed to fly non-stop for up to two years, only coming down at the end of that period to lay eggs. They can also survive cold periods by entering a state of torpor.

PENNINE BIRD HABITATS

Streams, rivers and lakes

Both the **great-crested grebe** and the **little grebe** live on natural lakes and reservoirs. In spring you can see the great-crested grebe's 'penguin dance', where they raise themselves from the water breast to breast by furiously paddling their feet, and then swing their heads from side to side. They also have their full plumage, including an elaborate collar that could well have served as inspiration for the Elizabethans. They nearly became extinct in Britain in the nineteenth century, but have now recovered despite plenty of enemies including pike, rooks, mink and even the wake from boats, which can flood their nests. The **little grebe** is small and dumpy but very well designed for hunting sticklebacks under water.

Yellow wagtails are summer visitors that are as likely to be seen on lakesides as in water meadows, pasture and even moors. How do you recognize them? They have a yellow underneath, unlike the **grey wagtail** which has a black chin and then a yellow belly. If the bird is by a fast-flowing stream it will almost certainly be a grey wagtail.

Reservoir water tends to be relatively acidic so supports little wildlife except wildfowl including **goosanders**, especially in winter, and the similar-looking **red-breasted mergansers**. They are both members of the sawbill family which use serrated bill edges to seize and hold small fish. The trout in the reservoirs will have been introduced for anglers.

In streams and rivers you may see **common sandpipers**. Most of them head for Africa in the winter, but about 50 are thought to brave it out in ever-milder Britain. You might see them stalking insects, their head held slowly and horizontally before a sudden snap marks the hunt to an end. **Dippers** are the only songbirds that can 'fly' underwater or walk along streambeds. You may see them 'curtseying' on rocks in the middle of swift-flowing streams before they dive under the surface. They fly extremely quickly, because their small wings were designed for maximum efficiency in the water and are far too small to keep the huge bodies airborne without enormous amounts of flapping and momentum.

Woodland

Although rare in the Pennines, broad-leaved woodland harbours a variety of bird-life. You may see, or more likely hear, a **green woodpecker**, the largest woodpecker in Britain. They are very shy and often hide behind branches. They trap insects by probing holes and cavities with their tongue, which has a sticky tip like a flycatcher.

The further north you go the more likely you are to see **pied flycatchers**, summer visitors from Africa. The male can have multiple mates and is known to keep territories well over a mile apart, perhaps to keep a quiet life.

Nuthatches are sparrow sized with blue backs, orange breasts and a black eye-stripe, and have the almost unique ability to clamber up and down trunks and branches. Here all year, in summer they eat insects and in the autumn crack open acorns and hazel nuts with hard whacks of their bill.

Treecreepers cling to trees in the same way as nuthatches and woodpeckers. They have a thin, downward-curved bill that is ideal for picking insects out of holes and crevices. They are brown above and silvery-white underneath, which should help you distinguish them from the similar sized and behaviourally similar **lesser-spotted woodpecker**, which is black and white and not seen on the more northern sections of the Pennine Way. The male woodpecker also has a red crown.

Coniferous woodland is not home to much wildlife at all, because the tree canopy is too dense. You may, however, see nesting **sparrowhawks**, Britain's second commonest bird of prey. It suffered a big decline in the 1950s due to the use of pesticides in farming. In all the British raptor (bird of prey) species the female is larger than the male, but the male sparrowhawk is one of the smallest raptors in Britain. It feeds entirely on fellow birds and has long legs and a long central toe for catching and holding them. It has a square ended tail and reasonably short wings for chasing birds into trees.

You may also see **short-eared owls** in young plantations because of the preponderance of their principal prey, the short-tailed vole. It also hunts over open moors, heaths and rough grasslands. This owl is probably the one that is most often seen in daylight. It has two ear-tufts on the top of its head which are, you've guessed it, shorter than the long-eared owl's.

You may also see a **black grouse** (see box p156), also known as **black game**. Conifer plantations are providing temporary havens for them while they try to regain some of their numbers. The males, black cocks, perform in mock-fights known as a lek in front of the females, **grey hens**. This happens throughout the year and if you see one fluffing up the white of its tail and cooing like a dove don't necessarily expect to see a female present, because they are quite happy to perform for anyone.

Coniferous woods are also home to the greeny-yellow **goldcrest**, Britain's smallest bird. It weighs less than 10 grams but along with the **coal tit** is possibly the dominant species in coniferous woods. Because it is one of the few species that can exploit conifers it is growing in number.

THE ENVIRONMENT AND NATURE

BLACK GROUSE
L: 580mm/23"

Moor, bog and grazing

Many birds have developed to live in the wettest, windiest, most barren places in England; the places along which the best of the Pennine Way passes. On heather moors you will almost certainly see **red-grouse**, for whom the heather is intensively managed to ensure a good supply of young shoots for food. They are reddy brown, slightly smaller than a pheasant and likely to get up at your feet and fly off making a lot of noise.

Moorland is also home to Britain's smallest falcon, the **merlin**. The male is slate-grey, the female a reddish brown. They eat small birds, catching them with low dashing flights. Their main threat comes from the expense of maintaining moorland for grouse shooting; as costs grow fewer and fewer farmers are doing this and with the disappearance of the moor we will see the disappearance of the merlin.

Bogs are breeding grounds for many species of waders, including the **curlew**, the emblem of the RSPB if not the Pennine Way. Long-legged, brown and buff coloured, they probe for worms and fish with their long, downward-curving bill. The curlew's forlorn bleat will follow you across many a moor.

Snipe and **Jack Snipe** live in wet areas. The former is the more common and bigger of the two (but is in itself smaller than a grouse), but they both share very similar plumages. Both have long bills for feeding in water, but the snipe's is particularly long. They rely on being camouflaged rather than escaping predators by flight, and hence often get up right at your feet. Once airborne their trajectory is fast and zigzag.

CURLEW
L: 600MM/24"

Golden Plover live in peaty terrain in winter and move to grassland in the summer. They are a little larger than a snipe, have golden spotted upper parts, are generally seen in a flock and can be recognized by their feeding action of running, pausing to look and listen for food (seeds and insects) and bobbing down to eat it. **Dunlins** also live in peaty terrain and are half the size of a golden plover but not dissimilar in colouring to the inexperienced eye. They are a very common wader.

You may also see but are more likely to hear the continuous and rapid song of the **skylark**. They tend to move from moorland to lower agricultural land in the

SKYLARK
L: 185MM/7.25"

LAPWING/PEEWIT
L: 320MM/12.5"

winter. Just bigger than a house sparrow, they have brown upper parts and chin with dark flakes and a white belly.

Patches of gorse and juniper scrub are often chosen as a nesting site for **linnets**, which flock together during the winter but operate in small colonies at other times. They are small birds that will also be seen on open farmland, as will the slightly larger **yellow hammer**, recognizable by its yellow head and chest. It too nests in gorse and juniper bushes.

The **lapwing** is relatively common, quite large and can be recognized by its whispy black plume on the back of its head and, in summer, the aerial acrobatics of the male. They fly high to dive steeply down, twisting and turning as if out of control before pulling out at the last minute.

The **meadow pipit** is a small, and a classic LBJ (little brown job), they make plenty of noise and on a still day will climb to about 15 metres (50ft) and then open their wings to parachute gently down. They can sometimes be recognized by their white outer tail feathers as they fly away from you.

The **peregrine falcon** had a hard time in the 20th century, being shot during the Second World War to protect carrier pigeons and then finding it hard to rear their young after eating insects that had fed on pesticide-soaked plants. Their recent comeback is therefore a sign that things are picking up again in the British countryside.

Buildings and cliffs

Swallows, **house martins** and **swifts** all nest in barns and other buildings. They are hard to tell apart, but as a simple guide: swallows are the largest, are blue-black above and have a white belly and a long-forked tail; swifts are the next down in size, are essentially all black with a shallow forked tail that is usually closed and probably fly the fastest; house martins are the smallest, have a relatively short tail and a completely white underneath and, most usefully for identification purposes, a white rump (on top, near the tail). As a walker, you may be able to relate to why a non-breeding swift will fly 100 miles to avoid rain. If insects are bugging you, thank nature for swifts. A single one will eat 10,000 of the pesky buzzers a day, so think how many more bites you would suffer if it were not for them.

Peregrine falcons, **kestrels** and **jackdaws** (similar to a crow but with a whitish back of the head) nest in cliffs. The kestrel, Britain's commonest and most familiar bird of prey, also nests in man-made structures and is sometimes seen in city centres. It can be distinguished from the sparrow hawk, the second most common raptor, by its pointed wings and hovering when hunting. The male has a blue-grey head and a rich chestnut above, while the female is a duller

THE ENVIRONMENT AND NATURE

chestnut both above and on her head. Jackdaws are very common in villages and towns; if you see a crow-like bird sitting on a chimney top, reckon on it being a jackdaw.

Owls may also nest in cliffs and barns. You are most likely to see a **little owl**, which is a non-native resident that will often occupy the same perch day after day. Local knowledge can be useful for finding one of these. **Barn owls** have been affected by intensive agriculture and are on the decline but are also one of the most widely distributed birds in the world.

MAMMALS

Roe deer are the smallest of Britain's native deer, and are hard to see. They normally inhabit woodland areas but you may see one in grassland or, if you're very lucky, swimming in a lake. The males (bucks) claim a territory in spring and will chase a female (doe) round and round a tree before she gives in to his pursuit. This leaves circles of rings round the base of the tree, which are known as 'roe rings'.

Badgers like to live in deciduous woodland. Their black-and-white striped head makes them highly recognizable, but you're most likely to see them at night. They are true omnivores eating almost anything including berries, slugs and dead rabbits. The female (sow) gathers dry grasses and bracken in February for her nest. She then tucks them between her chin and forequarters and shuffles backwards, dragging them into her home (sett). The young are born blind in February and March and stay underground until spring.

Badgers were thought to spread TB to cows and for this unproven allegation 25,000 were culled in the 1980s and 1990s. The jury is still out, but there's no doubt they do contract and carry the disease. Some conservationists argue that it is more likely that they catch it from cows rather than the other way round. Much hope for a solution is placed in a possible vaccine.

Foxes are common wherever there are animals or birds to be preyed on, or dustbins to scavenge from, which is just about everywhere. Britain is estimated to have forty times the fox population of northern France. They are believed to have been here since before the last Ice Age when the sabre-toothed tiger would have prevented them from enjoying their current supremacy in the food chain.

Although now banned, fox hunting is an emotive countryside issue. A lot of conservationists believe that the fox itself is the best control of its numbers. If an environment is unsuitable they tend not to try and inhabit it and, like some marsupials, a pregnant vixen will reabsorb her embryos if conditions are unfavourable for raising cubs.

Foxes do a useful job eating carrion, which sometimes includes dead lambs, and rabbits and if they could learn to lay off the capercaillie and other protected birds they'd even get the RSPB on their side.

The **otter** is a sensitive indicator of the state of our rivers. They nearly died out in the last century due to a number of attacks on them, their habitat and their environment, but law has protected them since 1981. Due to the work of conservationists they're now making a comeback, but even small amounts of pollution can set back the efforts to give them a strong foothold in the wild. They are reclusive so you'll be incredibly lucky if you see one. They not only eat fish, but water voles and small aquatic birds. Their most successful hunting tactic is to launch a surprise attack from below as an otter's eyes are set on the top of its head and they have unique muscles that compensate for the visual distortion caused by water.

Mink were introduced from North America and only exist in the wild because they escaped or were set free from mink farms. They are one of the most serious pests in the countryside; being an alien species nature has yet to work out how to balance their presence. They spend a lot of time in rivers feeding on aquatic birds and fish and can be distinguished from otters by their considerably smaller size and white chin patch.

The **stoat** is a small but fierce predator. They are native and fairly widespread and can be recognized by their elongated and elegant form, reddy-brown coats and white bellies. They are very adaptable, moving in wherever they can find a den, including old rabbit burrows, and may live for up to ten years. Minks, stoats, polecats, otters, badgers, weasels (the world's smallest carnivores) and pine martens are all from the same family.

The **red squirrel** is native, unlike the grey squirrel, but it is now rare to see one. They are smaller than their reviled grey cousins and feature a vibrant red coat and fabulously bushy tail (although their coat turns a little browner in winter). Note, too, the tufts that grow at the tips of their ears.

The alien **grey squirrel** has played a big part in the demise of the red squirrel, partly because it is able to eat the red squirrel's food before it ripens. Efforts to reintroduce the red squirrel have not had a great deal of success, partly because they're reluctant to move from tree to tree along the ground and therefore need a dense tree canopy, but also because they lack traffic sense, which forshortens their lives in urban areas.

The **common shrew** is a tiny animal that lives in woodland and hedgerows. It needs to eat every four hours, and in a 24-hour period will eat insects weighing twice its body weight, using its long sensitive nose to sniff them out. It spends a lot of time underground eating earthworms. The mother and babies are sometimes seen traversing open ground in a train-like procession, with each shrew holding the tale of the one in front. It is the second most common British mammal.

The **mole** is armed with powerful forearms that it uses to burrow a network of underground tunnels that act as traps for unsuspecting earthworms. They patrol these every four hours, either eating all the visitors on the spot or gathering them up to save for later after immobilizing them through decapitation.

In woodland or anywhere near buildings you may see the smallest of Britain's 15 resident species of **bat**, the **pipistrelle**. Bats have been here consistently since the Ice Age and are now a protected species. Even though the pipistrelle weighs a tiny 3-8 grams (about the same as a single clove of garlic,

THE ENVIRONMENT AND NATURE

or two sheets of kitchen roll), in one night it may eat as many as 3500 insects. Bats and **dormice** are the only British mammals to truly hibernate throughout the whole winter from October to April. They will wake, however, if the temperature increases to unseasonal levels.

REPTILES

The **adder**, or viper, is Britain's only poisonous snake but is harmless if left alone. It can be recognized by a black ziz-zag down its back and found in woodland and moorland. They hibernate in winter and when possible laze around in the morning and evening sun in spring and summer, eating everything from slugs to small birds. The males fight for females by rearing up and twisting themselves round each other as if trying to climb a tree; victory is often down to length. While this strenuous activity is going on the females are still asleep. They wake to find the victorious male rubbing his body against her and sticking his tongue out. It may sound all too familiar to many.

Although the **slow worm** looks like a snake, it is in fact a lizard, sharing their notched tongue (rather than a snake's forked tongue), moveable eyelids (snakes have no eyelids) and fixed jaw (snakes have a free jaw for swallowing large prey). They eat slugs and insects and inhabit thick vegetation and rotting wood. The **common lizard** inhabits grass, in woods, moorland or grassland. They feed on insects and spiders.

Conserving the Pennines

Some of us are painfully aware of the destruction of the countryside that following the end of the Second World War. In that time Britain lost some of its most precious habitats: over 150,000 miles of hedgerow, 95% of lowland hay meadows and 80% of chalk and limestone grassland to name but three. The otter which was once common is only now beginning to make a comeback, the large blue butterfly has become extinct, as have ten species of plant; several types of bat are endangered and even the common frog has become uncommon. The figures go on and on and are a sad reflection of our once-abundant countryside.

We now live in a time when 'conservation' and 'the environment' are well-used terms and it's tempting to be complacent in the belief that the countryside is in safe hands. While there have been a few significant improvements in recent years, many areas have continued to decline. Populations of wild birds, for instance, are good indicators of biodiversity as they are near the top of the food chain. The State of the Countryside 2001 report showed the serious decline in populations of 41 common farmland and woodland birds because of habitat destruction and pollution. In the Pennines the number of skylarks has dropped by 39% since 1990. The species that remain are increasingly being forced to live in ghettos which limits their chances of breeding successfully and could lead to damaging in-breeding. These trends are being mirrored throughout the world. If they continue the world could lose a quarter of its plant and animal species in the next thirty years.

As a nation we have lost touch not only with country matters, but with nature itself. Today most people's only contact with nature is through anthropomorphizing books or wildlife documentaries on television. This is hardly surprising. In the first census, in 1801, 70% of British people lived in the countryside. In the year 2000 that figure had fallen to a staggering 10%. Even though they may live in the countryside many in that 10% category have no real contact with the land or interest in rural affairs.

As walkers we are in a privileged position to re establish our relationship with nature and become interested and active in how it is looked after. It is after all, to some extent, all of our land; we depend on it for physical and spiritual sustenance. It's therefore useful to have some understanding of how it is currently being managed on our behalf.

GOVERNMENT AGENCIES AND SCHEMES

Government responsibility for the countryside is handled in England by **Natural England** (comprised of the formerly independent agencies English Nature, the Countryside Agency and the Rural Development Service). Natural England is responsible for 'enhancing biodiversity and landscape and wildlife in rural, urban, coastal and marine areas; promoting access, recreation and public well-being, and contributing to the way natural resources are managed, so they can be enjoyed now and for future generations'. Amongst other things it designates the level of protection for areas of land, as outlined below, and manages England's national trails (see box p60).

National Parks

National Park status is the highest level of landscape protection available in Britain and recognizes the importance of the area in terms of landscape, biodiversity and as a recreational resource. The Pennine Way passes through three National Parks: the Peak District, the Yorkshire Dales and Northumberland. Although they wield a considerable amount of power and can easily quash planning applications from the local council, their management is always a balance between conservation, the needs of visitors, and protecting the livelihoods of those who live within the park.

Following the Foot and Mouth outbreak in 2001 when footpaths countrywide were closed for months, the National Park Authorities suggested that Parks be used as a test bed for rural revival by setting up task forces to explain funding available to small rural businesses, generating ideas for projects, acting as the public element where necessary (eg in setting up farmers' markets) and advising on how to build on successes. It is hoped that these measures will help the government's stated objective, 'to move environmental and social goals closer to the heart of agricultural policy alongside its economic objectives'.

THE ENVIRONMENT AND NATURE

❑ National Trails

The Pennine Way is one of 15 National Trails in England and Wales. These are Britain's flagship long-distance paths which grew out of the post-war desire to protect the country's special places, a movement which also gave birth to National Parks and AONBs.

National Trails in England are designated and largely funded by Natural England and are managed on the ground by a National Trail Officer. They co-ordinate the maintenance work undertaken by the local highway authority and landowners to ensure that the trail is kept to nationally agreed standards.

The existence of the National Parks does, however, raise the question of what is being done to conserve and protect the countryside outside their boundaries? The policy of giving special protection to certain areas suggests that those areas not protected tend to be ignored when funding comes to be allocated. Since only 7% of the British Isles has National Park status, the conclusion to be drawn is that vast areas remain neglected and under threat.

Areas of Outstanding Natural Beauty (AONBs)

Land which falls outside the remit of a National Park but which is nonetheless deemed special enough for protection may be designated an AONB, the second level of protection after National Park status.

National Nature Reserves (NNRs) and Local Nature Reserves (LNRs)

NNRs are places where wildlife comes first. They were established to protect the most important areas of wildlife habitat and geological formations in Britain, and as places for scientific research. This does not mean they are 'no-go areas' for people. It means that we must be careful not to damage the wildlife of these fragile places.

LNRs are for both people and wildlife. They are living green spaces in towns, cities, villages and countryside which are important to people, and sup-

❑ Statutory bodies – contact details

- **Department for Environment, Food and Rural Affairs** (☎ 020-7238 6951, 🖳 www.defra.gov.uk) Government ministry responsible for sustainable development in the countryside.
- **Natural England** (☎ 0870-333 1181; 🖳 www.naturalengland.org.uk) See p59.
- **English Heritage** (🖳 www.english-heritage.org.uk) Organization whose central aim is to make sure that the historic environment of England is properly maintained. It is officially known as the Historic Buildings and Monuments Commission for England.
- **Forestry Commission** (☎ 0845-367 3787, 🖳 www.forestry.gov.uk). Government department for establishing and managing forests for a variety of uses (see box p50).
- **Peak District National Park** (🖳 www.peakdistrict.org).
- **Northumberland National Park** (🖳 www.northumberlandnationalpark.org.uk).
- **Yorkshire Dales National Park** (🖳 www.yorkshiredales.org.uk).

port a rich and vibrant variety of wildlife. They are places which have wildlife or geology of special local interest.

Sites of Special Scientific Interest (SSSIs)

SSSIs purport to afford extra protection to unique areas against anything that threatens the habitat or environment. They range in size from a small site where orchids grow, or birds nest, to vast swathes of upland, moorland and wetland.

The country through which the Pennine Way passes has its share of SSSIs but they are not given a high profile for the very reason that this would draw unwanted attention. They are managed in partnership with the owners and occupiers of the land but it seems this management is not always effective.

Special Areas of Conservation (SACs)

SACs are areas which have been given special protection under the European Union's Habitats Directive. They provide increased protection to a variety of wild animals, plants and habitats and are a vital part of global efforts to conserve the world's biodiversity.

❏ **Campaigning and conservation organizations – contact details**

● **Royal Society for the Protection of Birds** (RSPB; ☎ 01767-680551, 🖳 www.rspb.org.uk; The Lodge, Sandy, Bedfordshire SG19 2DL) (see p62).

● **Campaign to Protect Rural England** (CPRE; ☎ 020-7981 2800, 🖳 www.cpre.org.uk; 128 Southwark St, London SE1 0SW) The CPRE exists to promote the beauty and diversity of rural England by encouraging the sustainable use of land and other natural resources in both town and country.

● **National Trust** (☎ 0870-458 4000, 🖳 www.nationaltrust.org.uk; PO Box 39, Warrington WA5 7WD) A charity with 3.4 million members which aims to protect, through ownership, threatened coastline, countryside, historic houses, castles and gardens, and archaeological remains for everybody to enjoy.

● **The Wildlife Trusts** (☎ 0870-036 7711, 🖳 www.wildlifetrusts.org; The Kiln, Waterside, Mather Rd, Newark, Nottinghamshire, NG24 1WT) The umbrella organization for the 47 wildlife trusts in the UK; the trust is concerned with all aspects of nature conservation and owns over 50 nature reserves. Wildlife trusts along the Pennine Way include Derbyshire, Durham, Northumberland and Yorkshire.

● **World Wide Fund for Nature** (WWF; ☎ 01483-426444, 🖳 www.wwf.org.uk; Panda House, Weyside Park, Godalming, Surrey GU7 1XR) One of the world's largest conservation organizations, protecting endangered species and threatened habitats.

● **Woodland Trust** (☎ 01476-581135, 🖳 www.woodland-trust.org.uk; Autumn Park, Dysart Rd, Grantham, Lincs NG31 6LL) The trust aims to conserve, restore and re-establish native woodlands throughout the UK.

● **Friends of the Earth** (☎ 020-7490 1555, 🖳 www.foe.co.uk; 26-8 Underwood St, London N1 7JQ) International organization campaigning for a better environment.

● **Greenpeace** (☎ 020-7865 8100, 🖳 www.greenpeace.org; Greenpeace House, Canonbury Villas, London N1 2PN) International organization promoting peaceful activism in defence of the environment worldwide.

● **British Trust for Conservation Volunteers** (BTCV; ☎ 01302-572244, 🖳 www.btcv.org; 163 Balby Rd, Doncaster DN4 0RH) Encourages people to value their environment and take practical action to improve it.

THE ENVIRONMENT AND NATURE

CAMPAIGNING AND CONSERVATION ORGANIZATIONS

The idea of conservation started back in the mid-1800s with the founding of the **Royal Society for the Protection of Birds** (RSPB). The rise of its membership figures accurately reflect public awareness and interest in environmental issues as a whole: it took until the 1960s to reach 10,000, but then rocketed to 200,000 in the 1970s and mushroomed to over one million by the year 2000. A major spur to the movement's metamorphosis came in 1962 when Rachel Carson published a book called *Silent Spring* documenting the effects of agricultural and industrial chemicals on the environment. It was the long overdue wake-up call needed to bring environmental issues into the public eye. The RSPB now has 182 nature reserves in the UK.

There are now a large number of campaigning and conservation groups (see box p61). Independent of government but reliant on public support, they can concentrate their resources either on acquiring land which can then be managed purely for conservation purposes, or on influencing political decision-makers by lobbying and campaigning.

The huge increase in public interest and support during the last 20 years indicates that people are more conscious of environmental issues and believe that it cannot be left to our political representatives to take care of them for us without our voice. We are becoming the most powerful lobbying group of all; an informed electorate.

THE ENVIRONMENT AND NATURE

Minimum impact walking

Britain has little wilderness, at least not by the dictionary definition of land that is 'uncultivated and uninhabited'. But parts of the Pennine Way include the closest we have and it's a fragile environment. Trapped between massive conurbations, the Peak District and South Pennines in particular are among the most crowded recreational areas in England and inevitably this has brought its problems. As more and more people enjoy the freedom of the hills so the land comes under increasing pressure and the potential for conflict with other land-users is heightened. Everyone has a right to this natural heritage but with it comes a responsibility to care for it too.

You can do this while walking the Pennine Way by practising many of the suggestions in this section. Rather than being seen as a restriction, learning how to minimize your impact brings you closer to the land and to those who work it.

ECONOMIC IMPACT

Rural businesses and communities in Britain have been hit hard in recent years by a seemingly endless series of crises but there is a lot that the walker can do to help. Playing your part today involves much more than simply closing the gate and not dropping litter; the new ethos which is fast becoming fashionable is 'local' and with it come huge social and environmental benefits.

Buy local
Look and ask for local produce to buy and eat. Not only does this cut down on the amount of pollution and congestion that the transportation of food creates, so-called 'food miles', but also ensures that you're supporting local farmers and

producers; the very people who have moulded the countryside you have come to see.

Support local businesses
If you spend £1 in a local business 80p of that pound stays within the local economy where it can be spent again and again to do the most good for that community and landscape. If, on the other hand, you spend your money in a national chain store or restaurant the situation is reversed; only 20% (main-

Buy local and keep
shops like this from closing

ly the staff wages) stays within the local economy and the rest covers goods, transport and profit. The more money which circulates locally and is spent on local labour and products the more power the community has to resist the corporatization of the countryside which we are currently witnessing.

Encourage local cultural traditions and skills
No part of the countryside looks the same. Buildings, food, skills and language evolve out of the landscape and are moulded over hundreds of years to suit the locality. Encountering these cultural differences is a great part of the pleasure of walking in new places. Visitors' enthusiasm for local traditions and skills brings awareness and pride, nurturing a sense of place; an increasingly important role in a world where economic globalization continues to undermine the very things that provide security and a feeling of belonging.

ENVIRONMENTAL IMPACT

By choosing a walking holiday you've already taken a positive step towards minimizing your impact on the wider environment. By following these suggestions you can also tread lightly along the Pennine Way. Some of the latter practices become particularly relevant if you are wild camping.

Use public transport
Traffic congestion is becoming the norm in Britain although where there is a demand for it, public transport is improving and gets better with use. There are days in the Peak District, particularly after Bank Holidays, when a brown band of pollution smothers the horizon. Once the cars have gone, the band disperses.

The Pennines, especially the southern end, are not as remote as we like to think and these days noise pollution is also a growing problem. The wilderness of Kinder Scout is often now marred by the noise of planes heading for Manchester Airport. Elsewhere there's nothing more disappointing than sitting on top of a hill in front of a beautiful view only to have the background hum of traffic intrude on the peace. Nearly all of us contribute to this pollution in some way and the best way to stop it is to stay out of our cars and use public transport instead, becoming part of the solution rather than part of the problem.

Do you really need to use a baggage-forwarding service?
Think twice about effectively negating all the good you do in arriving by public transport and walking by then having your baggage vanned from one end of the Pennine Way to the other. For those who are able-bodied and not camping, it's hard to imagine what needs cannot be easily fitted into a 30-litre backpack. This self-sufficiency is part of the satisfaction of long-distance walking.

(**Opposite**) **Top**: Support local businesses. The family-run Pen-y-ghent Café in Horton-in-Ribblesdale (see p138) provides not only sustenance for passing walkers but also keeps a Pennine Way book for wayfarers to sign and operates a check-in/check-out service for day walkers. **Bottom**: Pen-y-ghent seen in the distance from the church at Horton. (Photos © Chris Scott).

Never leave litter

A piece of orange peel left on the ground takes six months to decompose; silver foil 18 months; a plastic bag 10 years; clothes 15 years; and a can 85 years.

Although you'll encounter it in popular areas, become fanatical about taking out all your litter and even that left by others; if you enjoyed the countryside, show it some respect by keeping it clean. As well as being unsightly litter kills wildlife, pollutes the environment and can be dangerous to farm animals. One good idea is to repackage any pre-packaged food into reusable containers as this reduces the amount of rubbish you have to get rid of.

Is it OK if it's biodegradable? Not really. Apple cores and especially banana skins and orange peel are unsightly, encourage flies, ants and wasps and so ruin a picnic spot for others. In high-use areas such as the Pennine Way bury them or better still take them with you.

Erosion

Stay on the main trail The effect of your footsteps may seem minuscule but when they are multiplied by thousands of walkers each year they become rather more significant. Although it can be a bit much to ask when the actual pathway is waterlogged, avoid taking shortcuts, widening the trail or creating more than one path; your footprints will be followed by many others.

Consider walking out of season The maximum disturbance caused by walkers coincides with the time of year when nature wants to do most of its growth and recovery. In high-use areas, like that along much of the Pennine Way, the trail often never recovers. Walking at less busy times eases this pressure while also generating year-round income for the local economy. Not only that, but it may make the walk more enjoyable as there are fewer people on the path and (where it's open) there's less competition for accommodation.

Respect wildlife

Care for all wildlife you come across and tempting as it may be to pick wild flowers leave them so the next people who pass can enjoy them too. Don't break branches off or damage trees in any way.

If you come across wildlife keep your distance and don't watch for too long. Your presence can cause considerable stress particularly if the adults are with their young or in winter when the weather is harsh and food scarce. Young animals are rarely abandoned. If you come across deer calves or young birds keep away so that their mother can return.

Outdoor toiletry

As more and more people discover the joys of the outdoors answering the call of nature is becoming an important issue. In some national parks in North

---

(**Opposite**) **Top**: Black Hill (see p87). Erosion is a serious problem on some parts of the trail; to counter it slabs and duckboards are being laid in places. **Bottom**: Dewy cobweb in the heather. (Photos © Chris Scott).

America visitors are required to pack out their excrement. This could soon be necessary here. Human excrement is not only offensive to our senses but, more importantly, can infect water sources.

Where to go Wherever possible **use a toilet**. Public toilets are marked in this guide and you'll also find facilities in pubs and cafés and on campsites.

If you do have to go outdoors choose a site at least **30 metres away from running water**. Carry a small trowel and **dig a hole** about 15cm (6") deep to bury your excrement. It will decompose quicker when in contact with the top soil or leaf mould. Do not squash it under rocks as this slows down the composting process. However, do not attempt to dig any holes on land that is of historical or archaeological interest, such as around Hadrian's Wall.

Toilet paper and tampons Toilet paper decomposes slowly and is easily dug up by animals and can then blow into water sources or onto the trail. The best method for dealing with it is to **pack it out**, along with **tampons** and **sanitary towels**.

ACCESS AND THE RIGHT TO ROAM

Britain is a crowded island with few places where you can wander as you please. But in November 2005 the Countryside & Rights of Way Act 2000 (CRoW), or 'Right to Roam' as dubbed by walkers, came into effect after a long campaign to allow greater public access to areas of countryside in England and Wales deemed to be uncultivated open country; this essentially means moorland, heathland, downland and upland areas. Some land is covered by restrictions (ie high-impact activities such as driving, cycling, horse-riding) and some land is excluded (gardens, parks and cultivated land). Full details are given on 🖳 www.countrysideaccess.gov.uk.

This confusing sign does not mean 'no access for walkers' but advises that you're leaving a Right to Roam area and thereafter must stick to footpaths.

With more freedom in the countryside comes a need for more responsibility from the walker. Remember that wild open country is still the workplace of farmers and home to all sorts of wildlife. Have respect for both and avoid disturbing domestic and wild animals.

The Countryside Code

The Countryside Code seems like common sense but some people still appear to have no understanding of how to treat the countryside they walk in. Every visitor has a responsibility to minimize their impact so that others can enjoy the same peaceful landscapes; it doesn't take much effort.

The Countryside Code was revised and relaunched in 2004, in part because of the changes brought about by the CRoW Act (see opposite). Below is an expanded version of the new Code, launched under the logo '**Respect, Protect and Enjoy**':

● **Be safe** You're responsible for your own safety so follow the simple guidelines outlined on pp68-70.

● **Leave all gates as you find them** Normally a farmer leaves gates closed to keep livestock in but may sometimes leave them open to allow livestock access to food or water.

❏ **The Countryside Code**
● Be safe – plan ahead and follow any signs
● Leave gates and property as you find them
● Protect plants and animals, and take your litter home
● Keep dogs under close control
● Consider other people

● **Leave livestock, crops and machinery alone** Help farmers by not interfering with their means of livelihood.

● **Take your litter home** 'Pack it in, pack it out'. Litter is not only ugly but can be harmful to wildlife. Small mammals often become trapped in discarded cans and bottles. Many walkers think that orange peel and banana skins do not count as litter. Even biodegradable foodstuffs attract common scavenging species such as crows and gulls to the detriment of less dominant species. See p65.

● **Keep your dog under control** Across farmland dogs should be kept on a lead. During lambing time they should not be taken with you at all (see box below).

● **Enjoy the countryside and respect its life and work** Access to the countryside depends on being sensitive to the needs and wishes of those who live and work there. Being courteous and friendly to those you meet will ensure a healthy future for all based on partnership and co-operation.

● **Keep to paths across farmland** Stick to the official path across arable or pasture land. Minimize erosion by not cutting corners or widening the path.

● **Use gates and stiles to cross fences, hedges and walls** The Pennine Way is well supplied with stiles where it crosses field boundaries. If you have to climb over a gate because you can't open it always do so at the hinged end.

● **Guard against all risk of fire** Accidental fire is a great fear of farmers and foresters. Never make a camp fire and take matches and cigarette butts out with you to dispose of safely.

● **Help keep all water clean** Leaving litter and going to the toilet near a water source can pollute people's water supplies. See pp65-6 for advice.

● **Take special care on country roads** Drivers often go dangerously fast on

❏ **Lambing and and grouse shooting**
Lambing takes place from mid-March to mid-May when dogs should not be taken along the path. Even a dog secured on a lead can disturb a pregnant ewe. If you see a lamb or ewe that appears to be in distress contact the nearest farmer.

Grouse shooting is an important part of the rural economy and management of the countryside. Britain is home to 20% of the world's moorland, and is under a duty to look after it. The season runs from 12 August to 10 December but shooting is unlikely to affect your walk.

MINIMUM IMPACT & OUTDOOR SAFETY

narrow winding lanes. To be safe, walk facing the oncoming traffic and carry a torch or wear highly visible clothing when it's getting dark.

● **Protect wildlife, plants and trees**   Care for and respect all wildlife you come across along the Way. Don't pick plants, break trees or scare wild animals. If you come across young birds that appear to have been abandoned leave them alone.

● **Make no unnecessary noise**   Enjoy the peace and solitude of the outdoors by staying in small groups and acting unobtrusively.

Outdoor safety

AVOIDANCE OF HAZARDS

Along with thoughtful judgments, good planning and preparation ensure most hazards can be dealt with. This information is just as important for those out on a day walk as for those walking the entire trail. Always make sure you have suitable **clothes** (see pp34-5) to keep you warm and dry, whatever the conditions and a spare change of inner clothes. Carry adequate food and water too.

A compass, whistle and torch are also advisable, as are a GPS, additional mapping, a first-aid kit and a mobile phone. The **emergency signal** is six blasts on the whistle or six flashes with a torch. For **Mountain Rescue** dial ☎ 999 although this should be treated as the last resort.

Safety on the Pennine Way
It's vital you take every precaution to ensure your own safety:
● Avoid walking on your own if possible.

● Make sure that somebody knows your plans for every day that you are on the trail. This could be a friend or relative whom you have promised to call every night, or the establishment you plan to stay in at the end of each day's walk. That way, if you fail to turn up or call that evening, they can raise the alarm.

● If visibility is suddenly reduced and you become uncertain of the correct trail, wait. You'll find that mist often clears, at least for long enough to allow you to get your bearings. If you are still uncertain, and the weather does not look like improving, return the way you came to the nearest point of civilization, and try again another time when conditions have improved.

● Fill your water container at every opportunity; carry some high-energy snacks.
● Always carry a torch, compass, map, whistle and wet-weather gear with you.
● Wear proper walking boots, not trainers.
● Be extra vigilant if walking with children or the unfit.

Dealing with an accident
● Use basic first aid to treat the injury to the best of your ability.
● Try to work out exactly where you are. If possible leave someone with the casualty while others go to get help. If there are only two people, you have a dilemma. If you decide to get help leave all spare clothing and food with the casualty.
● In an emergency dial ☎ 999.

WEATHER FORECASTS

The Pennines suffer from enormously unpredictable weather, so for the more remote northern sections it's advisable to find out the forecast before you set off for the day. Many hostels and tourist information centres have a summary of the weather forecast pinned up somewhere. Alternatively you can call the premium-rate weather line (see below). Pay close attention to it and base your plans for the day on what you hear. That said, even if the forecast is for a fine sunny day, always assume the worst and pack some wet-weather gear.

Telephone and online forecasts

Telephone forecasts are frequently updated and generally reliable. Calls are charged at the expensive premium rate: **Weather Call** ☎ 09068 500419 (Cumbria), ☎ 09068-500417 (Yorkshire).

For detailed **online** weather outlooks, including local five-day forecasts, log on to 🖳 www.bbc.co.uk/weather or 🖳 www.metoffice.gov.uk.

BLISTERS

It is important to try new boots before embarking on a long trek. Make sure the boots are comfortable and try to avoid getting them wet on the inside. Airing and massaging your feet at rest stops does wonders. If you feel any hot spots stop immediately and apply a few strips of zinc oxide tape and leave it on until it is pain free or the tape starts to come off.

If you have left it too late and a blister has developed you should surround it with 'moleskin' or any other blister kit to protect it from abrasion. Popping it can lead to infection. If the skin is broken keep the area clean with antiseptic and cover with a non-adhesive dressing material held in place with tape.

HYPOTHERMIA

Also known as exposure, hypothermia occurs when the body can't generate enough heat to maintain its normal temperature, usually as a result of being wet, cold, unprotected from the wind, tired and hungry. It's usually more of a problem in upland areas on the moors or of course outside summer.

Hypothermia is easily avoided by wearing suitable clothing, carrying and eating enough food and drink, being aware of the weather conditions and keeping an eye on the condition of your companions.

Besides feeling cold and tired, early signs to watch for include shivering. Find shelter as soon as possible and give them another warm layer of clothing and allow them to rest until feeling better. If possible warm the victim up with a hot drink and some chocolate or other high-energy food. If allowed to worsen, erratic behaviour, slurring of speech and poor co-ordination will become apparent and the victim can quickly progress into unconsciousness, followed by coma and death. Quickly get the victim out of any wind and rain, improvising a shelter if necessary. Rapid restoration of bodily warmth is essential and best achieved by bare-skin contact: someone should get into the same sleeping bag

MINIMUM IMPACT & OUTDOOR SAFETY

as the patient, both having stripped to the bare essentials, placing any spare clothing under or over them to build up heat. Send urgently for help.

HYPERTHERMIA

Heat exhaustion As the planet warms unprepared or careless walkers suffering heat exhaustion will become more common, even in the north of England. Trudging up hill on a hot day in a singlet and no headware is asking for it and simply drinking water is not enough. Attention must also be paid to **minerals** lost in sweat. The correct combination and concentration of salts is vital to the body's electrolytic balance. This governs the transmission of nervous signals to the brain and explains why your senses become impaired as you become seriously dehydrated. A slight salt deficiency manifests itself in headaches, lethargy and muscle cramps, though it can take a day or two for salt levels to run down enough for these symptoms to become noticeable.

If you feel groggy, taking some **salt in solution** may make you feel better. In fact, after any exertion on a hot day a cup of slightly salty water or, better still, a swig of an isotonic drink instantly replenishes the minerals and water you lost during that activity. If you don't want to contaminate your water bottle with salty water and don't have a cup handy, lick the back of your hand, sprinkle on some salt, lick it off and swig it down with some water. **Too much salt** in one go (easily done with salt tablets so avoid them) will make you nauseous and may induce vomiting, which means that you lose fluid and so return to Square One. Remember, salt must be ingested with a substantial volume of water.

A sachet of **rehydration powder** such as Dioralyte or Rehydrat replenishes lost minerals in the correct proportions and is a worthwhile part of a first-aid kit. Both are expensive for what they are, so you want to save them for when you're feeling really rough. So-called **isotonic sports drinks** like Gatorade or Game are a more economical way of doing the same thing but they do lack the precise medicinal range and balance of minerals found in pharmaceutical rehydration powders. Alternatively a lunchtime mug of instant soup will do wonders.

Heatstroke Heatstroke is another matter altogether; much more serious. A high body temperature and an absence of sweating are early indications, followed by symptoms similar to hypothermia (see p69) such as a lack of co-ordination, convulsions and coma. Death will follow if treatment is not given instantly. Rehydration sachets are not enough: shade the victim and sponge them down, wrap them in wet towels, fan them, and get help immediately.

SUNBURN

It can happen, even in northern England and even on overcast days. The only surefire way to avoid it is to cover exposed skin, especially your head or smother yourself in factor 15+ sunscreen throughout the day. Don't forget your lips, nose, the back of your neck.

PART 4: ROUTE GUIDE & MAPS

Using this guide

The trail guide and maps have been divided into 15 stages (walking from south to north, the direction taken by 80% of walkers on the Pennine Way), though these are not to be taken as rigid daily itineraries since people walk at different speeds and have different interests.

The **route overviews** introduce the trail for each of these stages. They're followed by information about **route-finding troublespots** highlighting places where even experienced walkers may want to pay close attention to navigation. To enable you to plan your itinerary, **practical information** is presented on the trail maps. This includes walking times for both directions, all places to stay and eat, as well as useful shops and other services. Further **details** are given in the text under the entry for each place. For an overview of all this information see the town and village facilities table, pp66-7.

TRAIL MAPS

Scale and walking times
The trail maps are to a scale of **1:20,000** (1cm = 200m; 3¹/₈ inches = one mile). **Walking times** are given along the side of each map; the arrow shows the direction to which the time refers. The black triangles indicate the points between which the times have been taken. **See box below about walking times.**

These time-bars are a rough guide and are not there to judge your walking ability. There are so many variables that affect walking speed from the weather conditions to how many beers you drank the previous evening. After the first hour or two of walking you'll be able to see how your speed relates to the timings on the maps.

Up or down?
The trail is shown as a dashed line. An arrow across the trail indicates the slope; two arrows show that it is steep. Note that the arrow points towards the higher part of the trail. If, for example, you are walking from A (at 80m) to B (at 200m) and the trail between the two is short and steep, it would be shown thus: A- - - - >>- - - -B. Reversed arrow heads indicate a downward gradient.

❏ **Important note – walking times**
Unless otherwise specified, **all times in this book refer only to the time spent walking.** You will need to add 20-30% to allow for rests, photography, checking the map, drinking water etc. When planning the day's hike count on 5-7 hours' actual walking.

Accommodation

Apart from in large towns where some selection has been necessary, all accommodation on or close to the trail is marked (or indicated off the maps) with details in the accompanying text.

Unless otherwise specified, **B&B rates** are per person (/pp) for the summer (high) season assuming two people sharing a room; see also pp16-17. The number and type of room is given for each entry: S = single room, D = double, T = Twin, F = family (ie sleeping three or more people).

Other map features

The numbered GPS waypoints refer to the list on pp256-62. Features are marked on the map when they are pertinent to navigation. In order to avoid cluttering the maps and making them unusable not all features have been marked each time they occur.

The route guide

EDALE

For many whose dream it has been to walk the Pennine Way, Edale will have assumed mystical significance. The very name conjures up a vision of gritstone cottages on the edge of wild moorland, and should you drive over Mam Tor and see the valley unrolling far below the impression is indeed auspicious. A stone church set against green pastoral hills, a single-lane road winding through the middle to a dead end and some beautiful old houses.

Having arrived by train or car would-be Pennine wayfarers make their way up the lane to the Old Nag's Head (see p74) for their farewell pint, but they do not linger. They are eager to be off, to break free, to step out on the longest long-distance footpath of them all, the fabled Pennine Way.

See the Annual Events box p24 for details about Edale Country Day in June.

Transport

Unless you get dropped off, the **train** is by far the easiest way to get to and from Edale. It's just half an hour from Sheffield and 45 minutes from Manchester. Hulley's No 260 **bus** service between Castleton and Edale operates on Sundays/Bank Holiday Mondays only. For further details see the public transport map and table, pp42-6. Car parking costs £4 a day or £5 overnight. For a **taxi** try Michael Rowland (☎ 01433-621924) or Brian Jackson (☎ 01433-620525).

Services

Pop into the **Moorland Centre** (☎ 01433-670207, 🖥 www.peakdistrict.gov.uk; Easter to end Oct Mon-Fri 9.30am-5pm, Sat & Sun 9.30am-5.30pm; Nov to Easter Mon-Fri 10am-3.30pm, Sat & Sun 9.30am-4.30pm). In addition to tourist information there are maps, guidebooks, snacks and souvenirs as well as a collection box for the Edale Mountain Rescue Team.

At the top end of the village there's a **post office** (☎ 01433-670220, open Mon, Tue, Thur 9am-1pm) with an **ATM** and a basic village **shop** (open daily 9am-4.30pm but closed for lunch 1-2pm in low season, Wed & Sun to 1pm only). There is no mobile phone coverage in the village but there are two **public phones**.

Where to stay

If you're coming from any distance it makes sense to spend a night in Edale before starting your walk giving you a whole day to complete the fairly arduous section to

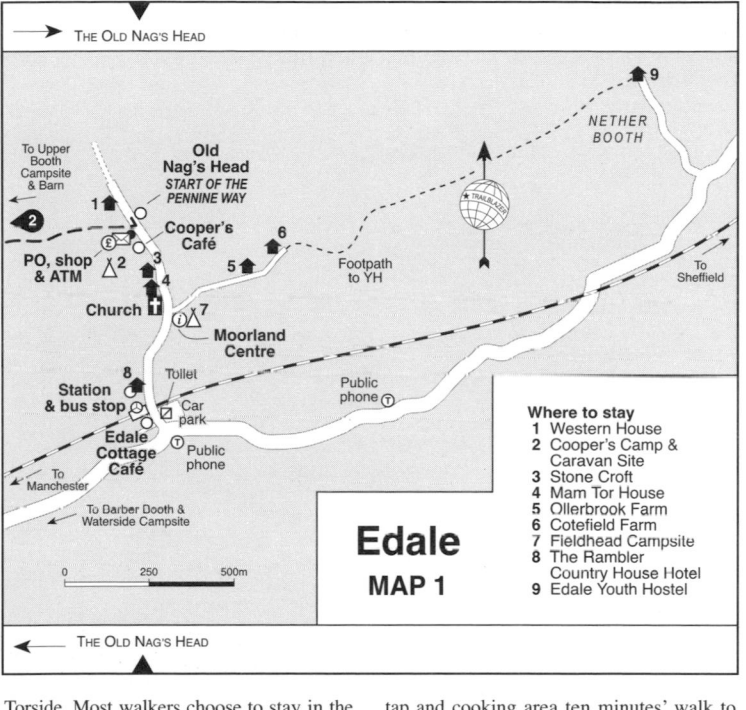

THE OLD NAG'S HEAD

Old Nag's Head
START OF THE PENNINE WAY

To Upper Booth Campsite & Barn

NETHER BOOTH

Cooper's Café

PO, shop & ATM

Footpath to YH

To Sheffield

Church

Moorland Centre

Station & bus stop

Toilet

Car park

Public phone

To Manchester

Edale Cottage Café

Public phone

To Darber Booth & Waterside Campsite

Where to stay
1 Western House
2 Cooper's Camp & Caravan Site
3 Stone Croft
4 Mam Tor House
5 Ollerbrook Farm
6 Cotefield Farm
7 Fieldhead Campsite
8 The Rambler Country House Hotel
9 Edale Youth Hostel

Edale

MAP 1

0   250   500m

THE OLD NAG'S HEAD

Torside. Most walkers choose to stay in the centre of the village but make sure you've booked ahead at peak times or at weekends.

The local community website ▢ **www .edale-valley.co.uk** lists many local establishments though some details are out of date; however, at the time of writing the website was being updated.

Note that some B&Bs may not be keen to take solo travellers at weekends.

In Edale There are two **campsites** in the centre of the village both of which are open all year: *Fieldhead* (☎ 01433-670386, ▢ www.fieldhead-campsite.co.uk) by the Moorland Centre, costs £4.50 per adult per night and *Cooper's Camp and Caravan Site* (☎/▢ 01433-670372, ▢ www.edale-valley.co.uk/coopers.htm), up the hill by the post office, charges £6 per person.

There's a simple **camping barn** (sleeping eight) with outside toilet, water

tap and cooking area ten minutes' walk to the east of the village at *Cotefield Farm* (☎ 01433-670273, ▢ www.edale-valley.co.uk/ cotefield.htm); for advance bookings call the YHA (☎ 0870-770 8868, ▢ www.yha .org.uk). It costs £6.50/pp (bring your own sleeping bag). There's also a 16-bed, self-catering **bunkhouse** at *Ollerbrook Farm* (☎ 01433-670235) costing £8 per person.

Walkers requiring B&B are fairly well catered for as long as they don't all turn up at once. The pleasantly lived-in *Mam Tor House* (☎ 01433-670253, ▢ www.mamtor house.co.uk; 2T/1F) next to the church has rooms bulging with books and charges £25. Nearby is *Stone Croft* (☎ 01433-670262, ▢ www.stonecroftguesthouse.co.uk; 2D, one en suite) which costs from £65-75 for a room.

Another cosy spot is *Western House* (☎ 01433-670014, ▢ www.cressbrook.co .uk/edale/westernhouse; 1D with private bathroom/1F en suite), just above the Nag's Head pub, which charges from £27.50 to £37.50/pp but requires two booked nights over a weekend.

The Rambler Country House Hotel (☎ 01433-670268; 3D/2T/4F) charges £38 for single occupancy and from £78 for two sharing, all en suite.

In Nether Booth Most nights you may find *Edale Youth Hostel* (bookings ☎ 0870-770 5808, 🖥 edale@yha.org.uk, open all day and all year) more of a 157-bed 'hyper-activity centre' over-run with school kids than the old ramblers' hostel it once was so beware before making the mile and a half walk east of Edale village, especially in the summer holidays as the hostel is usually fully booked with groups but at any time of the year it is best to book in advance. Dorm beds cost £12.50 for adults, £9 for under 18s. You can get there via a network of footpaths from the village or along the road. Evening meals are available and there is a bar.

In Barber Booth This small hamlet is about half a mile south-west of Edale (off Map 1, p73) or just under one mile south-east of Upper Booth (off Map 2) and if you're really stuck for accommodation *Waterside Campsite* (☎ 01433-670215) offers camping for £2.50/pp plus the same per tent and per vehicle.

Where to eat
Being the traditional start of the Pennine Way, a meal at the *Old Nag's Head* (☎ 01433-670291) at the top of the village is a must. Try the 'Nag's Special', a giant Yorkshire pudding full of lamb stew and chips for around £8; food is served daily 12-9.45pm, to 8pm on Sundays in the winter months.

The alternative is the less iconic *Rambler Country House Hotel* down the road or in the daytime try *Edale Cottage Café* near the station or *Cooper's Café* next to the post office.

EDALE TO CROWDEN   MAPS 1-9

Route overview

Traversing the peaty wastes of both the Kinder plateau and the tellingly named Bleaklow, distance-wise this **16-mile (26km, 6-7hrs)** stage is a jump in the deep end, not least because, at over **900m**, it includes the **second biggest total ascent** of the Pennine Way (the Cross Fell stage being nearly 1100m). A solid day's walk, it's a classic nevertheless, but these days for the right reasons.

The route was once so boggy and confusing that reputedly half of all who set out gave up. Today the worst of the mire has been subdued with stone slabs salvaged from demolished cotton mills and laid end to end to ensure the twin blessings of dry feet and a clearly navigable path.

The inaugural stage passes through the hamlet of **Upper Booth** (Map 2), a pleasant amble through the upper pastures of the valley. Thereafter follows the stiff ascent of **Jacob's Ladder** (Map 3) before open moorland is reached near **Edale Cross**. You'll meet the first of a handful of 'trig points' on top of **Kinder Low** where the route descends to take an impressive arc along the **Kinder Edges**, the plateau's western rim that at weekends can become thronged with day walkers.

Beyond the impressive but rarely flowing **Kinder Downfall** (Map 4) you leave the plateau rim for the steep stepped descent to William Clough (a Clough is a stream) and the Snake Path junction near **Mill Hill**. Here a slab causeway

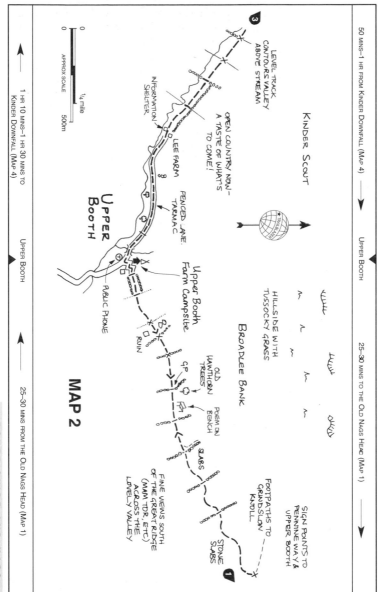

MAP 2

3

LEVEL TRACK
CONTOURS VALLEY
ABOVE STREAM

INFORMATION
SHELTER

KINDER SCOUT

OPEN COUNTRY NOW –
A TASTE OF WHAT'S
TO COME!

LEE FARM

UPPER
BOOTH

FENCED LANE.
TARMAC.

PUBLIC PHONE

HILLSIDE WITH
TUSSOCKY GRASS

BROADLEE BANK

Upper Booth
Farm Campsite

RUIN

G.P.

OLD
HAWTHORN
TREES

POEM ON
BENCH

SLABS

FOOTPATHS TO
PENNINE WAY &
UPPER BOOTH

GRINDSLOW
KNOLL

FINE VIEWS SOUTH
OF THE GREAT RIDGE
(MAM TOR, ETC.)
ACROSS THE
LOVELY VALLEY

STONE
SLABS

1

0
0
¼ mile
500m
APPROX SCALE

❏ **Kinder Scout**   **Map 3**

The Pennine Way used to go up Grindsbrook Clough to strike across the summit wastes of Kinder Scout, a challenging route that usually resulted in walkers becoming enmired and confused in the labyrinthine maze of peat channels. As generations of wandering boots eroded the peat the decision was taken to re-route the Way via the current, much more easily navigable, westerly path. But purists and the ignorant still march straight past the Old Nag's Head and up Grinds Brook. This is not a good idea.

For those who like to ignore this advice, the best way to cross the wilderness to Kinder Downfall is to follow a bearing of 310° from the top of Grindsbrook Clough where it emerges onto the plateau (SK105872 or N53° 22.9' W01° 50.6'). This should allow you to hit the easier edge path south of the Downfall (see Map 4 for the waypoint). With only a compass it's important not to stray north, even by a few degrees.

Up there, there are no landmarks or useful signs; misleading piles of stones or stakes indicating nothing. Even the wildlife lays low. The occasional golden plover pipes its warning call, a hare may spring up and run off at speed. Otherwise – nothing. Heed the plea of the golden plover and give it a wide berth.

unrolls invitingly across the bare moorland to **Snake Pass** (Map 6) on the A57. If you've had enough, hobble down to **Snake Pass Inn** (see p80) and drown your sorrows. Otherwise it's a good three hours to Torside, so buckle down and point your feet towards the sunken track known as **Devil's Dyke**, with Bleaklow your next objective.

In poor visibility (a caveat that can be invoked for any of the hill sections along the entire Pennine Way) the route to **Bleaklow Head** (Map 7) can be confusing and will need careful navigation. There are very few signs or waymarks to see you safely there, but if all is going well the meandering ascent along peat-lined gullies and past clear-water streams is an intimate, sheltered counterpoint to the preceding expanses of Kinder. Bleaklow itself is not so much a mountain as a peat soufflé that failed to rise and with good intuition or plain luck you'll reach the summit pile of stones skewered with a stake or two.

From this point it's all downhill to the **Longendale Valley** along the rim of **Clough Edge** (Map 8), a deep heather-clad gully, from where an underwhelming panorama of reservoirs and plantations reveal themselves far below.

Once the **B6105** is reached take heart as there's a good B&B close by (see p84). On the north side of the reservoir, **Crowden** (Map 9) is no more than a campsite and hostel-cum-activity centre, bringing you wearily but satisfyingly to the end of your first day. Only 240 miles to go.

Route-finding trouble spots (Edale to Crowden)

Even in thick mist the pathway to the summit to Kinder Low should present no difficulties, but watch out: the short hop from the trig point to the Kinder Edges path (Map 3) is not blatantly obvious, even in clear conditions.

It's the same story leaving Bleaklow summit (Map 7) where no single path leads to the mile post by the fence (GPS waypoint 006, see p256) at which point the route is clear. If in doubt or experiencing poor visibility follow a compass bearing or use GPS.

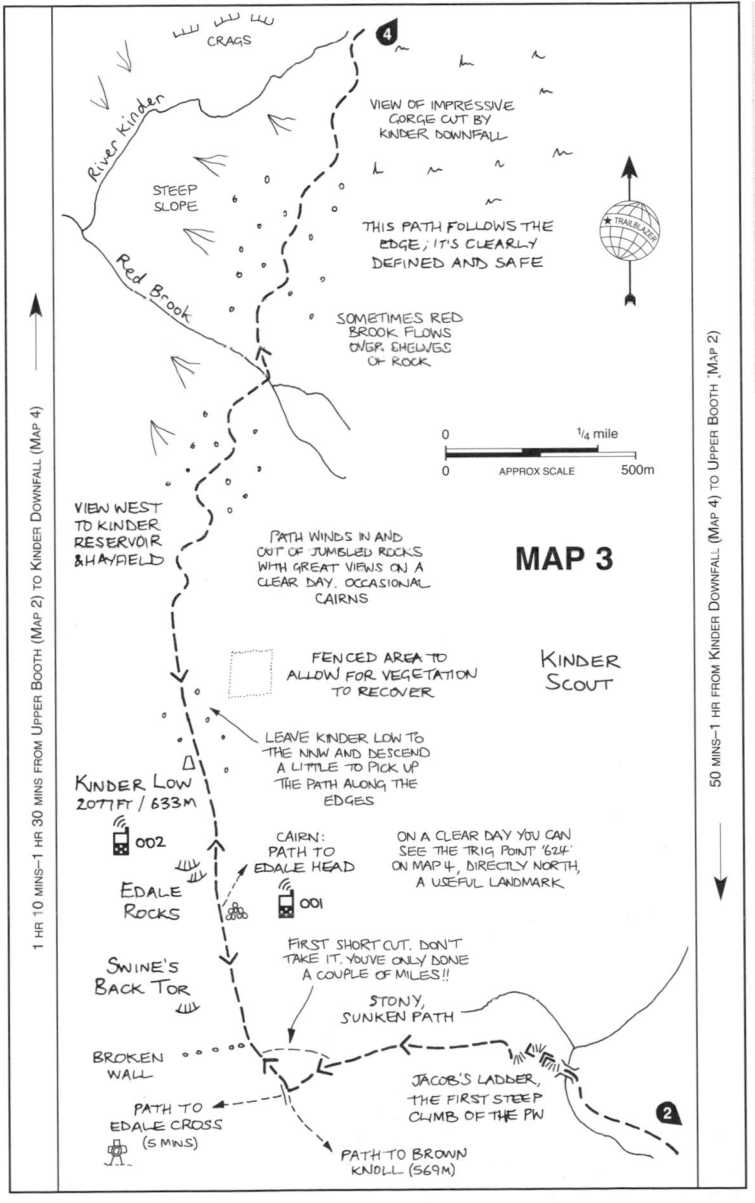

CRAGS

River Kinder

4

VIEW OF IMPRESSIVE
GORGE CUT BY
KINDER DOWNFALL

STEEP
SLOPE

Red Brook

THIS PATH FOLLOWS THE
EDGE, IT'S CLEARLY
DEFINED AND SAFE

SOMETIMES RED
BROOK FLOWS
OVER SHELVES
OF ROCK

TRAILBLAZER

0   ¼ mile
0   APPROX SCALE   500m

VIEW WEST
TO KINDER
RESERVOIR
& HAYFIELD

PATH WINDS IN AND
OUT OF JUMBLED ROCKS
WITH GREAT VIEWS ON A
CLEAR DAY. OCCASIONAL
CAIRNS

MAP 3

FENCED AREA TO
ALLOW FOR VEGETATION
TO RECOVER

KINDER
SCOUT

LEAVE KINDER LOW TO
THE NNW AND DESCEND
A LITTLE TO PICK UP
THE PATH ALONG THE
EDGES

KINDER LOW
2077 FT / 633 M

002

EDALE
ROCKS

CAIRN:
PATH TO
EDALE HEAD

001

ON A CLEAR DAY YOU CAN
SEE THE TRIG POINT '624'
ON MAP 4, DIRECTLY NORTH,
A USEFUL LANDMARK

SWINE'S
BACK TOR

FIRST SHORT CUT. DON'T
TAKE IT. YOU'VE ONLY DONE
A COUPLE OF MILES!!

STONY,
SUNKEN PATH

BROKEN
WALL

PATH TO
EDALE CROSS
(5 MINS)

JACOB'S LADDER,
THE FIRST STEEP
CLIMB OF THE PW

2

PATH TO BROWN
KNOLL (569M)

1 HR 10 MINS–1 HR 30 MINS FROM UPPER BOOTH (MAP 2) TO KINDER DOWNFALL (MAP 4)

50 MINS–1 HR FROM KINDER DOWNFALL (MAP 4) TO UPPER BOOTH (MAP 2)

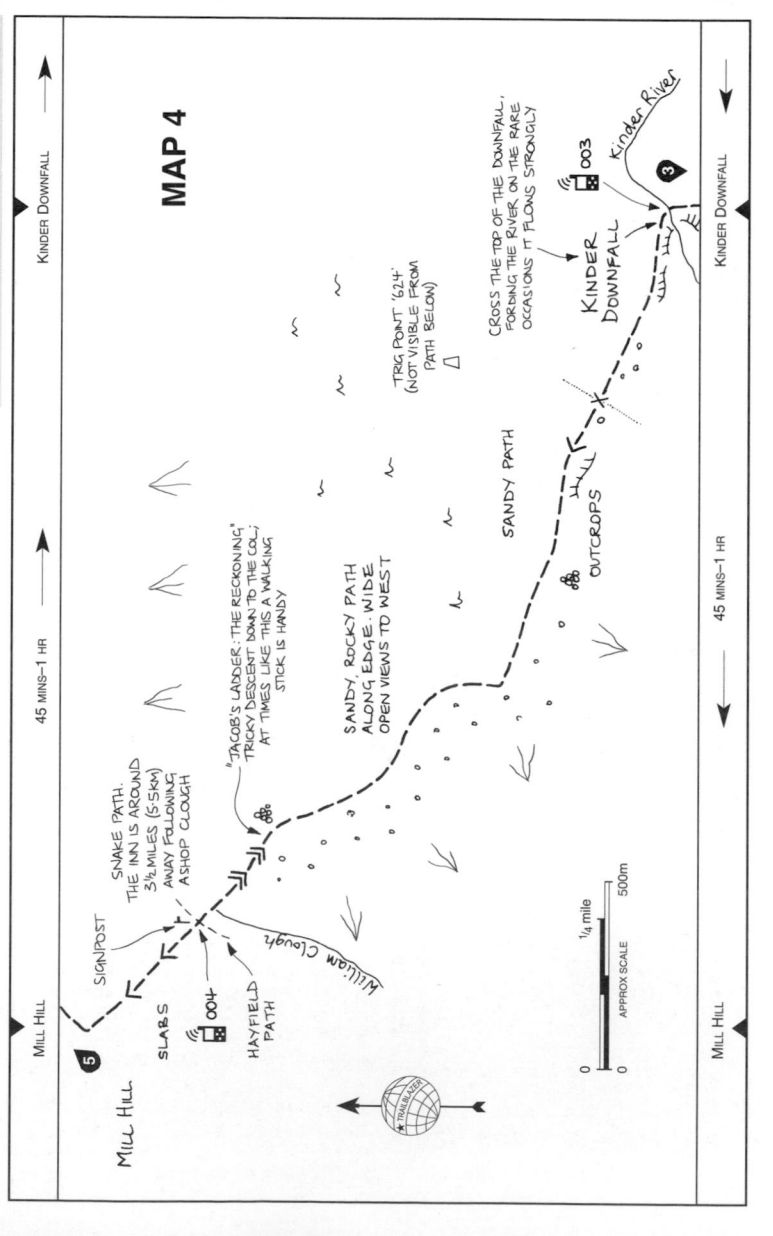

MAP 4

Mill Hill

Kinder Downfall

45 MINS–1 HR

SIGNPOST

SNAKE PATH.
THE INN IS AROUND
3½ MILES (5·5KM)
AWAY FOLLOWING
ASHOP CLOUGH

"JACOB'S LADDER: THE RECKONING"
TRICKY DESCENT DOWN TO THE COL;
AT TIMES LIKE THIS A WALKING
STICK IS HANDY

TRIG POINT '624'
(NOT VISIBLE FROM
PATH BELOW)

SLABS

HAYFIELD
PATH

004

William Clough

SANDY, ROCKY PATH
ALONG EDGE. WIDE
OPEN VIEWS TO WEST

SANDY PATH

OUTCROPS

CROSS THE TOP OF THE DOWNFALL,
FORDING THE RIVER ON THE RARE
OCCASIONS IT FLOWS STRONGLY

Kinder River

003

KINDER
DOWNFALL

3

¼ mile   500m

0   0

APPROX SCALE

0   0

TRAIL BLAZER

Mill Hill   45 MINS–1 HR   Mill Hill

Kinder Downfall

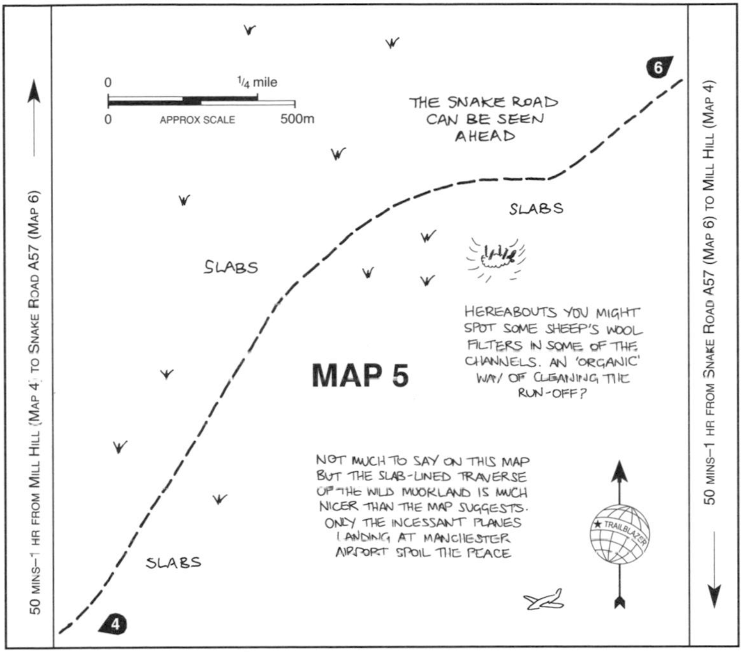

ROUTE GUIDE AND MAPS

6

THE SNAKE ROAD CAN BE SEEN AHEAD

0 ¼ mile
0 APPROX SCALE 500m

SLABS

SLABS

MAP 5

HEREABOUTS YOU MIGHT SPOT SOME SHEEP'S WOOL FILTERS IN SOME OF THE CHANNELS. AN 'ORGANIC' WAY OF CLEANING THE RUN-OFF?

NOT MUCH TO SAY ON THIS MAP BUT THE SLAB-LINED TRAVERSE OF THE WILD MOORLAND IS MUCH NICER THAN THE MAP SUGGESTS. ONLY THE INCESSANT PLANES LANDING AT MANCHESTER AIRPORT SPOIL THE PEACE

★ TRAILBLAZER

SLABS

4

50 MINS–1 HR FROM MILL HILL (MAP 4) TO SNAKE ROAD A57 (MAP 6)

50 MINS–1 HR FROM SNAKE ROAD A57 (MAP 6) TO MILL HILL (MAP 4)

❏ Peat

The Way has not become synonymous with miles of spirit-sapping bogs for nothing. Paving slabs have alleviated much of the misery, but why is it so darn soggy?

Peat and the underlying geology are to blame. The British Isles (and indeed much of the land mass of planet earth) was once covered in trees. Everywhere except the highest mountains and sandy beaches was wooded. Sabre-toothed tigers prowled in the forests alongside elephants and rhinos. Today these ancient woodlands and rampaging carnivores are no longer around. The reason for the disappearance of this habitat is not a natural phenomenon but the activities of early man.

Wet feet? Blame the cavemen!

When early Britons felled primeval forests for building and farming, groundwater was no longer absorbed and evaporated by the trees. Add the impermeability of the underlying gritstone and the saturated vegetation rotted where it lay, forming the peat, which you squelch through today. So, next time your boots fill with black peaty soup, don't curse nature, curse your axe-wielding forebears instead.

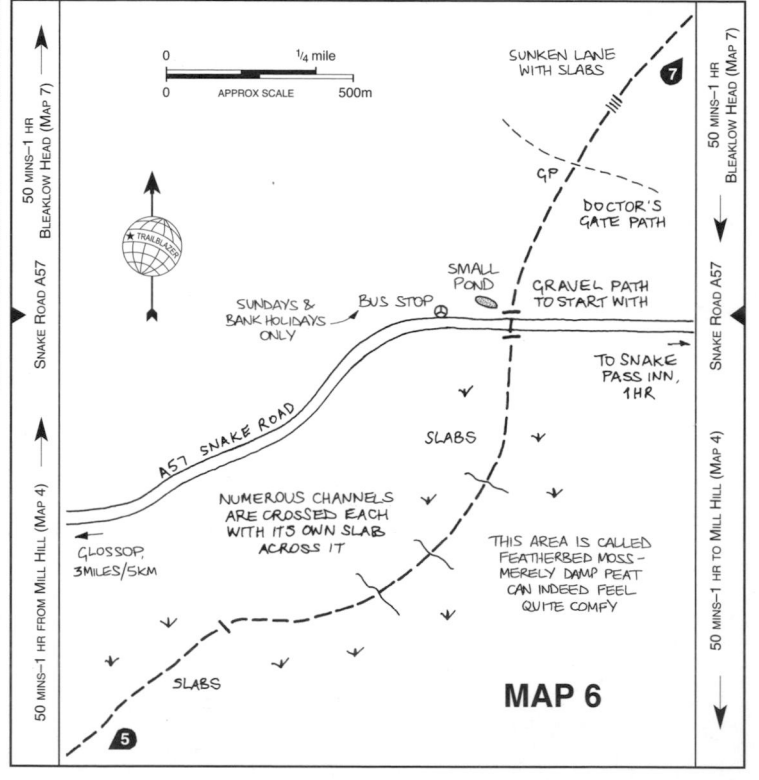

MAP 6

UPPER BOOTH **[Map 2, p75]**
Located two miles (3km) into the Pennine Way, Upper Booth can make a nice warm up the night before you start your walk proper. There's camping here at *Upper Booth Farm Campsite* (☎ 01433-670250, 🖥 www.upperboothcamping.co.uk) for £3 per person and a pitch in the **camping barn** for up to 12 people costs £5. Fresh free-range eggs and milk can be bought at this award-winning farm where conservation and business can be seen working hand in hand; an excellent example of how hill farming can be a sustainable and integral part of the local economy and community.

SNAKE PASS **[off Map 6]**
From Snake Pass, *Snake Pass Inn* (☎ 01433-651480; 🖥 www.snakepassinn.co .uk) (2S/6D all en suite) charges £40 for a single and £60 for a double). It is 2½ miles east down the A57, a pub full of history and character with a good choice of beer and meals at the Dambusters Bar. It's open all day, food is served daily 12 noon-9pm Wed-Sat, 12 noon-6pm on Sunday; in summer food may also be served on Mon and Tue as well. Of course a detour here means you probably won't make the Torside Valley tonight.

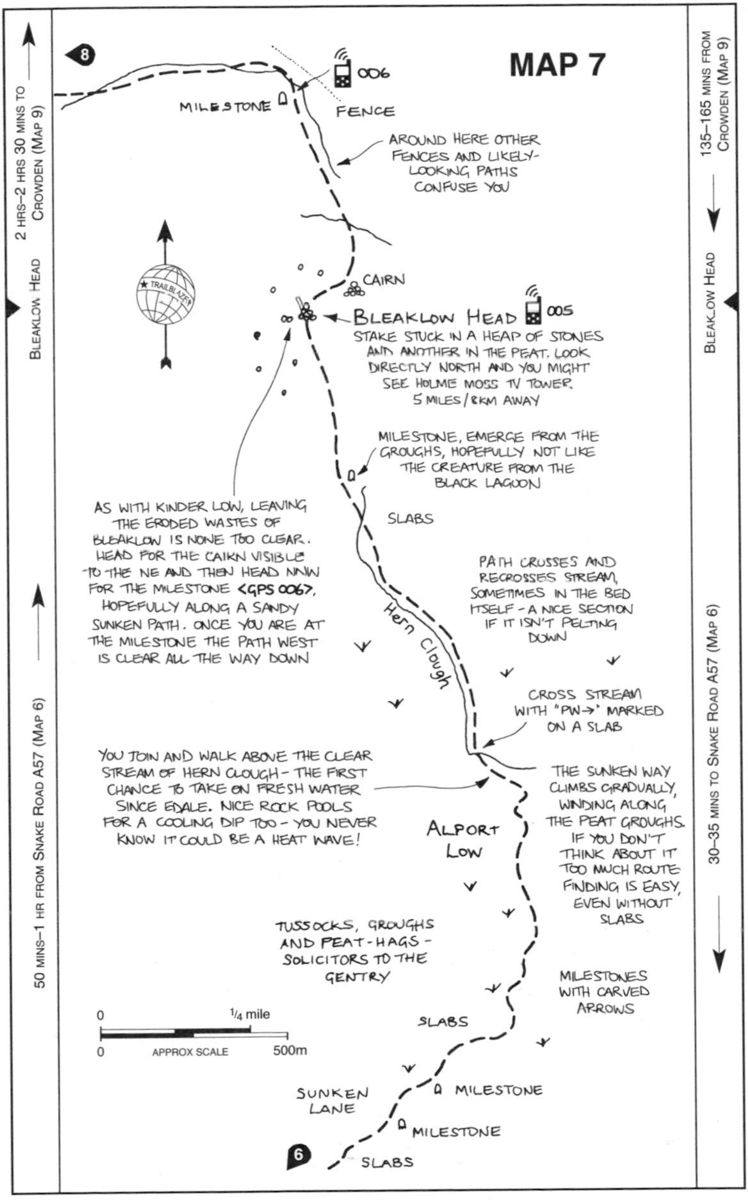

MAP 7

8

MILESTONE

006

FENCE

AROUND HERE OTHER FENCES AND LIKELY-LOOKING PATHS CONFUSE YOU

CAIRN

TRAILBLAZER

BLEAKLOW HEAD 005
STAKE STUCK IN A HEAP OF STONES AND ANOTHER IN THE PEAT. LOOK DIRECTLY NORTH AND YOU MIGHT SEE HOLME MOSS TV TOWER. 5 MILES / 8KM AWAY

MILESTONE, EMERGE FROM THE GROUGHS, HOPEFULLY NOT LIKE THE CREATURE FROM THE BLACK LAGOON

SLABS

AS WITH KINDER LOW, LEAVING THE ERODED WASTES OF BLEAKLOW IS NONE TOO CLEAR. HEAD FOR THE CAIRN VISIBLE TO THE NE AND THEN HEAD NNW FOR THE MILESTONE <GPS 007>, HOPEFULLY ALONG A SANDY SUNKEN PATH. ONCE YOU ARE AT THE MILESTONE THE PATH WEST IS CLEAR ALL THE WAY DOWN

PATH CROSSES AND RECROSSES STREAM, SOMETIMES IN THE BED ITSELF - A NICE SECTION IF IT ISN'T PELTING DOWN

Hern Clough

CROSS STREAM WITH "PW→" MARKED ON A SLAB

YOU JOIN AND WALK ABOVE THE CLEAR STREAM OF HERN CLOUGH - THE FIRST CHANCE TO TAKE ON FRESH WATER SINCE EDALE. NICE ROCK POOLS FOR A COOLING DIP TOO - YOU NEVER KNOW IT COULD BE A HEAT WAVE!

THE SUNKEN WAY CLIMBS GRADUALLY, WINDING ALONG THE PEAT GROUGHS. IF YOU DON'T THINK ABOUT IT TOO MUCH ROUTE FINDING IS EASY, EVEN WITHOUT SLABS

ALPORT LOW

TUSSOCKS, GROUGHS AND PEAT-HAGS - SOLICITORS TO THE GENTRY

MILESTONES WITH CARVED ARROWS

SLABS

0   1/4 mile
0   APPROX SCALE   500m

SUNKEN LANE

MILESTONE

MILESTONE

6

SLABS

2 HRS-2 HRS 30 MINS TO CROWDEN (MAP 9)

BLEAKLOW HEAD

50 MINS-1 HR FROM SNAKE ROAD A57 (MAP 6)

135-165 MINS FROM CROWDEN (MAP 9)

BLEAKLOW HEAD

30-35 MINS TO SNAKE ROAD A57 (MAP 6)

ROUTE GUIDE AND MAPS

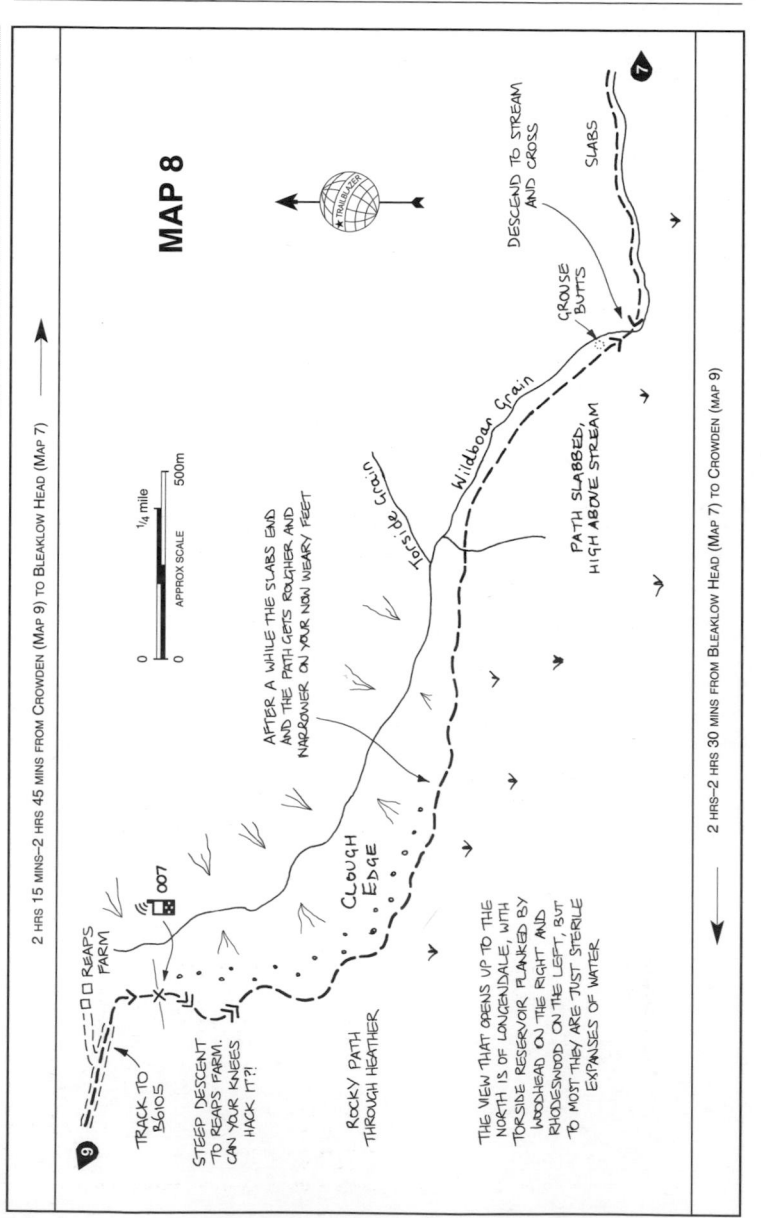

MAP 8

2 HRS 15 MINS–2 HRS 45 MINS FROM CROWDEN (MAP 9) TO BLEAKLOW HEAD (MAP 7)

2 HRS–2 HRS 30 MINS FROM BLEAKLOW HEAD (MAP 7) TO CROWDEN (MAP 9)

★ TRAILBLAZER

¼ mile

500m

0

0

APPROX SCALE

REAPS FARM

TRACK TO B6105

STEEP DESCENT TO REAPS FARM. CAN YOUR KNEES HACK IT?!

ROCKY PATH THROUGH HEATHER

CLOUGH EDGE

AFTER A WHILE THE SLABS END AND THE PATH GETS ROUGHER AND NARROWER ON YOUR NOW WEARY FEET

THE VIEW THAT OPENS UP TO THE NORTH IS OF LONGDENDALE, WITH TORSIDE RESERVOIR FLANKED BY WOODHEAD ON THE RIGHT AND RHODESWOOD ON THE LEFT, BUT TO MOST THEY ARE JUST STERILE EXPANSES OF WATER.

Torside Grain

Wildboar Grain

GROUSE BUTTS

DESCEND TO STREAM AND CROSS

SLABS

PATH SLABBED, HIGH ABOVE STREAM

9

7

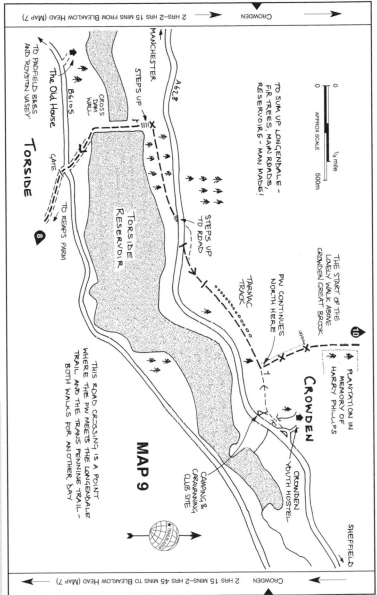

MAP 9

ROUTE GUIDE AND MAPS

Map 9, Crowden 83

ROUTE GUIDE AND MAPS

TORSIDE [Map 9, p83]

As you descend the Pennine Way from Clough Edge you reach Torside and the B6105 road. *The Old House B&B* (☎ 01457-857527, 🖳 www.oldhouse.torside .co.uk; 1D/1T/1F), only 500m west up the road, is friendly and a walker's favourite with en suite rooms from £25/pp, a nice TV lounge, a washing machine and drier. Evening meals are available but they also offer a lift to the *Peels Arms* (see below; a taxi back costs a fiver). They also have a 4-bed **bunkhouse** for £20/pp inc bedding and breakfast; a packed lunch costs £5. The bunkhouse has a kitchen in case walkers prefer to make their own breakfast. For people with limited time they offer a two-day Pennine Way package from £75/pp.

Windy Harbour Farm Hotel (☎ 01457-853107, 🖳 www.peakdistrict-hotel .co.uk; 6D/1T) is two miles along the B6105 en route to Padfield, but if you call or book ahead they'll come and pick you up. For B&B they charge £35 for single occupancy and £60 for two sharing. Evening meals are offered Mon-Fri (or take a 10-min walk to the *Peels Arms*); they also offer basic **camping** for £4 per person as long as the field is not too wet.

PADFIELD AND HADFIELD [off Map 9, p83]

Padfield is about 2½ miles to the west, adjacent to Hadfield, better known to many as the fictional 'Royston Vasey' from the *League of Gentlemen* TV series; not a distinction most 'local people' would cherish in reality. Hadfield also has a **railway station** with a frequent service to Manchester via Glossop (see the public transport table and map pp42-6).

The Peels Arms (☎ 01457-852719, 🖳 www.glossop.com/peels, Temple St; 1T/2D) is the best place for a meal (food is served Mon-Fri 12-2.30pm & 5-9pm, Sat 12-9pm, Sun 12-8pm, all day on Bank Holiday Mondays) and a drink; B&B costs from £25/pp.

Just over the road is *White House Farm* (☎ 01457-854695, 🖳 www.thepen nineway.co.uk/whitehousefarm; 2S/2T/1D) with B&B from £25/pp.

CROWDEN [Map 9, p83]

Crowden has long been synonymous with *Crowden Youth Hostel* (bookings ☎ 0870-770 5784, 🖳 crowden@yha.org.uk; open Easter-Oct). Part of the YHA franchise scheme, there are 38 beds in 1-, 2- and 4-bed-rooms (adults £12, under-18s £9) and a kitchen but if you prefer meals are served (evening meals are at 7.30pm).

The only other accommodation is the *Camping and Caravanning Club Site* (☎ 01457-866057, non-members £7.35) nearby, with good facilities including a shop and a drying room. The site is closed between November and March.

The only bus service is the National Express **coach** (No 350) between Manchester and Sheffield, which comes through Crowden three times a day (see the public transport map and table, pp42-6). If you need to call a **taxi**, try Goldline Taxis (☎ 01457-857777 or ☎ 01457-853333).

CROWDEN TO STANDEDGE   MAPS 9-15

Route overview

This section is a modest **11 miles (18km, 5-6¼hrs)**, one of the shortest days on the trail, and a fairly undemanding tonic after yesterday's baptismal exertions (although realistically, unless you plan to curl up in a ditch you must add another mile or two at the end to get to a place to stay).

The gradual ascent out of Torside to the gritstone outcrops of **Laddow Rocks** (Map 10) lining the Crowden Great Brook characterize an area of clas-

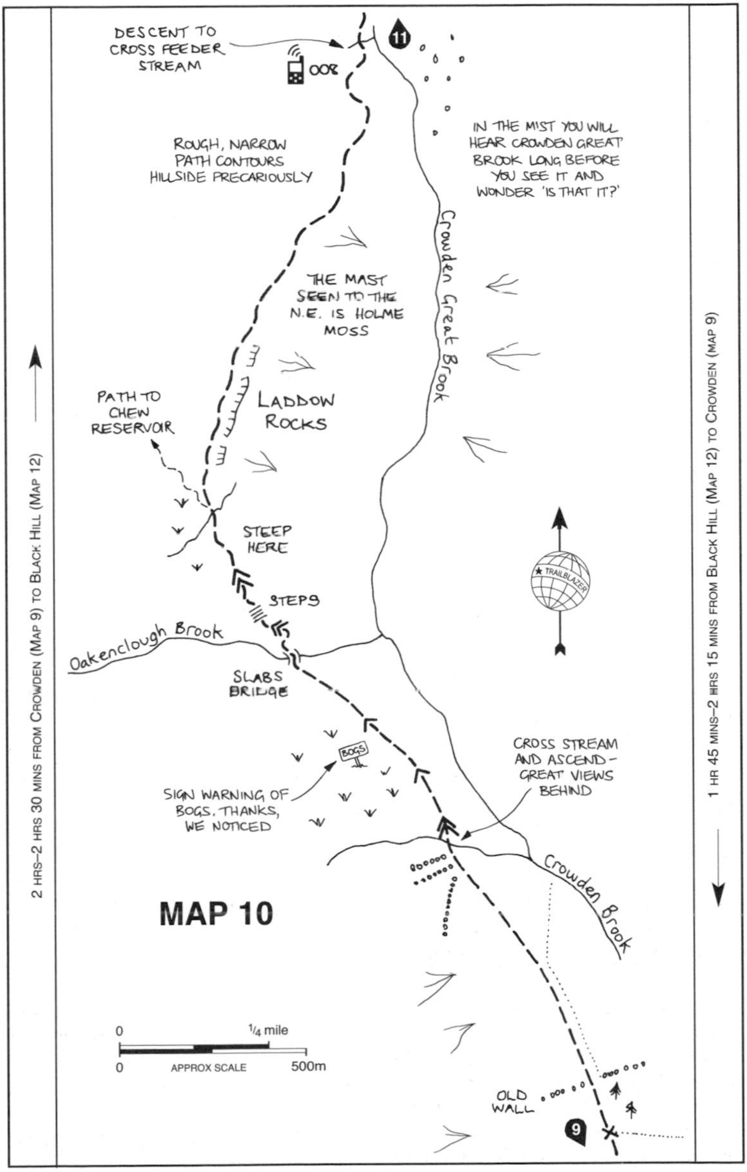

2 HRS–2 HRS 30 MINS FROM CROWDEN (MAP 9) TO BLACK HILL (MAP 12)
1 HR 45 MINS–2 HRS 15 MINS FROM BLACK HILL (MAP 12) TO CROWDEN (MAP 9)
DESCENT TO CROSS FEEDER STREAM
008
11
IN THE MIST YOU WILL HEAR CROWDEN GREAT BROOK LONG BEFORE YOU SEE IT AND WONDER 'IS THAT IT?'
ROUGH, NARROW PATH CONTOURS HILLSIDE PRECARIOUSLY
Crowden Great Brook
THE MAST SEEN TO THE N.E. IS HOLME MOSS
PATH TO CHEW RESERVOIR
LADDOW ROCKS
STEEP HERE
STEPS
TRAILBLAZER
Oakenclough Brook
SLABS BRIDGE
BOGS
CROSS STREAM AND ASCEND – GREAT VIEWS BEHIND
SIGN WARNING OF BOGS. THANKS, WE NOTICED
Crowden Brook
MAP 10
0
1/4 mile
0
APPROX SCALE
500m
OLD WALL
9

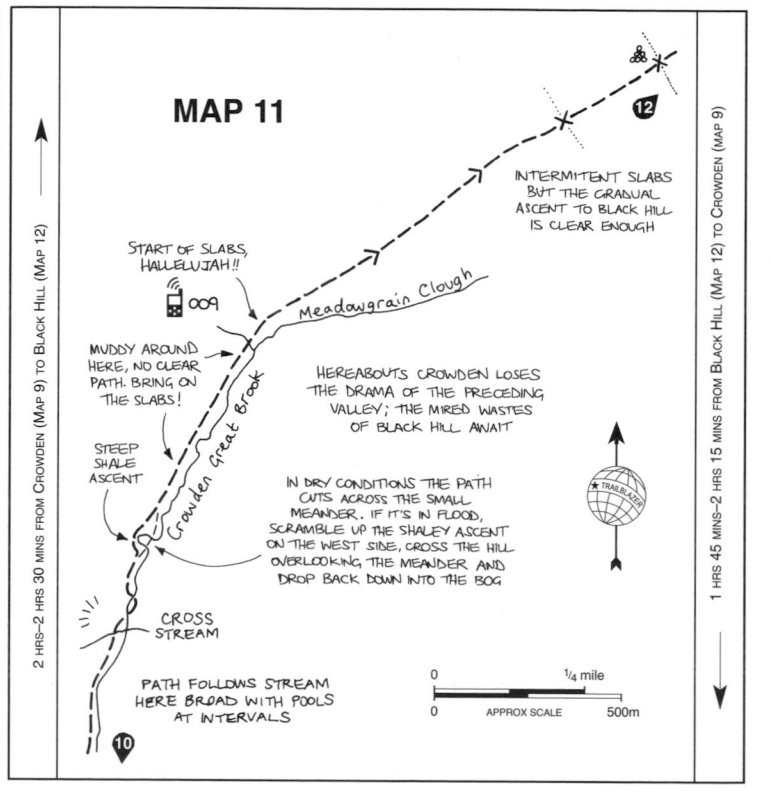

MAP 11

2 HRS–2 HRS 30 MINS FROM CROWDEN (MAP 9) TO BLACK HILL (MAP 12)

1 HRS 45 MINS–2 HRS 15 MINS FROM BLACK HILL (MAP 12) TO CROWDEN (MAP 9)

START OF SLABS, HALLELUJAH!!

009

INTERMITTENT SLABS BUT THE GRADUAL ASCENT TO BLACK HILL IS CLEAR ENOUGH

Meadowgrain Clough

Crowden Great Brook

MUDDY AROUND HERE, NO CLEAR PATH. BRING ON THE SLABS!

HEREABOUTS CROWDEN LOSES THE DRAMA OF THE PRECEDING VALLEY; THE MIRED WASTES OF BLACK HILL AWAIT

STEEP SHALE ASCENT

IN DRY CONDITIONS THE PATH CUTS ACROSS THE SMALL MEANDER. IF IT'S IN FLOOD, SCRAMBLE UP THE SHALEY ASCENT ON THE WEST SIDE, CROSS THE HILL OVERLOOKING THE MEANDER AND DROP BACK DOWN INTO THE BOG

★ TRAILBLAZER

CROSS STREAM

PATH FOLLOWS STREAM HERE BROAD WITH POOLS AT INTERVALS

0   1/4 mile

0   APPROX SCALE   500m

10

sic south Pennine countryside. In late spring bright bilberry bushes adorn the hillsides while below them dried and now soggy bracken takes on rich coppery hues. The march along the tops of Laddow has its moments of exposure – a sudden westerly gust while on the precipitous path could be most inopportune. But as you descend again to the Brook, just at the right moment wet feet are all but averted by a mill slab causeway that leads to the peat-soaked morass that answers aptly to the name of **Black Hill** (Map 12).

Many of these southerly days on the Pennine Way are bisected rather too frequently by east–west roads which intrude on the wilderness. **Wessenden Head** is one of them where the A635 carves its way across the moors, on a good day accompanied by the tantalizing aroma of frying bacon from the roadside snack van.

The successive hours string together a necklace of reservoirs: Wessenden (Map 13), Swellands and Black Moss (Map 14), a series of holding tanks serv-

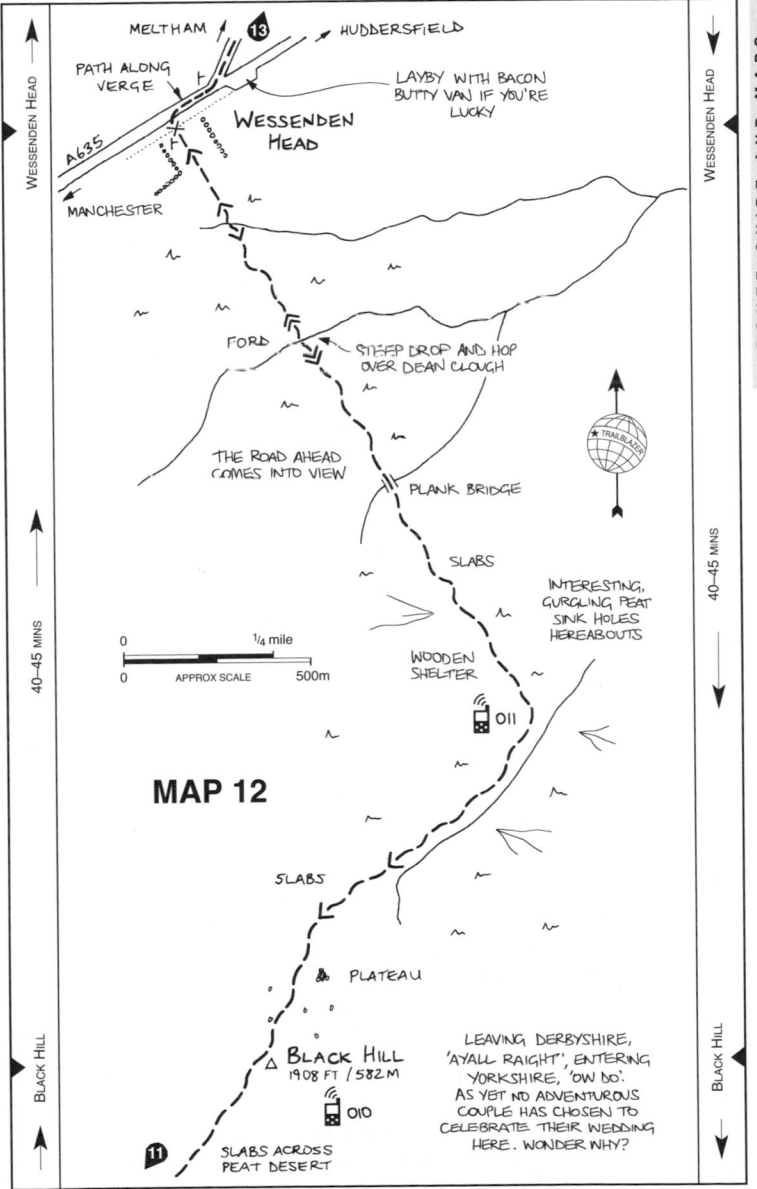

MELTHAM

13

HUDDERSFIELD

PATH ALONG VERGE

WESSENDEN HEAD

LAYBY WITH BACON BUTTY VAN IF YOU'RE LUCKY

A635

MANCHESTER

FORD

STEEP DROP AND HOP OVER DEAN CLOUGH

THE ROAD AHEAD COMES INTO VIEW

PLANK BRIDGE

SLABS

INTERESTING, GURGLING PEAT SINK HOLES HEREABOUTS

★ TRAILBLAZER

WESSENDEN HEAD

40–45 MINS

0   ¼ mile

0   APPROX SCALE   500m

WOODEN SHELTER

011

MAP 12

SLABS

PLATEAU

BLACK HILL
1908 FT / 582 M

010

11

SLABS ACROSS PEAT DESERT

LEAVING DERBYSHIRE, 'AYALL RAIGHT', ENTERING YORKSHIRE, 'OW DO'. AS YET NO ADVENTUROUS COUPLE HAS CHOSEN TO CELEBRATE THEIR WEDDING HERE. WONDER WHY?

WESSENDEN HEAD

40–45 MINS

BLACK HILL

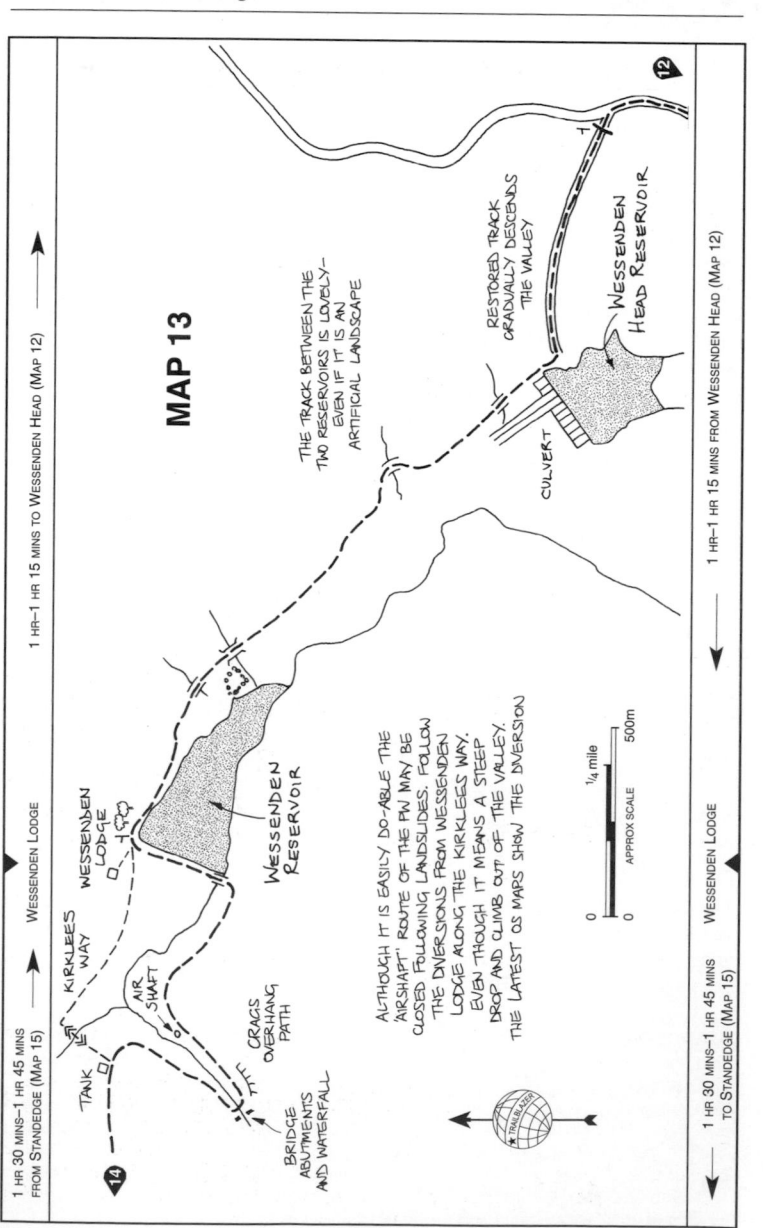

MAP 13

1 HR 30 MINS–1 HR 45 MINS FROM STANDEDGE (MAP 15) ⟶ WESSENDEN LODGE ⟶ 1 HR–1 HR 15 MINS TO WESSENDEN HEAD (MAP 12) ⟶

THE TRACK BETWEEN THE TWO RESERVOIRS IS LOVELY–EVEN IF IT IS AN ARTIFICIAL LANDSCAPE

RESTORED TRACK GRADUALLY DESCENDS THE VALLEY

WESSENDEN HEAD RESERVOIR

CULVERT

1 HR–1 HR 15 MINS FROM WESSENDEN HEAD (MAP 12)

KIRKLEES WAY

WESSENDEN LODGE

WESSENDEN RESERVOIR

AIR SHAFT

TRAIL

CRAGS OVERHANG PATH

BRIDGE ABUTMENTS AND WATERFALL

ALTHOUGH IT IS EASILY DO-ABLE THE 'AIRSHAFT' ROUTE OF THE PW MAY BE CLOSED FOLLOWING LANDSLIDES. FOLLOW THE DIVERSIONS FROM WESSENDEN LODGE ALONG THE KIRKLEES WAY. EVEN THOUGH THE KIRKLEES WAY DROP AND CLIMBS OUT OF THE VALLEY. THE LATEST OS MAPS SHOW THE DIVERSION

¼ mile

500m

APPROX SCALE

WESSENDEN LODGE ◀

1 HR 30 MINS–1 HR 45 MINS TO STANDEDGE (MAP 15)

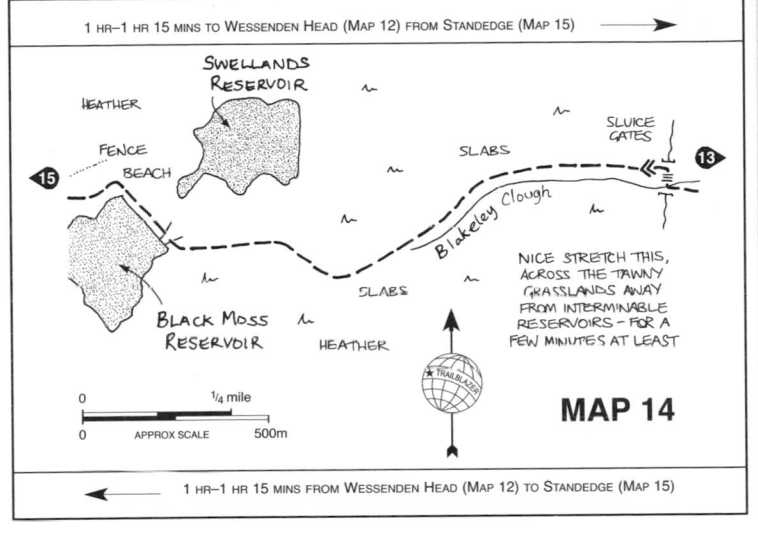

1 HR–1 HR 15 MINS TO WESSENDEN HEAD (MAP 12) FROM STANDEDGE (MAP 15)

SWELLANDS
RESERVOIR

HEATHER

FENCE

BEACH

15

SLUICE
GATES

SLABS

13

Blakeley Clough

NICE STRETCH THIS,
ACROSS THE TAWNY
GRASSLANDS AWAY
FROM INTERMINABLE
RESERVOIRS – FOR A
FEW MINUTES AT LEAST

SLABS

BLACK MOSS
RESERVOIR

HEATHER

TRAILBLAZER

0   ¼ mile

0   APPROX SCALE   500m

MAP 14

1 HR–1 HR 15 MINS FROM WESSENDEN HEAD (MAP 12) TO STANDEDGE (MAP 15)

ing the former industrial towns. The eye will be drawn to these successive stretches of water, scanning the surface for birdlife and rewarded, probably, by some Canada geese, a species of fowl which many birdwatchers dismiss as having no charm (an opinion which a goose might consider the kettle calling the pot black!). They were introduced in the 17th century as human migrants flowed in the opposite direction and have adapted readily to life in public parks in towns as well as in the countryside.

The approach to **Standedge Cutting** (Map 15) aims directly for the Great Western pub (see below), but turns sharp left along an old packhorse route before reaching the west end of the cutting at the Brun Clough Reservoir car park.

Route-finding trouble spots

The only place you could briefly go astray is on Map 11 where in heavy rain you might need to navigate round the flooded meander of Crowden Great Brook and squelch uncertainly north to thankfully meet the slabs (GPS Waypoint 008, see p256) leading up to Black Hill.

STANDEDGE   [Map 15, p91]

First's No 184 **bus** service passes through Standedge, and Diggle, en route between Huddersfield and Manchester; see the public transport map and table, pp42-6.

East of the Cutting

Arriving on the busy A62 at Standedge, the prospect of a bed for the night does not look too promising. *The Great Western* (☎ 01484-844315), which you'll have spotted from the Way, has fortunately re-opened. The pub itself is open all day and food is served Tue-Fri 12-2.30pm and 5-9pm, Sat 12-9pm, Sun 12-7pm; from late Mar to late Oct breakfast is served from 7am. They also offer basic **camping**; there's no charge but donations are welcomed.

The Carriage House (☎ 01484-844419), on the road towards Marsden, has less basic **camping** for around £3 with shower toilet facilities; if booked in advance they can provide breakfast for campers and will do basic food shopping as well. The pub specializes in Turkish food but they also have a full pub menu (food served Mon & Wed 6-8.30pm, Thur 5.30-9pm, Fri 5.30-9.30pm, Sat 12-10pm, Sun 12-8.30pm). At the time of writing the pub closed on Tuesdays but is open from 12 noon on Fridays.

Otherwise, short of waiting for the hourly Manchester–Huddersfield **bus**, the quickest way into **Marsden** (two miles) is to take the Standedge Trail eastwards from the Marker Stone on the PW at the south end of Redbrook Reservoir (Map 15; GPS waypoint 013, see p256).

There's surprisingly little choice in Marsden but the *Olive Branch Restaurant* (☎ 01484-844487, 🖳 www.olivebranch.uk.com; 3D), on the main Manchester Rd, has a mouthwatering menu of seafood, game and poultry and the restaurant is open Mon-Sat 6.30-9.30pm, Wed & Fri 12-1.45pm, Sun 1-8.30pm. A double costs £70 (single occupancy £55) for room only and from Monday to Thursday they do a £65 dinner and bed deal for solo travellers; breakfast costs £12.50.

DIGGLE [off Map 15]

On the outskirts of Diggle about 1½ miles south-west of the PW (all steeply downhill) is *New Barn* (☎ 01457-873937 or 0797-959 8232; 1S/1T/1D en suite/1F), Harrop Green Farm, which charges £25/pp. They have drying facilities and also offer packed lunches (£5). You can take First's No 184 **bus** (see the public transport map and table, pp42-6) back from the stop opposite up to the Way next morning.

A minute or two east of Diggle Hotel, *Sunfield Accommodation* (☎ 01457-874030, 🖳 sunfield.accom@lineone.net; 4D/1T/1F) offer en suite doubles for £50 or £35 for single occupancy.

West of the Cutting

B&B options west of the Cutting are not much more convenient. The closest to the Pennine Way on the **Diggle** side is *Rock Farm* (☎ 01457-870325 or 0790-955 6024; 1D en suite/1T; £25/pp) at the top of Manor Lane, Dean Head. To get there it's actually easier to continue over the A62 along the Pennine Bridleway track (west of the Pennine Way) which leads right to the farm. Or if you ring in advance they'll pick you up from the PW as well as drop you at the pub for a meal. You can get a taxi or walk back. They have drying facilities and also offer packed lunches (£5).

A bit further south but about as close (15 mins from the Way) is *Wellcroft House* (☎ 01457-875017; 🖳 www.wellcroft-house.co.uk; 1D/2T; £25/pp) on Bleak Hey Nook Lane. A listed 18th-century weavers' cottage, the rooms are very well equipped and there's a guest lounge. Evening meals are available; if booked in advance you will get a full meal but they are happy to make something if you haven't booked and decide not to go to the pub. Although most walkers seem to manage it, they'll pick you up if you can't walk another mile and can do you a packed lunch too.

Down in Diggle why not treat yourself at *Diggle Hotel* (☎ 01457-872741; 3D), a family-run free house with several real ales. Look out on the Specials board for the succulent *Lamb Henry* (see p19; the official dish of the Pennine Way) for around £8; it's not served all the time but is more common in the autumn. Food is served Mon-Fri 12-2.30pm & 5-9pm, Sat 12-9pm, Sun 12-8pm. Accommodation is also available here at £45 if you're sharing (£35 for single occupancy). At the time of writing the rooms were being refurbished and should be en suite in 2008.

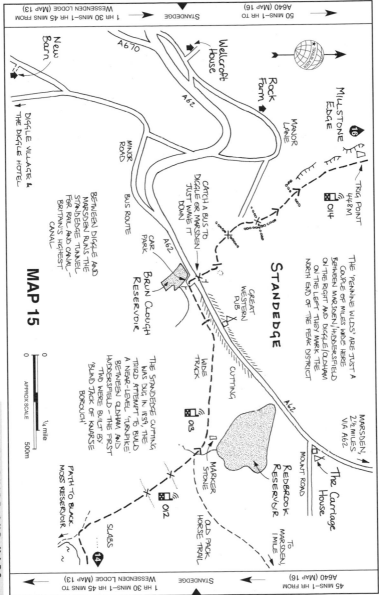

MAP 15

NEW BARN

DIGGLE VILLAGE & THE DIGGLE HOTEL

WELLCROFT HOUSE

ROCK FARM

MANOR LANE

MILLSTONE EDGE

TRIG POINT 448M

014

A670

A62

MINOR ROAD

BUS ROUTE

CATCH A BUS TO DIGGLE OR MARSDEN – JUST WAVE IT DOWN

BETWEEN DIGGLE AND MARSDEN RUNS THE STANDEDGE TUNNEL FOR RAIL AND CANAL – BRITAIN'S HIGHEST CANAL.

THE 'PENNINE WILDS' ARE JUST A COUPLE OF MILES WIDE HERE BETWEEN MARSDEN/HUDDERSFIELD ON THE RIGHT AND DIGGLE/OLDHAM ON THE LEFT. THEY MARK THE NORTH END OF THE PEAK DISTRICT

STANDEDGE

GREAT WESTERN PUB

CAR PARK

BRUN CLOUGH RESERVOIR

A62

CUTTING

WIDE TRACK

013

THE STANDEDGE CUTTING WAS DUG IN 1839, THE THIRD ATTEMPT TO BUILD A NEAR-LEVEL 'TURNPIKE' BETWEEN OLDHAM AND HUDDERSFIELD – THE FIRST TWO WERE BUILT BY 'BLIND JACK OF KNARSE BOROUGH'

MARKER STONE

012

REDBROOK RESERVOIR

MOUNT ROAD

THE CARTAGE HOUSE

MARSDEN, 2½ MILES VIA A62

TO MARSDEN, 1 MILE

OLD PACK HORSE TRAIL

PATH TO BLACK MOSS RESERVOIR

SLABS

APPROX SCALE

0 — ¼ mile
0 — 500m

STANDEDGE TO BLACKSHAW HEAD (CALDER VALLEY)
MAPS 15-22

Route overview
It has to be said that while much flatter than the previous two days and not without its agreeable moments, the **14 miles (23kms, 5-6¹/₂hrs)** to the Calder Valley is not the greatest day's walking on the Pennine Way. It starts enthusiastically enough with a traverse along **Millstone Edge**, the first of several gritstone edges, but several road crossings (not least of which is the the vertigo-inducing crossing high above the M62), along with the frequent hum of distant traffic and a string of man-made reservoirs does not distinguish this stage. The presence of rogue dirt bikers who gain easy access onto the moors between the A650 and the A58 can also spoil the day. Quite simply, the Lancashire and Yorkshire conurbations press in too close to the Pennine Way and almost smother it.

As the numerous reservoirs testify, the soggy moorland is well adapted to water catchment for these towns, but luckily the worst of the bogs are slabbed for your walking pleasure. Just beyond the M62, the wastes of **Redmires** (Map 18) certainly used to exact their annual tribute of walkers' boots and souls; now they quiver, subdued beneath the mighty flagstones.

Overlooking Littleborough, **Blackstone Edge** is an airy rampart. Soon you encounter the ancient **Aiggin Stone** and descend a short section of time- and cartwheel-worn 'Roman' pavement. Thereafter a less salubrious drain accompanies you nearly all the way to the White House pub (see p94) in preparation for the afternoon's level track circumventing several **reservoirs** (Map 19) before another moorland drain leads to a view of the distant monument of Stoodley Pike (see box p99). You reach Stoodley by way of **Coldwell Hill** (Map 20), along slabs which wend their way through stunted heather and grass, the Way designated intermittently with piles of stones, and come to another ancient crossroads known as **Withen's Gate**. If you're heading for **Mankinholes** (see p94), turn left here down the Calderdale Way for a mile and a bit.

If your objectives lie in the Calder Valley or beyond, **Stoodley Pike** (Map 21) demands a short rest to either admire the view or cower wretchedly from the rain. Underway again, it's downhill into farmland and through light woodland to the Rochdale Canal where a decision has to be made whether to towpath a mile or two into **Hebden Bridge** (see p99) or trek the same distance up some gruelling gradients to the nearest accommodation at **Blackshaw Head** (see p102).

Route-finding trouble spots
Good news, even in day-long 100-metre visibility, the only place the route is difficult to follow is along the braided paths alongside Blackstone Edge. Luckily, poles or cairns loom out of the murk just in time.

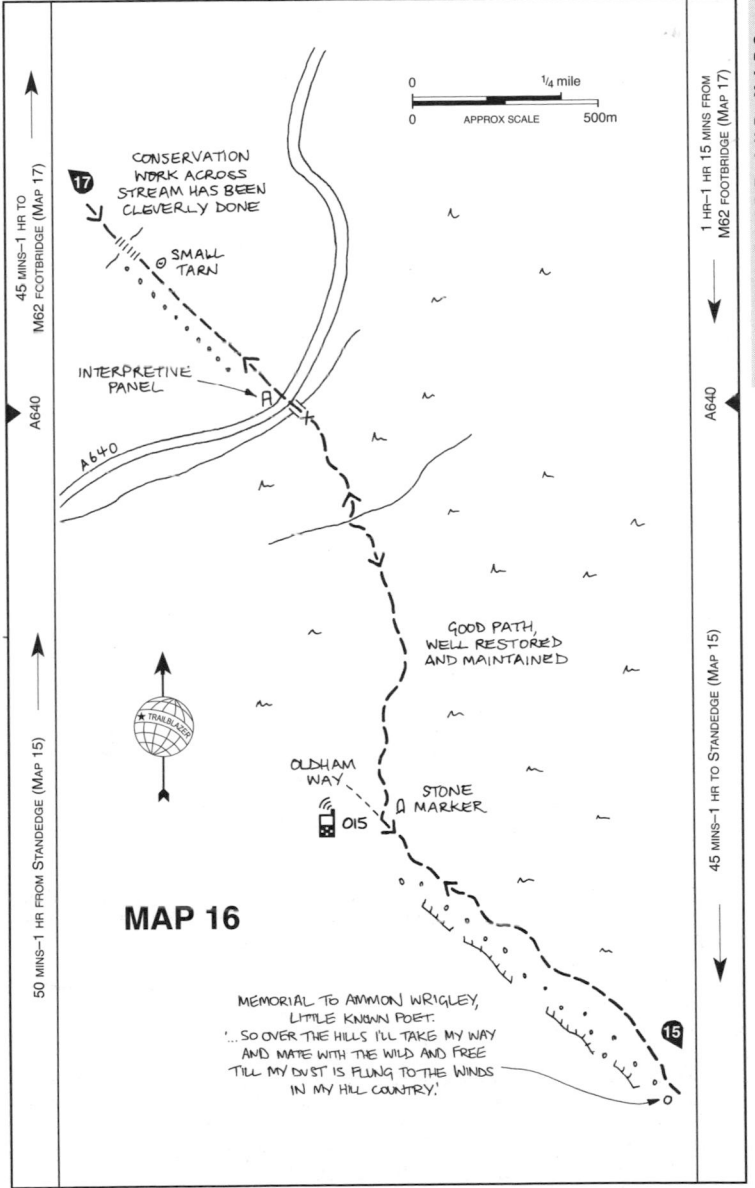

0   1/4 mile

0   APPROX SCALE   500m

45 MINS–1 HR TO M62 FOOTBRIDGE (MAP 17)

A640

50 MINS–1 HR FROM STANDEDGE (MAP 15)

1 HR–1 HR 15 MINS FROM M62 FOOTBRIDGE (MAP 17)

A640

45 MINS–1 HR TO STANDEDGE (MAP 15)

17

CONSERVATION WORK ACROSS STREAM HAS BEEN CLEVERLY DONE

SMALL TARN

INTERPRETIVE PANEL

A640

GOOD PATH, WELL RESTORED AND MAINTAINED

★ TRAILBLAZER

OLDHAM WAY

015

STONE MARKER

MAP 16

MEMORIAL TO AMMON WRIGLEY, LITTLE KNOWN POET. '... SO OVER THE HILLS I'LL TAKE MY WAY AND MATE WITH THE WILD AND FREE TILL MY DUST IS FLUNG TO THE WINDS IN MY HILL COUNTRY.'

15

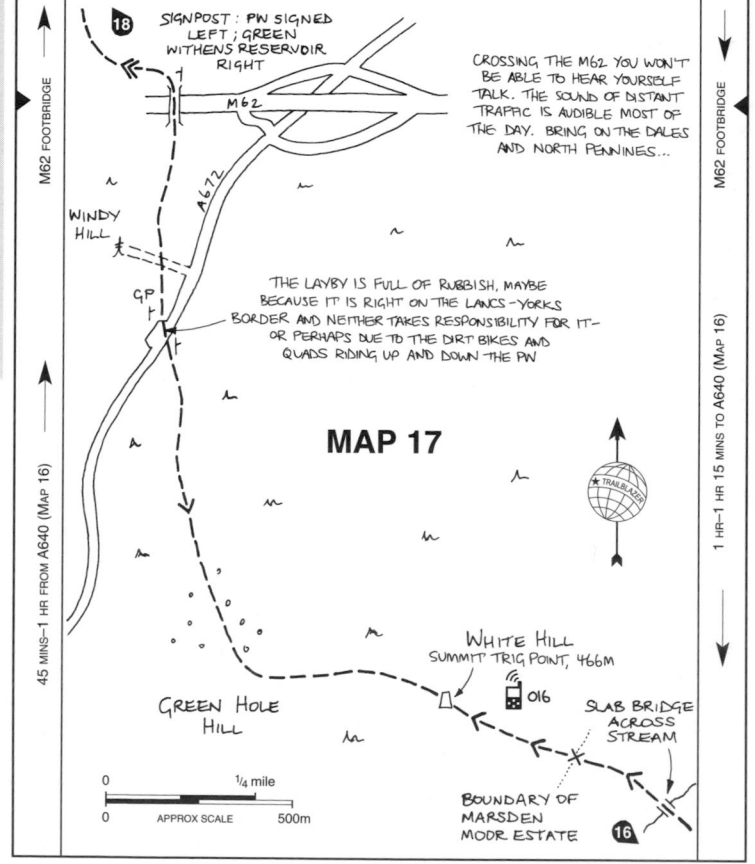

Within the map:

18

SIGNPOST: PW SIGNED
LEFT; GREEN
WITHENS RESERVOIR
RIGHT

M62

CROSSING THE M62 YOU WON'T
BE ABLE TO HEAR YOURSELF
TALK. THE SOUND OF DISTANT
TRAFFIC IS AUDIBLE MOST OF
THE DAY. BRING ON THE DALES
AND NORTH PENNINES...

A672

WINDY
HILL

GP

THE LAYBY IS FULL OF RUBBISH, MAYBE
BECAUSE IT IS RIGHT ON THE LANCS-YORKS
BORDER AND NEITHER TAKES RESPONSIBILITY FOR IT-
OR PERHAPS DUE TO THE DIRT BIKES AND
QUADS RIDING UP AND DOWN THE PW

MAP 17

★ TRAILBLAZER

WHITE HILL
SUMMIT TRIG POINT, 466M

016

SLAB BRIDGE
ACROSS
STREAM

GREEN HOLE
HILL

BOUNDARY OF
MARSDEN
MOOR ESTATE

16

0   1/4 mile
0   APPROX SCALE   500m

Left margin: ROUTE GUIDE AND MAPS

M62 FOOTBRIDGE

45 MINS-1 HR FROM A640 (MAP 16)

Right margin: M62 FOOTBRIDGE

1 HR-1 HR 15 MINS TO A640 (MAP 16)

BLACKSTONE EDGE/A58
[Map 19, p96]

It's rare that a pub pops up so opportunely so enjoy the ***White House*** (☎ 01706-378456), a former packhorse inn on the A58 near Blackstone Edge Reservoir, a perfectly serviceable place for a pint or a meal. It serves food 12 noon-2pm and 6.30-9pm Mon-Sat, and all day on Sunday 12-9pm; the bar shuts in the afternoon during the week.

First's No 528 hourly **bus** service between Rochdale and Halifax will stop here if requested (see public transport map and table, pp42-6).

MANKINHOLES   **[Map 20, p97]**

Unless you're content to curl up in a curlew's nest, the only accommodation between Standedge and the Calder Valley is in Mankinholes. It means a diversion off the route and unless you retrace your steps to Withen's Gate to rejoin the trail proper, you'll have missed out part of the Pennine Way and the resultant guilt could torment you for eternity.   *(cont'd on p99)*

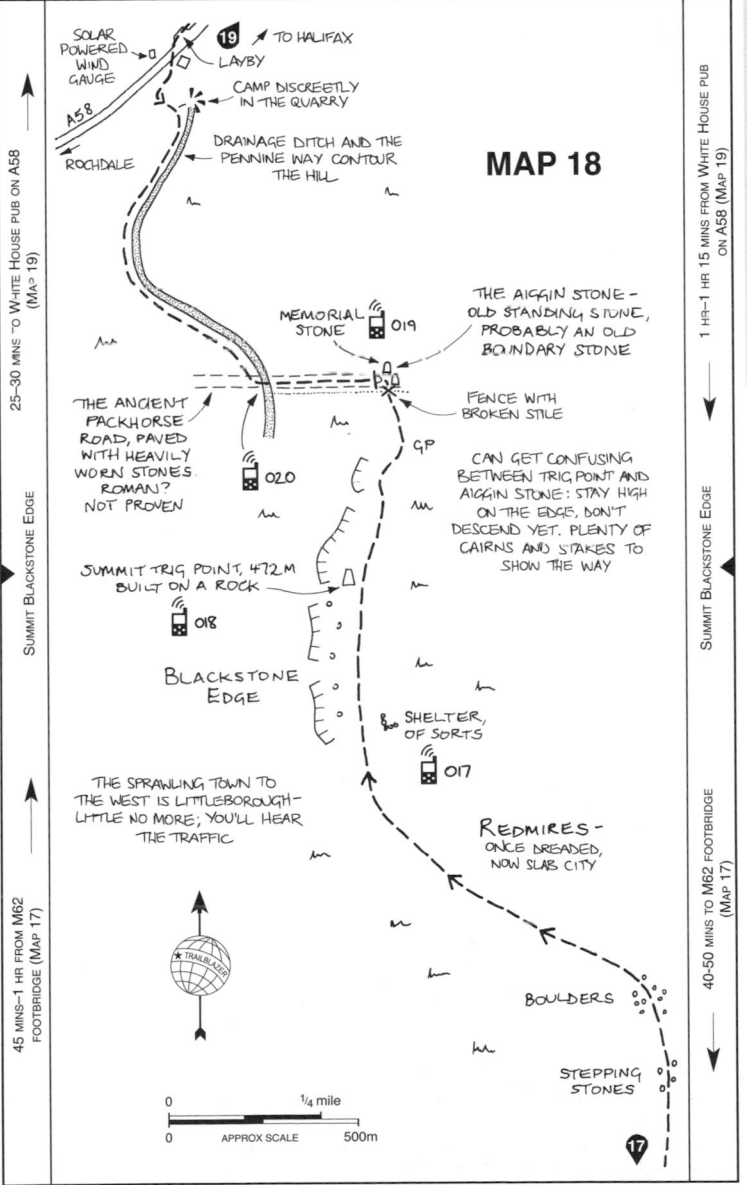

SOLAR POWERED WIND GAUGE

19 LAYBY ↗ TO HALIFAX

CAMP DISCREETLY IN THE QUARRY

A58

ROCHDALE

DRAINAGE DITCH AND THE PENNINE WAY CONTOUR THE HILL

MAP 18

25–30 MINS TO WHITE HOUSE PUB ON A58 (MAP 19)

1 HR–1 HR 15 MINS FROM WHITE HOUSE PUB ON A58 (MAP 19)

MEMORIAL STONE — 019

THE AIGGIN STONE – OLD STANDING STONE, PROBABLY AN OLD BOUNDARY STONE

FENCE WITH BROKEN STILE

THE ANCIENT PACKHORSE ROAD, PAVED WITH HEAVILY WORN STONES. ROMAN? NOT PROVEN

020

GP

CAN GET CONFUSING BETWEEN TRIG POINT AND AIGGIN STONE: STAY HIGH ON THE EDGE, DON'T DESCEND YET. PLENTY OF CAIRNS AND STAKES TO SHOW THE WAY

SUMMIT BLACKSTONE EDGE

SUMMIT TRIG POINT, 472M BUILT ON A ROCK

018

BLACKSTONE EDGE

SUMMIT BLACKSTONE EDGE

SHELTER, OF SORTS

017

THE SPRAWLING TOWN TO THE WEST IS LITTLEBOROUGH– LITTLE NO MORE; YOU'LL HEAR THE TRAFFIC

REDMIRES – ONCE DREADED, NOW SLAB CITY

★ TRAILBLAZER

45 MINS–1 HR FROM M62 FOOTBRIDGE (MAP 17)

40–50 MINS TO M62 FOOTBRIDGE (MAP 17)

BOULDERS

STEPPING STONES

0   ¼ mile

0   APPROX SCALE   500m

17

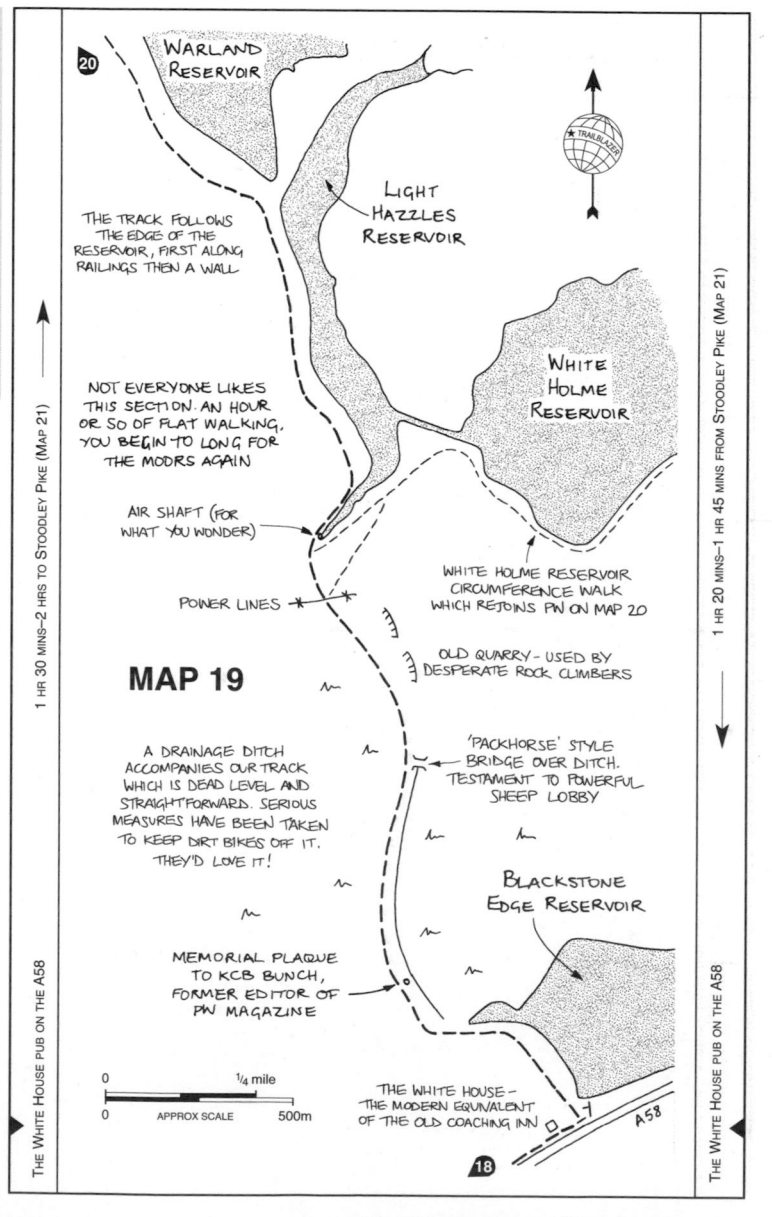

20

WARLAND RESERVOIR

LIGHT HAZZLES RESERVOIR

THE TRACK FOLLOWS THE EDGE OF THE RESERVOIR, FIRST ALONG RAILINGS THEN A WALL

WHITE HOLME RESERVOIR

NOT EVERYONE LIKES THIS SECTION. AN HOUR OR SO OF FLAT WALKING, YOU BEGIN TO LONG FOR THE MOORS AGAIN

AIR SHAFT (FOR WHAT YOU WONDER)

WHITE HOLME RESERVOIR CIRCUMFERENCE WALK WHICH REJOINS PW ON MAP 20

POWER LINES

MAP 19

OLD QUARRY - USED BY DESPERATE ROCK CLIMBERS

'PACKHORSE' STYLE BRIDGE OVER DITCH. TESTAMENT TO POWERFUL SHEEP LOBBY

A DRAINAGE DITCH ACCOMPANIES OUR TRACK WHICH IS DEAD LEVEL AND STRAIGHTFORWARD. SERIOUS MEASURES HAVE BEEN TAKEN TO KEEP DIRT BIKES OFF IT. THEY'D LOVE IT!

BLACKSTONE EDGE RESERVOIR

MEMORIAL PLAQUE TO KCB BUNCH, FORMER EDITOR OF PW MAGAZINE

0   ¼ mile

0   APPROX SCALE   500m

THE WHITE HOUSE - THE MODERN EQUIVALENT OF THE OLD COACHING INN

A58

18

1 HR 30 MINS-2 HRS TO STOODLEY PIKE (MAP 21)

1 HR 20 MINS-1 HR 45 MINS FROM STOODLEY PIKE (MAP 21)

THE WHITE HOUSE PUB ON THE A58

THE WHITE HOUSE PUB ON THE A58

★ TRAILBLAZER

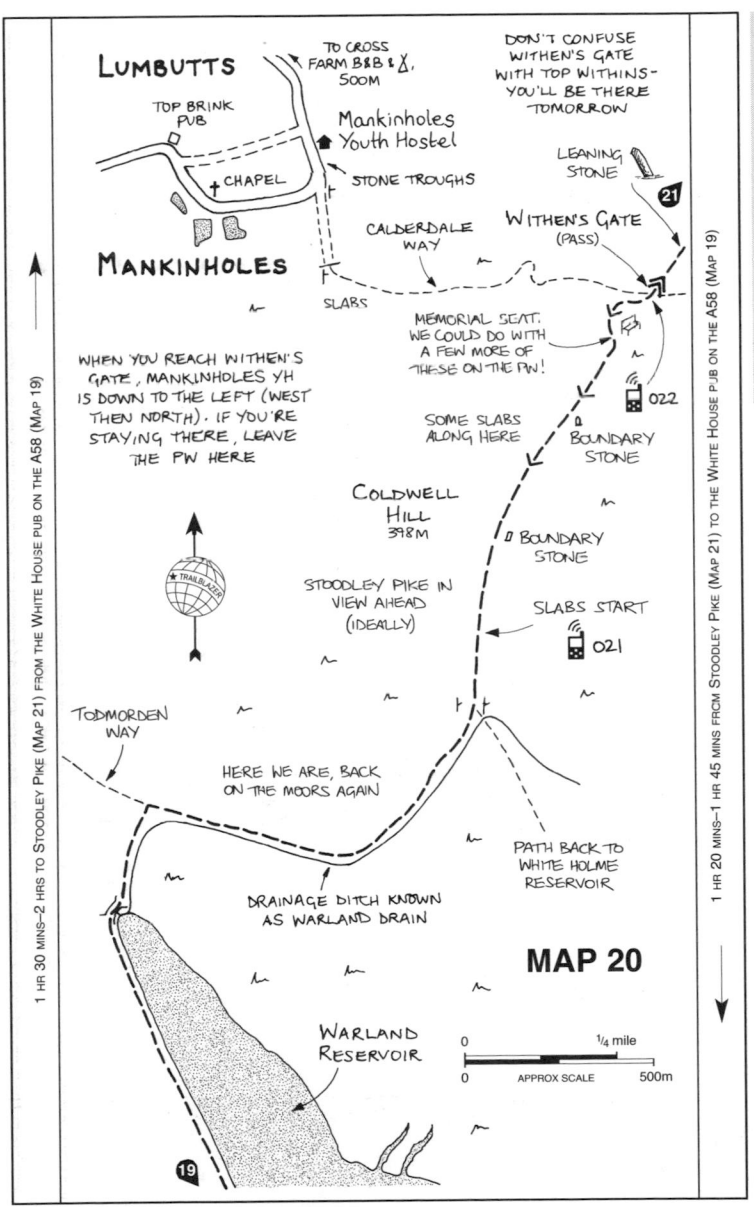

LUMBUTTS

TOP BRINK PUB

† CHAPEL

MANKINHOLES

TO CROSS FARM B&B & ⚹, 500M

Mankinholes Youth Hostel

STONE TROUGHS

CALDERDALE WAY

SLABS

DON'T CONFUSE WITHEN'S GATE WITH TOP WITHINS— YOU'LL BE THERE TOMORROW

LEANING STONE

21

WITHEN'S GATE (PASS)

MEMORIAL SEAT. WE COULD DO WITH A FEW MORE OF THESE ON THE PW!

022

WHEN YOU REACH WITHEN'S GATE, MANKINHOLES YH IS DOWN TO THE LEFT (WEST THEN NORTH). IF YOU'RE STAYING THERE, LEAVE THE PW HERE

SOME SLABS ALONG HERE

BOUNDARY STONE

COLDWELL HILL 398M

★ TRAILBLAZER

BOUNDARY STONE

STOODLEY PIKE IN VIEW AHEAD (IDEALLY)

SLABS START

021

TODMORDEN WAY

HERE WE ARE, BACK ON THE MOORS AGAIN

PATH BACK TO WHITE HOLME RESERVOIR

DRAINAGE DITCH KNOWN AS WARLAND DRAIN

MAP 20

WARLAND RESERVOIR

0   ¼ mile

0   APPROX SCALE   500m

19

1 HR 30 MINS–2 HRS TO STOODLEY PIKE (MAP 21) FROM THE WHITE HOUSE PUB ON THE A58 (MAP 19)

1 HR 20 MINS–1 HR 45 MINS FROM STOODLEY PIKE (MAP 21) TO THE WHITE HOUSE PUB ON THE A58 (MAP 19)

ROUTE GUIDE AND MAPS

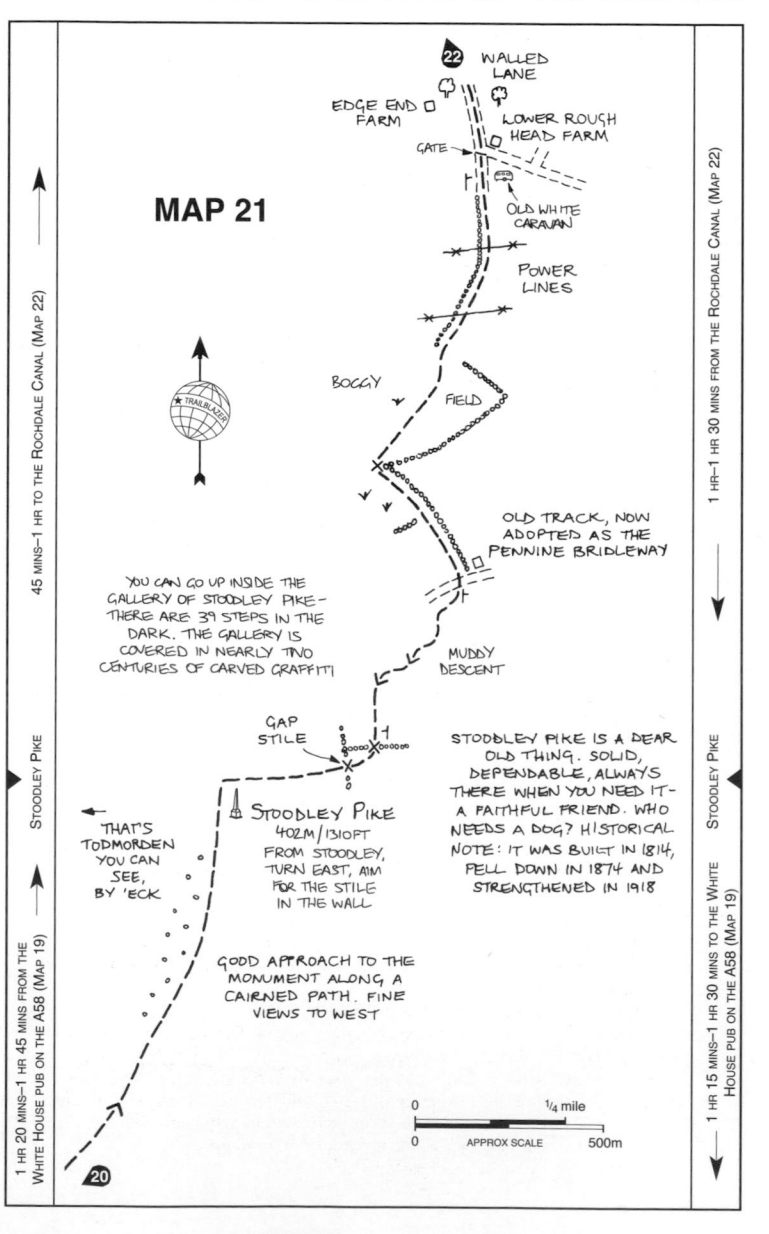

MAP 21

45 MINS–1 HR TO THE ROCHDALE CANAL (MAP 22)

1 HR–1 HR 30 MINS FROM THE ROCHDALE CANAL (MAP 22)

22

WALLED
LANE

EDGE END
FARM

LOWER ROUGH
HEAD FARM

GATE

OLD WHITE
CARAVAN

POWER
LINES

BOGGY

FIELD

OLD TRACK, NOW
ADOPTED AS THE
PENNINE BRIDLEWAY

YOU CAN GO UP INSIDE THE
GALLERY OF STOODLEY PIKE –
THERE ARE 39 STEPS IN THE
DARK. THE GALLERY IS
COVERED IN NEARLY TWO
CENTURIES OF CARVED GRAFFITI

MUDDY
DESCENT

GAP
STILE

STOODLEY PIKE IS A DEAR
OLD THING. SOLID,
DEPENDABLE, ALWAYS
THERE WHEN YOU NEED IT –
A FAITHFUL FRIEND. WHO
NEEDS A DOG? HISTORICAL
NOTE: IT WAS BUILT IN 1814,
FELL DOWN IN 1874 AND
STRENGTHENED IN 1918

STOODLEY PIKE
402M/1310FT
FROM STOODLEY,
TURN EAST, AIM
FOR THE STILE
IN THE WALL

THAT'S
TODMORDEN
YOU CAN
SEE,
BY 'ECK

GOOD APPROACH TO THE
MONUMENT ALONG A
CAIRNED PATH. FINE
VIEWS TO WEST

1 HR 20 MINS–1 HR 45 MINS FROM THE
WHITE HOUSE PUB ON THE A58 (MAP 19)

STOODLEY PIKE

STOODLEY PIKE

1 HR 15 MINS–1 HR 30 MINS TO THE WHITE
HOUSE PUB ON THE A58 (MAP 19)

TRAILBLAZER

0   1/4 mile
0   500m
APPROX SCALE

20

(cont'd from p94) Most walkers continue down to the Calder Valley but unless you haul on up the other side, the bright lights of Hebden Bridge also require a diversion of a mile or two. Saved from the bean counters' axe the traditional *Mankinholes Youth Hostel* (☎ 0870-770 5952, 🖳 mankinholes@yha.org .uk, open Feb-Dec) is an old manor house charging £14 (under 18s £10) for one of its 32 beds. It is licensed but

HEBDEN BRIDGE [see Map 22a, p101]

It was along the Calder Valley that the Industrial Revolution was born and Hebden Bridge, a half-hour stroll east of the Pennine Way along the Rochdale Canal towpath, is well worth the short detour.

Since the mills closed it's attracted a large 'alternative' population (in 2005 it was named Europe's funkiest place to live) and as a result there are plenty of lively pubs, restaurants, interesting shops and a vibrant arts scene. The Picture House **cinema** (☎ 01422-842807) shows matinées at

does not provide meals, so you'll have to cook your own or go to the *Top Brink* pub (☎ 01706-812696), which serves food Mon-Tue 5.30-9.30pm, Wed-Fri 12-2.30pm and 5.30-9.30pm, Sat 12-10pm, Sun and Bank Holidays 12-9.30pm.

Those preferring B&B can get it at *Cross Farm* (☎ 01706-813481; 2D/2T) from £25 per person; basic **camping** (with facilities in a barn) costs £3.50 per person.

3pm at the weekend and the main programme is at 7.45pm daily. There are regular performances at the **Little Theatre** (🖳 www.hebdenbridgelittletheatre.co.uk) beside the Holme St Arts Centre; see the website for details. See box p24 for details about the Arts Festival in July.

If you need to save energy, visit the **Alternative Technology Centre** by the canal. Here you'll learn that over a third of energy consumed in the UK goes on transportation, so good on you for walking!

❏ Stoodley Pike   [see Map 21]

This needle-shaped monument above the Calder Valley (Calderdale) was erected on a site where there had been an ancient burial cairn, assumed to be that of a chieftain. It seems plausible, the height being a commanding one and the ideal spot to erect a memorial.

It was also an ideal site for a beacon since the chain that warned of the approach of the Spanish Armada included Halifax's Beacon Hill and Pendle Hill above Clitheroe, Stoodley being the link between the two.

Be that as it may, in 1814 it was decided to celebrate the defeat of Napoleon by erecting a monument by public subscription and local bigwigs were quick to put their name down. Then as now a chance to appear influential was not to be missed. Unfortunately Napoleon escaped from Elba, raised his armies and overthrew the restored monarchy, cutting short the erection of the monument. After Wellington finally put paid to Bonaparte at Waterloo, the work began again and it was completed before the end of 1815.

Disaster struck in 1854 when the tower collapsed as the country was going to war again, this time in the Crimea, an evil omen indeed. Rebuilt, it has survived to this day although they do say it wobbled a bit on the eve of the Falklands War.

For walkers along the Pennine Way the 37-metre (120ft) high spire is a landmark that beckons them from afar. Roughly at the 40-mile (60km) mark from Edale, it marks a change in the countryside. The peat moors are largely behind us and ahead lie more pastoral scenes as the gritstone gives way to limestone.

Tomorrow to fresh woods and pastures new.

ROUTE GUIDE AND MAPS

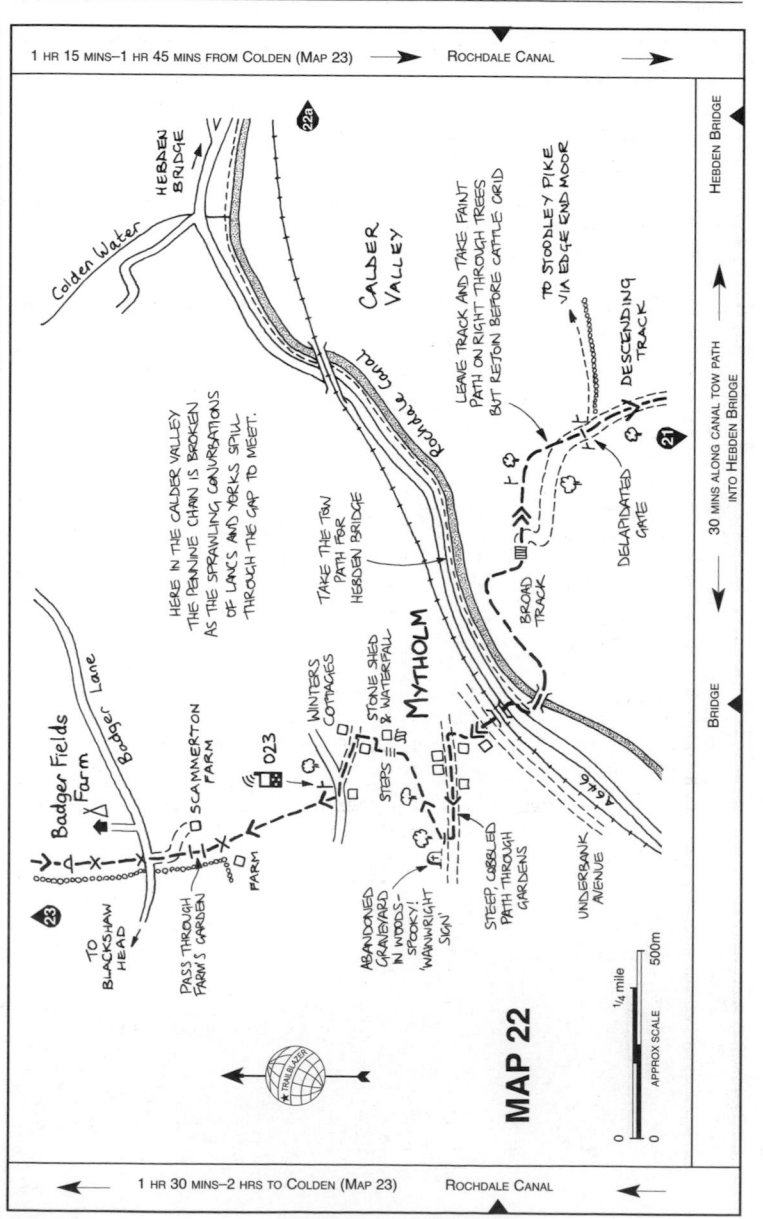

1 HR 15 MINS–1 HR 45 MINS FROM COLDEN (MAP 23) ➡ ROCHDALE CANAL ➡

HEBDEN BRIDGE

HEBDEN BRIDGE

Colden Water

CALDER VALLEY

Rochdale Canal

22a

HERE IN THE CALDER VALLEY THE PENNINE CHAIN IS BROKEN AS THE SPRAWLING CONURBATIONS OF LANCS AND YORKS SPILL THROUGH THE GAP TO MEET.

TAKE THE TOW PATH FOR HEBDEN BRIDGE

LEAVE TRACK AND TAKE FAINT PATH ON RIGHT THROUGH TREES BUT RETURN BEFORE CATTLE GRID

TO STOODLEY PIKE VIA EDGE END MOOR

DESCENDING TRACK

BROAD TRACK

DELAPIDATED GATE

21

WINTERS COTTAGES

STONE SHED & WATERFALL

MYTHOLM

SCAMMERTON FARM

☐23

Badger Fields Farm

Badger Lane

FARM

STEPS

PASS THROUGH FARM'S GARDEN

ABANDONED GRAVEYARD IN WOODS- SPOOKY! 'WAINWRIGHT' SIGN

STEEP COBBLED PATH THROUGH GARDENS

UNDERBANK AVENUE

A646

BRIDGE

30 MINS ALONG CANAL TOW PATH INTO HEBDEN BRIDGE

23

TO BLACKSHAW HEAD

MAP 22

¼ mile

500m

0

0 APPROX SCALE

★ TRAILBLAZER

BRIDGE

1 HR 30 MINS–2 HRS TO COLDEN (MAP 23) ROCHDALE CANAL

ROUTE GUIDE AND MAPS

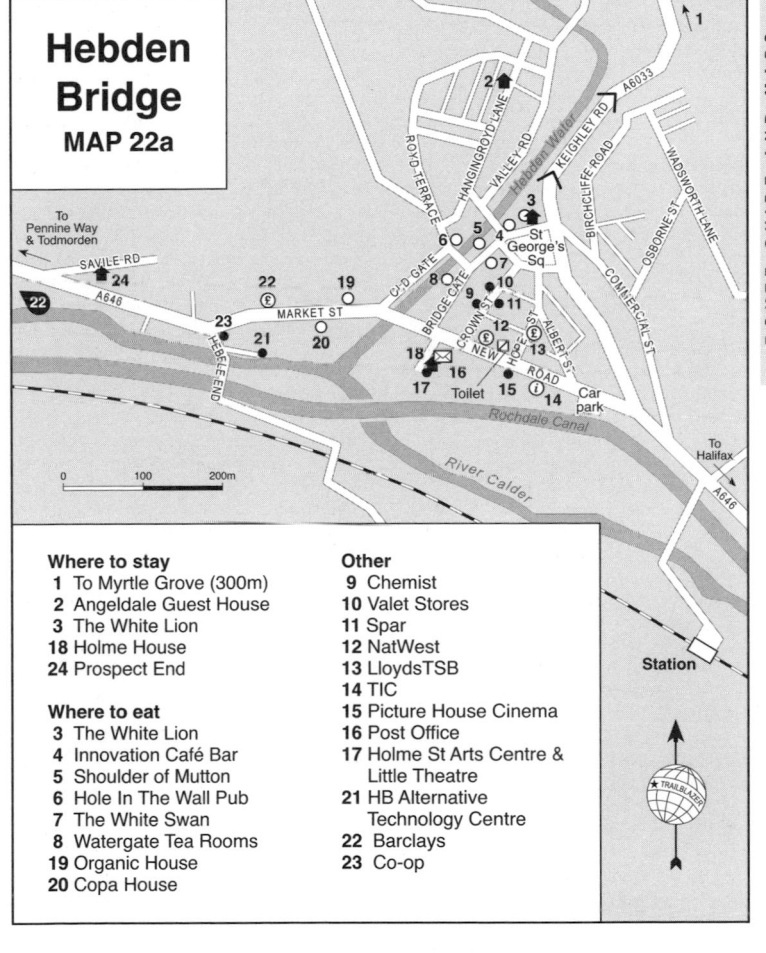

Hebden Bridge MAP 22a

Where to stay
1 To Myrtle Grove (300m)
2 Angeldale Guest House
3 The White Lion
18 Holme House
24 Prospect End

Where to eat
3 The White Lion
4 Innovation Café Bar
5 Shoulder of Mutton
6 Hole In The Wall Pub
7 The White Swan
8 Watergate Tea Rooms
19 Organic House
20 Copa House

Other
9 Chemist
10 Valet Stores
11 Spar
12 NatWest
13 LloydsTSB
14 TIC
15 Picture House Cinema
16 Post Office
17 Holme St Arts Centre &
   Little Theatre
21 HB Alternative
   Technology Centre
22 Barclays
23 Co-op

Transport

There are frequent **trains** from Leeds, Bradford, Manchester and Preston. There are no direct **buses** from any major cities, but First operates regular services to Burnley, Rochdale, Todmorden, Haworth, Keighley and Halifax; see the public transport map and table (pp42-6) for details.

Services

The **tourist information centre** (☎ 01422-843831, 🖳 www.hebdenbridge.co.uk) is in the middle of the town. It's open Apr-Oct Mon-Fri 9.30am-5.30pm, Sat/Sun 10.30am-5pm; Nov-Mar Mon-Fri 10am-5pm, Sat/Sun 10.30am-4.15pm.

There are three major **banks**, all with **cash machines** and there's also a **post**

office. Valet Stores on Crown St sells **walking gear** and there's a small Spar **supermarket** (open 8.30am-11pm weekdays) opposite. Alternatively try the Co-op (till 8.30am-9pm weekdays) on the main road.

Where to stay

There are no campsites in town, but several B&Bs and hotels. On the western edge is **Prospect End** (☎ 01422-843586, 🖳 www .prospectend.co.uk, 8 Prospect Tce, Savile Rd; 1D/1T both en suite) with doubles from £35 per person (single occupancy £50). In order to reach it from the Way you'll have to walk in on the A646, not the towpath.

The very central **Holme House** (☎ 01422-847588, 🖳 www.holmehouseheb denbridge.co.uk; 1T/2D), on New Rd, is a classy Georgian house charging £35 per person (single occupancy £55). There's a £7.50 surcharge at weekends.

Angeldale Guest House (☎ 01422-847321, 🖳 www.angeldale.co.uk; 2D/2T/2F), at the top of Hangingroyd Lane, is also fairly central with doubles from £28 per person (en suite £32). During the week single occupancy costs from £35 but at the weekend the rate is the room rate.

Myrtle Grove (☎ 01422-846078, 🖳 www.myrtlegrove.btinternet.co.uk, Old Lees Rd; 1D en suite) is just north of the town centre up the hill, a veggie-friendly place; two sharing costs £70, single occupancy (from £35) on weekdays only.

The White Lion Hotel (☎ 01422-842197, 🖳 www.whitelionhotelhb.co.uk, Bridge Gate; 2T/5D/3F) has en suite doubles from £65; single occupancy £48.

Where to eat

If sandwiches and full English breakfasts (FEBs) are getting a bit galling, make the

most of the variety and choice in Hebden. There are some particularly good cafés along Market St. **Organic House** (☎ 01422-843429, 🖳 www.organic-house.co .uk; Mon-Sat 9-5.30pm, snacks only after 3pm, Sun 10am-5pm) does a range of wholesome dishes including a spinach, potato and feta tart, warm cheese sauce and salad for £5.95.

Nearby, **Copa House** (☎ 01422-845524) is open Tue-Sun 10am-4pm and Thur-Sat 6pm to late – booking is advised for the evening. They serve home-made soup and sandwiches during the day. The evening menu changes regularly but at the time of writing included Gorgonzola risotto with peas and broad beans (£7.95) as well as a selection of meat and fish dishes and some tasty desserts such as sticky toffee pudding with vanilla ice cream (£4.50).

The **Innovation Café Bar** (☎ 01422-844094), in Hebden Bridge Mill, does home-made soups and crêpes; alternatively, corned beef hash with salad costs £4.50. It's open Mon-Sat 9.45am-5pm, Sun 10am-5pm.

On Bridge Gate, off the square, the **Shoulder of Mutton** serves pub grub from £4. Just down the road on the left is the **White Swan**, with similarly priced food. Nearby is the licensed **Watergate Tea Rooms** (☎ 01422-842978, daily 10.30am-4.30pm) which does great home-made food such as a giant Yorkshire pudding. 'The Works' breakfast costs £5.70; a veggie version is also available.

Just across the pedestrian bridge over Hebden Water is the **Hole in the Wall**, a pub offering rump steaks for £6.95 and 16oz T-bones for £9.50. **The White Lion** (see 'Where to stay') does pub food daily 12 noon-9pm from around £6.

BLACKSHAW HEAD [Map 22, p100]

Where the trail crosses Badger Lane there is **Badger Fields Farm** (☎ 01422-845161, 🖳 www.badgerfields.com; 2T/1D) where Mrs Whitaker offers B&B for £52 for two sharing or £33 single occupancy, with drying facilities, evening meals for £13 and a

packed lunch for a fiver. **Camping** is £3.

Blackshaw Head has no services but a **bus** (Wymetro E) runs frequently to Hebden Bridge (see public transport map and table, pp42-6) and it's only a mile to the *New Delight* pub (see p107).

CALDER VALLEY TO ICKORNSHAW   MAPS 22-31

Route overview

Though it starts with a hefty climb out of the Calder Valley, this **17-mile (25km, 6-8hrs)** section offers an array of landscapes from shady dells, dry-stone-walled pastures, the ever-present reservoirs and of course, heather-clad moorland. Route-finding has its moments, but others have managed; so can you!

Set off by zig-zagging up through **Mytholm**, an as-yet ungentrified outlier of Hebden Bridge. Behind you Stoodley Pike follows your every move, and soon you're clear of the valleyside and return among the pastures where the incongruous council terraces of **Colden** (Map 23) rise into view, grittily embedded below **Heptonstall Moor**. Once traversed, the peaty wastes drop down past a reservoir to the sheltered confluence of babbling brooks at **Graining Water** (Map 25), overlooked from one side by crags and from the other by the Pack Horse Inn (see p107).

An amble above this stream and a quiet road section leads to the **Walshaw Dean** series of reservoirs, forsaken before they get too tedious as you again climb the tawny moors to **Withins Height** (Map 27). Once crested you get a view of the dramatically situated ruin said to be the inspiration for the house in Emily Brontë's *Wuthering Heights* (see box p112).

Hereabouts paths leave the Way to **Haworth** (3½ miles, 6km) and the full 'Brontë Experience' (see maps 27 and 28). Otherwise, all that remains is to drop down to **Ponden Reservoir** and decide whether to stay here or plod on to the mildly greater opportunities to be found around Ickornshaw and Cowling.

To get there the route climbs round the spur of the reservoir and up out of the Worth Valley onto **Ickornshaw Moor** (Map 30). As you come down the north side of the moor you'll spot several shooting huts; nearby Cowling has ancient shooting rights for the moorlands surrounding you.

Correctly negotiating the styles and gates of pastures below brings you to the **waterfall** at Lumb Head Beck and a walled track that leads eventually to the A6068 on which lie Ickornshaw and Cowling.

Route-finding trouble spots

Clear weather poses no problems but drifting aimlessly with the mist across Heptonstall Moor might be something you come to regret. However, once past the turn off to Clough Hole Bridge you should make it to the far side.

Withins Height Moor has a clear slabbed path, though you want to be sure you stick to the Pennine Way and not veer off into Haworth unnecessarily. And with your wits about you Ickornshaw Moor should pose no problems either; just remember to keep track after the shooters' huts while field-hopping your way to the waterfall from where you're nearly home and, who knows, maybe even dry.

COLDEN   **[Map 23, p104]**
Within a mile of leaving the valley, we come upon signs pointing the way to **Aladdin's Cave**, promising untold excesses such as sweets, cakes, groceries and

drinks. This is *Highgate Farm* (☎ 01422-842897) run by the redoubtable May Stocks who has a natural instinct what wayfarers want and has provided for them accordingly. (cont'd on p107)

ROUTE GUIDE AND MAPS

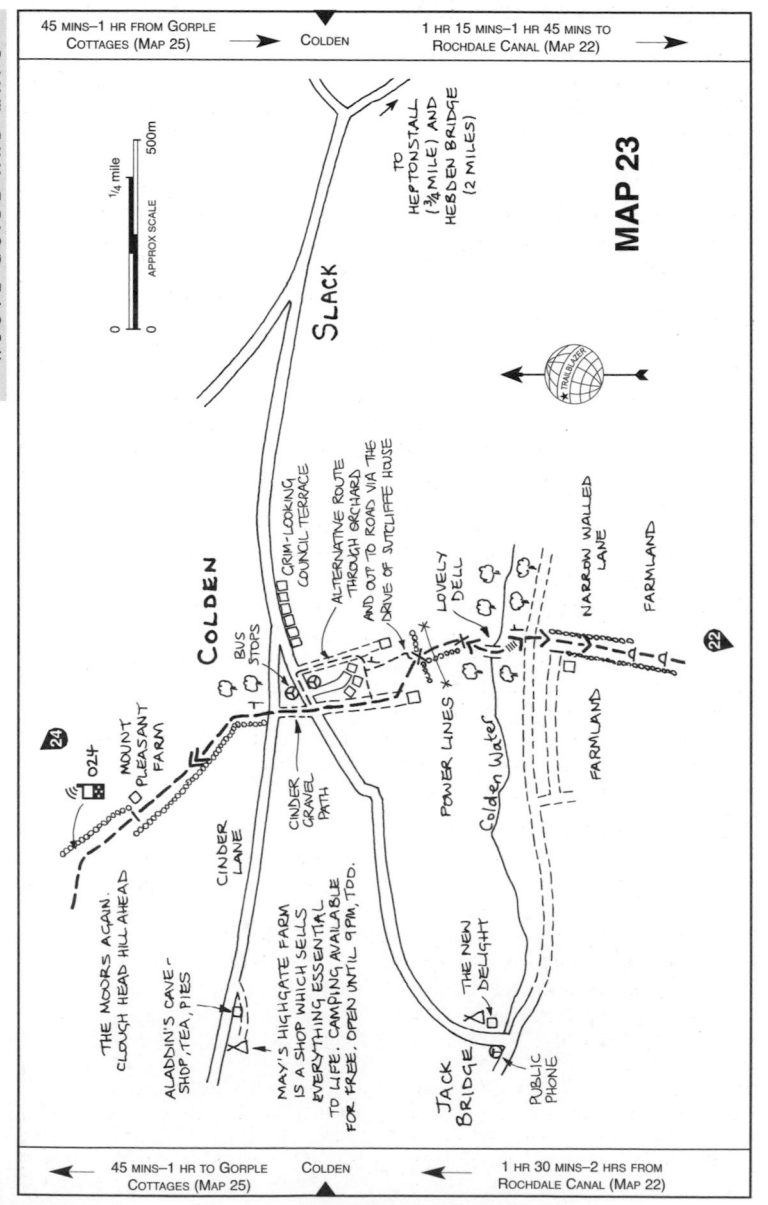

MAP 23

TO HEPTONSTALL (¾ MILE) AND HEBDEN BRIDGE (2 MILES)

SLACK

COLDEN

GRIM-LOOKING COUNCIL TERRACE

ALTERNATIVE ROUTE THROUGH ORCHARD AND OUT TO ROADS VIA THE DRIVE OF SUTCLIFFE HOUSE

LOVELY DELL

NARROW WALLED LANE

FARMLAND

BUS STOPS

POWER LINES

FARMLAND

COLDEN WATER

MOUNT PLEASANT FARM

CINDER LANE

CINDER GRAVEL PATH

THE MOORS AGAIN. CLOUGH HEAD HILL AHEAD

ALADDIN'S CAVE – SHOP, TEA, PIES

MAY'S HIGHGATE FARM IS A SHOP WHICH SELLS EVERYTHING ESSENTIAL TO LIFE. CAMPING AVAILABLE FOR FREE. OPEN UNTIL 9PM, TOO.

THE NEW DELIGHT

JACK BRIDGE

PUBLIC PHONE

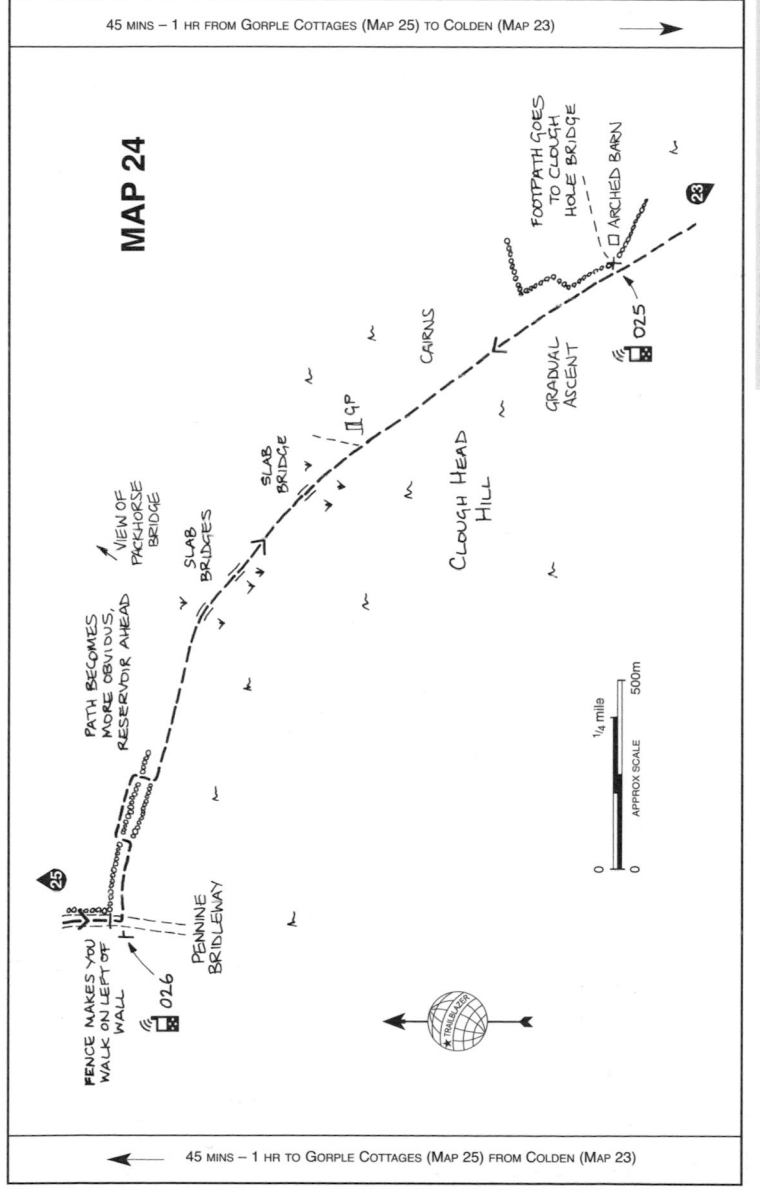

45 MINS – 1 HR FROM GORPLE COTTAGES (MAP 25) TO COLDEN (MAP 23)

MAP 24

FOOTPATH GOES TO CLOUGH HOLE BRIDGE

☐ ARCHED BARN

23

025

GRADUAL ASCENT

CAIRNS

19P

SLAB BRIDGE

VIEW OF PACKHORSE BRIDGE

SLAB BRIDGES

CLOUGH HEAD HILL

PATH BECOMES MORE OBVIOUS, RESERVOIR AHEAD

25

026

PENNINE BRIDLEWAY

FENCE MAKES YOU WALK ON LEFT OF WALL

¼ mile

500m

APPROX SCALE

0

0

TRAILBLAZER

45 MINS – 1 HR TO GORPLE COTTAGES (MAP 25) FROM COLDEN (MAP 23)

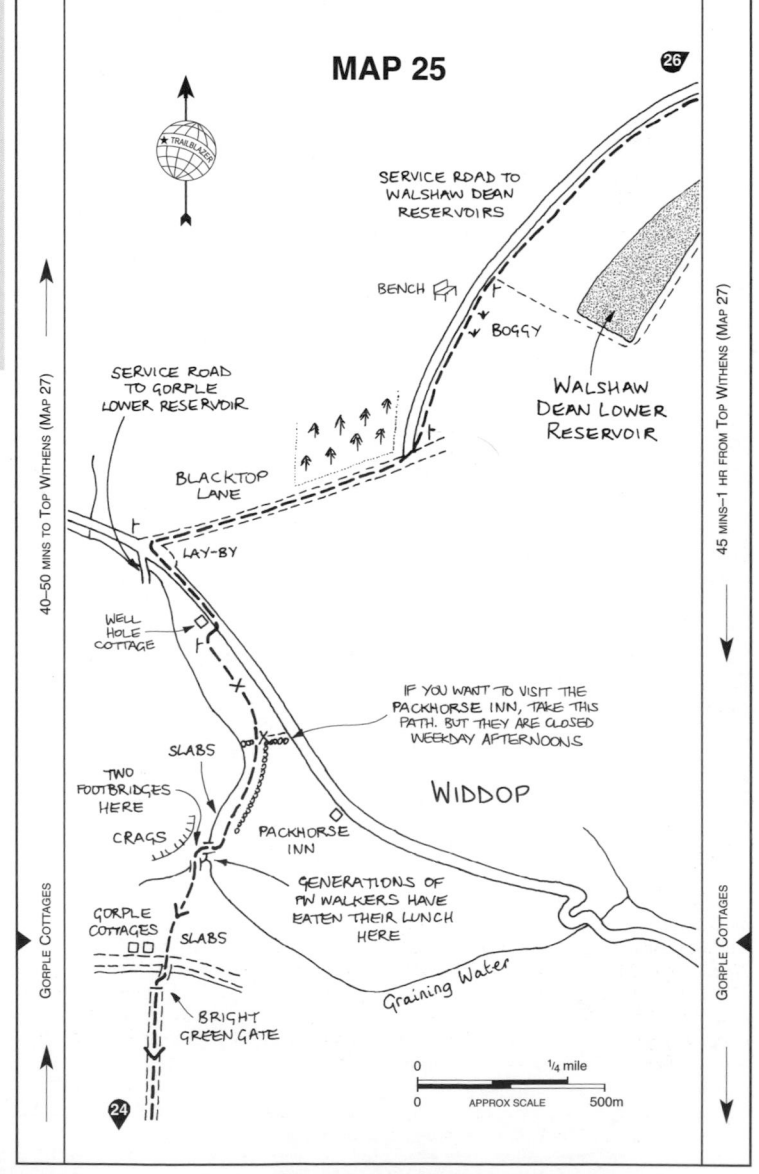

MAP 25

26

SERVICE ROAD TO WALSHAW DEAN RESERVOIRS

BENCH

BOGGY

WALSHAW DEAN LOWER RESERVOIR

SERVICE ROAD TO GORPLE LOWER RESERVOIR

BLACKTOP LANE

LAY-BY

WELL HOLE COTTAGE

IF YOU WANT TO VISIT THE PACKHORSE INN, TAKE THIS PATH. BUT THEY ARE CLOSED WEEKDAY AFTERNOONS

SLABS

TWO FOOTBRIDGES HERE

CRAGS

WIDDOP

PACKHORSE INN

GENERATIONS OF PW WALKERS HAVE EATEN THEIR LUNCH HERE

GORPLE COTTAGES

SLABS

Graining Water

BRIGHT GREEN GATE

40–50 MINS TO TOP WITHENS (MAP 27)

45 MINS–1 HR FROM TOP WITHENS (MAP 27)

GORPLE COTTAGES

GORPLE COTTAGES

24

0   ¼ mile

0   APPROX SCALE   500m

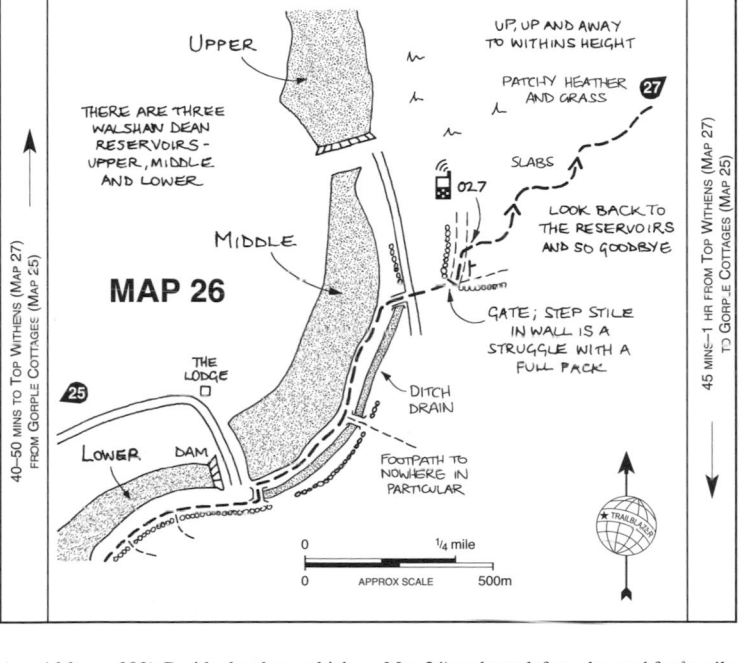

UPPER

THERE ARE THREE
WALSHAW DEAN
RESERVOIRS -
UPPER, MIDDLE
AND LOWER

MIDDLE

MAP 26

THE
LODGE

LOWER   DAM

UP, UP AND AWAY
TO WITHINS HEIGHT

PATCHY HEATHER
AND GRASS

SLABS

☎ 027

LOOK BACK TO
THE RESERVOIRS
AND SO GOODBYE

GATE; STEP STILE
IN WALL IS A
STRUGGLE WITH A
FULL PACK

DITCH
DRAIN

FOOTPATH TO
NOWHERE IN
PARTICULAR

40–50 MINS TO TOP WITHENS (MAP 27)
FROM GORPLE COTTAGES (MAP 25)

45 MINS–1 HR FROM TOP WITHENS (MAP 27)
TO GORPLE COTTAGES (MAP 25)

0   ¼ mile

0   APPROX SCALE   500m

(cont'd from p103) Beside the shop, which is open daily 7am-9pm, May allows basic **camping** for free.

Further north, just over a mile off the Way, there's camping for £5 per person at *Pennine Camp and Caravan Site* (off Map 24; ☎ 01422-842287, approx Apr-Oct), High Greenwood House. To get there take the path down to Clough Hole Bridge (see Map 24) and turn left up the road for ¾ mile to the campsite.

The New Delight (☎ 01422-846178; food served daily Easter to end Aug 12-2.30pm and 6-9pm), at **Jack Bridge**, provides a haven for thirsty or just plain miserable Pennine Way walkers with ales including Mansfield Cask and the locally brewed Moorhouses. **Camping** costs £4/pp.

WIDDOP   [Map 25]

The next pub north from Colden is the *Pack Horse Inn* (Map 25; ☎ 01422-842803; 2D/1T en suite), a few hundred metres off-route. In summer food is served Tue-Sun noon-2pm and 7-9.30pm, Oct to Easter at weekends only. If you spent the night in Hebden, lunchtime could be about now but note that they're closed Mondays year-round and they also close in the afternoon; in the winter months they only open in the evening. B&B (Tue-Sun only) costs from £48 per room.

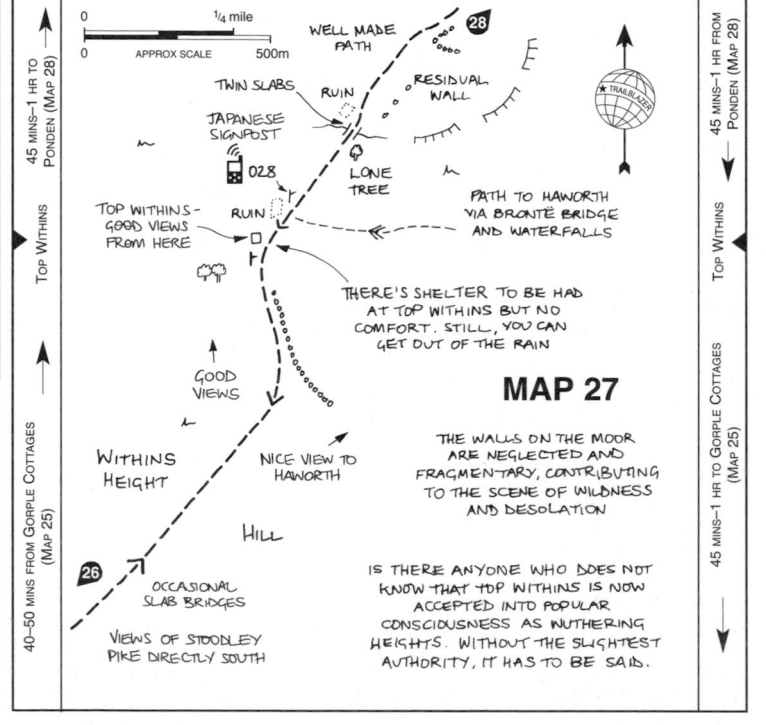

45 MINS–1 HR TO PONDEN (MAP 28)

TOP WITHINS

40–50 MINS FROM GORPLE COTTAGES (MAP 25)

WELL MADE PATH

TWIN SLABS   RUIN

JAPANESE SIGNPOST

028

TOP WITHINS– GOOD VIEWS FROM HERE   RUIN

RESIDUAL WALL

LONE TREE

PATH TO HAWORTH VIA BRONTË BRIDGE AND WATERFALLS

THERE'S SHELTER TO BE HAD AT TOP WITHINS BUT NO COMFORT. STILL, YOU CAN GET OUT OF THE RAIN

GOOD VIEWS

WITHINS HEIGHT

NICE VIEW TO HAWORTH

HILL

OCCASIONAL SLAB BRIDGES

VIEWS OF STOODLEY PIKE DIRECTLY SOUTH

0   ¼ mile

0   APPROX SCALE   500m

MAP 27

THE WALLS ON THE MOOR ARE NEGLECTED AND FRAGMENTARY, CONTRIBUTING TO THE SCENE OF WILDNESS AND DESOLATION

IS THERE ANYONE WHO DOES NOT KNOW THAT TOP WITHINS IS NOW ACCEPTED INTO POPULAR CONSCIOUSNESS AS WUTHERING HEIGHTS. WITHOUT THE SLIGHTEST AUTHORITY, IT HAS TO BE SAID.

45 MINS–1 HR FROM PONDEN (MAP 28)

TOP WITHINS

45 MINS–1 HR TO GORPLE COTTAGES (MAP 25)

PONDEN   [Map 28]

With Ponden in sight, you can **camp** with a view at *Upper Heights Farm* (☎ 01535-645585) for £5. By March 2008 the new shower and toilet block should be ready and from then they plan to be open year-round. Since the pub in Stanbury (see below) is a fair old walk away it's best to ensure you can be self sufficient.

Ponden is now much smaller than it was when weaving was dominant in the area. **Ponden Mill** has been turned into a

'retail experience' and the houses along the Haworth road have been gentrified.

On the west side of the reservoir *Ponden House* (☎ 01535-644154, 🖥 www .pondenhouse.co.uk; 2T/2D) is a tastefully converted old barn right on the trail. Rooms cost from £55 (£60 en suite, single occupancy £30) or **camp** round the back for £5. Evening meals go for £16, probably a good idea unless you want to walk the mile to the nearest pub. Campers can come in and get a breakfast for around £6.

STANBURY   [Map 28]

If Ponden is full and you have no intention of staying in Haworth, a walk down the road brings you to Stanbury and *The Old Silent Inn* (☎ 01535-647437, 🖥 www.old-silent-inn.co.uk; 2S/1T/5D/1F all en suite),

an upmarket hostelry which gained its name after Bonnie Prince Charlie hid out here in 1688 with a nod and a wink from the locals. To do likewise will cost a hefty £55 for a single, £65 for a twin or double, all with breakfast. Meals and bar meals are

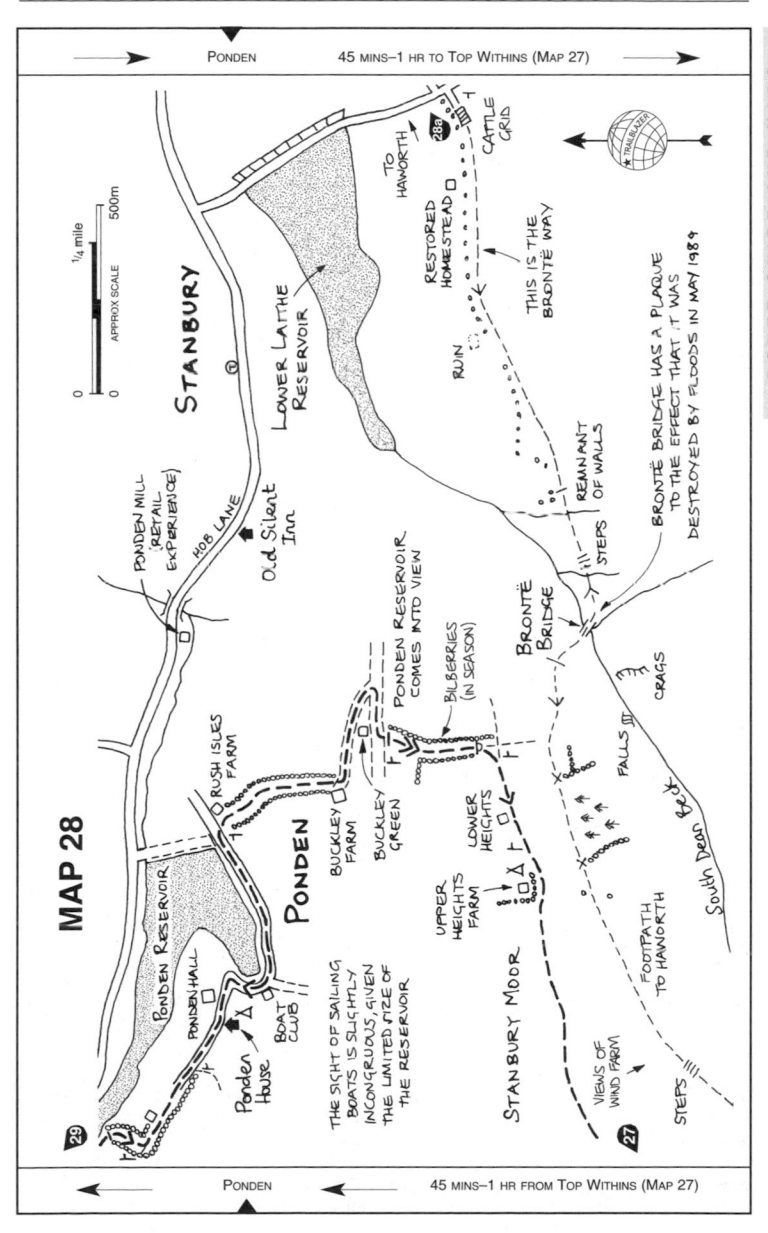

MAP 28

PONDEN   45 MINS–1 HR TO TOP WITHINS (MAP 27)

STANBURY

PONDEN MILL
(RETAIL
EXPERIENCE)

HOB LANE

Old Silent Inn

LOWER LAITHE RESERVOIR

TO HAWORTH

CATTLE GRID

28a

RESTORED HOMESTEAD

THIS IS THE BRONTË WAY

RUIN

REMNANT OF WALLS

STEPS

BRONTË BRIDGE

BRONTË BRIDGE HAS A PLAQUE
TO THE EFFECT THAT IT WAS
DESTROYED BY FLOODS IN MAY 1989

CRAGS

PONDEN RESERVOIR
COMES INTO VIEW

BILBERRIES
(IN SEASON)

RUSH ISLES FARM

BUCKLEY FARM

BUCKLEY GREEN

LOWER HEIGHTS

UPPER HEIGHTS FARM

FALLS

South Dean Beck

FOOTPATH TO HAWORTH

STEPS

VIEWS OF WIND FARM

STANBURY MOOR

PONDEN RESERVOIR

PONDEN HALL

PONDEN

PONDEN HOUSE

BOAT CLUB

THE SIGHT OF SAILING
BOATS IS SLIGHTLY
INCONGRUOUS, GIVEN
THE LIMITED SIZE OF
THE RESERVOIR

29

27

¼ mile   500m

APPROX SCALE

0   0

available Mon-Fri 12-2.15pm & 6-9pm, Sat 12-9pm, Sun 12-8pm.

If this doesn't suit Keighley & District's No 664 **bus** stops here en route between Keighley and Haworth (see public transport map and table, pp42-6 for details).

HAWORTH [see Map 28a]

The Pennine Way does not go through Haworth, but there are good reasons for taking the detour off the Way via the Brontë Bridge and Falls to seek whatever solace may be required: refreshment, accommodation (which is in short supply on the Way itself), literary inspiration; all are there in abundance but the extra 3¹/₂ miles (6km) down also involves 3¹/₂ miles back up!

This gritstone town's appeal is firmly based on its association with the Brontë sisters. Year-round the streets throng with visitors, most of whom have probably never read the works of Emily, Charlotte or Anne. However, such is the romantic appeal of the family, whose home can still be visited, that the crowds continue to be drawn here from all over the world. And Haworth has long been a major destination on the UK tour circuit for Japanese visitors; you'll have spotted PW signs in Japanese near Top Withens and others directing tourists up the picturesque cobbled Main St.

Transport

The **train station** is a stop on the Keighley and Worth Valley Railway Line (☎ 01535-645214, ☐ www.kwvr.co.uk), a preserved line which runs steam trips at weekends throughout the year and also daily during holiday periods between Keighley (where it links up with the main Leeds–Settle–Carlisle line) and Oxenhope.

Bus transport (First and Keighley & District) from Haworth connects with Bradford, Keighley, Oxenhope, Stanbury and Hebden Bridge (see public transport map and table, pp42-6).

Taxi companies include Brontë Taxis (☎ 01535-644442) and Crown Taxis (☎ 01535-662020).

Services

Haworth has services aplenty including two **post offices**, a Spar **supermarket** (7am-10.30pm daily), souvenir shops, a bookshop, newsagents' and numerous fudge outlets. The **tourist information centre** (☎ 01535-642329, ☐ www.visitbrontecoun try.com) is open daily May-Aug 9.30am-5.30pm, Sep-Apr daily 9.30am-5pm and is situated at the top of the cobbled Main St in a commanding position that's hard to miss.

There are **no banks** in Haworth but there is a **cash machine** in the Spar supermarket near the station.

Halfway up the cobbled Main St, on the corner of 'Purvs Lane', is **Spooks**, an interesting 'alternative' bookshop. If your walk isn't going quite as well as you'd planned you could have a tarot reading (£20) but perhaps the money would be better spent on an aromatherapy massage, also available here for £20.

The **Parsonage (Brontë Museum**; ☎ 01535-642323, ☐ www.bronte.info; open daily 10am-5.30pm Apr-Sep and 11am-5pm Oct-Mar, closed Jan, £5.50) is at the top of the town. It tells the fascinating story of the family (see box p112) and their tragic life including the only son, Branwell, who gave his life up to riotous living. With such talented sisters, who could blame him?

Where to stay

Haworth Youth Hostel (☎ 0870-770 5858, ☐ haworth@yha.org.uk, Longlands Drive, open all year) is on the other side of town, 1¹/₂ miles up a long hill, passing most of the other services on the way. This grand Victorian mansion has nearly 100 beds but the popularity of the town means that it gets very busy at peak times. Adults are charged £14, under 18s £10. The hostel is open all day, there's an evening meal at 6.30pm and a bar.

One of the best B&Bs, *The Apothecary Guest House* (☎ 01535-643642, ☐ www .bronte-country.com/accomm/apothecary, 86 Main St; 2S/3D/1T/1F all en suite or with a private bathroom), is ideally located

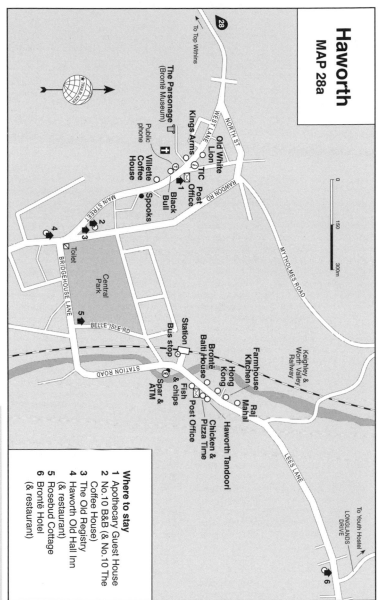

Haworth
MAP 28a

To Top Withins

The Parsonage
(Brontë Museum)

Public phone

Villette Coffee House

Kings Arms

Old White Lion

TIC

Post Office

Black Bull

Spooks

Toilet

Central Park

Station

Bus stop

Brontë Balti House

Hong Kong

Farmhouse

Raj Mahal

Keighley & Worth Valley Railway

Haworth Tandoori

Chicken & Pizza Time

Fish & chips

Post Office

Spar & ATM

To Youth Hostel

LONGLANDS DRIVE

LEES LANE

MYTHOLMES ROAD

STATION ROAD

BRIDGEHOUSE LANE

BELLE ISLE RD

MAIN STREET

WEST LANE

NORTH ST

RAWDON RD

0   150   300m

Where to stay
1 Apothecary Guest House
2 No.10 B&B (& No.10 The Coffee House)
3 The Old Registry
4 Haworth Old Hall Inn (& restaurant)
5 Rosebud Cottage
6 Brontë Hotel (& restaurant)

❏ The Brontës of Haworth

Haworth cannot be separated from the Brontës. Their home, the Parsonage, still stands and is open to the public, attracting tens of thousands of visitors every year from across the world. A shop sells the complete works in book form, on disc and on tape plus lavender-scented pot-pourris.

The churchyard above which the Parsonage stands can be a haunting place on a wet evening, calling to mind Mrs Gaskell's account of life in Haworth. Standing at the top of the village, the graveyard's eternal incumbents poisoned the springs which fed the pumps from which the villagers drew their water. Small wonder that typhoid and fever often afflicted the community.

Mrs Gaskell's description sums up the oppressive nature of Haworth in Victorian times, an echo of which can be heard even today:

The rain ceased, and the day was just suited to the scenery – wild and chill – with great masses of cloud, glooming over the moors, and here and there a ray of sunshine ... darting down into some deep glen, lighting up the tall chimney, or glistening on the windows and wet roof of the mill which lies couching at the bottom. The country got wilder and wilder as we approached Haworth; for the last four miles we were ascending a huge moor at the very top of which lies the dreary, black-looking village. The clergyman's house was at the top of the churchyard. So through that we went – a dreary, dreary place, literally paved with rain-blackened tombstones, and all on the slope.
Mrs Gaskell *The Life of Charlotte Brontë*, 1857

The three Brontë sisters, Emily (*Wuthering Heights*, 1847), Charlotte (*Jane Eyre*, 1847) and Anne (*The Tenant of Wildfell Hall*, 1848), were brought up by their father and an aunt in the Parsonage where Reverend Brontë had taken a living in 1820. The only boy in the family, Branwell, had every hope and expectation lavished on him, taking precedence over his more talented sisters as the son, but squandered his life in drink and drugs, dying in 1848.

The lonely, unassuming sisters wrote under male pseudonyms but still their talents went largely unrecognized during their lifetimes and they all died comparatively young from the unhealthy conditions that plagued their village. Today their reputation as novelists endures, and *Wuthering Heights* in particular – set so obviously in the Haworth locality – continues to entrance readers with its vivid portrait of thwarted passion and unfulfilled lives shaped by the bleak, unforgiving landscape of the Yorkshire moors.

right in the heart of town, surrounded by places to eat. Their prices are a reasonable £25-30 for a single and £45-50 for two sharing.

At the bottom of Main St *The Old Registry* (☎ 01535-646503, 🖥 www.theold registryhaworth.co.uk, 2-4 Main St; 9D/1T

all en suite from £65 to £80; up to £10 more Fri & Sat, up to £15 less on Sun) is furnished with an eye for detail and an emphasis on luxury and pampering. Residents who choose to eat in can have a pizza and a drink in their bar open Mon-Sat 6-8pm.

(Opposite) Top: The ruins of Top Withins (see p108), said to be the inspiration for *Wuthering Heights*. (Photo © Chris Scott). **Bottom**: The Parsonage where the Brontës lived and wrote is now a museum that's well worth the detour to Haworth. (Photo © Keith Carter).

Next door at No 10 is the more modest-sized *No 10 B&B* (☎ 01535-644694, 🖥 www.10thecoffeehouse.co.uk; 2D en suite, from £70), where one room overlooks the cobbled street and the other the valley; one room has a four-poster bed. Not far away is *Haworth Old Hall Inn* (☎ 01535-642709, 🖥 www.hawortholdhall.co.uk, Sun St; 1T/1D both en suite) where either room costs from £65,

Rosebud Cottage (☎ 01535-640321, 🖥 www.rosebudcottage.co.uk, 1 Belle Isle Rd; 1S/2D/1T all en suite) is a well-run establishment with rooms at £32.50 for the single and £65 for two sharing a double or twin; an evening meal costs £15.

Brontë Hotel (☎ 01535-644112, 🖥 www.bronte-hotel.co.uk, Lees Lane; 3S/2T/3D /3F) is a larger establishment not far from the youth hostel and might be just the ticket for a group of walkers wanting accommodation under the same roof. It's geared for over-nighters with good clean rooms, most en suite and with ample scope for eating and drinking downstairs (see column opposite). You can expect to pay £27 for a single, £37 en suite, £50 for a twin or £65 en suite and £70 for an en suite family room.

Where to eat

Three of Haworth's pubs, the *Old White Lion*, *Kings Arms*, and *Black Bull*, are clustered together at the top of the cobbled street. However, one of the best, *Haworth Old Hall Inn* (see column opposite) stands apart and is particularly recommended for its real ales. They are open all day and a range of bar meals in generous portions is served Mon-Fri 12-3pm & 5.30-9pm, Sat 12-4pm & 5-9.30pm, Sun 12 noon-4pm & 5-8pm. Another place to consider is the *Brontë Hotel* (see column opposite) where food is served Mon-Fri 12-2pm & 7-9pm, Sat 12-2pm & 7-9.30pm, Sun 12-8.30pm.

The cobbled Main St has a plethora of eating places. For lunches and afternoon teas you can't do better than *Villette Coffee House* (☎ 01535-644967) where such delights as Yorkshire curd tarts, large flat Yorkshire Parkins, delicious sticky ginger buns and a rich spicy scone known as a Fat Rascal can all be savoured. Cream teas are £2.20 and their all-day breakfast is a feast for £3.30. They are open daily in season 8.30am-5/6pm – until the last customer leaves – and in winter till 4 or 4.30pm.

No 10 The Coffee House (see No 10 B&B) serves a variety of tea and freshly ground coffees as well as home-made cakes baked daily on the premises in a relaxing environment; they are open Thur-Sat and Bank Holiday Mondays 12.30-6.30pm.

In the eastern, non-touristy, part of town is a collection of takeaways and restaurants. *Raj Mahal* (☎ 01535-643890; 51 Mill Hey; daily 5.30-11.30pm, to 12 midnight on Fri and Sat) is a notable Indian restaurant, or try the nearby *Brontë Balti* or *Haworth Tandoori*. There are also **takeaways** (a Chinese, Hong Kong, and Chicken & Pizza Time), a *fish and chip* shop, and the *Farmhouse Kitchen* over the road.

ROUTE GUIDE AND MAPS

(**Opposite**): Main St and most of the other cobbled streets of Haworth are busy with tourists throughout the year. (Photo © Chris Scott).

ROUTE GUIDE AND MAPS

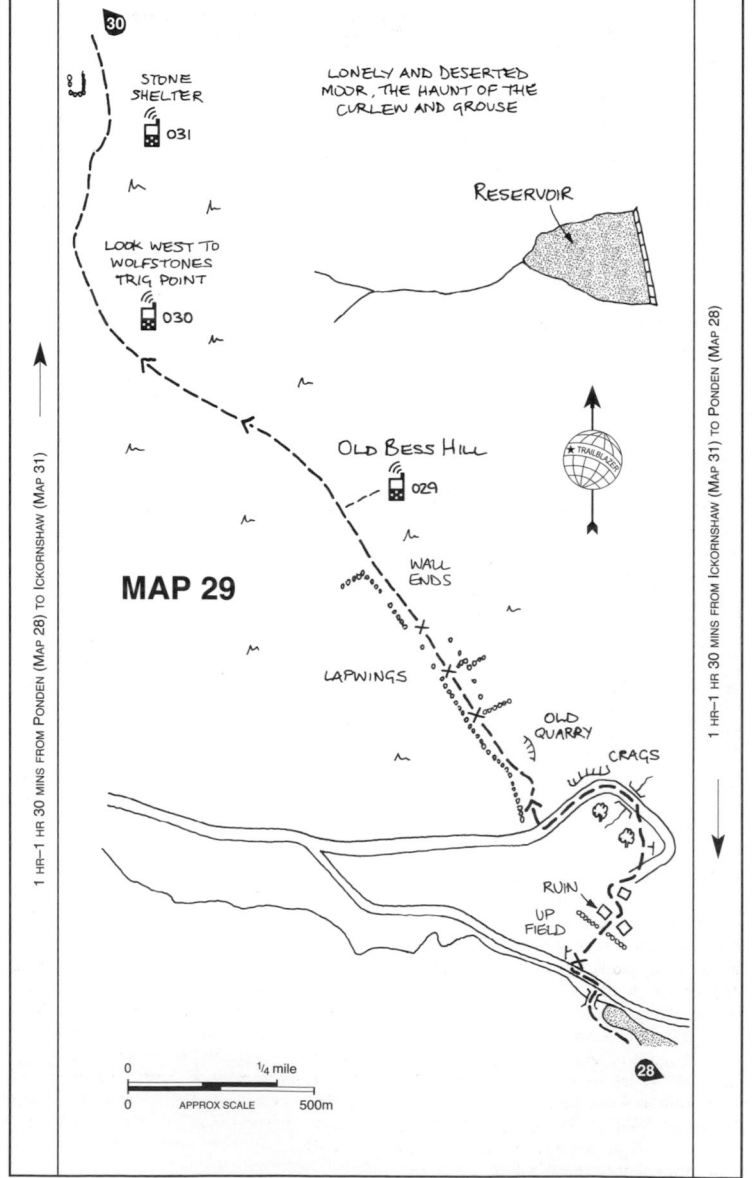

1 HR–1 HR 30 MINS FROM PONDEN (MAP 28) TO ICKORNSHAW (MAP 31)

1 HR–1 HR 30 MINS FROM ICKORNSHAW (MAP 31) TO PONDEN (MAP 28)

STONE SHELTER
031

LONELY AND DESERTED MOOR, THE HAUNT OF THE CURLEW AND GROUSE

RESERVOIR

LOOK WEST TO WOLFSTONES TRIG POINT
030

OLD BESS HILL
029

WALL ENDS

MAP 29

LAPWINGS

OLD QUARRY

CRAGS

RUIN

UP FIELD

★ TRAILBLAZER

0   ¼ mile
0   APPROX SCALE   500m

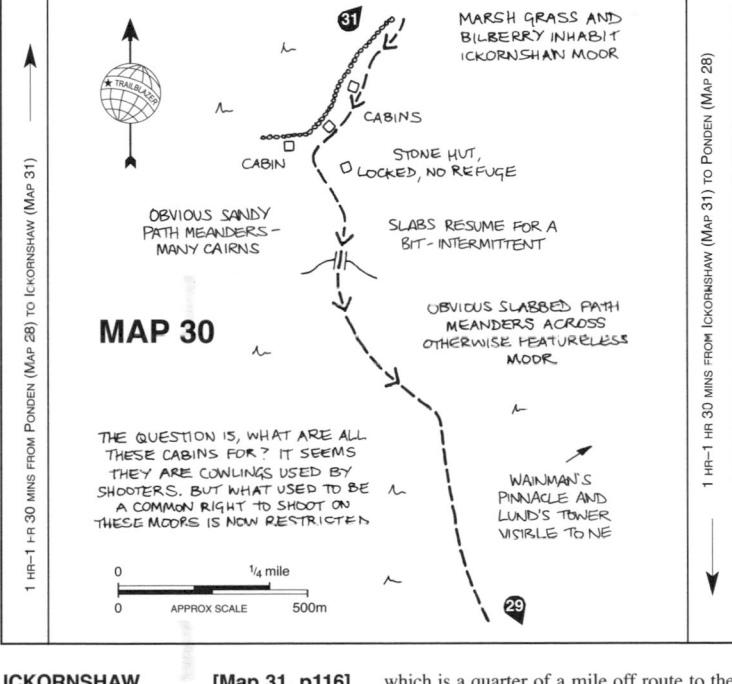

Within the map:

MARSH GRASS AND BILBERRY INHABIT ICKORNSHAW MOOR

CABINS

STONE HUT, LOCKED, NO REFUGE

CABIN

OBVIOUS SANDY PATH MEANDERS – MANY CAIRNS

SLABS RESUME FOR A BIT - INTERMITTENT

MAP 30

OBVIOUS SLABBED PATH MEANDERS ACROSS OTHERWISE FEATURELESS MOOR

THE QUESTION IS, WHAT ARE ALL THESE CABINS FOR? IT SEEMS THEY ARE COWLINGS USED BY SHOOTERS. BUT WHAT USED TO BE A COMMON RIGHT TO SHOOT ON THESE MOORS IS NOW RESTRICTED

WAINMAN'S PINNACLE AND LUND'S TOWER VISIBLE TO NE

★ TRAILBLAZER

0   ¼ mile
0   APPROX SCALE   500m

1 HR–1 HR 30 MINS FROM PONDEN (MAP 28) TO ICKORNSHAW (MAP 31)

1 HR–1 HR 30 MINS FROM ICKORNSHAW (MAP 31) TO PONDEN (MAP 28)

31

29

ICKORNSHAW   [Map 31, p116]

The Pennine Way crosses the busy A6068 between Colne and Keighley at Ickornshaw. To blend in say 'Ick-<u>corn</u>-sher', with the emphasis on the 'corn' and no one need ever know your dark secret. Ickornshaw is an off-shoot of Cowling

COWLING   [Map 31, p116]

Cowling has a useful **grocery shop/post office** (early closing Wed), a pub (no food served), a Chinese *takeaway* (Mei Mei) and a reasonably priced gourmet restaurant, *The Harlequin* (☎ 01535-633277, 🖥 enq@the harlequin.org.uk) that makes a wonderful change from takeaways and pub fare.

The menu changes weekly but includes an extensive selection of meat and fish dishes as well as some vegetarian dishes. Food is served Wed to Sat noon-2pm and 6-9.30pm, 12-7pm on Sunday. If that's too fancy for you the nearest pub meal will be at

which is a quarter of a mile off route to the east (see below). The nearest B&B is *Winterhouse Barn* (☎ 01535-632234, 🖥 www.thepennineway.co.uk/winterhouse barn; 2T/1D), where you'll pay £20 per person or £4 for **camping** in a field round the back with a toilet and shower block.

the *Dog & Gun* another mile down the road.

If you're shopping and eating in Cowling it won't give you nightmares to stay there too. *Woodland House* (☎ 01535-637886, 🖥 www.woodland-house.co.uk; 2 Woodland St, 1T/1D en suite, 1T with private bathroom) is an especially walker-friendly B&B charging £27.50 for single occupancy and £50 for two sharing.

Both Burnley & Pendle and Keighley & District operate **bus** services here (see public transport map and table, pp42-6) for details.

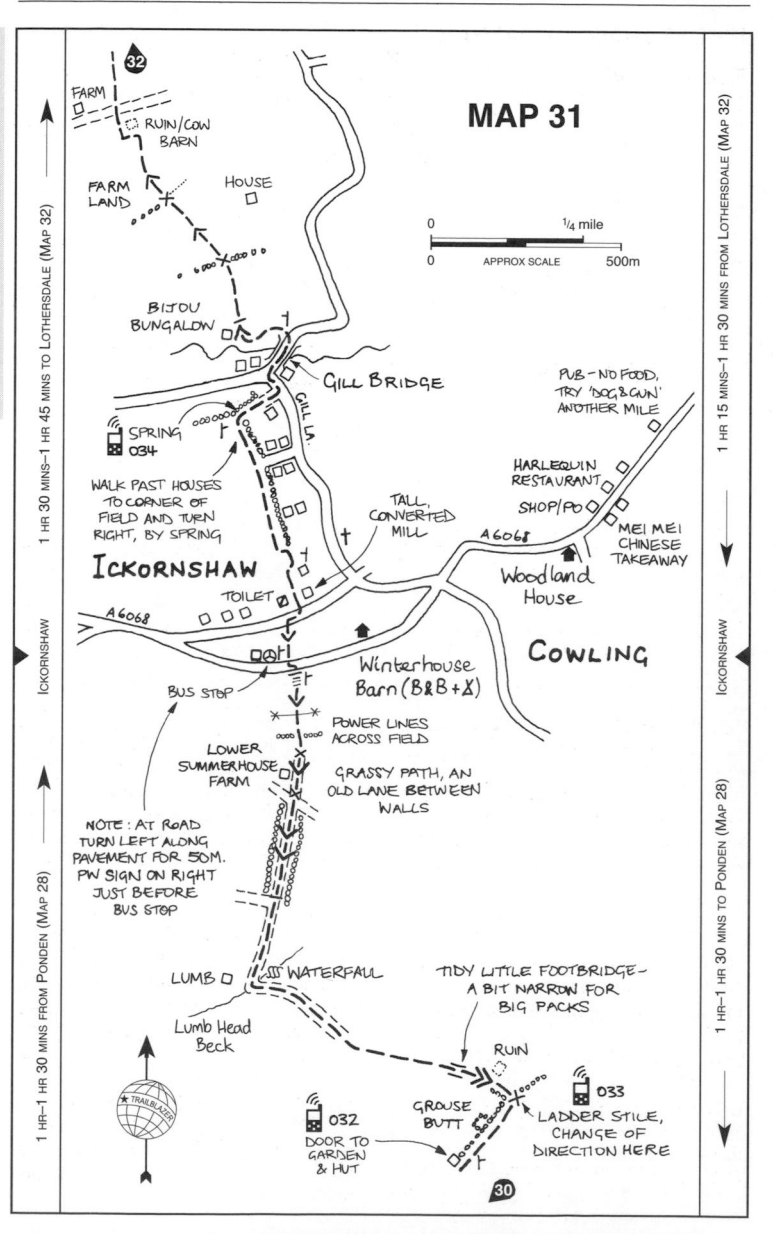

MAP 31

32

FARM

RUIN/COW BARN

HOUSE

FARM LAND

BIJOU BUNGALOW

0   ¼ mile
0   500m
APPROX SCALE

GILL BRIDGE

PUB – NO FOOD, TRY 'DOG & GUN' ANOTHER MILE

SPRING 034

HARLEQUIN RESTAURANT

SHOP/PO

MEI MEI CHINESE TAKEAWAY

GILL LA.

WALK PAST HOUSES TO CORNER OF FIELD AND TURN RIGHT, BY SPRING

TALL, CONVERTED MILL

A6068

Ickornshaw

Woodland House

TOILET

A6068

Cowling

BUS STOP

Winterhouse Barn (B&B + X)

POWER LINES ACROSS FIELD

LOWER SUMMERHOUSE FARM

GRASSY PATH, AN OLD LANE BETWEEN WALLS

NOTE: AT ROAD TURN LEFT ALONG PAVEMENT FOR 50M. PW SIGN ON RIGHT JUST BEFORE BUS STOP

LUMB

WATERFALL

Lumb Head Beck

TIDY LITTLE FOOTBRIDGE – A BIT NARROW FOR BIG PACKS

RUIN

TRAILBLAZER

032
DOOR TO GARDEN & HUT

GROUSE BUTT

033
LADDER STILE, CHANGE OF DIRECTION HERE

30

1 HR 30 MINS–1 HR 45 MINS TO LOTHERSDALE (MAP 32)

ICKORNSHAW

1 HR 30 MINS–1 HR 30 MINS FROM PONDEN (MAP 28)

1 HR 15 MINS–1 HR 30 MINS FROM LOTHERSDALE (MAP 32)

ICKORNSHAW

1 HR–1 HR 30 MINS TO PONDEN (MAP 28)

ICKORNSHAW TO MALHAM

MAPS 31-41

Route overview

This **17-mile (25km, 6-7hrs)** walk delivers you first class into the famed Yorkshire Dales and, better still, on the way drops you after 8 or 11 miles walking on the doorstep of two great cafés.

Leaving Ickornshaw via **Gill Bridge**, another 'up-and-over' pastoral interlude brings you to a wooded valley and **Lothersdale** (Map 32) from whose centre sprouts a huge out-of-place mill chimney. This is the last of the South Pennine milltowns and the country begins to change as you prepare to traverse the riverine lowlands of the Aire Gap. It's something you'll hopefully get a fine view of from **Pinhaw Beacon** (Map 33) whose panorama can reveal Pen-y-ghent, 16 miles distant, the lowest of the Three Peaks and a challenge soon to come. Though off route, Earby has more accommodation and eating options than **Thornton-in-Craven** (Map 34).

The Way leaves Thornton, passing pristine retirement bungalows to cross a series of fields and reach the towpath of the **Leeds–Liverpool Canal** (Map 35) just before the unusual bridge-on-a-bridge at **East Marton**. Beyond the narrow boats is the charming *Abbots Harbour Restaurant* (see p121), a perfect place to synchronize an arrival with a rumbling tummy.

At East Marton our route leaves the canal and takes to the green, wildflower-speckled fields again, climbing to diminutive **Scaleber Hill** (Map 36) from where the church tower of Gargrave jauntily signals '*Come hither, wayfarer!*'.

Gargrave (Map 37), the Gateway to the Dales, is an interlude worth prolonging and it would be a glum walker indeed who did not avail themselves of the services of the *Dalesman Café* (see p124). That done, the uphill road-walk out of the town soon branches off to cross **Eshton Moor** (Map 38; actually walls, plantations and pasture), an airy ramble to meet the meandering arcs of the River Aire for the second time; it was the Aire you crossed via the bridge in Gargrave. Riverside walking is on the agenda for the remaining two hours or so as you pass through **Airton** (Map 39) and **Kirkby Malham** to reach the tourist magnet that is **Malham**, venue for a thousand school field trips and the end of this section for Pennine wanderers.

Route-finding trouble spots

Possible difficulties are limited to correctly **negotiating the rolling fields** and stiles before the Aire River; the sole moorland stretch over Pinhaw Beacon is straightforward. In the pastures signs get knocked down or overgrown and in the meadows, approaching Scaleber Hill or over Eshton Moor, a single clear path rarely develops. GPS lights the way of course, but even without a receiver a moment's contemplation will set you on the right track.

LOTHERSDALE   **[Map 32, p118]**

With no B&Bs at the time of writing, all that's left here is the friendly *Hare and Hounds* (☎ 01535-630977) with good pub food for £6-7 (food served Tue-Sat 12

noon-2pm Mon-Sat 6-9pm Sun 12-9pm; the pub closes during the afternoon). However, Keighley & District's No 80 **bus** service calls in here; see public transport map and table, pp42-6.

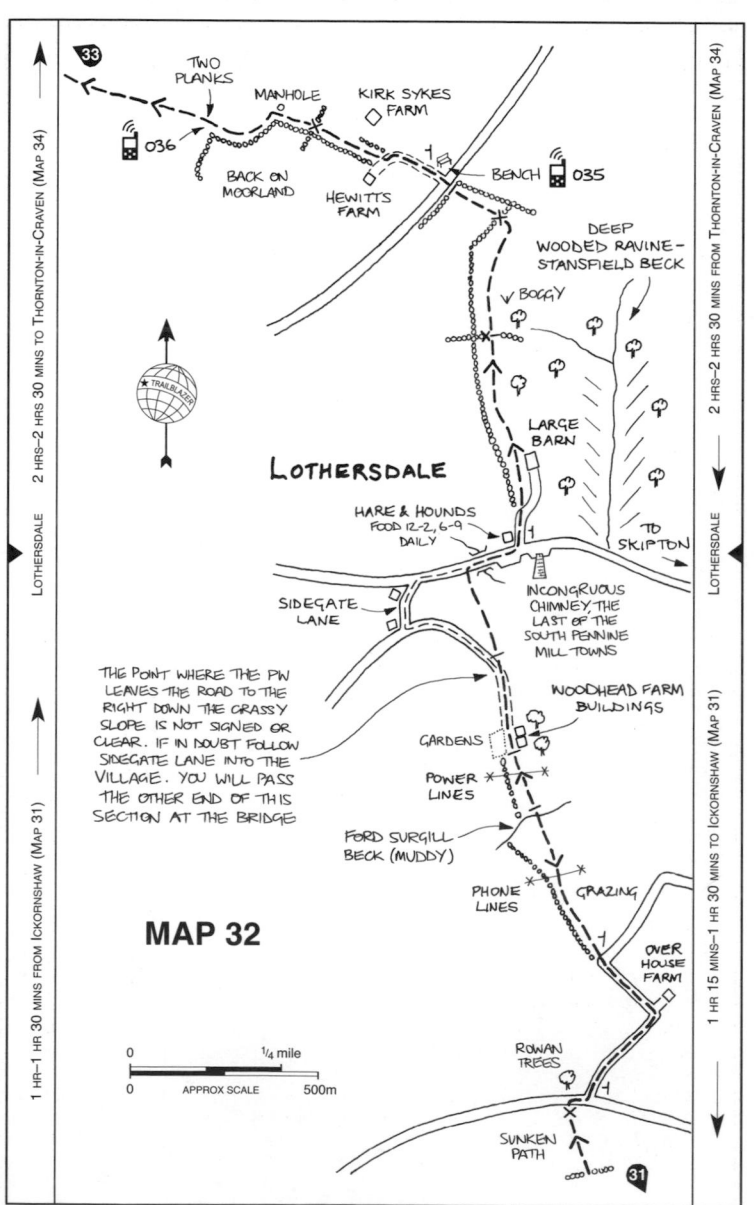

33

TWO PLANKS

MANHOLE

KIRK SYKES FARM

036

BACK ON MOORLAND

HEWITTS FARM

BENCH 035

DEEP WOODED RAVINE - STANSFIELD BECK

V BOGGY

LARGE BARN

LOTHERSDALE

HARE & HOUNDS
FOOD 12-2, 6-9 DAILY

TO SKIPTON

SIDEGATE LANE

INCONGRUOUS CHIMNEY, THE LAST OF THE SOUTH PENNINE MILL TOWNS

THE POINT WHERE THE PW LEAVES THE ROAD TO THE RIGHT DOWN THE GRASSY SLOPE IS NOT SIGNED OR CLEAR. IF IN DOUBT FOLLOW SIDEGATE LANE INTO THE VILLAGE. YOU WILL PASS THE OTHER END OF THIS SECTION AT THE BRIDGE

WOODHEAD FARM BUILDINGS

GARDENS

POWER LINES

FORD SURGILL BECK (MUDDY)

PHONE LINES

GRAZING

OVER HOUSE FARM

MAP 32

ROWAN TREES

SUNKEN PATH

31

0   ¼ mile
0   APPROX SCALE   500m

2 HRS–2 HRS 30 MINS TO THORNTON-IN-CRAVEN (MAP 34)

LOTHERSDALE

1 HR–1 HR 30 MINS FROM ICKORNSHAW (MAP 31)

2 HRS–2 HRS 30 MINS FROM THORNTON-IN-CRAVEN (MAP 34)

LOTHERSDALE

1 HR 15 MINS–1 HR 30 MINS TO ICKORNSHAW (MAP 31)

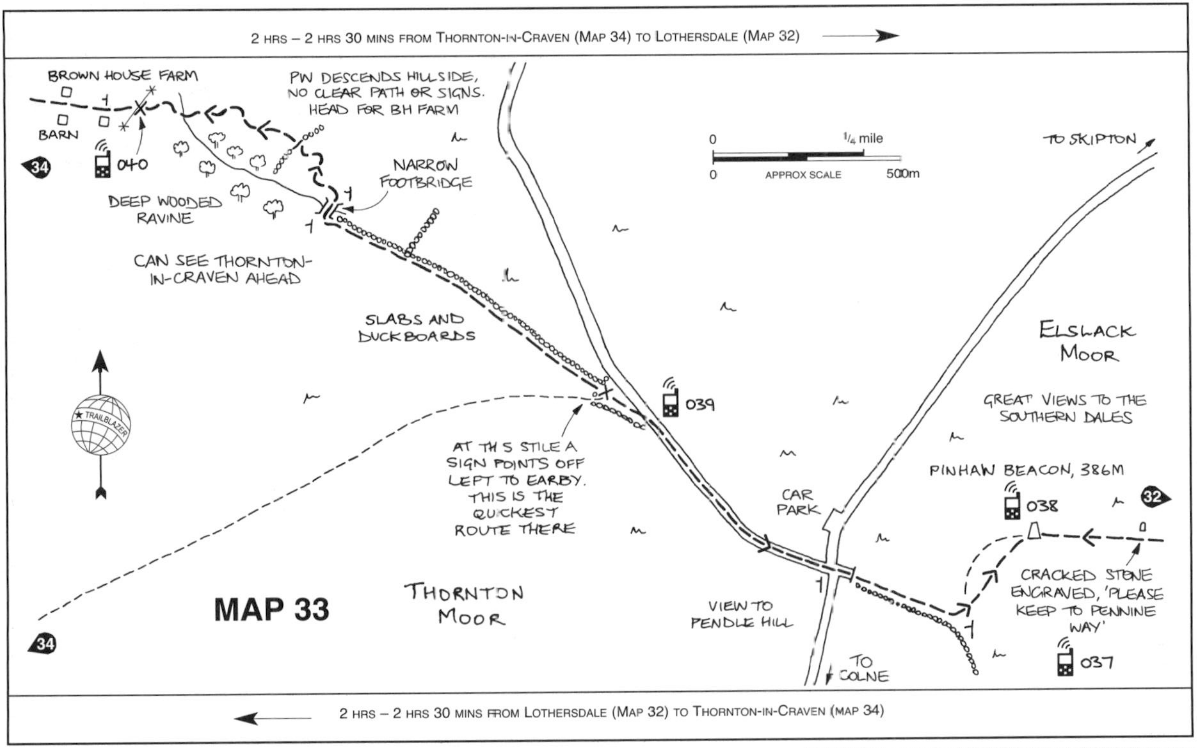

2 HRS – 2 HRS 30 MINS FROM THORNTON-IN-CRAVEN (MAP 34) TO LOTHERSDALE (MAP 32)
BROWN HOUSE FARM
BARN
34
040
DEEP WOODED RAVINE
PW DESCENDS HILLSIDE, NO CLEAR PATH OR SIGNS. HEAD FOR BH FARM
NARROW FOOTBRIDGE
CAN SEE THORNTON-IN-CRAVEN AHEAD
SLABS AND DUCKBOARDS
0
1/4 mile
0
APPROX SCALE
500m
TO SKIPTON
ELSLACK MOOR
039
GREAT VIEWS TO THE SOUTHERN DALES
TRAILBLAZER
AT THIS STILE A SIGN POINTS OFF LEFT TO EARBY. THIS IS THE QUICKEST ROUTE THERE
PINHAW BEACON, 386M
32
038
CAR PARK
CRACKED STONE ENGRAVED, 'PLEASE KEEP TO PENNINE WAY'
MAP 33
THORNTON MOOR
VIEW TO PENDLE HILL
34
037
TO COLNE
2 HRS – 2 HRS 30 MINS FROM LOTHERSDALE (MAP 32) TO THORNTON-IN-CRAVEN (MAP 34)

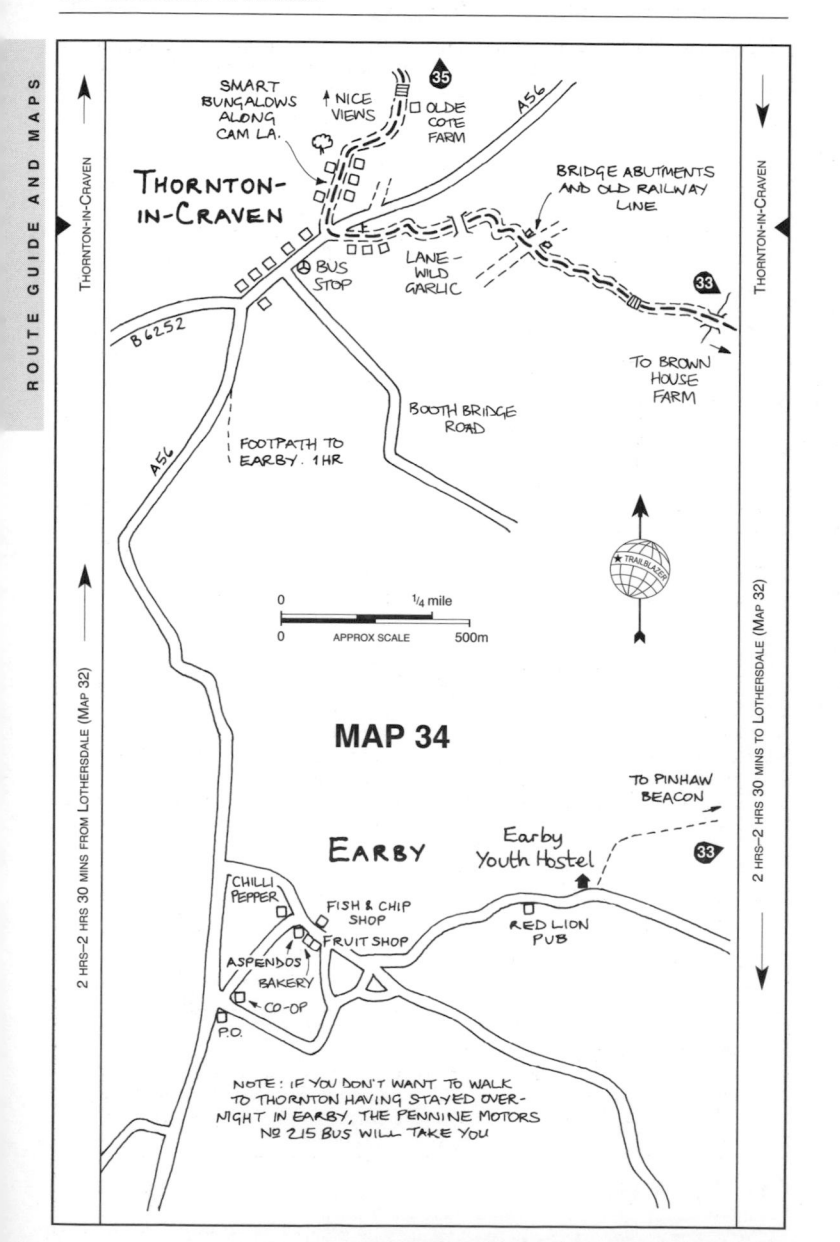

SMART BUNGALOWS ALONG CAM LA.

↑ NICE VIEWS

35

OLDE COTE FARM

A56

BRIDGE ABUTMENTS AND OLD RAILWAY LINE

THORNTON-IN-CRAVEN

BUS STOP

LANE-WILD GARLIC

33

TO BROWN HOUSE FARM

B6252

A56

FOOTPATH TO EARBY. 1HR

BOOTH BRIDGE ROAD

0   ¼ mile

0   APPROX SCALE   500m

TRAILBLAZER

MAP 34

TO PINHAW BEACON

EARBY

Earby Youth Hostel

33

CHILLI PEPPER

FISH & CHIP SHOP

FRUIT SHOP

RED LION PUB

ASPENDOS BAKERY

CO-OP

P.O.

NOTE: IF YOU DON'T WANT TO WALK TO THORNTON HAVING STAYED OVER-NIGHT IN EARBY, THE PENNINE MOTORS Nº 215 BUS WILL TAKE YOU

ROUTE GUIDE AND MAPS

THORNTON-IN-CRAVEN

THORNTON-IN-CRAVEN

2 HRS–2 HRS 30 MINS FROM LOTHERSDALE (MAP 32)

2 HRS–2 HRS 30 MINS TO LOTHERSDALE (MAP 32)

THORNTON-IN-CRAVEN [Map 34]

There's no longer any chance of accommodation here but Pennine Motor Services operate regular **buses** along the A56 to Burnley and Skipton and Tyrer Tours No 280 runs between Preston and Skipton (see public transport map and table, pp42-6).

See box p24 for details of the village fête in July.

EARBY [Map 34]

The only accommodation here, 1½ miles (2km) off the trail, is at the 22-bed *Earby Youth Hostel* (☎ 0870-770 5802, 🖳 earby@yha.org.uk, open Easter to Oct). Adults are charged £13, under 18s £9.50. It opens at 5pm and is self-catering only.

Earby, however, is quite a large community. There's a pub, *The Red Lion*, near the hostel, *Chilli Pepper* (☎ 01282-843943, open Mon-Thur 5-11pm, Fri & Sat 5-12 midnight, Sun 3-11pm), a good Indian restaurant and takeaway, *Aspendos* (pizzas and kebabs to take away), a *fish and chip* shop, a **fruit shop**, a **bakery**, a **post office** and a Co-op **supermarket**.

Pennine Motor Services' **bus** No 215 calls in here daily (see public transport map and table, pp42-6).

EAST MARTON [Map 35, p122]

There are two B&Bs of note in the enclave of East Marton, a hidden treasure known only to canal users and walkers looking for a mooring or way station alongside the Pennine Way.

Next to Abbots Harbour (see below) is *Sawley House* (☎ 01282-843207; 1T/1D) where for £25/pp you can enjoy the atmosphere of a farmhouse that dates back to the 12th century. For those who prefer to **camp**, £6 will see you securely ensconced, with showers at your disposal, too, and the restaurant next door.

Abbots Harbour (Sawley House number, daily 10am-4.30pm, closed Thurs) deserves an accolade for its atmosphere and food. This is a cracking good place to eat. A bacon sandwich is £2.60, all-day breakfast £6.50 and the lunch menu includes home-cooked favourites such as shepherd's pie (£8.20), a fate which most sheep would accept willingly.

The *Cross Keys* (☎ 01282-844326) is the nearest pub, up the lane facing the main road; it serves food Mon-Fri 12-2.30pm & 6-9pm, Sat 12-9.30pm, Sun 12-8pm and serves Copper Dragon as well as rotating guest beers which may include the ever-effective Black Sheep Bitter.

Should you need to get out of town fast ring SD Cars (☎ 01282-814310) for a **taxi**. Lancashire United **bus** No X80 stops in West Marton, a mile away, en route between Preston and Skipton (see public transport map and table, pp42-6) a mile away.

❏ **Important note – walking times**

Unless otherwise specified, **all times in this book refer only to the time spent walking**. You will need to add 20-30% to allow for rests, photography, checking the map, drinking water etc. When planning the day's hike count on 5-7 hours' actual walking.

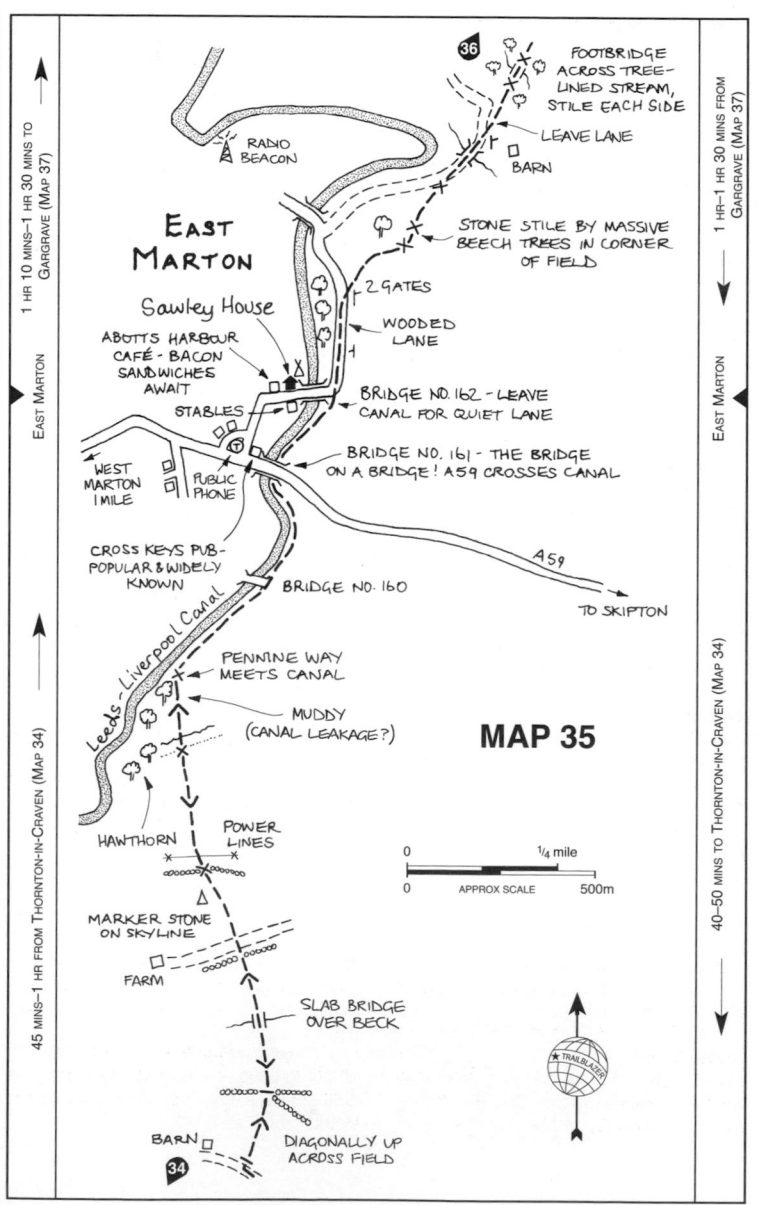

36

FOOTBRIDGE
ACROSS TREE-
LINED STREAM,
STILE EACH SIDE

LEAVE LANE

BARN

RADIO
BEACON

EAST
MARTON

Sawley House

STONE STILE BY MASSIVE
BEECH TREES IN CORNER
OF FIELD

2 GATES

ABBOTTS HARBOUR
CAFÉ - BACON
SANDWICHES
AWAIT

WOODED
LANE

STABLES

BRIDGE NO. 162 - LEAVE
CANAL FOR QUIET LANE

WEST
MARTON
1 MILE

PUBLIC
PHONE

BRIDGE NO. 161 - THE BRIDGE
ON A BRIDGE! A59 CROSSES CANAL

CROSS KEYS PUB -
POPULAR & WIDELY
KNOWN

BRIDGE NO. 160

A59

TO SKIPTON

Leeds - Liverpool Canal

PENNINE WAY
MEETS CANAL

MUDDY
(CANAL LEAKAGE?)

MAP 35

HAWTHORN

POWER
LINES

MARKER STONE
ON SKYLINE

FARM

0   1/4 mile

0   APPROX SCALE   500m

SLAB BRIDGE
OVER BECK

BARN

DIAGONALLY UP
ACROSS FIELD

34

★ TRAILBLAZER

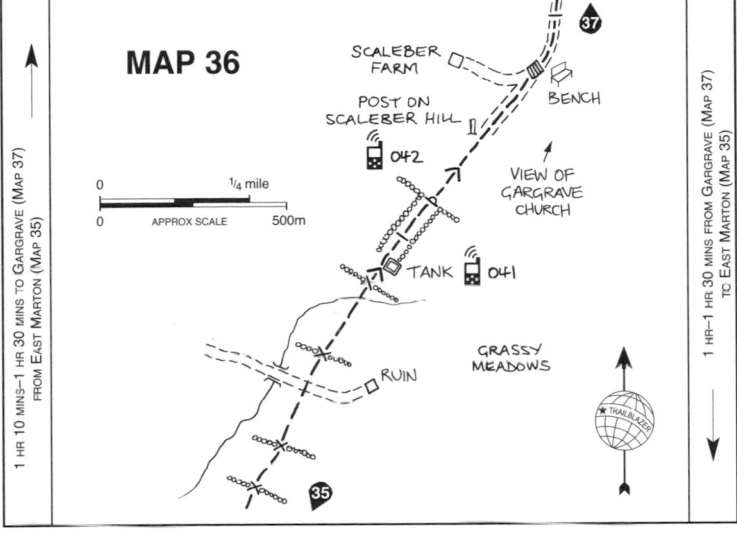

MAP 36

SCALEBER FARM

POST ON SCALEBER HILL 042

BENCH

VIEW OF GARGRAVE CHURCH

TANK 041

0   1/4 mile

0   APPROX SCALE   500m

GRASSY MEADOWS

RUIN

★ TRAILBLAZER

1 HR 10 MINS—1 HR 30 MINS TO GARGRAVE (MAP 37) FROM EAST MARTON (MAP 35)

1 HR—1 HR 30 MINS FROM GARGRAVE (MAP 37) TO EAST MARTON (MAP 35)

ROUTE GUIDE AND MAPS

GARGRAVE   [see Map 37a, p124]

This small attractive town has most things you will want. Say hello to the Aire river which you'll be following later in the day.

Services

All shops are on the main road and close together. There is a **pharmacy**, a well-stocked Co-op **supermarket** (Mon-Sat 8am-8pm, Sun 10am-6pm).

The **post office** (early closing Tue) offers a fax service. There is a **cash machine** at the Co-op.

If one person in your party looks as if they may not make it, it may be worth reserving some turf at the **florist**: they claim it to be 'top quality – suitable for graves.'

See box p24 for details of the agricultural show here in August.

Transport

Gargrave is a stop on the Leeds to Carlisle railway. Pennine Motor Services (PMS), Stagecoach and Royal Mail Postbus operate

bus services to Malham, Airton and Skipton (see public transport map and table, pp42-6).

Where to stay

Surprisingly, at the time of writing, the choice in Gargrave is limited to just two pubs and a campsite, so plan ahead or take a bus (Pennine Motor Services No 580) to Skipton. (See ☐ www.skiptonweb.co.uk/ tourist for details of the many accommodation possibilities in Skipton as well as other tourist information).

Coming off the Pennine Way, just before the bridge you'll pass *The Masons Arms* (☎ 01756-749304, ☐ www.masons armsgargrave.com; 4D/2T), on the corner close to the church, which has en suite rooms costing from £65; single occupancy costs £45 but is not available on a Saturday night.

The Old Swan Inn (☎ 01756-749232; 1S/2D/1T) has en suite doubles for £60 (£30 for the single) but these rates do not include breakfast.

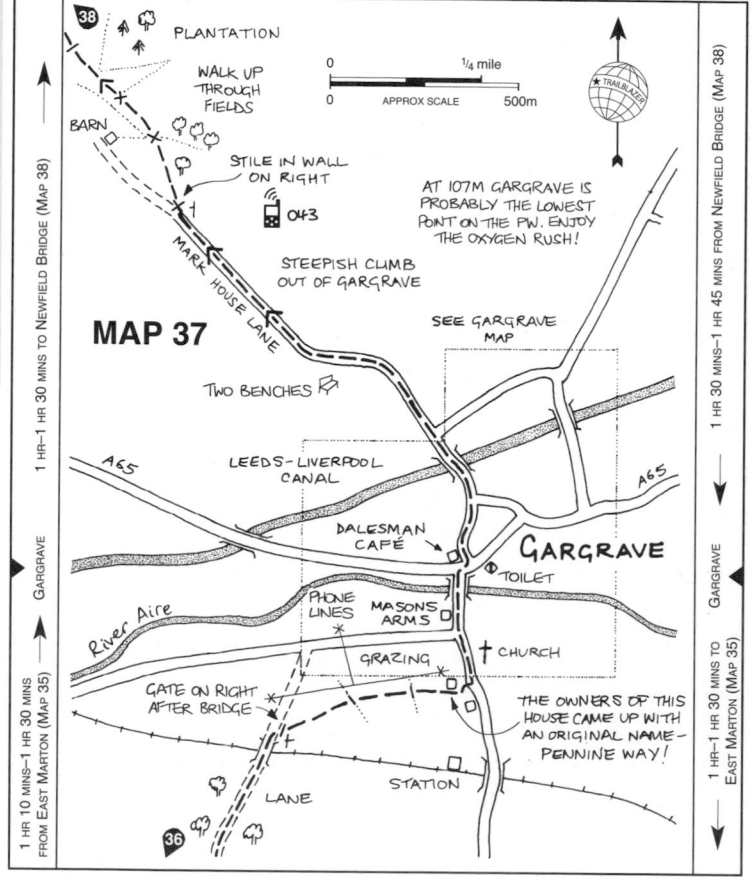

MAP 37

38

PLANTATION

WALK UP
THROUGH
FIELDS

0   ¼ mile
0   500m
APPROX SCALE

TRAILBLAZER

BARN

MARK HOUSE LANE

STILE IN WALL
ON RIGHT

043

AT 107M GARGRAVE IS
PROBABLY THE LOWEST
POINT ON THE PW. ENJOY
THE OXYGEN RUSH!

STEEPISH CLIMB
OUT OF GARGRAVE

SEE GARGRAVE
MAP

TWO BENCHES

A65

LEEDS-LIVERPOOL
CANAL

A65

DALESMAN
CAFÉ

GARGRAVE

TOILET

River Aire

PHONE
LINES

MASONS
ARMS

CHURCH

GRAZING

GATE ON RIGHT
AFTER BRIDGE

THE OWNERS OF THIS
HOUSE CAME UP WITH
AN ORIGINAL NAME-
PENNINE WAY!

LANE

STATION

36

Side labels:
ROUTE GUIDE AND MAPS

1 HR-1 HR 30 MINS TO NEWFIELD BRIDGE (MAP 38)

GARGRAVE

1 HR 10 MINS-1 HR 30 MINS FROM EAST MARTON (MAP 35)

1 HR 30 MINS-1 HR 45 MINS FROM NEWFIELD BRIDGE (MAP 38)

GARGRAVE

1 HR-1 HR 30 MINS TO EAST MARTON (MAP 35)

Carry on up that road and you'll get to,
Eshton Road Caravan Site (☎ 01756-749229) with **camping** for £4 per person.

Where to eat

As you cross the bridge over the River Aire you will be facing the *Dalesman Café* (☎ 01756-749250; Tue-Sun 9am-5pm, but also open most Bank Holiday Mondays), a well-primed place for some tucker. It offers a great range of good-value food (ham, eggs and chips, £4.95) as well as indul-

gences such as quality ice cream and 200 different varieties of sweets sold out of jars in the old-fashioned way.

Nearby is a very good Indian restaurant, *Bollywood Cottage* (☎ 01756-749252), open Tue-Sun 5.30-11.30pm. To eat in there are balti dishes from around £5, tandooris from £7.

Just up West St is the *White Cottage Tea Room* (☎ 01756-748229; open year-round except for November, Mon-Fri 11am-5pm, Sat & Sun 10am-5pm).

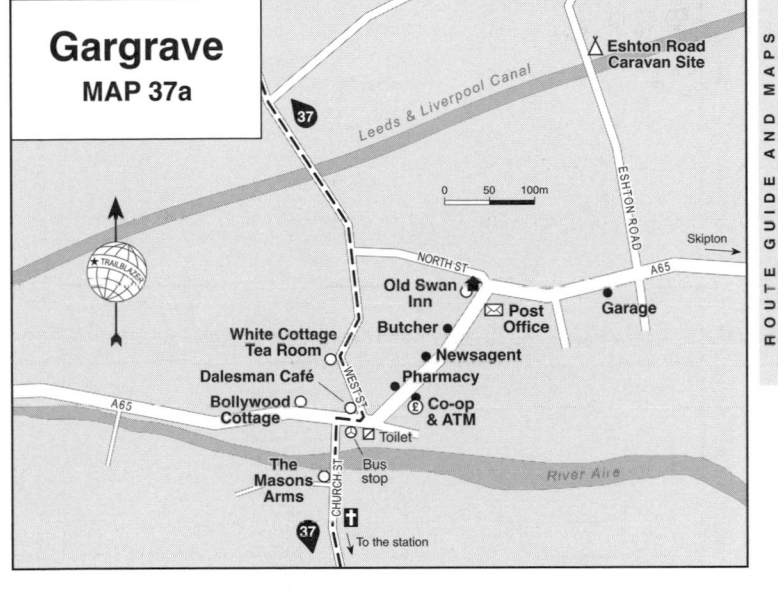

Everything is home made and the menu includes delicious triple-decker sandwiches – try and get through their ham with Wensleydale and chutney – and other dishes such as soup or ploughman's lunches.

The Masons Arms (see p123) is friendly; their interesting pub food costs around £6 and is served daily 12-2pm & 6-9pm, except Wednesday evenings when the etimes are 7-9pm.

The Old Swan Inn (see p123) serves pub food in summer between 12 noon and 2pm Mon-Sat (to 4pm on Sun) and daily 6-9pm, in winter 5-8pm Tue-Fri and to 9pm on Sat and Sun and has a variety of traditionally themed rooms such as a flagstone floor 'Snug' and a 'Parlour' with a rocking chair.

AIRTON [Map 39, p127]

Right by the left bank of the river, Airton is home to little more than two places to stay: *Quaker Hostel* (☎ 01729-830263, 🖳 bob minor@aol.com; 14 beds), attached to the Quaker Meeting House. It's not a fancy place, reminiscent of some of the older Youth Hostels before most became what they are today. A bed costs only £8 and there are cooking facilities. Advance booking is recommended.

The other place, towards the other end

of the scale, is *Lindon Guesthouse* (☎ 01729-830418; 1T/2D en suite), which is a little way out of the village along the Malham road. The house is better appointed than the average Pennine Way walker may expect. B&B is £59 for two sharing; packed lunches are available.

Both Stagecoach and the Royal Mail post **bus** (see public transport map and table, pp42-6) call here en route between Skipton and Malham.

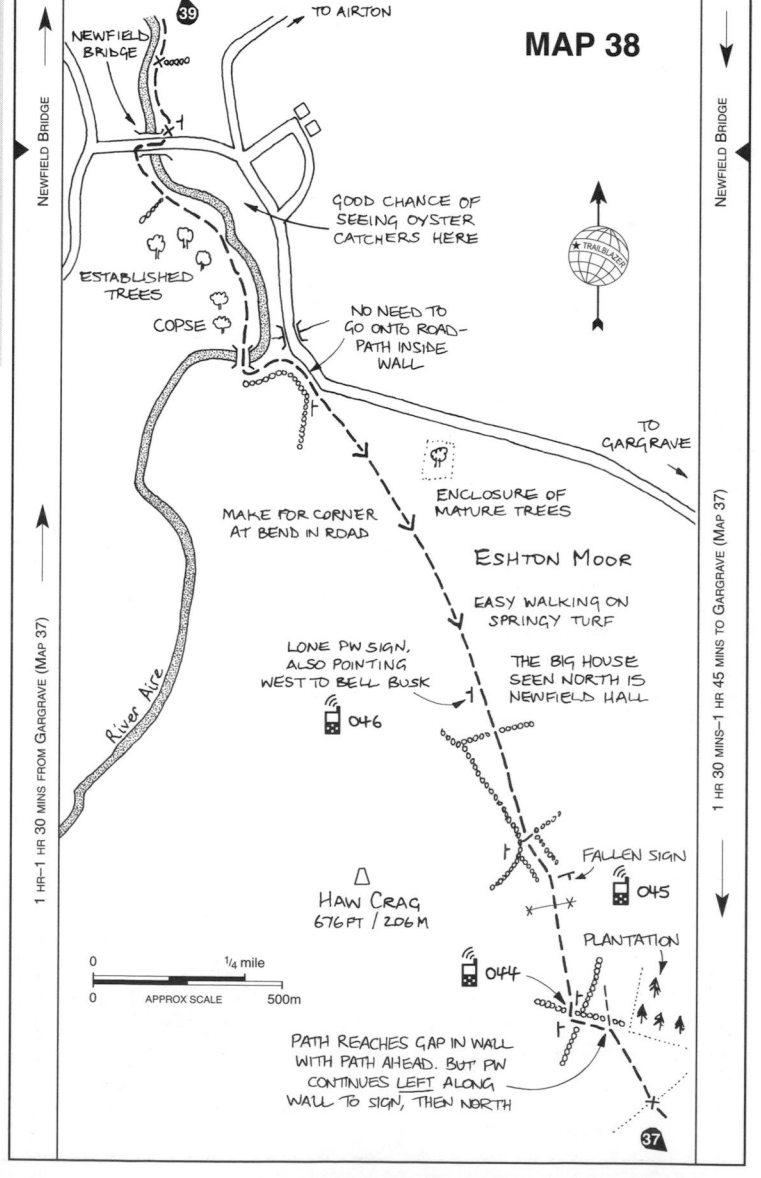

NEWFIELD BRIDGE

TO AIRTON

MAP 38

NEWFIELD BRIDGE

39

NEWFIELD BRIDGE

GOOD CHANCE OF SEEING OYSTER CATCHERS HERE

★ TRAILBLAZER

ESTABLISHED TREES

COPSE

NO NEED TO GO ONTO ROAD – PATH INSIDE WALL

TO GARGRAVE

ENCLOSURE OF MATURE TREES

MAKE FOR CORNER AT BEND IN ROAD

ESHTON MOOR

EASY WALKING ON SPRINGY TURF

1 HR–1 HR 30 MINS FROM GARGRAVE (MAP 37)

River Aire

LONE PW SIGN, ALSO POINTING WEST TO BELL BUSK

📱 046

THE BIG HOUSE SEEN NORTH IS NEWFIELD HALL

1 HR 30 MINS–1 HR 45 MINS TO GARGRAVE (MAP 37)

FALLEN SIGN

📱 045

△ HAW CRAG 676PT / 206M

PLANTATION

📱 044

0   ¼ mile

0   APPROX SCALE   500m

PATH REACHES GAP IN WALL WITH PATH AHEAD. BUT PW CONTINUES <u>LEFT</u> ALONG WALL TO SIGN, THEN NORTH

37

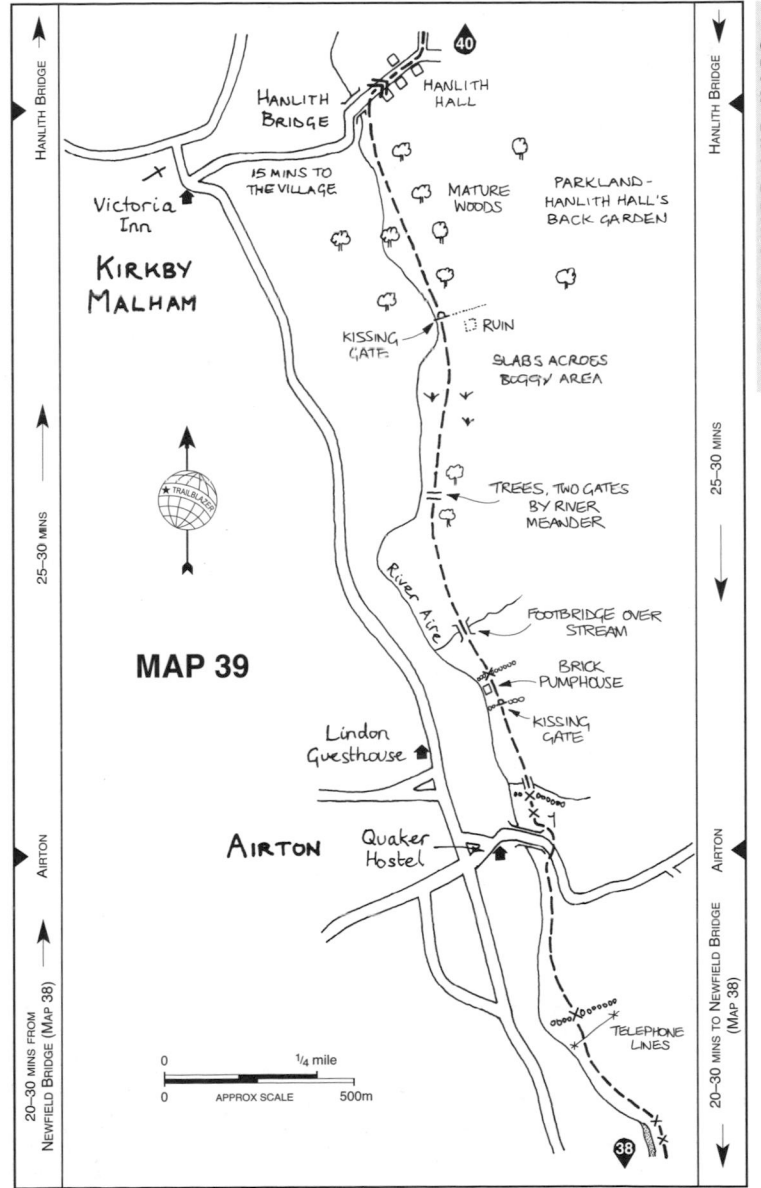

MAP 39

KIRKBY MALHAM [Map 39, p127]

Standing back from the river the village is another gem, carefully preserved by its inhabitants and unspoilt by anything as common as a shop. The church has a set of stocks into which anyone putting up a satellite dish would probably be clapped and pelted with rotting fruit.

But there is a pub, *The Victoria Inn* (☎ 01729-830499; 2T/2D), where the recently renovated rooms cost £60 (£35 for single occupancy). Food is served Fri-Sun 12-3pm & Tue-Sun 6-9pm. The pub closes in the afternoon but is open all day in the summer months.

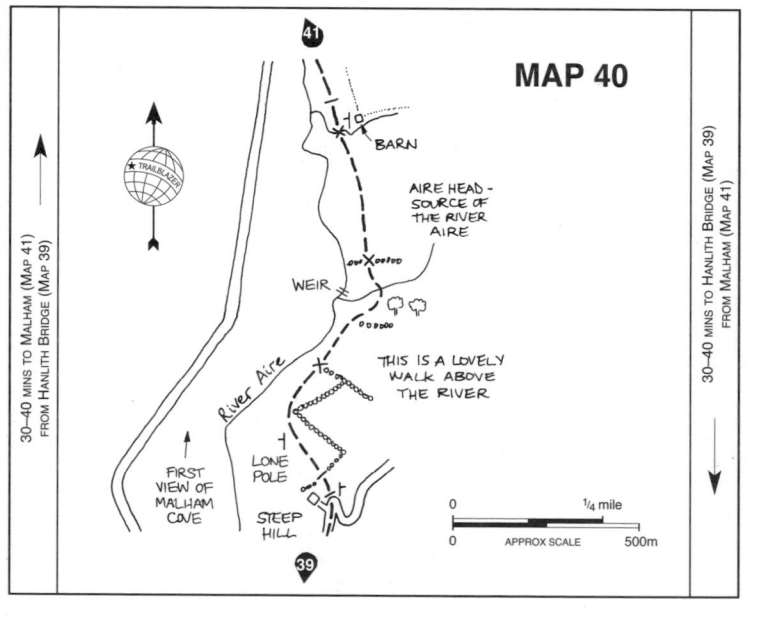

MAP 40

BARN

AIRE HEAD – SOURCE OF THE RIVER AIRE

WEIR

THIS IS A LOVELY WALK ABOVE THE RIVER

River Aire

FIRST VIEW OF MALHAM COVE

LONE POLE

STEEP HILL

★ TRAILBLAZER

30-40 MINS TO MALHAM (MAP 41)
FROM HANLITH BRIDGE (MAP 39)

30-40 MINS TO HANLITH BRIDGE (MAP 39)
FROM MALHAM (MAP 41)

0   ¼ mile
0   APPROX SCALE   500m

MALHAM [see Map 41a, p130]

You would be wise to plan your overnight stay here on a weekday or certainly a non-holiday period. For no greater reason than its dramatic limestone amphitheatre this little stone village with its pretty river is among the most touristy places between Haworth and the Roman wall, receiving as many annual visitors as Ayers Rock. On the positive side that means there's plenty of accommodation.

Services

The **Yorkshire Dales National Park Information Centre** (☎ 01969-652380,

www.malhamdale.com; Apr-Oct daily 10am-5pm, Nov-Mar Sat-Sun only 10am-4pm) is just to the south of the village and is worth a visit for its interactive displays about the geology and history of the area. The website is useful for the area in general, including yet more accommodation (what follows overleaf is a selection). For **shops** there's the Cove Centre (Mon-Sat 10am-4.30pm, Sun 11.30am-5.30pm), fork left at the small triangular green in the centre of the village, where you will get everything you need for your trip, including camping fuel and clotted cream fudge

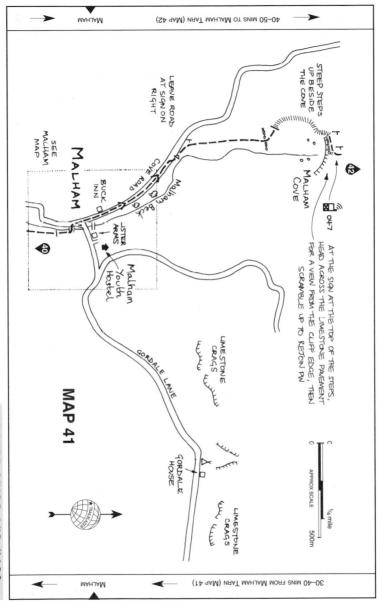

MAP 41

40-50 MINS TO MALHAM TARN (MAP 42)

MALHAM

STEEP STEPS UP BESIDE THE COVE

LEAVE ROAD AT SIGN ON RIGHT

SEE MALHAM MAP

MALHAM

Malham Cove Road

Malham Beck

BUCK INN

USTER ARMS

Malham Youth Hostel

Malham Cove

AT THE SIGN AT THE TOP OF THE STEPS, HEAD ACROSS THE LIMESTONE PAVEMENT FOR A VIEW FROM THE CLIFF EDGE, THEN SCRAMBLE UP TO REJOIN PW

042

42

40

GORDALE LANE

GORDALE HOUSE

LIMESTONE CRAGS

LIMESTONE CRAGS

TRAILBLAZER

APPROX SCALE

¼ mile

500m

30-40 MINS FROM MALHAM TARN (MAP 41)

MALHAM

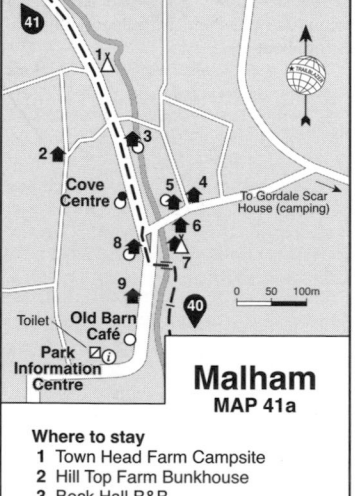

Malham
MAP 41a

Where to stay
1 Town Head Farm Campsite
2 Hill Top Farm Bunkhouse
3 Beck Hall B&B
4 Malham Youth Hostel
5 Lister Arms
6 Eastwood House
7 Miresfield Farm (B&B & camping)
8 The Buck Inn
9 River House Hotel

(don't get them mixed up!). There is also a small village shop on the Green.

See box p24 for details of various events held here in the summer.

Transport

Both Stagecoach and the Royal Mail post **bus** run from here to Airton, Gargrave and Skipton (see public transport map and table, pp42-6). For a 24-hour service call **Skipton Taxis** (☎ 01756-794994/701122).

Where to stay

After the lean pickings in the last few places in Malham your cup runneth over but then again, so do visitor numbers. If it's B&B accommodation you're after, note that during peak times some places will accept bookings only for a **two-day stay at weekends** and, as in some other places,

solo travellers need expect no favours on pricing. As far as room quantities and ambience goes, most of the 'B&Bs' in Malham can be classified in the 'small hotel' category. It's a busy place.

To **camp** in an awesome setting walk one mile east to *Gordale Scar House* (☎ 01729-830333), where they charge £2.50 per person, £2 per tent. There's a toilet and shower block; a shower costs 10p.

North of the village there's spacious year-round camping at *Town Head Farm* (☎ 01729-830287) where a pitch costs £3.50 per person, £1 per tent. There's also camping for £4.50 per person at *Miresfield Farm* (see below).

There's **bunkhouse** accommodation at *Hill Top Farm* (☎ 01729-830320, 🖳 www.malhamdale.com/bunkbarn.htm); there are 32 spaces in rooms for 2-11 people (the smaller rooms can be booked for private use), showers, a drying room and a fully equipped kitchen and it costs £10/pp.

Near the centre of the village is the very popular *Malham Youth Hostel* (☎ 01729-830321, bookings ☎ 0870-770 5946, 🖳 malham@yha.org.uk, open all year). The 82-bed purpose-built hostel opens at 5pm and an evening meal is served at 7pm, though as always there is also a self-catering kitchen. There's also a shop selling basic foods such as tinned goods, milk, eggs and bread. Adults pay £14, under 18s £10.

Miresfield Farm (☎ 01729-830414, 🖳 www.malhamdale.com/miresfield.htm; 5D /5T) charges £32 per person although the lonely singleton pays £40, or £45 at weekends. *Beck Hall* (☎ 01729-830332, 🖳 www.beckhallmalham.com; 5T/7D/4F) is in a nice setting across a footbridge by the river and charges from just £25-35 per person, even at weekends, if you book early enough. The rooms are all en suite with a shower except for one which has a private bathroom. In addition there is the centrally located *Eastwood House* (☎ 01729-830409, 🖳 eastwood_house@hotmail .com; 1D/2F en suite) costing £30/pp midweek and £35/pp at the weekend. They will pick people up from Horton-in-Ribblesdale if they have been unable to find accommodation there and will take them back the next morning.

If you're looking for more comfort try *The Buck Inn* (☎ 01729-830317, 💻 www .buckinnmalham.co.uk; 2T/6D/2F) on your left as you come into the village. The rooms are all en suite and cost £68-95 (single occupancy £45-55). Over the road the *Lister Arms* (☎ 01729-830330, 💻 www.lis terarms.co.uk; 5D/1T/3F en suite) charges £70 (£80 Fri-Sun minimum two nights, single occupancy £60-65) all with breakfast.

Doubles or twins at *River House Hotel* (☎ 01729-830315, 💻 www.riverhouseho tel.co.uk; 2T/4D/1F en suite) cost from £70 (single occupancy from £50).

Places to eat

Lister Arms (see above) feels like the better of the two pubs and has a great restaurant menu and is open daily 6-9pm. Main cours-es are around £9. They also have a bar menu (daily 12-2pm and 6-9pm) with dishes for about £6.

Pub grub is also served at *The Buck Inn* (see column opposite, daily 12-2pm and 7-9pm) and at *Beck Hall* (see p130; Tue-Sun 11.30am-5.30pm) where they sell salads, sandwiches, baked potatoes and they also do a cream tea. *River House Hotel* (see column opposite) has a restaurant, open Tue-Sat 6.30-8pm, which is also open to non-residents; booking in advance is recommended.

For something simpler try *The Cove Centre* (see p128) where you can get a bowl of soup, a packed lunch or a baked potato. There's also the *Old Barn Café* (closed Wed & Thur) near the Park Information Centre. An all-day breakfast costs £5, jacket potatoes are £4; they also serve cakes as well as afternoon teas. They're open daily until 5.30pm.

MALHAM TO HORTON-IN-RIBBLESDALE   MAPS 41-48

Route overview

Catching your breath from the airy rim of **Malham Cove** you know you're in for a sensational day's walk, a full **15 miles (24kms, 6-8hrs)** of striding that, on a fine day, lifts the Pennine Way up into the best of your expectations. Limestone country envelopes the walker, its springy turf and expansive views returning the investment made so far in weary legs and peat-stained socks.

Gone are the smog-blackened gritstone farmsteads of Calderdale and the Worth Valley. At last you're in proper walking country. Look around from any of the summits today and for the first time in days no pinnacle, radio mast or obelisk mars the horizon.

The hills, too, are distinctively majestic. The massive bulk of **Fountains Fell** (see box p138) and Pen-y-ghent are real mountains, challenges worthy of your effort and determination. Limestone, we salute you!

You don't get off quite scot-free. Towards the end of this stage, the ascent of **Pen-y-ghent** (Map 46), the 'hill of the winds', is the job in hand. A daunting climb with a series of steep rocky steps, it's easier than it looks. As is so often the case, it's the long downhill stretch to **Horton-in-Ribblesdale** (Map 48) that may well do you in.

Route-finding trouble spots

Even in poor weather and exacerbated by the elevations involved, it's hard to see anywhere the route might be lost. Pen-y-ghent up and down is as clear as a bell; the possible exception might be the ascent of Fountains Fell, so be alert.

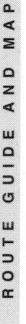

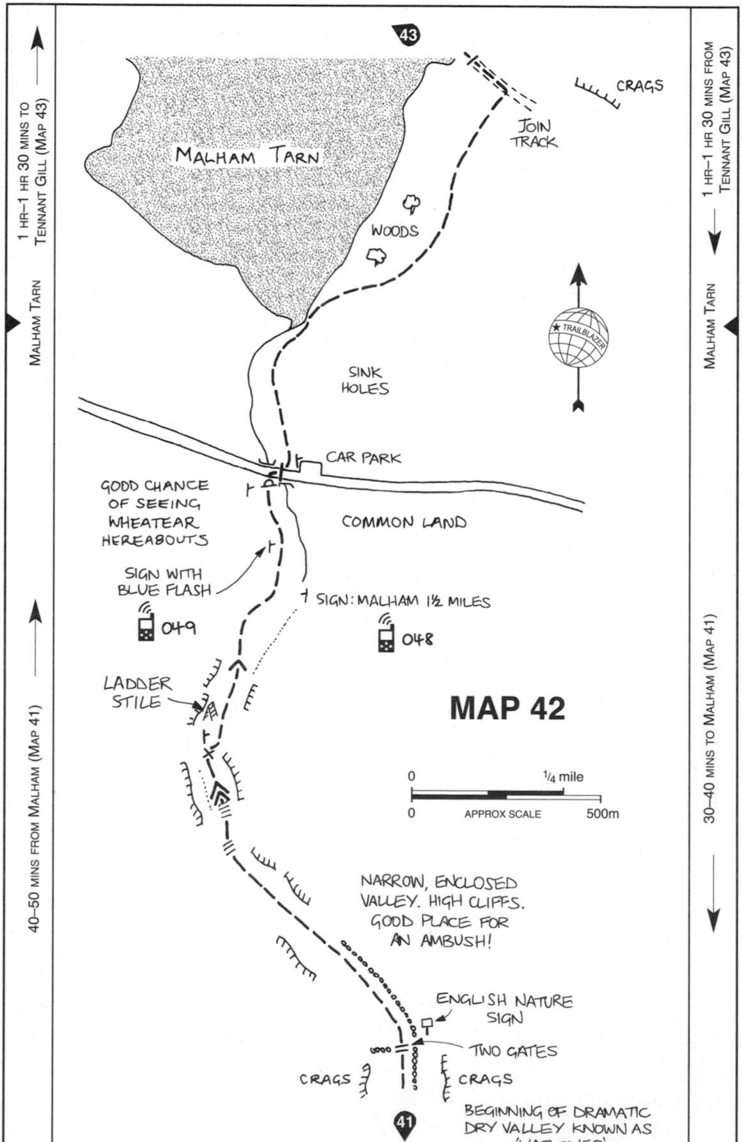

1 HR–1 HR 30 MINS TO
TENNANT GILL (MAP 43)

MALHAM TARN

1 HR–1 HR 30 MINS FROM
TENNANT GILL (MAP 43)

MALHAM TARN

40–50 MINS FROM MALHAM (MAP 41)

30–40 MINS TO MALHAM (MAP 41)

43

CRAGS

MALHAM TARN

JOIN
TRACK

WOODS

★ TRAILBLAZER

SINK
HOLES

CAR PARK

GOOD CHANCE
OF SEEING
WHEATEAR
HEREABOUTS

COMMON LAND

SIGN WITH
BLUE FLASH

049

SIGN: MALHAM 1½ MILES

048

LADDER
STILE

MAP 42

0   ¼ mile

0   500m
APPROX SCALE

NARROW, ENCLOSED
VALLEY. HIGH CLIFFS.
GOOD PLACE FOR
AN AMBUSH!

ENGLISH NATURE
SIGN

TWO GATES

CRAGS

CRAGS

41

BEGINNING OF DRAMATIC
DRY VALLEY KNOWN AS
'WATLOWES'

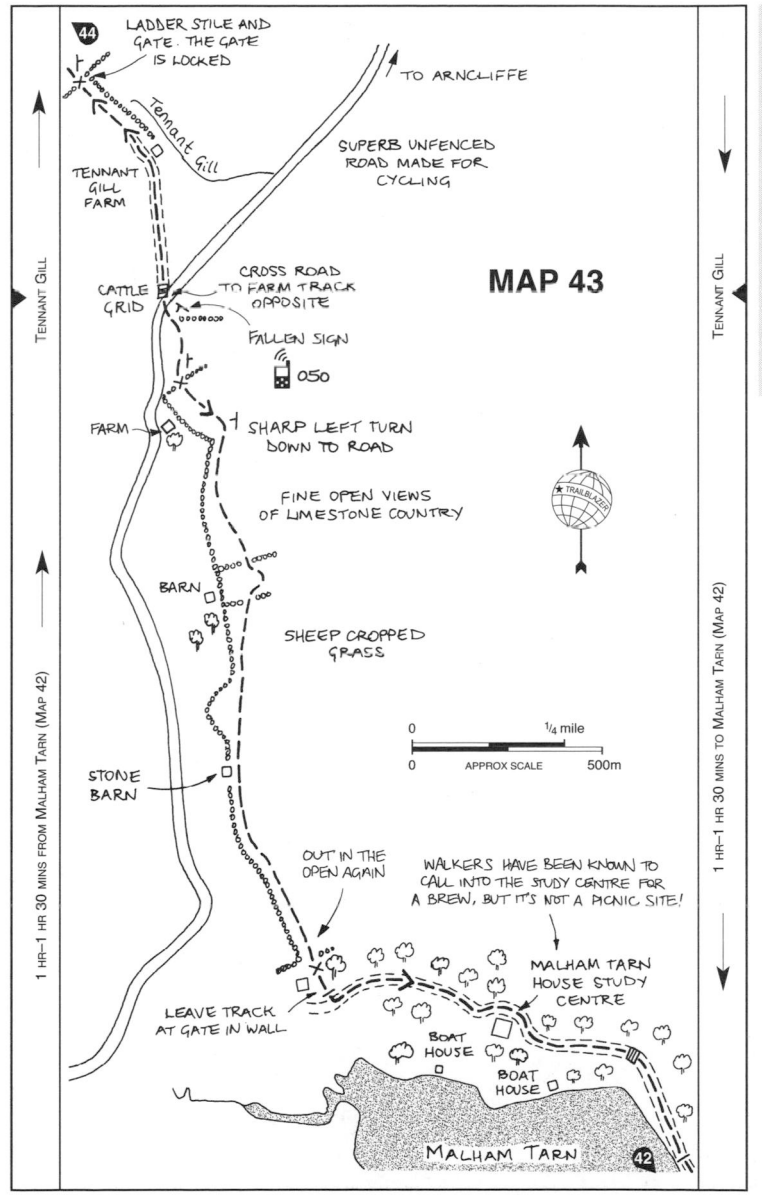

44 LADDER STILE AND GATE. THE GATE IS LOCKED

TO ARNCLIFFE

Tennant Gill

SUPERB UNFENCED ROAD MADE FOR CYCLING

TENNANT GILL FARM

TENNANT GILL

CATTLE GRID

CROSS ROAD TO FARM TRACK OPPOSITE

MAP 43

TENNANT GILL

FALLEN SIGN

050

FARM

SHARP LEFT TURN DOWN TO ROAD

FINE OPEN VIEWS OF LIMESTONE COUNTRY

TRAILBLAZER

BARN

SHEEP CROPPED GRASS

1 HR–1 HR 30 MINS FROM MALHAM TARN (MAP 42)

STONE BARN

0   1/4 mile

0   APPROX SCALE   500m

1 HR–1 HR 30 MINS TO MALHAM TARN (MAP 42)

OUT IN THE OPEN AGAIN

WALKERS HAVE BEEN KNOWN TO CALL INTO THE STUDY CENTRE FOR A BREW, BUT IT'S NOT A PICNIC SITE!

MALHAM TARN HOUSE STUDY CENTRE

LEAVE TRACK AT GATE IN WALL

BOAT HOUSE

BOAT HOUSE

MALHAM TARN

42

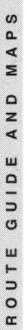

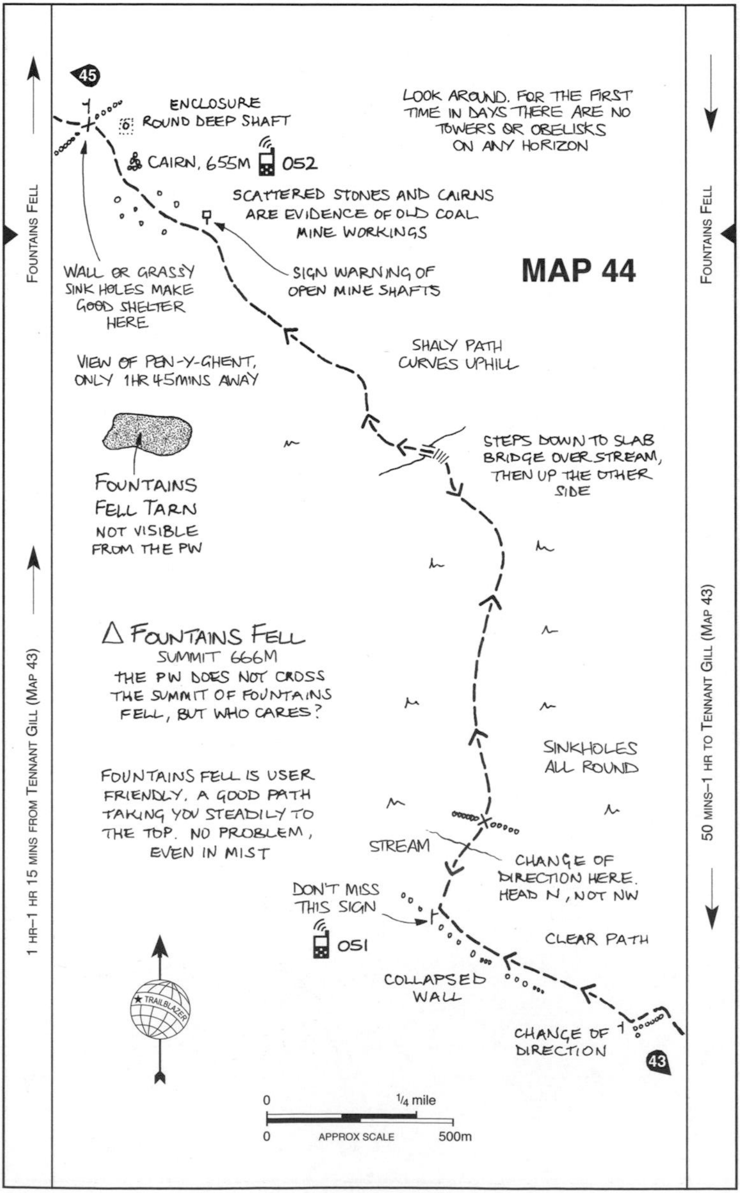

45

ENCLOSURE
ROUND DEEP SHAFT

LOOK AROUND. FOR THE FIRST
TIME IN DAYS THERE ARE NO
TOWERS OR OBELISKS
ON ANY HORIZON

CAIRN, 655M 052

SCATTERED STONES AND CAIRNS
ARE EVIDENCE OF OLD COAL
MINE WORKINGS

SIGN WARNING OF
OPEN MINE SHAFTS

MAP 44

WALL OR GRASSY
SINK HOLES MAKE
GOOD SHELTER
HERE

VIEW OF PEN-Y-GHENT,
ONLY 1HR 45MINS AWAY

SHALY PATH
CURVES UPHILL

FOUNTAINS
FELL TARN
NOT VISIBLE
FROM THE PW

STEPS DOWN TO SLAB
BRIDGE OVER STREAM,
THEN UP THE OTHER
SIDE

△ FOUNTAINS FELL
SUMMIT 666M
THE PW DOES NOT CROSS
THE SUMMIT OF FOUNTAINS
FELL, BUT WHO CARES?

FOUNTAINS FELL IS USER
FRIENDLY. A GOOD PATH
TAKING YOU STEADILY TO
THE TOP. NO PROBLEM,
EVEN IN MIST

SINKHOLES
ALL ROUND

STREAM

CHANGE OF
DIRECTION HERE.
HEAD N, NOT NW

DON'T MISS
THIS SIGN

051

CLEAR PATH

COLLAPSED
WALL

CHANGE OF
DIRECTION

43

TRAILBLAZER

0   ¼ mile

0   APPROX SCALE   500m

Fountains Fell

Fountains Fell

1 HR–1 HR 15 MINS FROM TENNANT GILL (MAP 43)

50 MINS–1 HR TO TENNANT GILL (MAP 43)

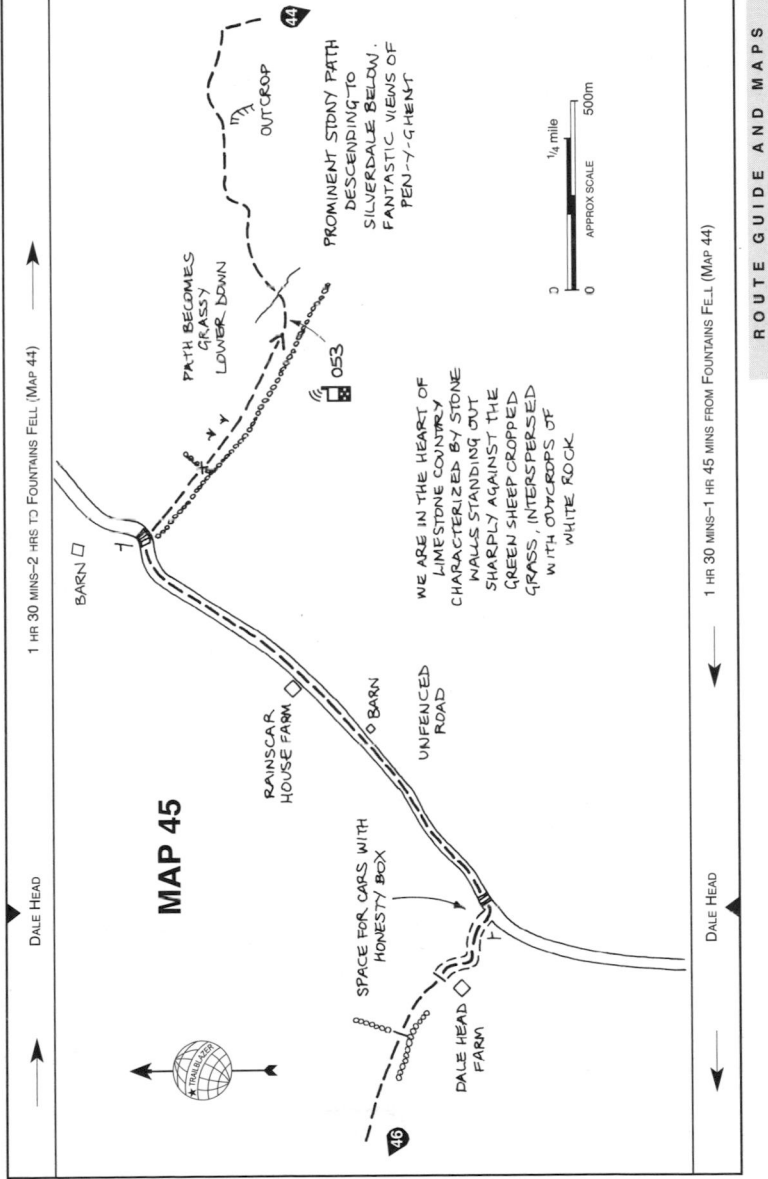

MAP 45

DALE HEAD

1 HR 30 MINS–2 HRS TO FOUNTAINS FELL (MAP 44)

1 HR 30 MINS–1 HR 45 MINS FROM FOUNTAINS FELL (MAP 44)

DALE HEAD

BARN

RAINSCAR HOUSE FARM

BARN

UNFENCED ROAD

SPACE FOR CARS WITH HONESTY BOX

DALE HEAD FARM

46

44

PATH BECOMES GRASSY LOWER DOWN

OUTCROP

053

PROMINENT STONY PATH DESCENDING TO SILVERDALE BELOW. FANTASTIC VIEWS OF PEN-Y-GHENT

WE ARE IN THE HEART OF LIMESTONE COUNTRY CHARACTERIZED BY STONE WALLS STANDING OUT SHARPLY AGAINST THE GREEN SHEEP CROPPED GRASS, INTERSPERSED WITH OUTCROPS OF WHITE ROCK

TRAILBLAZER

¼ mile
APPROX SCALE
0   500m

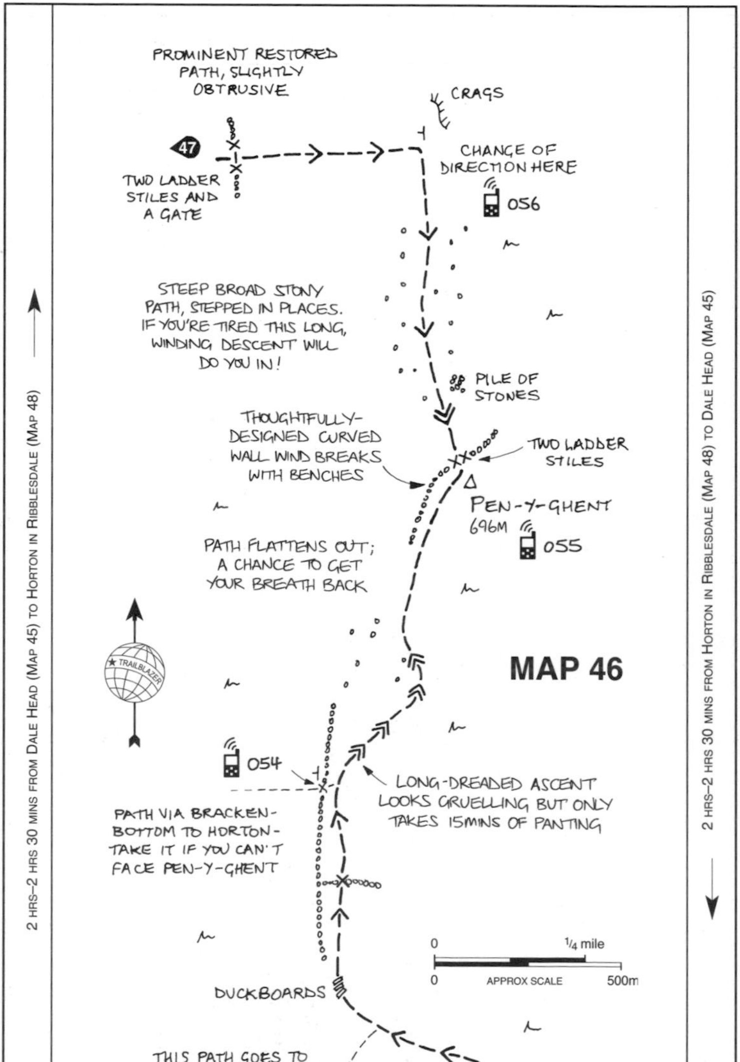

2 HRS–2 HRS 30 MINS FROM DALE HEAD (MAP 45) TO HORTON IN RIBBLESDALE (MAP 48)
2 HRS–2 HRS 30 MINS FROM HORTON IN RIBBLESDALE (MAP 48) TO DALE HEAD (MAP 45)
MAP 46
PROMINENT RESTORED PATH, SLIGHTLY OBTRUSIVE
CRAGS
47
TWO LADDER STILES AND A GATE
CHANGE OF DIRECTION HERE
056
STEEP BROAD STONY PATH, STEPPED IN PLACES. IF YOU'RE TIRED THIS LONG, WINDING DESCENT WILL DO YOU IN!
PILE OF STONES
THOUGHTFULLY-DESIGNED CURVED WALL WIND BREAKS WITH BENCHES
TWO LADDER STILES
PEN-Y-GHENT
696M
055
PATH FLATTENS OUT; A CHANCE TO GET YOUR BREATH BACK
TRAILBLAZER
054
LONG-DREADED ASCENT LOOKS GRUELLING BUT ONLY TAKES 15MINS OF PANTING
PATH VIA BRACKEN-BOTTOM TO HORTON - TAKE IT IF YOU CAN'T FACE PEN-Y-GHENT
0
1/4 mile
0
APPROX SCALE
500m
DUCKBOARDS
THIS PATH GOES TO HELWITH BRIDGE AND DUBCOTE FARM - SEE MAP 48
45

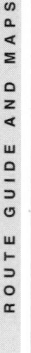

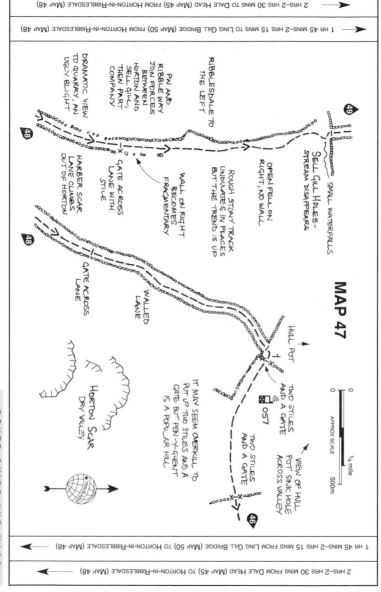

MAP 47

DRAMATIC VIEW
TO QUARRY, AN
UGLY BLIGHT

PW AND
RIBBLE WAY
JOIN FORCES
BETWEEN
HORTON AND
SELL GILL,
THEN PART
COMPANY

RIBBLESDALE TO
THE LEFT

SELL GILL HOLES –
SMALL WATERFALLS

STREAM DISAPPEARS

OPEN FELL ON
RIGHT, NO WALL

49

48

GATE ACROSS
LANE WITH
STILE

WALL ON RIGHT
BECOMES
FRAGMENTARY

ROUGH STONY TRACK
UNDULATES IN PLACES
BUT THE TREND IS UP

HARBER SCAR
LANE CLIMBS
OUT OF HORTON

48

GATE ACROSS
LANE

WALLED
LANE

HORTON SCAR
DRY VALLEY

HULL POT

TWO STILES
AND A GATE

IT MAY SEEM OVERKILL TO
PUT UP TWO STILES AND A
GATE BUT PEN-Y-GHENT
IS A POPULAR HILL

VIEW OF HULL
POT, SINK HOLE
ACROSS VALLEY

TWO STILES
AND A GATE

46

057

APPROX SCALE

0   ¼ mile
0   500m

❏ **Fountains Fell**   **[see Map 44, p134]**

Named after its original owners, the Cistercian monks of Fountains Abbey near Ripon, Fountains Fell possessed substantial coal deposits beneath its cap of millstone grit. It probably still does, but not in sufficient quantity to make extraction economically viable.

The most active period of coal extraction was the early 1800s when a road was constructed to the summit plateau where shafts were sunk. The remnants of this road now constitutes the generally agreeable gradient of the Pennine Way.

The output of coal was estimated at around 1000 tons a year which required some 10,000 packhorse loads to carry it away.

Very little now remains of the coal industry on Fountains Fell and the shafts have mostly been filled in. The ruins of the colliery building are in evidence but give no real idea of what was once a flourishing industry. We can spare a thought for the miners who had to work in this inhospitable place, spending the week in makeshift accommodation (known as 'shops') within yards of their labours and getting up in the small hours to trudge to work in all weathers.

HORTON-IN-RIBBLESDALE [Map 48]

There are no services along the route until you get to Horton, a famous landmark on the Pennine Way, as much for the presence of the Pen-y-ghent Café as for the charm of the village itself.

Services

There's a well-stocked **post office/shop** (daily 9am-6pm, to 1pm on Wed and 5.30pm Sun) while Pen-y-ghent café (☎ 01729-860333, in summer Mon and Wed-Fri 9am-5.30pm, Sat-Sun 8am-5.30pm, closed Tue; they open later in the winter months), over the road, doubles as the **tourist information centre** (and can provide current weather forecasts) and also sells camping gear, snacks, maps and books.

Transport

Horton is on the Leeds–Carlisle railway and **trains** are frequent, making it an ideal place to begin or end a walk along the Way.

The only **bus** service (to Ingleton via Settle) is operated by Kirkby Lonsdale Coach Hire (see public transport map and table, pp42-6).

For a **taxi** call Settle Taxis (☎ 01729-824824/822219).

Where to stay

In the centre of the village *Holme Farm Camping* (☎ 01729-860281) costs £2 per tent plus £2 per person and is conveniently situated next to the Golden Lion Hotel.

Braecrest B&B (☎ 01729-860389; 1D/1T/1F) is a basic B&B over the river on the west side of town which charges £23 per person (shared facilities).

Of the two pubs most walkers prefer *Crown Hotel* (☎ 01729-860209, 🖳 www.crown-hotel.co.uk; 2S/8D/3F), probably as it's right on the Way. They charge £24.40/pp or £29.50 for an en suite room.

The *Golden Lion Hotel* (☎ 01729-860206, 🖳 www.goldenlionhotel.co.uk; 2D/3T) down the road charges £40 for single occupancy (£60 Fri & Sat), otherwise it's £30/pp. They also have 55-beds in two **bunk rooms** at £12/pp as well as space outside to pitch **tents** if the campsite next door is full (you can use the pub's facilities).

If all these are full try *Eastwood House* (see p130) in Malham.

Where to eat

As old as the Pennine Way itself, the legendary *Pen-y-ghent Café* is the obvious port of call being a 'One Stop Shop' for the

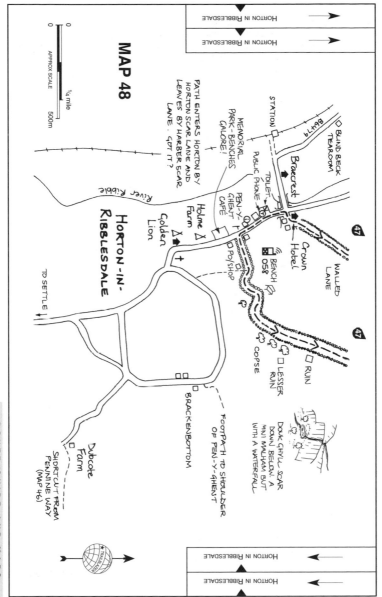

MAP 48

APPROX SCALE

0

¼ mile

0

500m

HORTON IN RIBBLESDALE →

HORTON IN RIBBLESDALE →

PATH ENTERS HORTON BY
HORTON SCAR LANE AND
LEAVES BY HARBER SCAR
LANE. GOT IT?

MEMORIAL
PARK - BENCHES
GALORE!

River Ribble

STATION

B6479

BLIND BECK
TEAROOM

Braecrest

PUBLIC PHONE

TOILET

PEN-Y-
GHENT
CAFÉ

Holme
Farm

Golden
Lion

HORTON-IN-
RIBBLESDALE

PO/SHOP

BENCH
OS8

Crown
Hotel

WALLED
LANE

47

47

COPSE

LESSER
RUIN

RUIN

DOUK GHYLL SCAR
DOWN BELOW. A
MINI MALHAM BUT
WITH A WATERFALL

TO SETTLE ←

FOOTPATH TO SHOULDER
OF PEN-Y-GHENT

BRACKENBOTTOM

Dubcote
Farm

SHORTCUT FROM
PENNINE WAY
(MAP 46)

HORTON IN RIBBLESDALE ←

HORTON IN RIBBLESDALE ←

TRAILBLAZER

❑ **Fell running**

Whilst puffing steadily up the Cam High Road, you may be ignominiously overtaken by a wiry person in brief shorts, the scantiest of vests and strange-looking lightly studded shoes. He or she is a fell runner, participant in a sport that is taken very seriously hereabouts.

The routes involve the muddiest tracks and the steepest hills, the sort of terrain that most people would dismiss as un-runnable. It goes to extremes too, and the **Three Peaks Challenge** is one of them. On this event people have to run 26 miles (42km) from Pen-y-ghent Café up three peaks – Pen-y-ghent, Whernside and Ingleborough – which you can see around you, and back in less than 12 hours. The fastest time is less than three hours. See also the box on p24.

walker with basic kit for sale as well as home-made cakes and filling meals. The Bayes family who run it are very helpful and friendly and provide a superb service for the walker. They are immensely knowledgeable about the area.

As well as operating a check-in/check-out service for day-walkers in the area, since the Pennine Way was opened they've been keeping a **Pennine Way book** for Wayfarers to sign as they pass. There are so many volumes there's now quite a library but it's a wonderful record of everyone who's passed along the Way. Be sure to sign it.

Food on offer here includes filling staples such as beans on toast, vegetable chowder soup with a roll, and chilli con

carne (£4.50). They also offer takeaway sandwiches – ham or strong cheese (£1.95).

The Crown Hotel (see p138) does pub grub daily 12-2pm and 6-8.30pm with a nice garden round the back, and *The Golden Lion* (see p138; bar food served daily 12-2pm & 6-9pm, Fri & Sat to 9.30pm) offers the same type of fare at similar prices; there's not much to choose between them.

Just outside the village at its northern end is the *Blindbeck Tea Room* (☎ 01729-860396) which serves home-made cakes and scones as well as hot and cold snacks. Blindbeck is open 10am-6pm Mon-Fri and usually 9am-6pm at the weekends; they close earlier in the winter months.

HORTON-IN-RIBBLESDALE TO HAWES   MAPS 48-55

Route overview

A **14-mile (23km, 5-6 hrs)** section, this stage involves a single long ascent up onto Dodd Fell to end with a relatively sudden drop down into Upper Wensleydale and the town of Hawes. For much of the way we follow wall-bound stony tracks, old packhorse trails (see box opposite) used for centuries as thoroughfares over the wild limestone moors. It has to be said that these ever-present walls mute the exhilaration of being out on the moors and the rough track will get to your feet (though it's not as tough as the descent from Cross Fell in a few days' time).

Climbing out of Horton by way of Harber Scar Lane from the doorstep of the Crown Hotel, the lane passes gurgling potholes and tops out on **Jackdaw Hill** (Map 49; 400m/1312ft). It then follows a prominent 'green road' past more pot holes and limestone outcrops to reach the delightful **Ling Gill** ravine where the beck has carved a deep gash, creating a unique reserve for trees, wildflowers and wildlife beyond the range of usual predators. So steep is it that even the signboard's invitation to considerately explore the interior of the reserve may not be enough to motivate you.

No matter. The trail crosses **Ling Gill Bridge** (Map 50) and more uphill 'packhorsing' follows, the path easily followed to the high crossroads known as **Cam End**, halfway between Horton and Hawes. The view of Three Peaks country with Ribblehead Viaduct clearly visible in the wide valley between Ingleborough and Whernside is an impressive sight. Make the most of it for you must turn your back and follow the broad track of Cam High Road as it contours the hillside above dense forestry to reach **Kidhow Gate** (Map 53). Here farmers have been gathering their sheep for driving to market for as long as flocks have been grazed on the springy turf of these wide open moors.

Another 'green road', West Cam Road, leads along the shoulder of **Dodd Fell** high above the mysterious valley of Snaizeholme, a long level trudge enclosed by walls and fences that seem reluctant to end. But briefly end they do and you flit freely across the fells around and down **Rottenstone Hill** (Map 54) where **Hawes** (Map 55) beckons from far below. A smaller version of Haworth but without the 'Wutherobilia', Hawes is a welcoming village with all the services a walker could possibly need for rest and recuperation.

Route-finding trouble spots

For most of this stage even a lame packhorse with a coal sack over its head would have no problems. For you, apart from the all-hay diet, the experience should be similar. Apart from the perimeter of Hawes itself, the sole drama might be coming off Rottenstone Hill in thick mist where the grassy path thins out until cairns lead to a stream crossing by a wall (GPS Waypoint 067, see p260).

❏ **Packhorse roads**

The trackways that criss-cross the mid-Pennines are the remains of a once-thriving traffic in goods transported on the backs of packhorses.

These hardy animals were tough, stocky breeds known variously as jaggers after the German Jaeger ponies from which their stock came, or galloways after the Scottish breed particularly suited to carrying loads over rough country.

Wool, coal, hides, iron, lead, stone, charcoal and peat were carried down to the towns, the tracks used taking the shortest way across unenclosed country, often to avoid local taxes. Over the years the way would become heavily worn and sunken and we find names such as Hollow Way (Holloway) on maps where the traffic has cut a deep groove. Stones would be used to fill up holes and reinforce the road.

Most of the upland roads were abandoned when **turnpike** tollways were adopted for wheeled traffic and it was only farmers who continued to use the old tracks to get up onto the high fells. Now walkers use them more than farmers. With the advent of all-terrain quad bikes there was no need to follow the tracks; farmers simply ride straight across a field to the nearest gate.

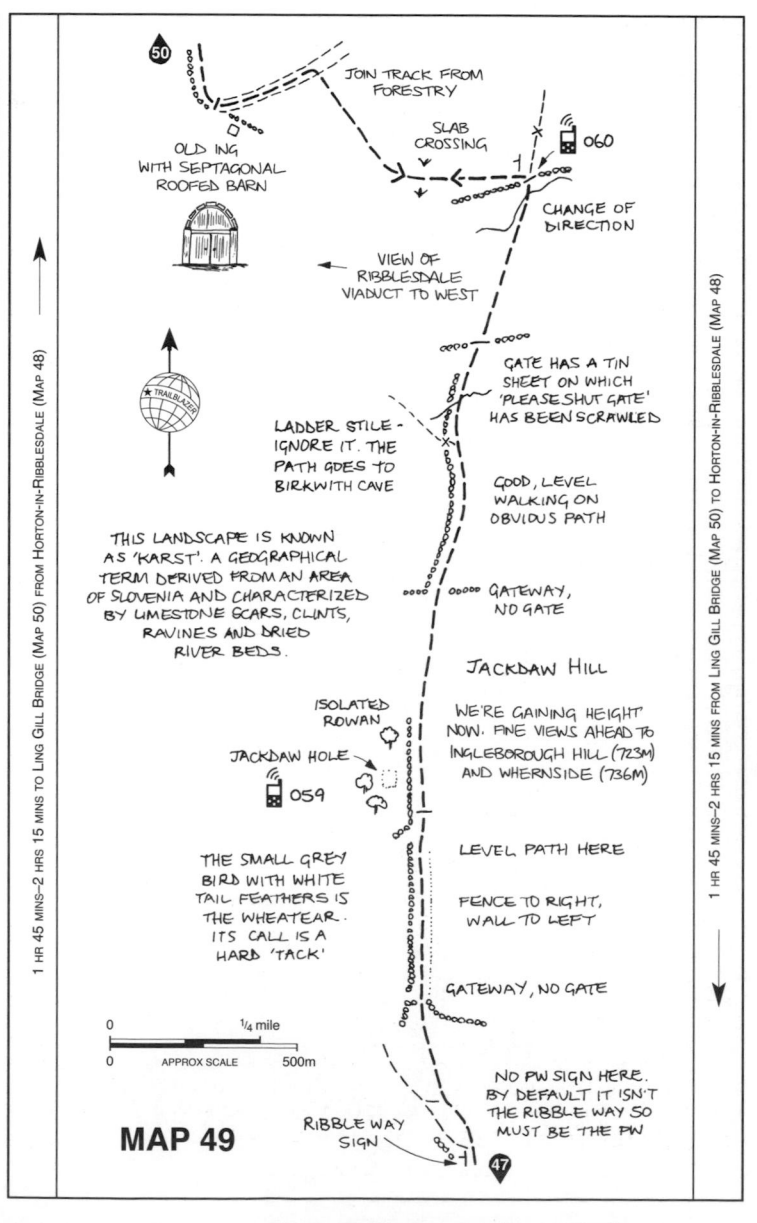

1 HR 45 MINS–2 HRS 15 MINS TO LING GILL BRIDGE (MAP 50) FROM HORTON-IN-RIBBLESDALE (MAP 48)

1 HR 45 MINS–2 HRS 15 MINS FROM LING GILL BRIDGE (MAP 50) TO HORTON-IN-RIBBLESDALE (MAP 48)

JOIN TRACK FROM FORESTRY

SLAB CROSSING

060

CHANGE OF DIRECTION

OLD ING WITH SEPTAGONAL ROOFED BARN

VIEW OF RIBBLESDALE VIADUCT TO WEST

TRAILBLAZER

GATE HAS A TIN SHEET ON WHICH 'PLEASE SHUT GATE' HAS BEEN SCRAWLED

LADDER STILE - IGNORE IT. THE PATH GOES TO BIRKWITH CAVE

GOOD, LEVEL WALKING ON OBVIOUS PATH

THIS LANDSCAPE IS KNOWN AS 'KARST'. A GEOGRAPHICAL TERM DERIVED FROM AN AREA OF SLOVENIA AND CHARACTERIZED BY LIMESTONE SCARS, CLINTS, RAVINES AND DRIED RIVER BEDS.

GATEWAY, NO GATE

JACKDAW HILL

ISOLATED ROWAN

JACKDAW HOLE

059

WE'RE GAINING HEIGHT NOW. FINE VIEWS AHEAD TO INGLEBOROUGH HILL (723M) AND WHERNSIDE (736M)

LEVEL PATH HERE

THE SMALL GREY BIRD WITH WHITE TAIL FEATHERS IS THE WHEATEAR. ITS CALL IS A HARD 'TACK'

FENCE TO RIGHT, WALL TO LEFT

GATEWAY, NO GATE

0   ¼ mile

0   APPROX SCALE   500m

NO PW SIGN HERE. BY DEFAULT IT ISN'T THE RIBBLE WAY SO MUST BE THE PW

MAP 49

RIBBLE WAY SIGN

47

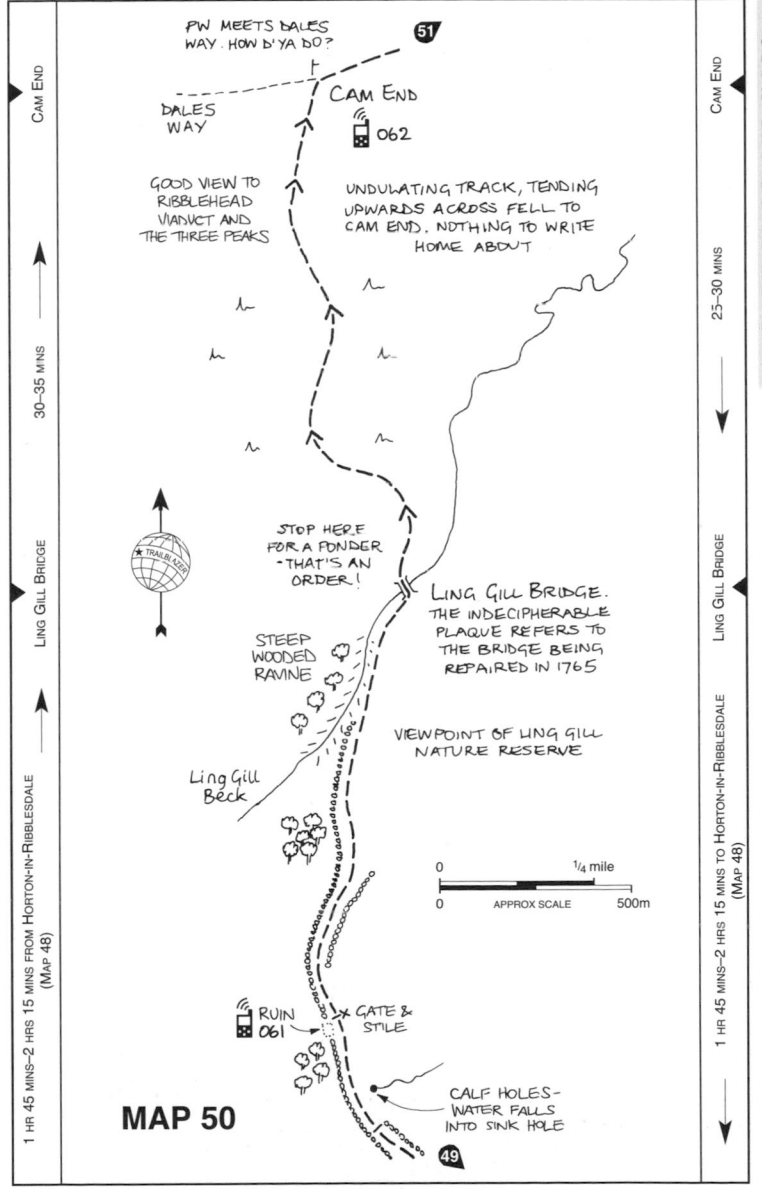

PW MEETS DALES WAY. HOW D'YA DO?

51

CAM END

📱 062

DALES WAY

UNDULATING TRACK, TENDING UPWARDS ACROSS FELL TO CAM END. NOTHING TO WRITE HOME ABOUT

GOOD VIEW TO RIBBLEHEAD VIADUCT AND THE THREE PEAKS

STOP HERE FOR A PONDER - THAT'S AN ORDER!

★ TRAILBLAZER

LING GILL BRIDGE. THE INDECIPHERABLE PLAQUE REFERS TO THE BRIDGE BEING REPAIRED IN 1765

STEEP WOODED RAVINE

VIEWPOINT OF LING GILL NATURE RESERVE

Ling Gill Beck

0		¼ mile
0	APPROX SCALE	500m

📱 RUIN 061 ✕ GATE & STILE

CALF HOLES - WATER FALLS INTO SINK HOLE

MAP 50

49

CAM END

CAM END

25-30 MINS

LING GILL BRIDGE

LING GILL BRIDGE

1 HR 45 MINS-2 HRS 15 MINS TO HORTON-IN-RIBBLESDALE (MAP 48)

30-35 MINS

LING GILL BRIDGE

LING GILL BRIDGE

1 HR 45 MINS-2 HRS 15 MINS FROM HORTON-IN-RIBBLESDALE (MAP 48)

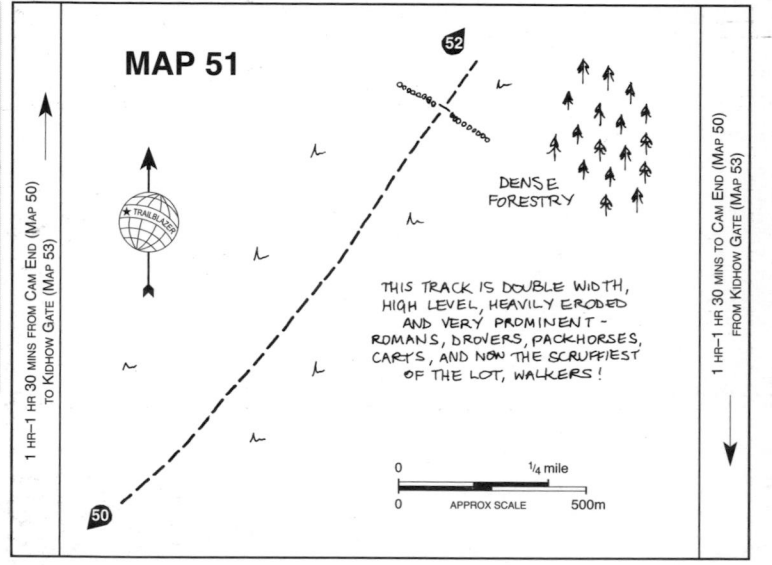

MAP 51

1 HR–1 HR 30 MINS FROM CAM END (MAP 50) to KIDHOW GATE (MAP 53)

52

★ TRAILBLAZER

DENSE
FORESTRY

THIS TRACK IS DOUBLE WIDTH,
HIGH LEVEL, HEAVILY ERODED
AND VERY PROMINENT –
ROMANS, DROVERS, PACKHORSES,
CARTS, AND NOW THE SCRUFFIEST
OF THE LOT, WALKERS!

1 HR–1 HR 30 MINS TO CAM END (MAP 50) FROM KIDHOW GATE (MAP 53)

0   ¼ mile

0   APPROX SCALE   500m

50

(Opposite) Top: The dramatic valley of Watlowes (see p132), looking south. (Photo ©
Keith Carter). Bottom: Pen-y-ghent, one of the peaks in the twenty-six-mile Three Peaks
Challenge (see p140) which starts from the Pen-y-ghent Café in Horton-in-Ribblesdale and
also includes the summits of Whernside and Ingleborough. (Photo © Chris Scott).

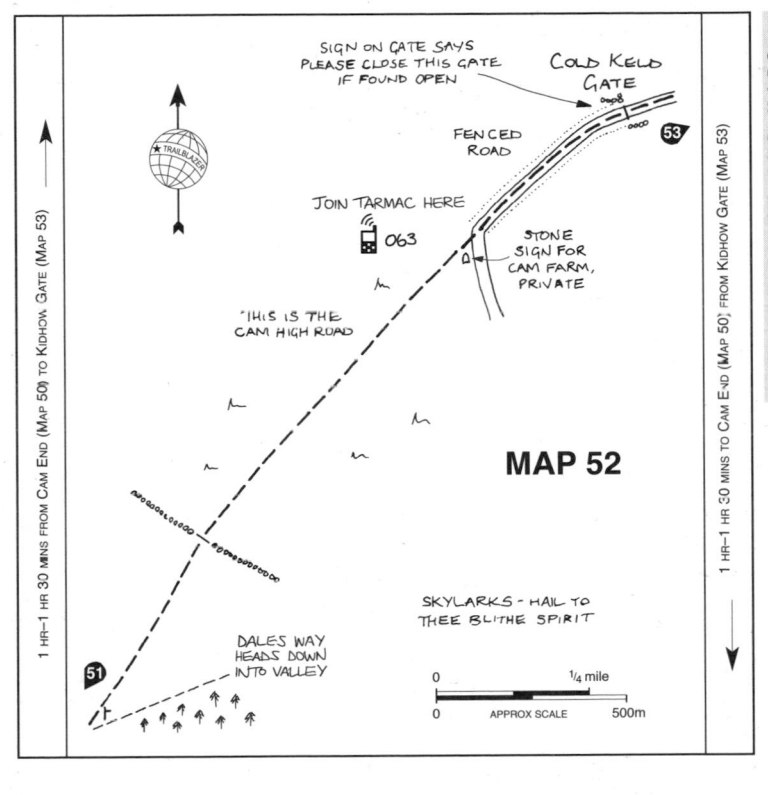

SIGN ON GATE SAYS
PLEASE CLOSE THIS GATE
IF FOUND OPEN

COLD KELD
GATE

FENCED
ROAD

53

JOIN TARMAC HERE

063

STONE
SIGN FOR
CAM FARM,
PRIVATE

'THIS IS THE
CAM HIGH ROAD'

MAP 52

SKYLARKS - HAIL TO
THEE BLITHE SPIRIT

DALES WAY
HEADS DOWN
INTO VALLEY

51

★ TRAILBLAZER

1 HR–1 HR 30 MINS FROM CAM END (MAP 50) TO KIDHOW GATE (MAP 53)

1 HR–1 HR 30 MINS TO CAM END (MAP 50) FROM KIDHOW GATE (MAP 53)

0   ¼ mile

0   APPROX SCALE   500m

(Opposite) Top: The peaceful village of Garrigill (see p200). **Bottom**: Great Dunn Fell. The white geodesic forms of the radar tracking station are a useful landmark. (Photos © Chris Scott).

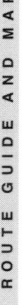

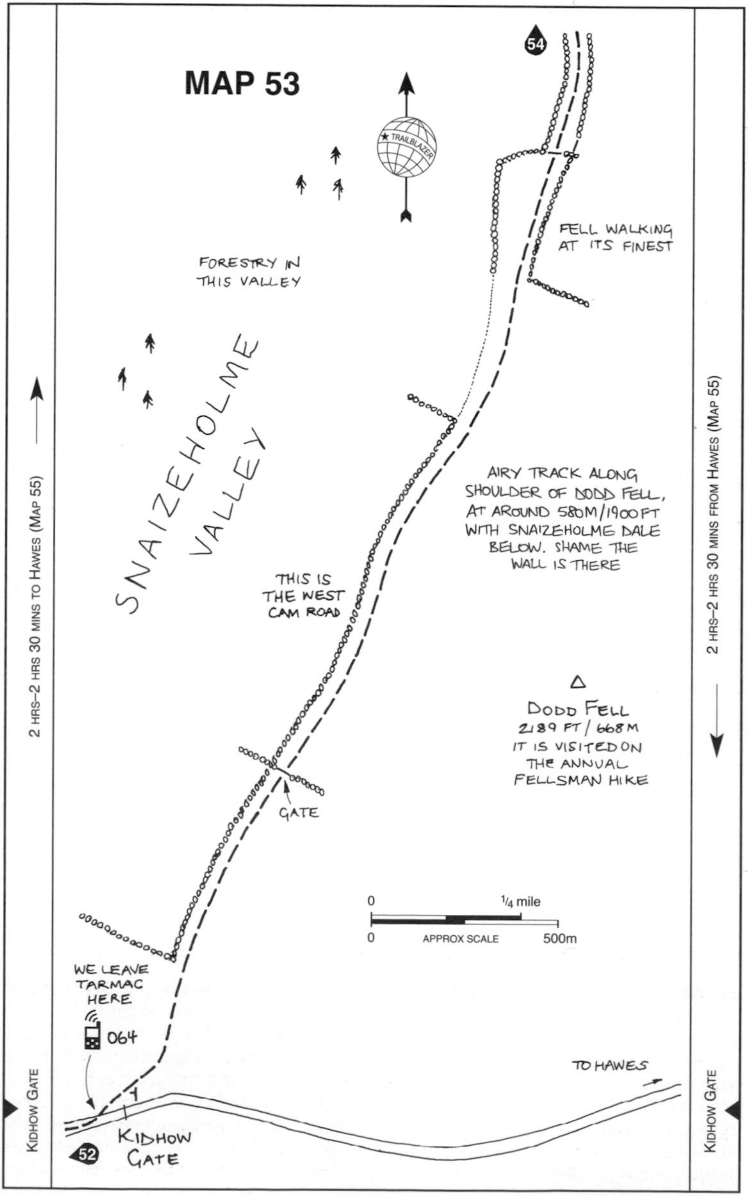

MAP 53

★ TRAILBLAZER

FELL WALKING
AT ITS FINEST

FORESTRY IN
THIS VALLEY

SNAIZEHOLME VALLEY

AIRY TRACK ALONG
SHOULDER OF DODD FELL,
AT AROUND 580M/1900 FT
WITH SNAIZEHOLME DALE
BELOW. SHAME THE
WALL IS THERE

THIS IS
THE WEST
CAM ROAD

△
DODD FELL
2189 FT / 668 M
IT IS VISITED ON
THE ANNUAL
FELLSMAN HIKE

GATE

0   ¼ mile
0   APPROX SCALE   500m

WE LEAVE
TARMAC
HERE
064

TO HAWES

2 HRS–2 HRS 30 MINS TO HAWES (MAP 55)

2 HRS–2 HRS 30 MINS FROM HAWES (MAP 55)

KIDHOW GATE

KIDHOW GATE

KIDHOW
GATE

54

52

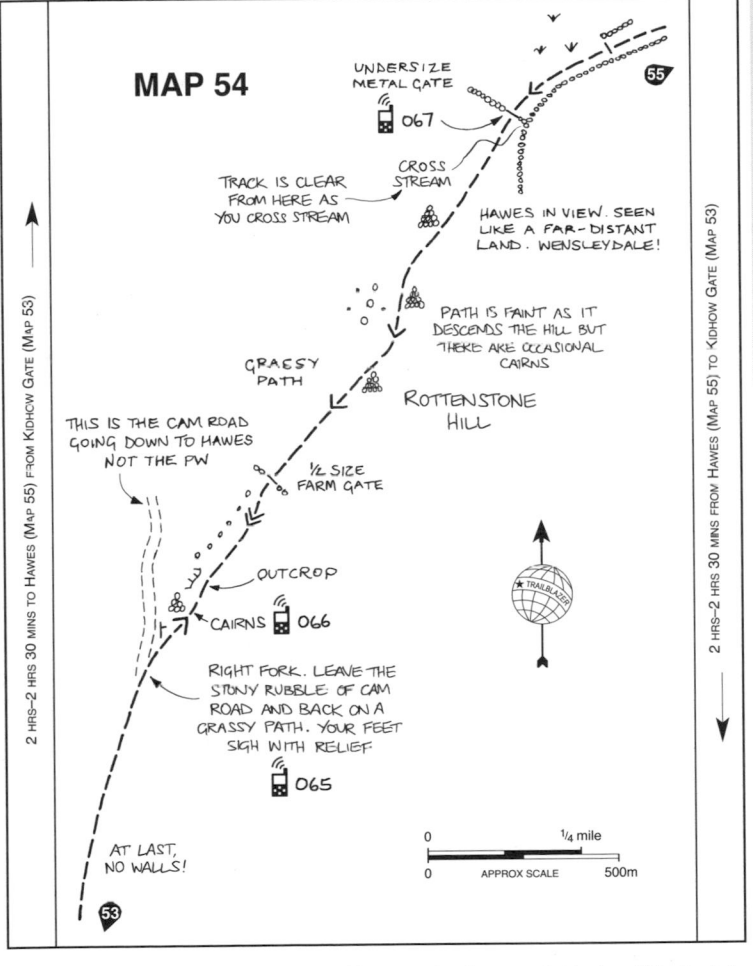

MAP 54

UNDERSIZE METAL GATE

067

CROSS STREAM

TRACK IS CLEAR FROM HERE AS YOU CROSS STREAM

HAWES IN VIEW. SEEN LIKE A FAR-DISTANT LAND. WENSLEYDALE!

PATH IS FAINT AS IT DESCENDS THE HILL BUT THERE ARE OCCASIONAL CAIRNS

GRASSY PATH

ROTTENSTONE HILL

THIS IS THE CAM ROAD GOING DOWN TO HAWES NOT THE PW

½ SIZE FARM GATE

OUTCROP

CAIRNS 066

RIGHT FORK. LEAVE THE STONY RUBBLE OF CAM ROAD AND BACK ON A GRASSY PATH. YOUR FEET SIGH WITH RELIEF.

065

AT LAST, NO WALLS!

55

53

2 HRS–2 HRS 30 MINS TO HAWES (MAP 55) FROM KIDHOW GATE (MAP 53)

2 HRS–2 HRS 30 MINS FROM HAWES (MAP 55) TO KIDHOW GATE (MAP 53)

★ TRAILBLAZER

| 0 | | ¼ mile |
| 0 | APPROX SCALE | 500m |

HAWES   [Map 55a, p149]

There's nothing pretentious about Hawes. It's a down-to-earth Yorkshire town with a vibrant centre full of pubs and cafés. If you're in need of a break this could be the place to relax for a day or so. There's plenty to see: a good local museum, a traditional ropemaker – and this is the home of the world-famous Wensleydale cheese.

At the award-winning **Wensleydale Creamery** (☎ 01969-667664, 🖳 www .wensleydale.co.uk; open Mon-Sat 9.30am-5pm, Sun 10am-4.30pm) the 900-year-old art of local cheese-making was nearly lost, only to be saved by the international popularity of Wensleydale-cheese-munching characters Wallace & Gromit. Blending Wensleydale with cranberries soon became

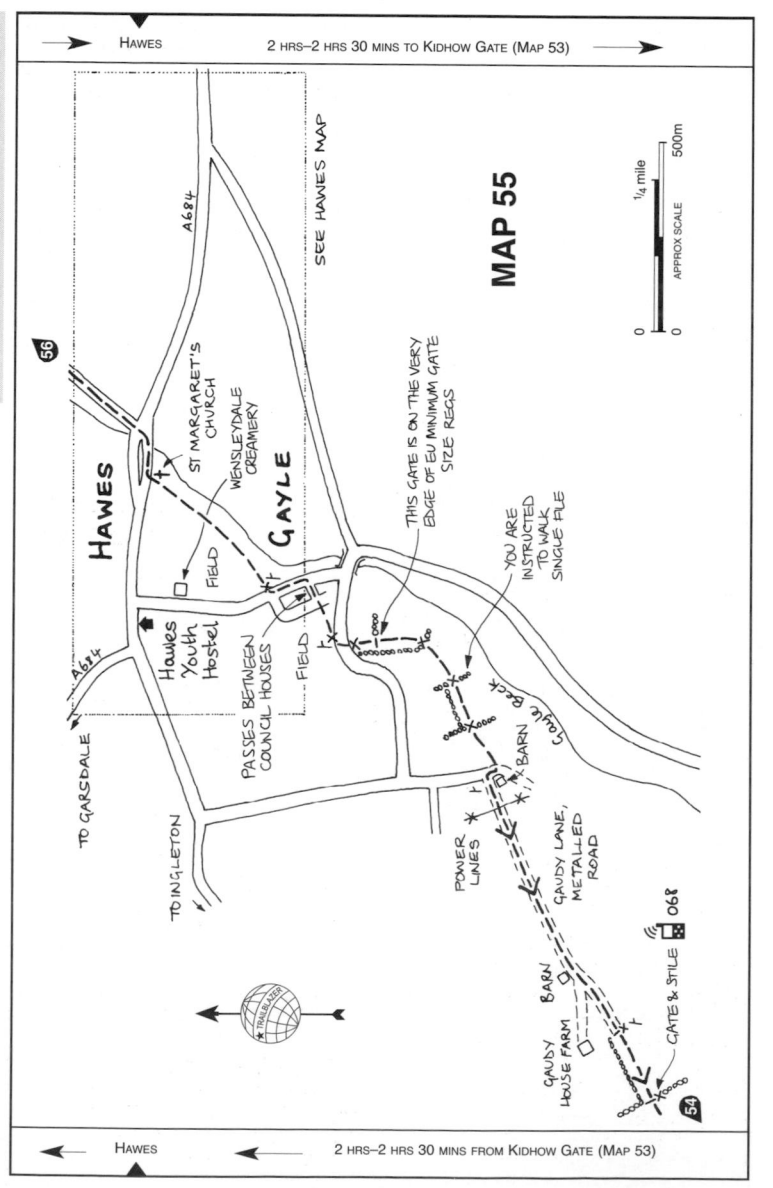

HAWES → 2 HRS–2 HRS 30 MINS TO KIDHOW GATE (MAP 53) →

SEE HAWES MAP

MAP 55

¼ mile

500m

APPROX SCALE

56

A684

HAWES

ST MARGARET'S CHURCH

WENSLEYDALE CREAMERY

GAYLE

THIS GATE IS ON THE VERY EDGE OF EU MINIMUM GATE SIZE REGS

YOU ARE INSTRUCTED TO WALK SINGLE FILE

FIELD

Hawes Youth Hostel

A684

TO GARSDALE

PASSES BETWEEN COUNCIL HOUSES

FIELD

GAYLE BECK

TO INGLETON

BARN

POWER LINES

GAUDY LANE, METALLED ROAD

TRAILBLAZER

GAUDY BARN

GAUDY HOUSE FARM

GATE & STILE

068

54

← HAWES ← 2 HRS–2 HRS 30 MINS FROM KIDHOW GATE (MAP 53)

a best-seller, with Carrot and Orange a kids' favourite and the recent Cheddar with Cherrybell Peppers and Sundried Tomatoes set to become a hit with gourmand *fromageurs*. Phone in advance if you want to go on the Cheese Experience Tour as cheese is not made every day.

The informative **Dales Countryside Museum** (£3) is open daily 10am-5pm (last entry to the museum is at 4pm). Nearby the **Hawes Ropemaker** is not something you'll find in every town.

See box p24 for details of events held here in the summer.

Transport
The best way to **Garsdale station** for the Carlisle–Leeds line is by taxi. Hawes is on

a number of **bus** routes (see public transport map and table, pp42-6), though none is particularly frequent. For a **taxi** try Cliff Ellis (☎ 01969-667598).

Services
The **National Park Centre** and **Tourist Information Centre** (☎ 01969-666210, ✉ hawes@yorkshiredales.org.uk) are in the Dales Countryside Museum. A useful **website** for information on the town is ✉ www.wensleydale.org/hawes.

There's a **Spar supermarket** (Mon-Fri 8am-7pm, Sat 8am-7.30pm, Sun 10am-5pm) while **Elijah Allen & Sons** is a wonderful old grocery store that shows how it used to be done and has been run by the same family since 1870.

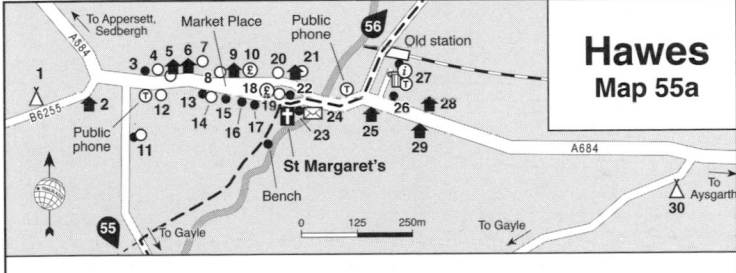

Hawes
Map 55a

Where to stay
1 Honeycott Caravan Park
2 Hawes Youth Hostel
5 Cockett's Hotel
6 The Board Hotel
9 The Bull's Head Hotel
21 Laburnum House
25 Spring Bank House
28 Ebor House
29 Fair View House
30 Bainbridge Ings Camping

Where to eat
4 Paul's Pizzas
5 Cockett's Hotel
7 Prachin
8 Bay Tree Café & Bistro
11 Wensleydale Creamery
12 The Chippie
14 Wensleydale Pantry

Where to eat (cont'd)
19 The White Hart
20 Wilson's
21 Laburnum House Tearoom

Other
3 Littlefair Ironmongery
10 Barclays
11 Wensleydale Creamery
13 Spar
15 Stewart R Cunningham
16 Elijah Allen & Sons
17 Chemist and Wine Merchant
18 HSBC
22 Launderette
23 Three Peaks (Gear Shop)
24 Post Office
26 Hawes Ropemaker
27 Dales Countryside Museum,
   National Park Centre & Tourist Info

For **outdoor gear** there's Three Peaks, which has a selection of boots if yours have had it, or try Stewart R Cunningham (daily 9.30am-5pm). The **ironmonger** Littlefair has some camping fuels.

There's a **launderette** (Mon-Sat 9.30am-4pm, closed Wed), a **post office** (early closing Wed) and both **banks** have cash machines. There's also a **chemist**, which doubles as a **wine merchant** so you can buy both the cause and the cure in one shop!

Where to stay

You can **camp** either side of the village. If you're feeling energetic head for *Bainbridge Ings Caravan and Camping Site* (☎ 01969-667354, 💻 www.bainbridge-ings.co.uk; late Mar/Apr-Oct), three-quarters of a mile east of the Market Place, where you can pitch your tent in beautiful countryside for £3.50 per person. They sell milk and eggs. A bit nearer (on the B6255 to the west) but maybe too caravan-oriented is *Honeycott Caravan Park* (☎ 01969-667310, 💻 www .honeycott.co.uk; Mar-Oct) which also charges £3.50 per person.

It may have a comparatively bland exterior but inside *Hawes Youth Hostel* (☎ 01969-667368, bookings ☎ 0870-770 5854, 💻 hawes@yha.org.uk, open daily Mar-Oct) has all the trimmings including 52 beds for £14 (under 18s £10). It opens at 5pm and dinner is at 7pm sharp. There is also a self-catering kitchen and the hostel has a licence.

There's a clutch of **B&Bs** at the east of town which include *Ebor House* (☎ 01969-667337, 💻 www.eborhouse.co.uk; 2S/1F/ 1T/3D) which charges £55 or £70 for en suites. The single rooms cost £30 and have a private shower room; they also offer packed lunches (£4.50).

Laburnum House (☎ 01969-667717, 💻 www.stayatlaburnumhouse.co.uk, The Holme; 1T/2D/1F) has all en suite rooms costing £52 and is just off Market Place. *Spring Bank House* (☎ 01969-667376, Townfoot; 2D/1T) has en suite rooms for £55 and they can do a packed lunch to help zip you over Great Shunner Fell.

Fair View House (☎ 01969-667348, 💻 www.fairview-hawes.co.uk; 1S/2D/1F) is another imposing Victorian property where two sharing pay £60 and there's a (non en-suite) single for £30.

Probably the best **hotel** is *Cockett's* (☎ 01969-667312, 💻 www.cocketts.co.uk; 2T/3D/1F, all en suite), which charges £64-80 for twins/doubles and a bit more for one of their four-poster rooms; the brow-beaten single occupant pays £50. They can do a packed lunch.

Two people sharing a room at *The Board Hotel* (☎ 01969-667223, 💻 www .theboardhotel.co.uk; 3D) pay £60 (single occupancy in summer costs £40) while at *The Bull's Head Hotel* (☎ 01969-667437, 💻 www.bullsheadhotel.com; 4D/2T/1F en suite) they will pay from £55.

Where to eat

The Buttery Restaurant at Wensleydale Creamery (see p147) is a fully licensed restaurant where few could resist a free cheese sample for a starter.

Back in town, *Bay Tree Café & Bistro* offers quiches and hot or cold filled baguettes with tasty fillings while the best dinner in town is waiting for you at *Cockett's* where two courses (£16.95) could include a smoked bacon, avocado and blue Wensleydale salad finished with a chive vinaigrette dressing followed by a baked fillet of plaice stuffed with spinach and mushrooms finished with a spring onion and white wine sauce. Well worth the slog from Horton, if not Edale itself! The restaurant is open daily (except Tuesday) 7-8.30pm.

Less fancy is *The White Hart*, a welcoming locals' pub, which stays open all day and from 12 noon to 2pm and 7-8.30pm will cook up a square meal for around £8.

If you're due for a curry *Prachin* (☎ 01969-6673142, Tue-Sun 6-11pm) over the road imports succulent Indian and Bangladeshi morsels daily from Bradford.

For daytime snacks *Wilson's* (daily 10.30am-5pm) greets you as you stumble past the church off the Pennine Way with a 'full-carb' giant Yorkshire pudding with chips and gravy (£4). *Wensleydale Pantry*

(☎ 01969-667202) is open daily from 8.30am to 4.30pm (to 8.30pm in the summer) and has meals for around £7. Close by, *Laburnum House Tearoom* (see p150) serves home-made food and also has a 'soup 'n' sandwich' menu in a nice setting.

They are open daily 10am-5pm.

For a takeaway, besides *Prachin* there's *Paul's Pizzas*, and *The Chippie* (cod, chips and mushy peas for £4). I don't know about you but writing all that has made me hungry!

HAWES TO TAN HILL

Route overview

MAPS 55-64

This stage is back on par with the Malham section, a highly satisfying **16½-mile (27km, 6-7hrs)** trek to the northern edge of the Yorkshire Dales. You start off ambling playfully through the meadows to the village of **Hardraw** (Map 56) where you must steel yourself for the five-mile (8km) slog to the 716-metre (2349ft) summit of **Great Shunner Fell** (Map 59). However, the ascent is largely free of walls and climbing the shoulder of Great Shunner offers views east to the Buttertubs Pass road and west to the distinctive stepped peaks of the northern dales of which Great Shunner is one. On the far side cairns, slabs and our old friend peat bring us round to the enclosed perfection of **Swaledale** in whose verdant arms rests the village of **Thwaite** (Map 61). For once a fine café, part of Kearton Country Hotel (see p158) crops up right around lunchtime; a better place to recharge the batteries for the afternoon's exertions could not be found.

With digestion underway, the route leads first through the hay meadows surrounding the village to soar high above the valley of the infant River Swale along the exposed shoulder of **Kisdon Hill** (Map 62). Negotiating scree and rubble the path drops back into woodland and down to cross this river by a waterfall. Continuing straight soon brings you to curious little **Keld**, an isolated limestone settlement at the intersection with the Coast to Coast Path (another Trailblazer title which no walker's library should be without!). Keld has a campground, shop, a couple of B&Bs and now a small hotel. It's worth popping in for a look-see and an ice cream even if you're set on Tan Hill.

Refreshed again, you rise above Keld to traverse the upland valley of Stonesdale, a muddy prospect at times, and then, with a final flourish, soar like a bleating curlew onto **Stonesdale Moor** (Map 63). The lonely silhouette of the **Tan Hill Inn** (Map 64 and p161) soon crops up against the setting sun and a glass of Theakston's finest calls to you lovingly from the bar.

Route-finding trouble spots

Even in mist, once set right on the path to Great Shunner Fell it would be hard to part from it and it's the same story coming off the far side into Thwaite.

Helpful signage is a bit sparse as you level off from the climb out of Thwaite around Kisdon House, but again the gradual descent into Keld is straightforward. Only the next stage, pre-occupied with the latter reaches of the mushy Stonesdale Valley, up to where it turns up onto Stonesdale Moor at Lad Gill could cause route-finding discord. Once on the moor it's plain sailing to Tan Hill but if you've failed to even get that far, the metalled road on the far side of Stonesdale Beck parallels the Way and also leads straight to the Inn.

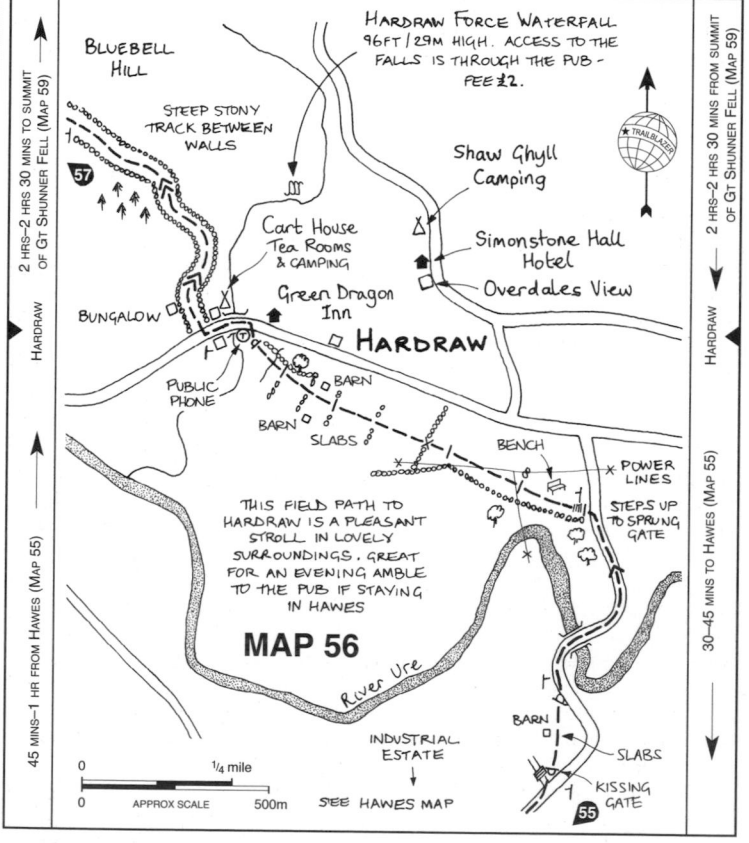

2 HRS–2 HRS 30 MINS TO SUMMIT OF GT SHUNNER FELL (MAP 59)

HARDRAW

45 MINS–1 HR FROM HAWES (MAP 55)

2 HRS–2 HRS 30 MINS FROM SUMMIT OF GT SHUNNER FELL (MAP 59)

HARDRAW

30–45 MINS TO HAWES (MAP 55)

BLUEBELL HILL

HARDRAW FORCE WATERFALL
96FT / 29M HIGH. ACCESS TO THE FALLS IS THROUGH THE PUB – FEE £2.

STEEP STONY TRACK BETWEEN WALLS

★ TRAILBLAZER

Shaw Ghyll Camping

57

Cart House Tea Rooms & CAMPING

Simonstone Hall Hotel

Green Dragon Inn

Overdales View

BUNGALOW

HARDRAW

PUBLIC PHONE

BARN

BARN

SLABS

BENCH

POWER LINES

STEPS UP TO SPRUNG GATE

THIS FIELD PATH TO HARDRAW IS A PLEASANT STROLL IN LOVELY SURROUNDINGS. GREAT FOR AN EVENING AMBLE TO THE PUB IF STAYING IN HAWES

MAP 56

River Ure

INDUSTRIAL ESTATE

BARN

SLABS

KISSING GATE

55

SEE HAWES MAP

0   1/4 mile
0   APPROX SCALE   500m

HARDRAW   [Map 56]

Hardraw's *Green Dragon Inn* (☎ 01969-667392, 🖳 www.greendragonhardraw.com; 2S/2T/5D/1F en suite) is known for its fine ales. B&B is £70 per room and **camping** next door costs £4. Food is served between 10am and 9.30pm with meals from £7. There is live music most Saturday nights; see box p24 for details of the brass band contest held here in September.

Camping is also possible over the river at *Cart House Tea Rooms* (☎ 01969-667691) for £3/pp plus £2 per tent. They are open March to the end of October; the tea rooms are open daily 10am-5pm for snacks, light lunches and afternoon teas.

To the east of the village the very quiet *Shaw Ghyll Campsite* (☎ 01969-667359, 🖳 rogerstott@aol.com; Easter to end Oct) charges £10 per tent and booking is advised. There is a toilet block and a shower costs 50p (in a meter).

If you're not too muddy or sweaty and feel like some luxury treat yourself at *Simonstone Hall Hotel* (☎ 01969-667255, 🖳 www.simonstonehall.com; 20 rooms). B&B costs from £140 per room and there is a fine restaurant (daily 7-8.45pm and open to non-residents). You won't want to leave.

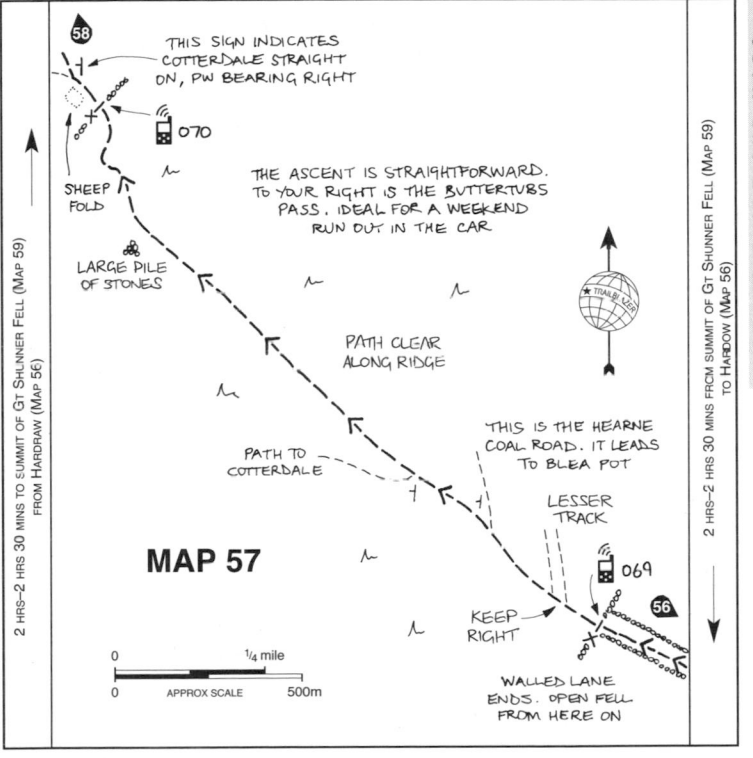

ROUTE GUIDE AND MAPS

❏ Field barns

As you pass through the Yorkshire Dales the prevalence of field barns will have been obvious. Swaledale is particularly noted for these isolated stone barns which are also known as laithes. It has been estimated that within a thousand-metre radius of the village of Muker there are 60 barns of this type. They were part and parcel of the traditional farming methods of the area which saw grazing land enclosed between stone walls, the cattle kept in the barns between October and May, fed on hay stored in the upper roof space of the barn. Cows were milked where they stood and their manure was spread on the surrounding fields. Typically, a field barn would house four or five cows, hence a farmer with a large herd would need plenty of barns to keep them in.

Today, field barns are largely redundant due to farmers making hay on a semi-industrial basis with automated machinery, the hay being baled and stored in huge modern barns close to the farm buildings for convenience. Field barns are used mainly for storage. In some cases farmers have converted them into tourist accommodation, thanks to the availability of grants encouraging them to do so.

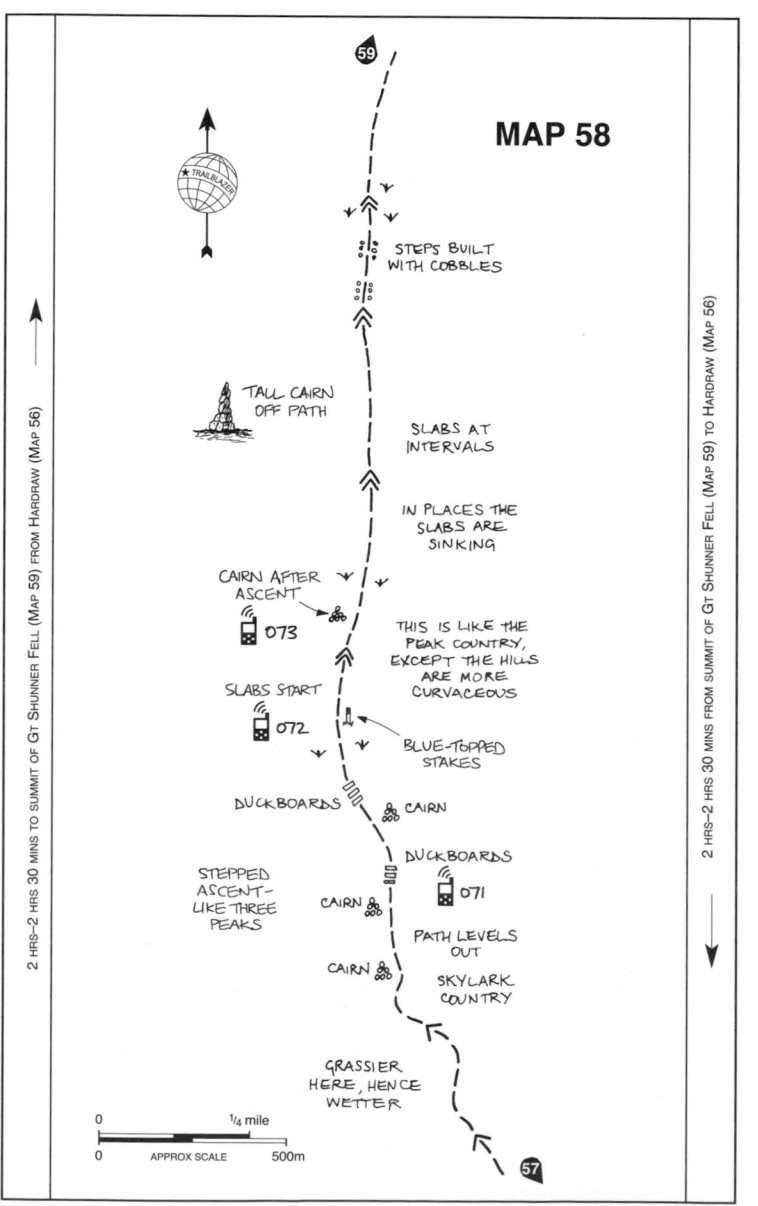

MAP 58

59

STEPS BUILT
WITH COBBLES

TALL CAIRN
OFF PATH

SLABS AT
INTERVALS

IN PLACES THE
SLABS ARE
SINKING

CAIRN AFTER
ASCENT

073

THIS IS LIKE THE
PEAK COUNTRY,
EXCEPT THE HILLS
ARE MORE
CURVACEOUS

SLABS START

072

BLUE-TOPPED
STAKES

DUCKBOARDS

CAIRN

DUCKBOARDS

071

STEPPED
ASCENT-
LIKE THREE
PEAKS

CAIRN

PATH LEVELS
OUT

CAIRN

SKYLARK
COUNTRY

GRASSIER
HERE, HENCE
WETTER

57

0   ¼ mile

0   APPROX SCALE   500m

2 HRS–2 HRS 30 MINS TO SUMMIT OF GT SHUNNER FELL (MAP 59) FROM HARDRAW (MAP 56)

2 HRS–2 HRS 30 MINS FROM SUMMIT OF GT SHUNNER FELL (MAP 59) TO HARDRAW (MAP 56)

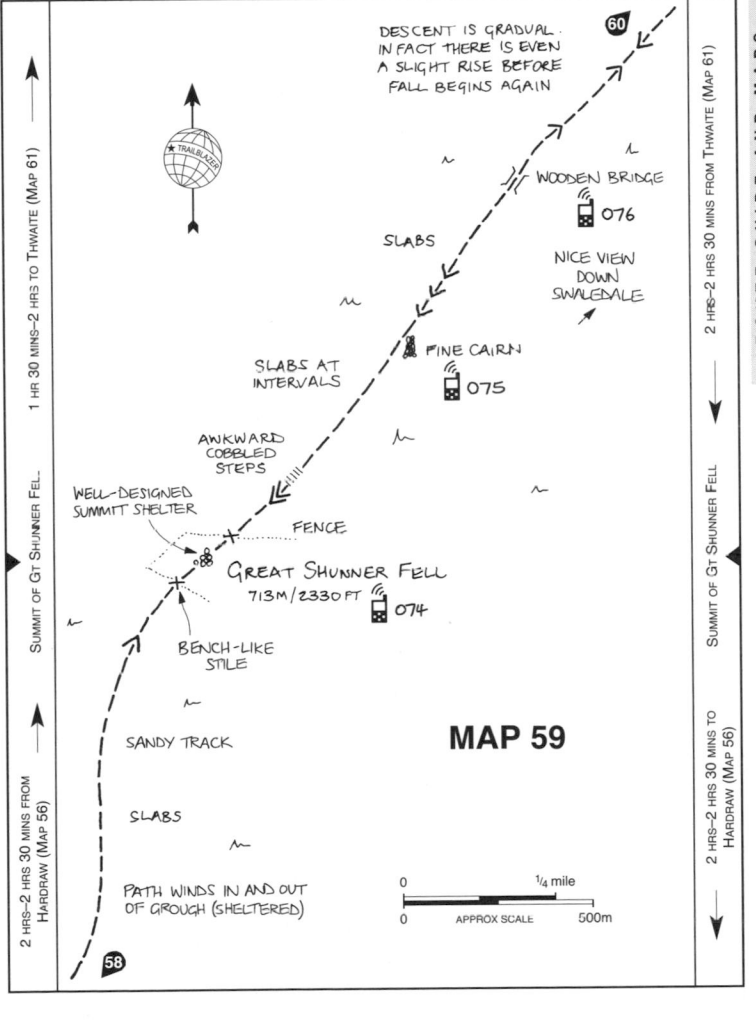

ROUTE GUIDE AND MAPS

1 HR 30 MINS–2 HRS TO THWAITE (MAP 61)

SUMMIT OF GT SHUNNER FELL

2 HRS–2 HRS 30 MINS FROM HARDRAW (MAP 56)

2 HRS–2 HRS 30 MINS FROM THWAITE (MAP 61)

SUMMIT OF GT SHUNNER FELL

2 HRS–2 HRS 30 MINS TO HARDRAW (MAP 56)

DESCENT IS GRADUAL. IN FACT THERE IS EVEN A SLIGHT RISE BEFORE FALL BEGINS AGAIN

60

★ TRAILBLAZER

WOODEN BRIDGE
076

SLABS

NICE VIEW DOWN SWALEDALE

FINE CAIRN
075

SLABS AT INTERVALS

AWKWARD COBBLED STEPS

WELL-DESIGNED SUMMIT SHELTER

FENCE

GREAT SHUNNER FELL
713M / 2330 FT 074

BENCH-LIKE STILE

SANDY TRACK

MAP 59

SLABS

PATH WINDS IN AND OUT OF GROUGH (SHELTERED)

0   1/4 mile
0   APPROX SCALE   500m

58

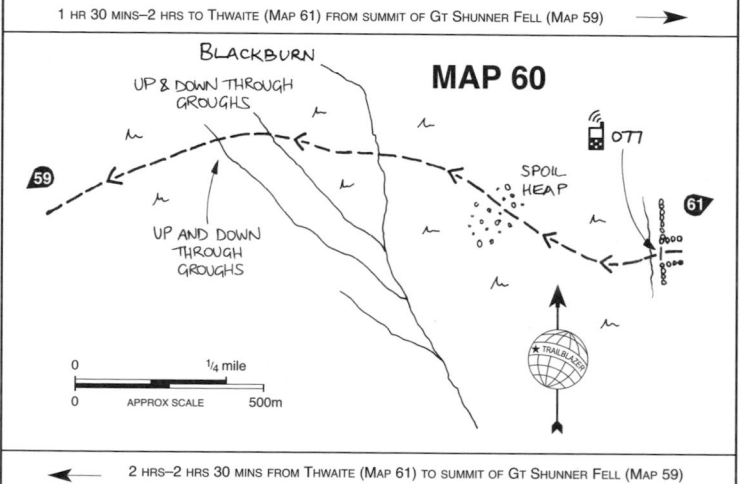

1 HR 30 MINS–2 HRS TO THWAITE (MAP 61) FROM SUMMIT OF GT SHUNNER FELL (MAP 59) ⟶

BLACKBURN

UP & DOWN THROUGH GROUGHS

MAP 60

077

SPOIL HEAP

59

UP AND DOWN THROUGH GROUGHS

61

0   ¼ mile
0   APPROX SCALE   500m

★ TRAILBLAZER

⟵ 2 HRS–2 HRS 30 MINS FROM THWAITE (MAP 61) TO SUMMIT OF GT SHUNNER FELL (MAP 59)

❏ Black Grouse

Pennine Way walkers are unlikely to get as far as Bowes without seeing or at least hearing grouse. Their distinctive nagging croak which has been likened to the warning 'go-back, go-back, go-back' is a familiar sound on wild heather moors, as familiar as the lonely bubbling call of the curlew or the insistent pipe of the golden plover.

While the red grouse is the primary target of many a landowner's gun, the black grouse is a different matter altogether. Shot almost to extinction across most of Northern England, it is now only plentiful in the Scottish hills where the vast space and better cover have enabled it to survive in some numbers. In the Pennines only a few remnants remain and these are carefully protected by gamekeepers and conservationists alike. Most keepers now appreciate the bird for its own sake and, like their changing attitudes to birds of prey, are simply glad it has survived.

In Baldersdale black grouse have been seen in the vicinity of the former youth hostel where their curious courtship ritual was described to me by the warden. The hen birds line up on the branch of a tree like spectators grabbing the best seats in the stands to watch the cock birds perform their 'lek', a display acted out on a piece of prepared ground on which they parade, each trying to outdo the others in their strutting and posturing. Their lyre-shaped tail feathers are fanned out in a magnificent demonstration intended to win the hens' affections.

There are reports that the black grouse is making a comeback; Pennine Way walkers would be the richer if this is so.

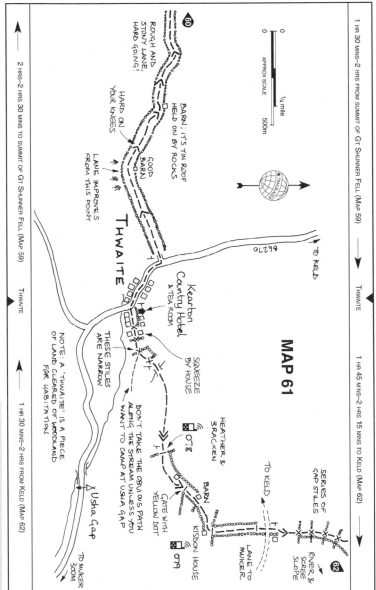

MAP 61

1 HR 30 MINS–2 HRS FROM SUMMIT OF GT SHUNNER FELL (MAP 59) ⟶ THWAITE ⟶ 1 HR 45 MINS–2 HRS 15 MINS TO KELD (MAP 62) ⟶

⟵ 2 HRS–2 HRS 30 MINS TO SUMMIT OF GT SHUNNER FELL (MAP 59) THWAITE ▶ ⟵ 1 HR 30 MINS–2 HRS FROM KELD (MAP 62)

APPROX SCALE

0 ¼ mile
0 500m

TRAILBLAZER

60

ROUGH AND STONY LANE, HARD GOING!

HARD ON YOUR KNEES

BARN: IT'S TIN ROOF HELD ON BY ROCKS

GOOD BARN

LANE IMPROVES FROM THIS POINT

Thwaite

TO KELD

B6270

Kearton Country Hotel & Tea Room

THESE STILES ARE NARROW

SQUEEZE BY HOUSE

NOTE: A 'THWAITE' IS A PIECE OF LAND CLEARED OF WOODLAND FOR HABITATION

HEATHER & BRACKEN

OT6

DON'T TAKE THE OBVIOUS PATH ALONG THE STREAM UNLESS YOU WANT TO CAMP AT USHA GAP

△ Usha Gap

BARN

GATE WITH YELLOW DOT

TO KELD

KISDON HOUSE

OT9

LANE TO MUKER

TO MUKER 300M

SERIES OF GAP STILES

62

RIVER & SCREE SLOPE

ROUTE GUIDE AND MAPS

Map 61, Thwaite 157

THWAITE [Map 61, p157]

The village is notable for the welcome café and tea room at *Kearton Country Hotel* (☎ 01748-886277, 🖥 www.keartoncountryho tel.co.uk; 6D/5T/1F) where you can have morning coffee, a pint with bar meals or choose something from the proper lunch menu; the cappuccinos alone deserve an industry award. B&B costs from £35.50 per person plus £10 per person for half board. Lunch is served daily 12-5pm and evening meals 6.30-7.30pm.

MUKER [off Map 61, p157]

Half a mile beyond Usha Gap you reach Muker. This is a very pleasant little place and a favourite of James Herriot (the Yorkshire vet who wrote *All Creatures Great and Small*). It has a church, a small **shop** and a fine pub, the *Farmers Arms* (☎ 01748-886297), which serves food daily 12-2.30pm and 6-8.45pm.

There are several B&Bs: *Muker Village Store and Teashop* (☎ 01748-886409, 🖥 www.mukervillage.co.uk) comprises the village shop, a tearoom (Easter to end Oct, Wed-Mon 11am-ish to when it goes quiet; weekends only in winter) and B&B (1D or T; £30/pp). *Swale Farm* (☎ 01748-886479, 🖥 www.dalesandvales walks.co.uk/swalefarm.html; 1T/1D both en suite), in the village centre, charges just £25/pp. *Chapel House* (☎ 01748-886822, 🖥 www.mukerchapel.co.uk; 1D) in the old Methodist chapel charges £30 if sharing or £35 for single occupancy.

KELD [Map 62]

Until the former YH got converted into a hotel in 2007 (Keld Lodge), Keld used to be an accommodation and eating bottleneck, exacerbated as a stop on the popular Coast to Coast path. Now the pressure is off for all walkers. Harrogate District's Little Red **Bus** No 30/30A service runs to Richmond via Thwaite (see public transport map and table, pp42-6).

You can **camp** at *Park Lodge* (☎ 01748-886274) where it costs £3.75 per person and there's a **café** and **shop** (Easter

For **campers**, just over half a mile east through the meadows brings you to the campsite at *Usha Gap* (☎ 01748-886214, 🖥 www.ushagap.btinternet.co.uk), a lovely riverside field where you can pitch for £4 including showers.

Thwaite is a stop on Harrogate District's Little Red **Bus** No 30/30A between Keld and Richmond (see public transport map and table, pp42-6).

Feeling chilly? Then you'll be delighted to learn that for 30 years Muker has also been the home of **Swaledale Woollens** (☎ 01748-886251, 🖥 www.swaledalewoollens.co.uk), its products made from the yarn of Swaledale sheep. The shop boasts that it actually saved the village following the depression caused by the collapse of the mining industry. Following a meeting in the pub, a decision was made to set up a local cottage industry producing knitwear, and today 30 home-workers are employed in knitting the jumpers, hats and many other items available in the store, which is near the pub.

See box p24 for details about Swaledale's Arts Festival held here in May.

Harrogate District's Little Red **Bus** No 30/30A service stops here en route between Richmond and Keld (see public transport map and table, pp42-6).

to end Sep; daily 9am-6pm). Half a mile west of Keld is *Park House Campsite* (☎ 01748-886549, 🖥 park.house@btinternet .co.uk). It's a lovely riverside site and they charge £3 per person. There's a food shop and indoor sitting area, a place you may not want to vacate as Keld can be rather popular with midges too.

Keld Lodge (☎ 01748-886259, 🖥 www.keldlodge.com; 3S/4D/4T or F), the former youth hostel, has been converted into a small licensed hotel with en suites for £35/pp and £25 for the one en suite single 'pod' room which has bunk beds in. Along

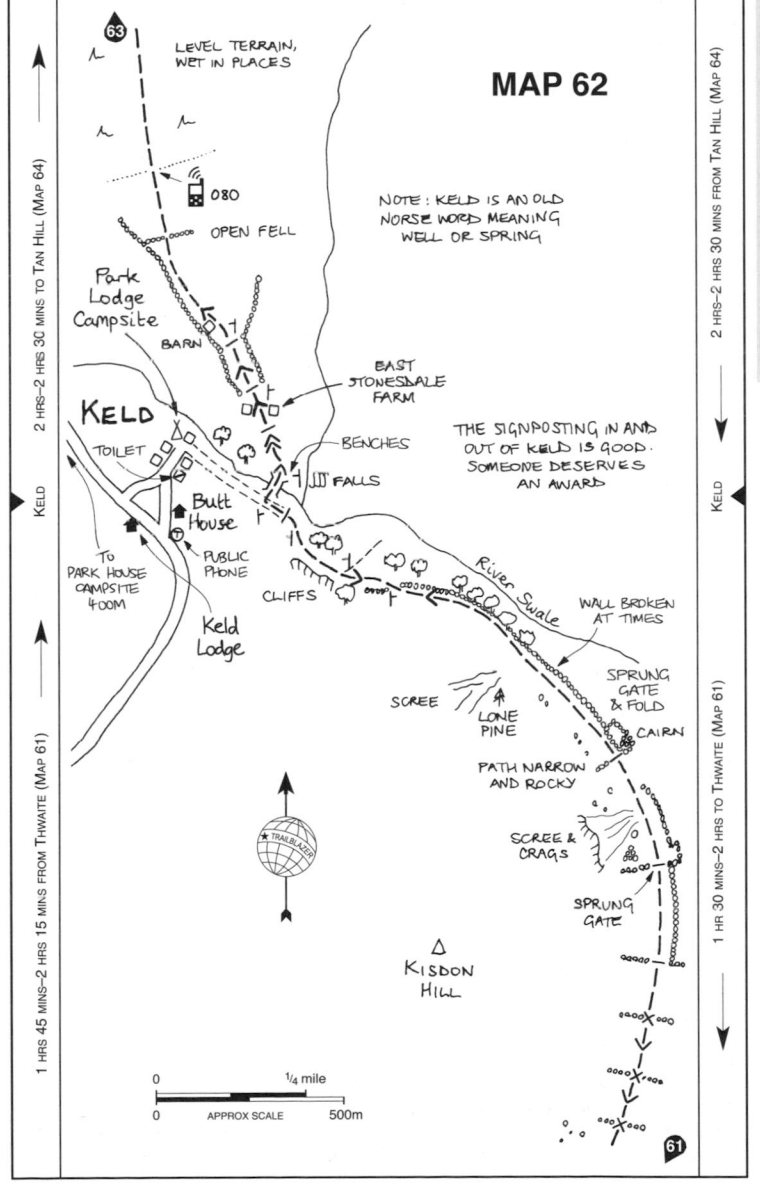

MAP 62

63

LEVEL TERRAIN, WET IN PLACES

080

OPEN FELL

NOTE: KELD IS AN OLD NORSE WORD MEANING WELL OR SPRING

Park Lodge Campsite

BARN

KELD

TOILET

EAST STONESDALE FARM

BENCHES

THE SIGNPOSTING IN AND OUT OF KELD IS GOOD. SOMEONE DESERVES AN AWARD

Butt House

FALLS

PUBLIC PHONE

River Swale

TO PARK HOUSE CAMPSITE 400M

Keld Lodge

CLIFFS

WALL BROKEN AT TIMES

SCREE

LONE PINE

SPRUNG GATE & FOLD

CAIRN

PATH NARROW AND ROCKY

★ TRAILBLAZER

SCREE & CRAGS

SPRUNG GATE

△ KISDON HILL

0   ¼ mile

0   APPROX SCALE   500m

61

2 HRS—2 HRS 30 MINS TO TAN HILL (MAP 64)

KELD

1 HRS 45 MINS—2 HRS 15 MINS FROM THWAITE (MAP 61)

2 HRS—2 HRS 30 MINS FROM TAN HILL (MAP 64)

KELD

1 HR 30 MINS—2 HRS TO THWAITE (MAP 61)

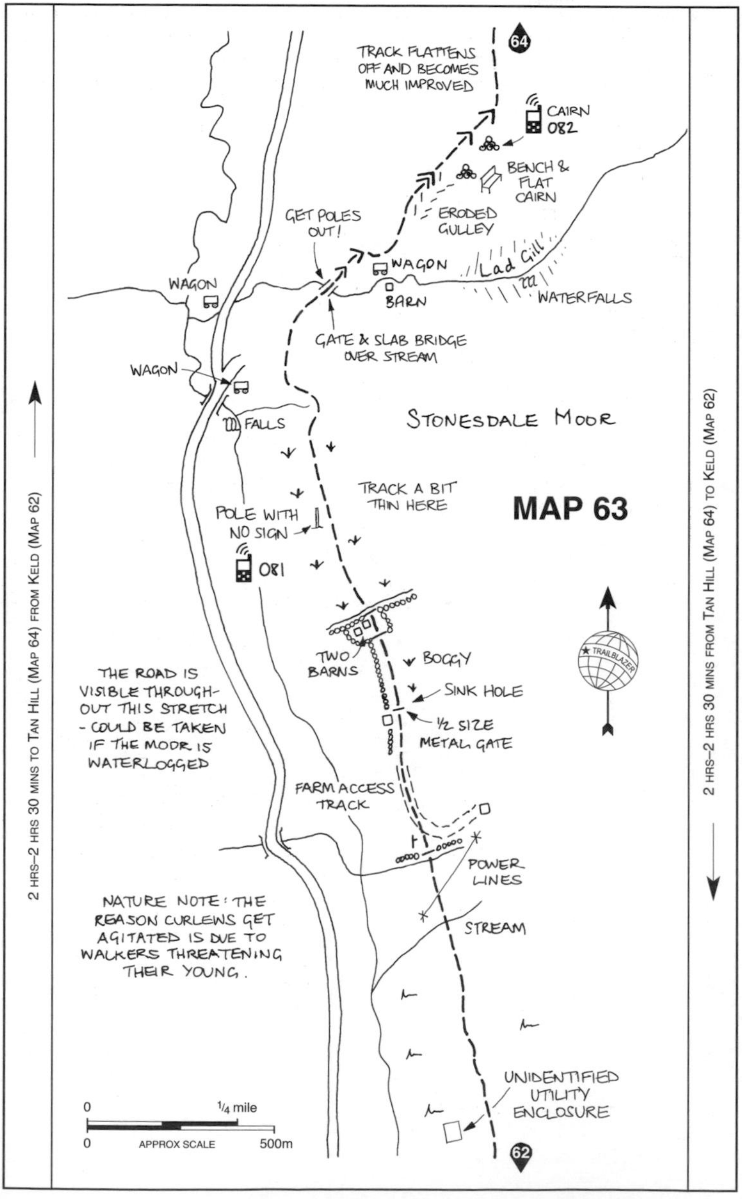

64

TRACK FLATTENS OFF AND BECOMES MUCH IMPROVED

CAIRN 082

BENCH & FLAT CAIRN

ERODED GULLEY

GET POLES OUT!

WAGON

WAGON

WAGON BARN

Lad Gill

WATERFALLS

GATE & SLAB BRIDGE OVER STREAM

WAGON

FALLS

STONESDALE MOOR

POLE WITH NO SIGN

081

TRACK A BIT THIN HERE

MAP 63

★ TRAILBLAZER

TWO BARNS

BOGGY

SINK HOLE

½ SIZE METAL GATE

THE ROAD IS VISIBLE THROUGHOUT THIS STRETCH - COULD BE TAKEN IF THE MOOR IS WATERLOGGED

FARM ACCESS TRACK

POWER LINES

NATURE NOTE: THE REASON CURLEWS GET AGITATED IS DUE TO WALKERS THREATENING THEIR YOUNG.

STREAM

UNIDENTIFIED UTILITY ENCLOSURE

0   ¼ mile

0   APPROX SCALE   500m

62

2 HRS–2 HRS 30 MINS TO TAN HILL (MAP 64) FROM KELD (MAP 62)

2 HRS–2 HRS 30 MINS FROM TAN HILL (MAP 64) TO KELD (MAP 62)

with a bar there's a **restaurant** (meals cost from around £8) and a drying room. Part-owned by Brigantes (see p20), using their baggage services gets you preferential booking and a £5 discount.

Doreen Whitehead's *Butt House* (☎ 01748-886374; 1S/2T/1D) is mentioned wherever Pennine Way walkers gather. B&B costs £30 per person; if the single room is taken you'll pay an extra £6 for single occupancy of a double or twin, if available. They are licensed too, which may just give your evening meal a welcome kick. Unfortunately, at the time of writing Doreen and her husband were planning to sell up and move. However, they expect the new owners to continue doing B&B so it's worth ringing to find out the latest.

TAN HILL [Map 64, p162]

Tan Hill Inn (☎ 01833-628246, 🖳 www .tanhillinn.com; 2D/5T/1F) charges £35 per head for single occupancy and £60 for two sharing an en suite room – the rooms are all en suite apart from the family room. Besides the pub there are no facilities here apart from some rocks to shelter behind but at £2, **camping** round the back is as cheap as it gets, and the money is donated to charity. There is a tap and outside loo.

Outside all is as quiet as a lapwing's grave but a good night inside can be a different matter; stories have been told of things getting quite animated late at night as a result of the many evenings when the pub lives music.

Food is available daily between 12 noon and 2.30pm and in the evening between 7pm and 9pm but the owners say they can make a sandwich any time. The pub itself is open all day year-round.

❏ Kentucky Fried Turkeys versus Tan Hill Inn

England's highest pub hit the news in 2007 when web-trawling lawyers behind the Kentucky Fried Chicken fast-food chain set out to sue the Tan Hill Inn for daring to use KFC's phrase 'Family Feast' on the online menu for their annual Christmas dinner. Googling the forbidden words results in over 2 million hits but the pub's owners were sternly informed that "'*Family Feast' is a registered trademark of Kentucky Fried Chicken (Great Britain) Limited.*" .

Arriving in April and signed by a 'Mr Giles Pratt' the owner assumed it was an overdue April Fool joke and initially ignored it. When the threats continued the owner rang her solicitors and was advised that the claim was indeed no joke. Of course the owner stood by her guns and local solicitors offered to take on the case for free.

A storm of media interest ensued and the pub's website crashed while jokes about the nutritional value of KFC's fare did the rounds. The KFC lawyers merely succeeded in making turkeys of themselves and the claim was withdrawn as they conceded a once-a-year traditional roast turkey Christmas dinner at a moorland pub could not be confused with a cardboard bucket full of fried chicken and chips with coleslaw and a fizzy drink.

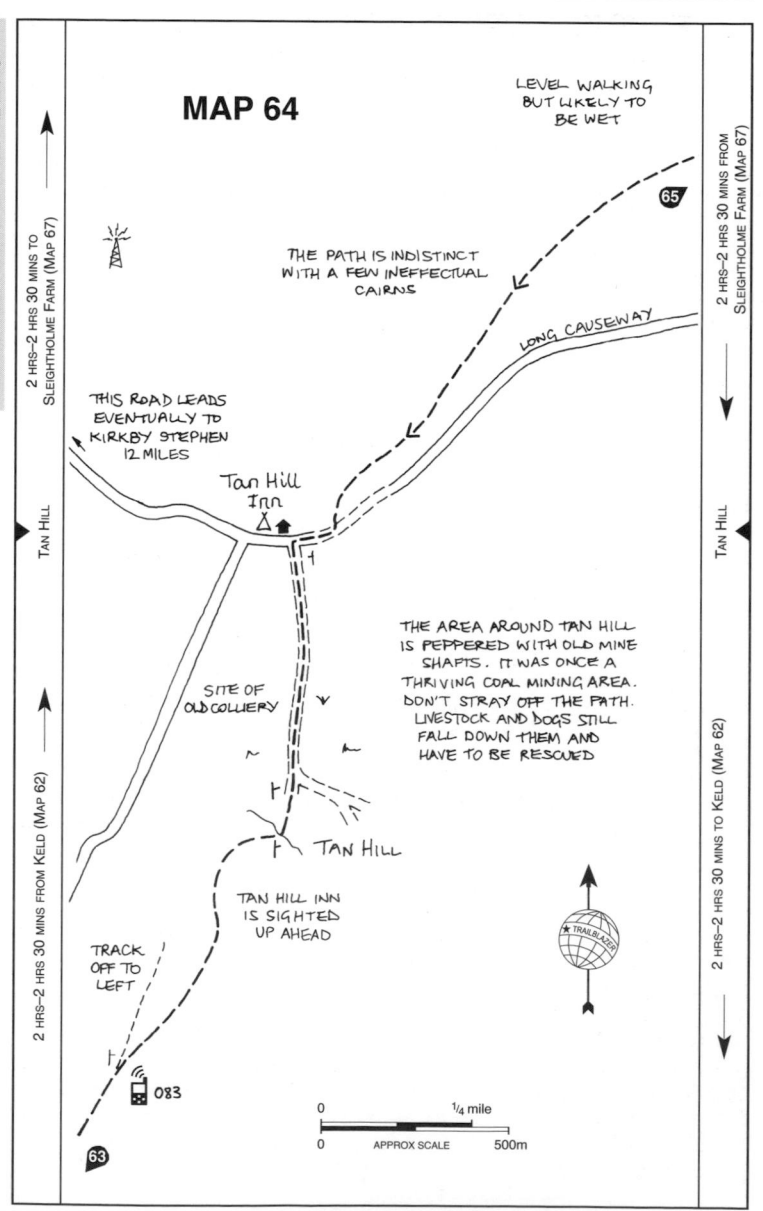

MAP 64

LEVEL WALKING
BUT LIKELY TO
BE WET

65

2 HRS–2 HRS 30 MINS TO SLEIGHTHOLME FARM (MAP 67)

2 HRS–2 HRS 30 MINS FROM SLEIGHTHOLME FARM (MAP 67)

THE PATH IS INDISTINCT
WITH A FEW INEFFECTUAL
CAIRNS

LONG CAUSEWAY

THIS ROAD LEADS
EVENTUALLY TO
KIRKBY STEPHEN
12 MILES

Tan Hill
Inn

Tan Hill

Tan Hill

THE AREA AROUND TAN HILL
IS PEPPERED WITH OLD MINE
SHAFTS. IT WAS ONCE A
THRIVING COAL MINING AREA.
DON'T STRAY OFF THE PATH.
LIVESTOCK AND DOGS STILL
FALL DOWN THEM AND
HAVE TO BE RESCUED

SITE OF
OLD COLLIERY

TAN HILL

TAN HILL INN
IS SIGHTED
UP AHEAD

2 HRS–2 HRS 30 MINS FROM KELD (MAP 62)

2 HRS–2 HRS 30 MINS TO KELD (MAP 62)

★ TRAILBLAZER

TRACK
OFF TO
LEFT

083

63

0   ¼ mile

0   APPROX SCALE   500m

TAN HILL TO MIDDLETON-IN-TEESDALE   MAPS 64-72

Route overview

Having spent a memorable night at Tan Hill Inn, today's **17-mile (25km, 6-7hrs)** day has the distinct novelty of starting off downhill. It's something you may appreciate if the Tan Hill Experience has hit you hard.

Downhill it may be but you're descending into the sheep-swallowing wastes of **Sleightholme Moor** (Map 65) and as you near Frumming Beck you may find your still-waking limbs forced into grough-hopping lunges over the peaty trenches until the path thankfully gains the better-drained northern bank. White-topped posts mark the way intermittently and all passes agreeably by your side until you bridge it and take to a road which leads down to Sleightholme Farm. It's a stage of the walk during which the continuing peels of lapwing and curlew may quite possibly begin to get on your wick.

Having re-crossed Sleightholme Beck, you clamber up and over **Wytham Moor** (Map 67) and (if you don't take the Bowes Variant, see below) drop down to the River Greta at **God's Bridge**.

Bowes Variant At Trough Heads (Map 67; GPS waypoint 087/787, see p258) a branch of the Pennine Way splits east for **8½ miles via Bowes** (see maps 67a-c) to reconverge at Baldersdale (totalling three extra miles). Cooked up by the hallowed Alfred Wainright before Baldersdale became an overnight-ing option, so influential was his original guidebook that the Bowes Loop became absorbed into the official route.

This longer route has noticeably **fewer ups and downs** and is a little more scenically appealing, although route finding can have a few irritating moments. Currently **accommodation options** on *both* routes are rather lean until Middleton, so if you're not camping in the wilds, make sure you book ahead.

Here at the Stainmore Gap you scurry under the A66 via a litter-strewn underpass. The roar of the traffic reminds you of the M62 back in the far distant past, before you'd earned your Pennine Way spurs. Depending on the wind, it takes till well after **Ravock Castle** (Map 68; merely a scattering of stones) on top of Bowes Moor before you're finally free of the din.

You now drop into, and climb stiffly out of, Sled Dale over **Race Yate** (Map 69) to drop back among the reservoirs which now fill **Baldersdale**. If you can reach, pat yourself on the back; this is the **halfway mark** on the Pennine Way. Yes, you're *only* halfway.

You may choose to overnight here; if so Clove Lodge bunkhouse (see p172) is your only option. For those as yet unsatiated, it's six or seven miles to Middleton, including a hill climb over to Lunedale and another over **Harter Fell**; this may well dampen any excess energy you had stored up for the town, though it invites you in with a good range of accommodation, eating and re-provisioning options.

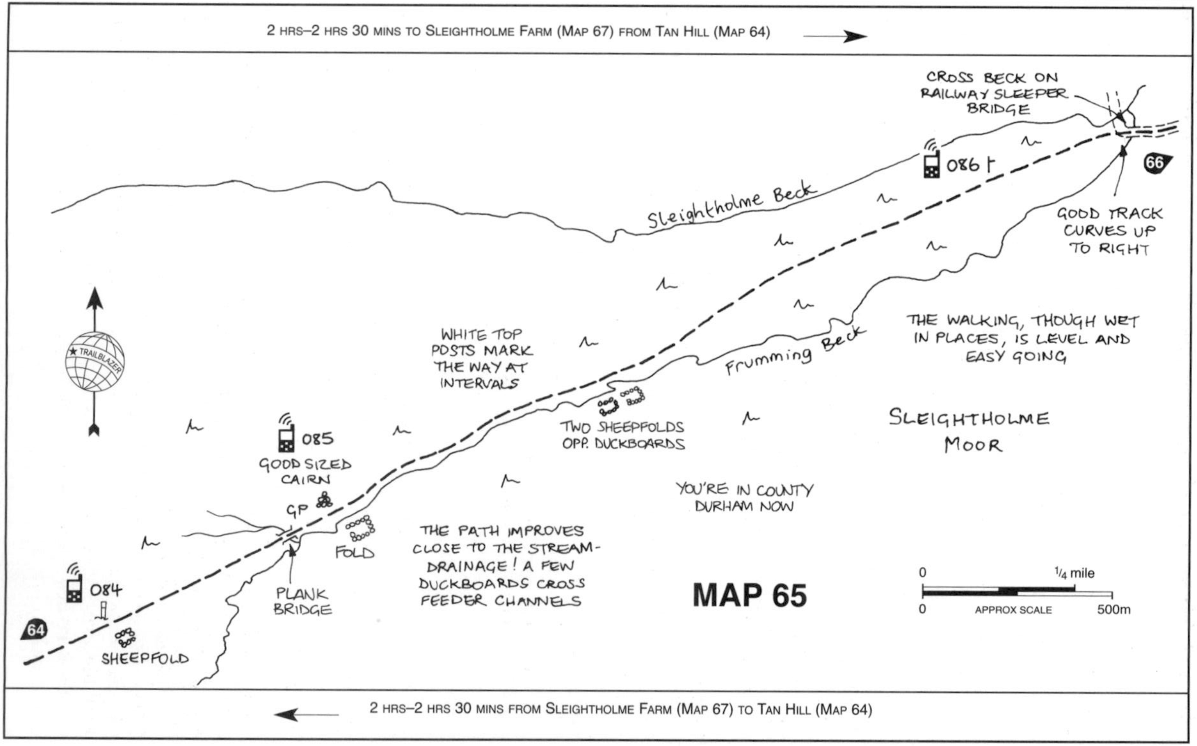

ROUTE GUIDE AND MAPS

2 HRS–2 HRS 30 MINS TO SLEIGHTHOLME FARM (MAP 67) FROM TAN HILL (MAP 64) →

66

CROSS BECK ON RAILWAY SLEEPER BRIDGE

GOOD TRACK CURVES UP TO RIGHT

086

THE WALKING, THOUGH WET IN PLACES, IS LEVEL AND EASY GOING

SLEIGHTHOLME MOOR

Sleightholme Beck

Frumming Beck

YOU'RE IN COUNTY DURHAM NOW

MAP 65

¼ mile

APPROX SCALE

0   500m

TWO SHEEPFOLDS OPP. DUCKBOARDS

WHITE TOP POSTS MARK THE WAY AT INTERVALS

THE PATH IMPROVES CLOSE TO THE STREAM- DRAINAGE! A FEW DUCKBOARDS CROSS FEEDER CHANNELS

085

GOOD SIZED CAIRN

G.P.

FOLD

PLANK BRIDGE

084

SHEEPFOLD

64

★ TRAILBLAZER

2 HRS–2 HRS 30 MINS FROM SLEIGHTHOLME FARM (MAP 67) TO TAN HILL (MAP 64) ←

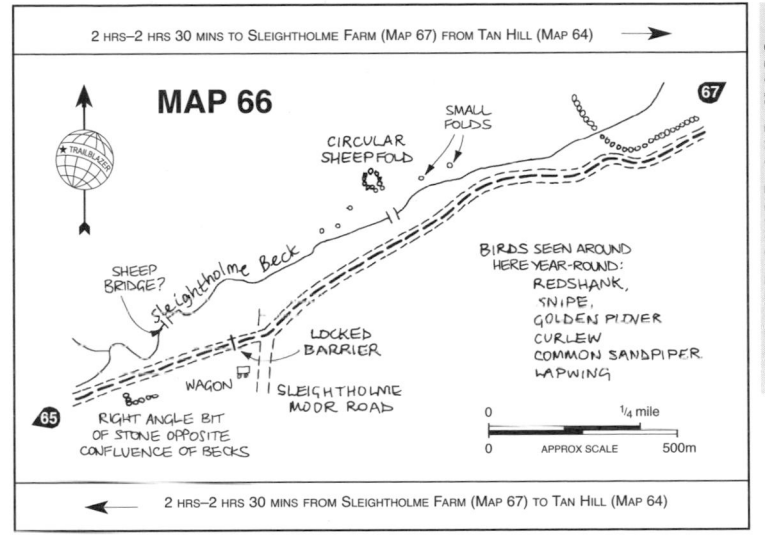

2 HRS–2 HRS 30 MINS TO SLEIGHTHOLME FARM (MAP 67) FROM TAN HILL (MAP 64)

MAP 66

TRAILBLAZER

SMALL FOLDS

CIRCULAR SHEEP FOLD

SHEEP BRIDGE?

Sleightholme Beck

LOCKED BARRIER

BIRDS SEEN AROUND HERE YEAR-ROUND:
REDSHANK,
SNIPE,
GOLDEN PLOVER
CURLEW
COMMON SANDPIPER
LAPWING

WAGON

SLEIGHTHOLME MOOR ROAD

65

RIGHT ANGLE BIT OF STONE OPPOSITE CONFLUENCE OF BECKS

0 .... 1/4 mile

0 .... APPROX SCALE 500m

2 HRS–2 HRS 30 MINS FROM SLEIGHTHOLME FARM (MAP 67) TO TAN HILL (MAP 64)

Route-finding trouble spots

Irregular white-topped posts light the way across Sleightholme Moor; in thick mist a GPS may help. From there over the A66 to Baldersdale is clear, with the only other hitch – fair weather or foul – being the successful navigation over the walls and pastures leading up and around the shoulder of Harter Fell. The Bowes loop too has its confusions, mostly across the discreetly signed field.

BOWES [Map 67a, p167]

There is little to do here but a stroll to the pub could include a look at the **churchyard** where Dickens found inspiration for the character of Smike in *Nicholas Nickleby*. See box p24 for details of the farming show held here in September.

The **post office** (early closing Wed) is along the main street. The tiny **village shop** is open Mon-Fri 7.30am-12.30pm & 2-5.30pm, Sat/Sun 8am-12pm.

Nowadays the accommodation choice is not so great here with the *Ancient Unicorn* (☎ 01833-628321, 🖳 www.ancient-unicorn.com; 4T or D/1F) being a pub with great bar meals (daily 12-2pm Sun-

Wed 7-9pm; Thur-Sat 6-9.30pm) but B&B goes for a hefty £70 for twins or doubles (single occupancy £40).

Campers can pitch at *West End Farm* (☎ 01833-628239) for £3 per person but the noise from the A66 may be a distraction.

Classic Coaches operates a **bus** to Kirkby Stephen, which is on the Leeds to Carlisle railway line, and both Classic Coaches and Central Coaches go to Barnard Castle where other services connect with Darlington which is on the London to Edinburgh line (see transport map and table, pp42-6).

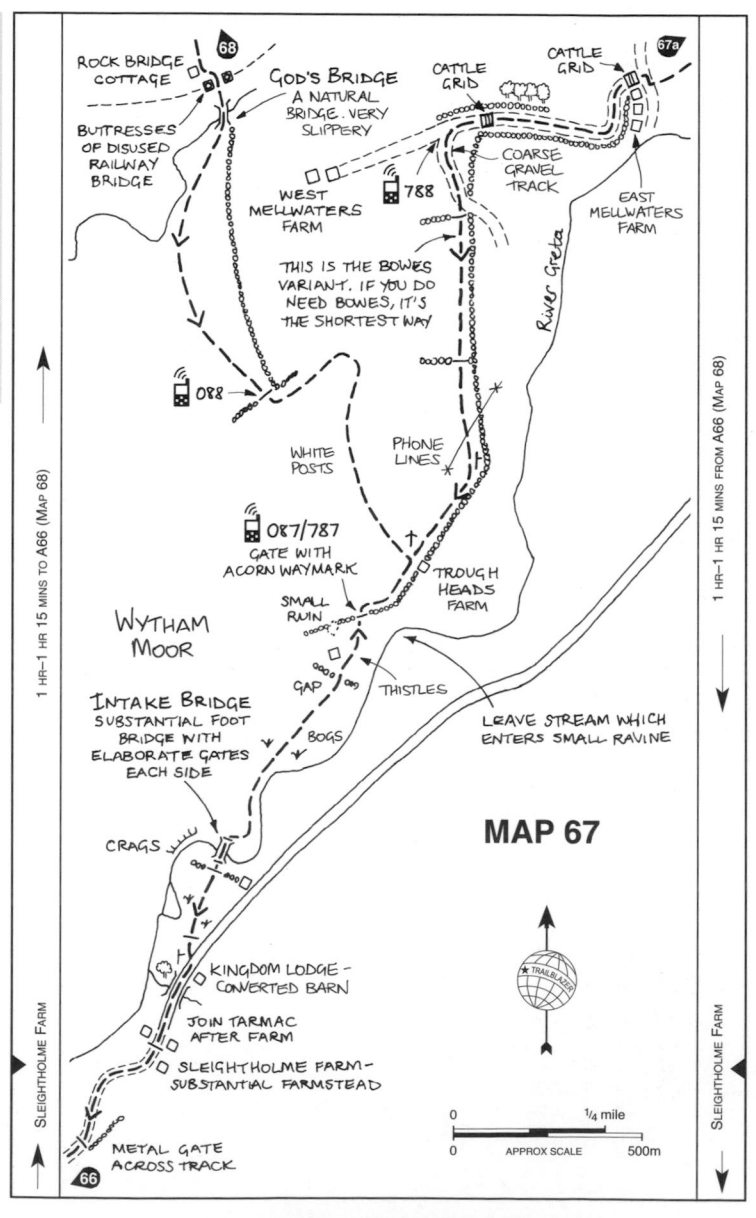

ROUTE GUIDE AND MAPS

ROCK BRIDGE COTTAGE

68

GOD'S BRIDGE
A NATURAL BRIDGE. VERY SLIPPERY

CATTLE GRID

CATTLE GRID

67a

BUTTRESSES OF DISUSED RAILWAY BRIDGE

WEST MELLWATERS FARM

788

COARSE GRAVEL TRACK

EAST MELLWATERS FARM

THIS IS THE BOWES VARIANT. IF YOU DO NEED BOWES, IT'S THE SHORTEST WAY

088

River Greta

WHITE POSTS

PHONE LINES

087/787
GATE WITH ACORN WAYMARK

SMALL RUIN

TROUGH HEADS FARM

WYTHAM MOOR

INTAKE BRIDGE
SUBSTANTIAL FOOT BRIDGE WITH ELABORATE GATES EACH SIDE

GAP

BOGS

THISTLES

LEAVE STREAM WHICH ENTERS SMALL RAVINE

CRAGS

MAP 67

KINGDOM LODGE – CONVERTED BARN

JOIN TARMAC AFTER FARM

SLEIGHTHOLME FARM – SUBSTANTIAL FARMSTEAD

METAL GATE ACROSS TRACK

66

0   ¼ mile

0   APPROX SCALE   500m

1 HR–1 HR 15 MINS TO A66 (MAP 68)

1 HR–1 HR 15 MINS FROM A66 (MAP 68)

SLEIGHTHOLME FARM

SLEIGHTHOLME FARM

TRAILBLAZER

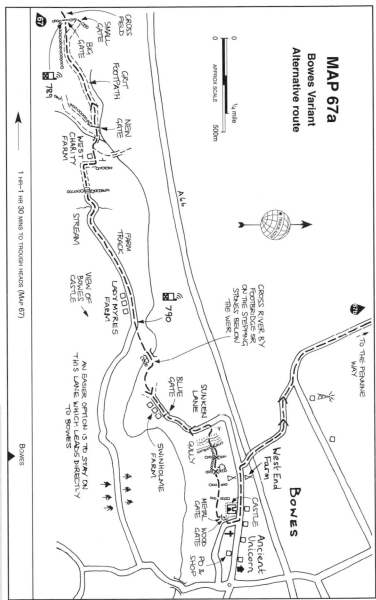

MAP 67a
Bowes Variant
Alternative route

APPROX SCALE

0

¼ mile

0

500m

CROSS FIELD

SMALL GATE

BIG GATE

67

GRIT FOOTPATH

789

NEW GATE

WEST CHARITY FARM

STREAM

FARM TRACK

LADY MYRES FARM

VIEW OF BOWES CASTLE

790

A66

CROSS RIVER BY FOOTBRIDGE OR ON THE STEPPING STONES BELOW THE WEIR

67b

TO THE PENNINE WAY

SUNKEN LANE

BLUE GATE

GULLY

SWINHOLME FARM

AN EASIER OPTION IS TO STAY ON THIS LANE WHICH LEADS DIRECTLY TO BOWES

METAL GATE

WOOD GATE

CASTLE GATE

WEST END FARM

Ancient Unicorn

PO & SHOP

BOWES

1 HR-1 HR 30 MINS TO TROUGH HEADS (MAP 67)

BOWES

ROUTE GUIDE AND MAPS

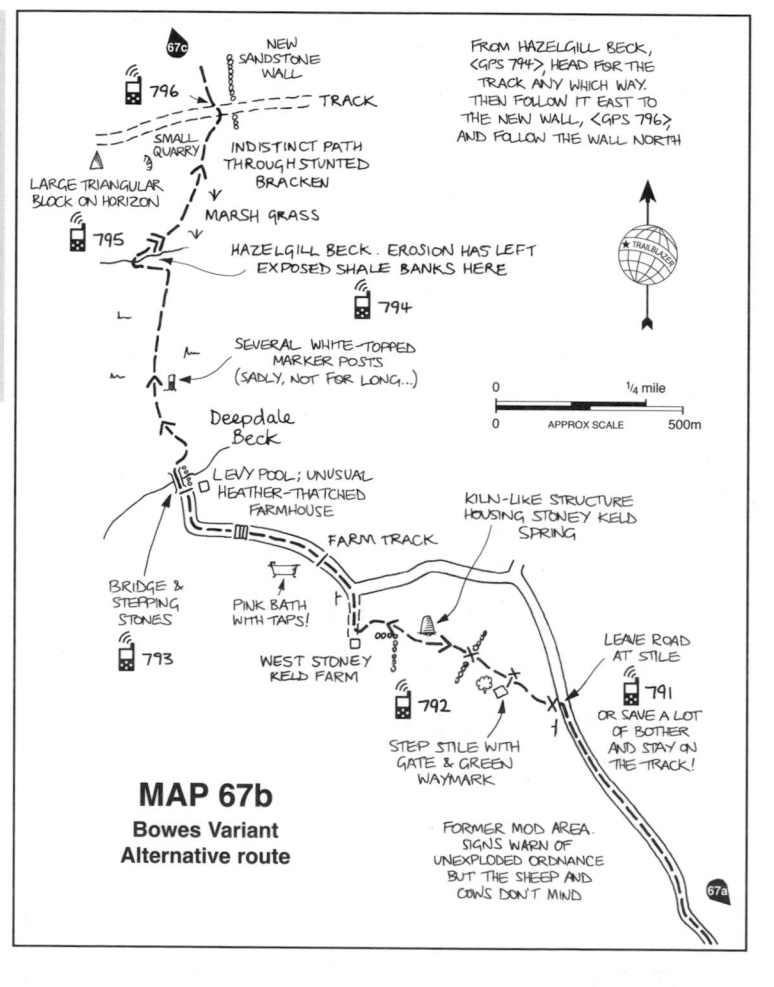

NEW SANDSTONE WALL

67c

796

TRACK

SMALL QUARRY

INDISTINCT PATH THROUGH STUNTED BRACKEN

LARGE TRIANGULAR BLOCK ON HORIZON

795

MARSH GRASS

HAZELGILL BECK. EROSION HAS LEFT EXPOSED SHALE BANKS HERE

794

FROM HAZELGILL BECK, <GPS 794>, HEAD FOR THE TRACK ANY WHICH WAY. THEN FOLLOW IT EAST TO THE NEW WALL, <GPS 796> AND FOLLOW THE WALL NORTH

TRAILBLAZER

SEVERAL WHITE-TOPPED MARKER POSTS (SADLY, NOT FOR LONG...)

0   ¼ mile

0   APPROX SCALE   500m

Deepdale Beck

LEVY POOL; UNUSUAL HEATHER-THATCHED FARMHOUSE

FARM TRACK

KILN-LIKE STRUCTURE HOUSING STONEY KELD SPRING

BRIDGE & STEPPING STONES

793

PINK BATH WITH TAPS!

WEST STONEY KELD FARM

792

STEP STILE WITH GATE & GREEN WAYMARK

LEAVE ROAD AT STILE

791

OR SAVE A LOT OF BOTHER AND STAY ON THE TRACK!

MAP 67b

**Bowes Variant
Alternative route**

FORMER MOD AREA. SIGNS WARN OF UNEXPLODED ORDNANCE BUT THE SHEEP AND COWS DON'T MIND

67a

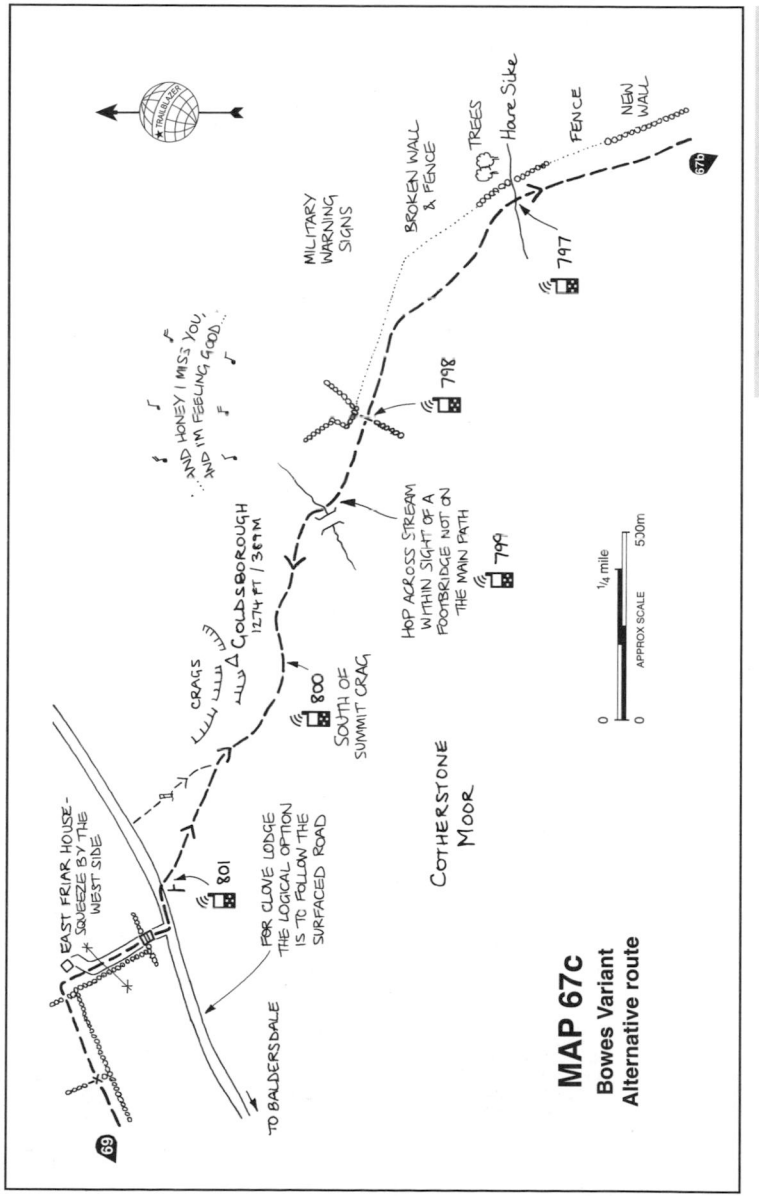

MAP 67c
Bowes Variant
Alternative route

TO BALDERSDALE

69

EAST FRIAR HOUSE –
SQUEEZE BY THE
WEST SIDE

801

FOR CLOVE LODGE
THE LOGICAL OPTION
IS TO FOLLOW THE
SURFACED ROAD

CRAGS

△ GOLDSBOROUGH
1274 FT / 365M

800
SOUTH OF
SUMMIT CRAG

COTHERSTONE
MOOR

AND HONEY I MISS YOU,
AND I'M FEELING GOOD.

MILITARY
WARNING
SIGNS

HOP ACROSS STREAM
WITHIN SIGHT OF A
FOOTBRIDGE NOT ON
THE MAIN PATH

799

798

BROKEN WALL
& FENCE

TREES

Hare Sike

FENCE

NEW
WALL

747

67d

APPROX SCALE
¼ mile
0   530m

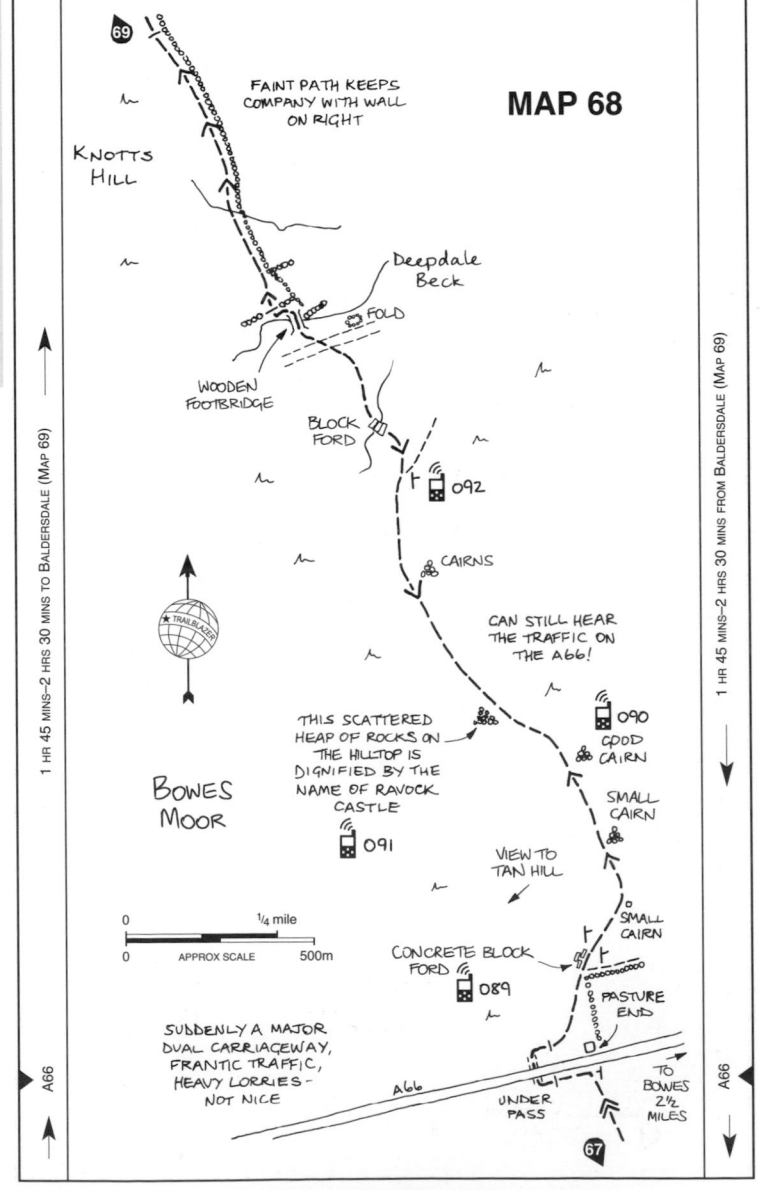

MAP 68

69

FAINT PATH KEEPS
COMPANY WITH WALL
ON RIGHT

KNOTTS
HILL

Deepdale
Beck

FOLD

WOODEN
FOOTBRIDGE

BLOCK
FORD

092

CAIRNS

CAN STILL HEAR
THE TRAFFIC ON
THE A66!

090
GOOD
CAIRN

THIS SCATTERED
HEAP OF ROCKS ON
THE HILLTOP IS
DIGNIFIED BY THE
NAME OF RAVOCK
CASTLE

SMALL
CAIRN

BOWES
MOOR

091

VIEW TO
TAN HILL

★ TRAILBLAZER

SMALL
CAIRN

0   ¼ mile

CONCRETE BLOCK
FORD

0   500m
APPROX SCALE

089

PASTURE
END

SUDDENLY A MAJOR
DUAL CARRIAGEWAY,
FRANTIC TRAFFIC,
HEAVY LORRIES –
NOT NICE

A66

TO
BOWES
2½
MILES

UNDER
PASS

67

1 HR 45 MINS–2 HRS 30 MINS TO BALDERSDALE (MAP 69)

1 HR 45 MINS–2 HRS 30 MINS FROM BALDERSDALE (MAP 69)

A66

A66

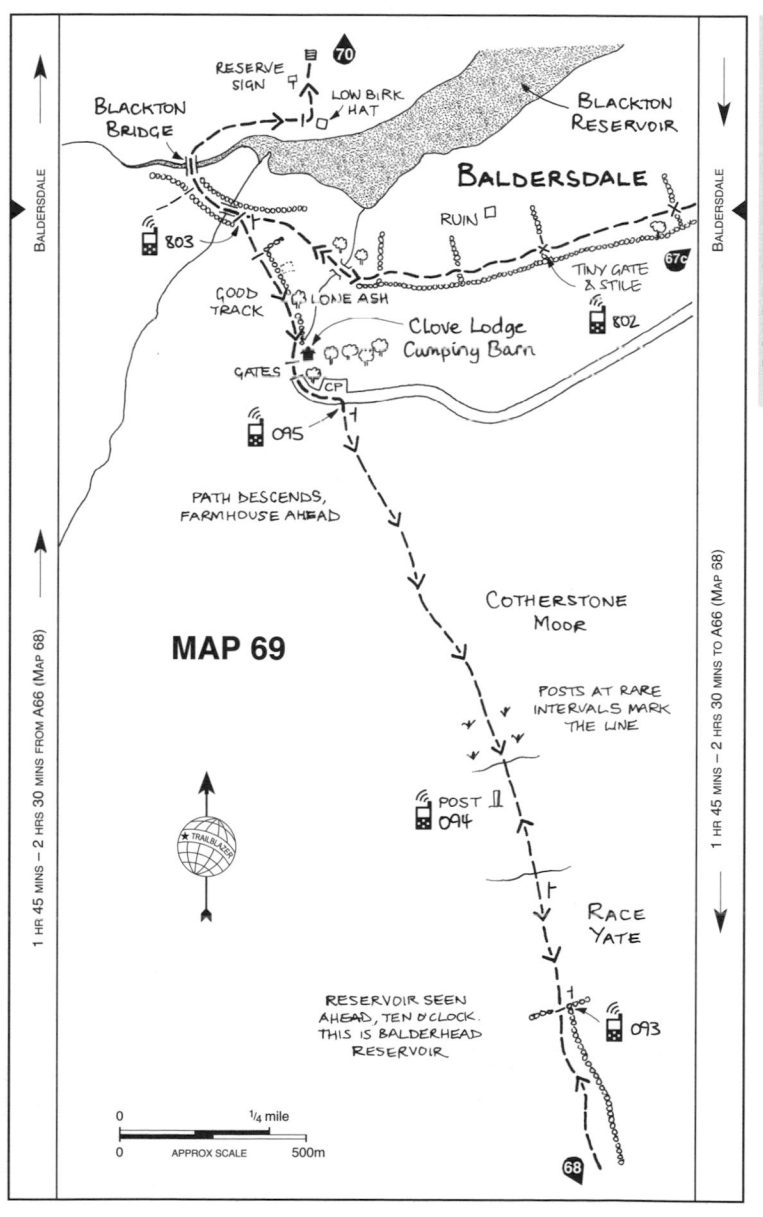

RESERVE SIGN

70

LOW BIRK HAT

BLACKTON BRIDGE

BLACKTON RESERVOIR

BALDERSDALE

803

RUIN

TINY GATE & STILE

67c

GOOD TRACK

LONE ASH

Clove Lodge Camping Barn

802

GATES

CP

095

PATH DESCENDS, FARMHOUSE AHEAD

COTHERSTONE MOOR

MAP 69

POSTS AT RARE INTERVALS MARK THE LINE

TRAILBLAZER

POST

094

RACE YATE

RESERVOIR SEEN AHEAD, TEN O'CLOCK. THIS IS BALDERHEAD RESERVOIR

093

68

BALDERSDALE

BALDERSDALE

1 HR 45 MINS – 2 HRS 30 MINS FROM A66 (MAP 68)

1 HR 45 MINS – 2 HRS 30 MINS TO A66 (MAP 68)

0   1/4 mile

0   APPROX SCALE   500m

BALDERSDALE [Map 69, p171]
These days all that's left in Baldersdale for the weary Pennine wayfarer is *Clove Lodge* (☎ 01833-650030, 💻 www.clove lodge.co.uk). They have a very cosy four-bed holiday cottage (1D/1D or T en suite) where B&B costs £35/pp if the cottage has not already been booked as a weekly let; however, if the cottage is full there's usual-ly space in the house for B&B guests. An evening meal costs £15 and it's £4.75 for a packed lunch. It's not a bad place to lay up for a rest day at the halfway point.

The Alston Road Garage (see public transport map and table, pp42-6) bus service to/from Middleton will call at both Baldersdale and Lunedale if prebooked at least an hour in advance.

❏ **Hannah Hauxwell**
Right on the edge of Blackton Reservoir beside the Pennine Way stands the farm of Low Birk Hat (see Map 69, p171), home for many years to a remarkable woman. Hannah Hauxwell came to public attention through a number of television pro-grammes and books (both formats are still available) telling the story of the life of someone living at subsistence level in Baldersdale as recently as the 1970s. With a cow which had one calf a year, she allowed herself £250 a year for living expenses, with-out electricity or gas, surviving the harsh winters by the simple expedient of putting on another coat.

Later Hannah Hauxwell became famous for her courage and her natural under-standing of the world and its follies when she travelled for the cameras recording her impressions of cities around the world. Her curiosity and common-sense enabled her to put her finger on the unusual and get pleasure from the commonplace.

Now retired and living more comfortably nearby, Hannah will be long remem-bered by those who followed her adventures. Her farm where at one time her father alone supported a family of seven, both sets of parents, himself, his wife and their daughter, has since been much modernized and a glimpse over the wall reveals mere-ly an echo of the hard livelihood it once accommodated. See also box p186.

Hannah's Meadow (see Map 70) Part of the legacy of Hannah Hauxwell has been the preservation of her farmland which has been given the status of a study area for meadow grasses and wild flowers.

Purchased by Durham Wildlife Trust in 1988, the site was later designated a Site of Special Scientific Interest (see p61) qualifying by having 23 of the 47 species of rare and characteristic plants listed by English Nature (now known as Natural England). The meadows were never ploughed, being cut for hay in August and thereafter grazed by cows resulting in herb-rich meadows. Numerous kinds of birds are visitors to the meadows and no fewer than 16 kinds of dung-beetle have been identified.

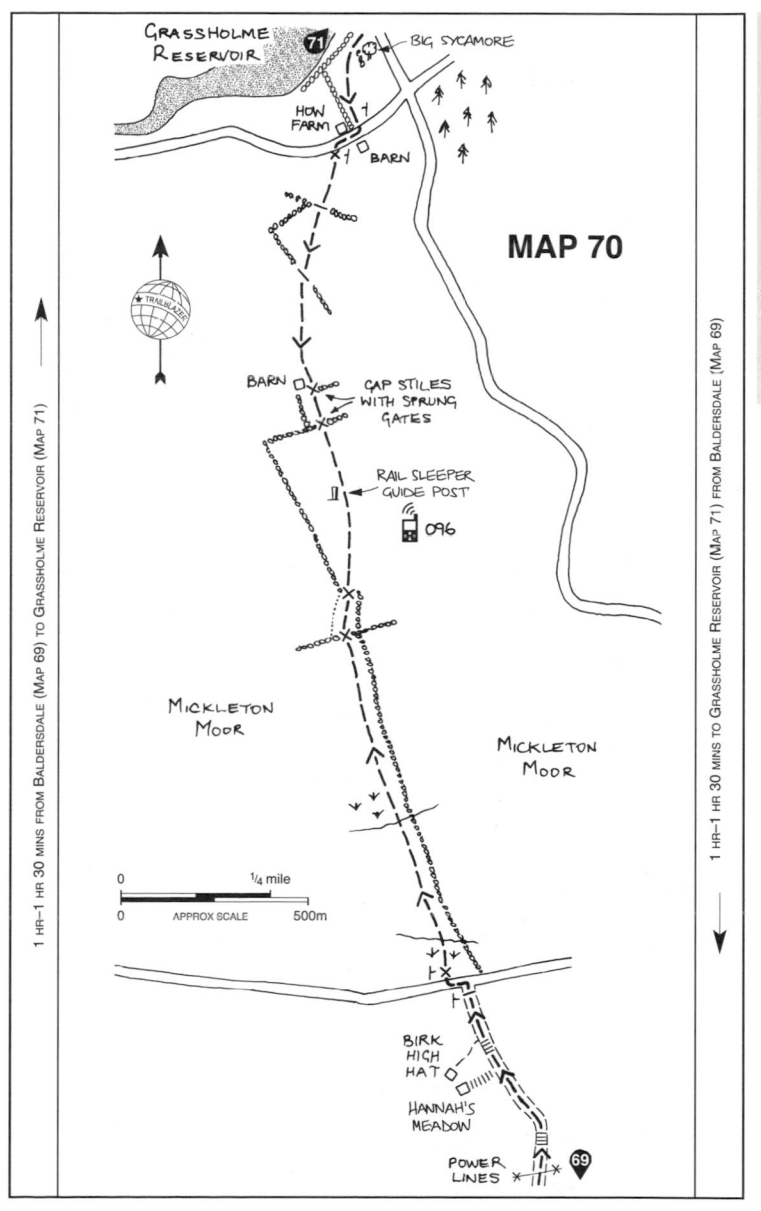

GRASSHOLME RESERVOIR

71

BIG SYCAMORE

HOW FARM

BARN

MAP 70

TRAILBLAZER

BARN

GAP STILES WITH SPRUNG GATES

RAIL SLEEPER GUIDE POST

096

MICKLETON MOOR

MICKLETON MOOR

0   ¼ mile

0   APPROX SCALE   500m

BIRK HIGH HAT

HANNAH'S MEADOW

POWER LINES

69

1 HR–1 HR 30 MINS FROM BALDERSDALE (MAP 69) TO GRASSHOLME RESERVOIR (MAP 71)

1 HR–1 HR 30 MINS TO GRASSHOLME RESERVOIR (MAP 71) FROM BALDERSDALE (MAP 69)

ROUTE GUIDE AND MAPS

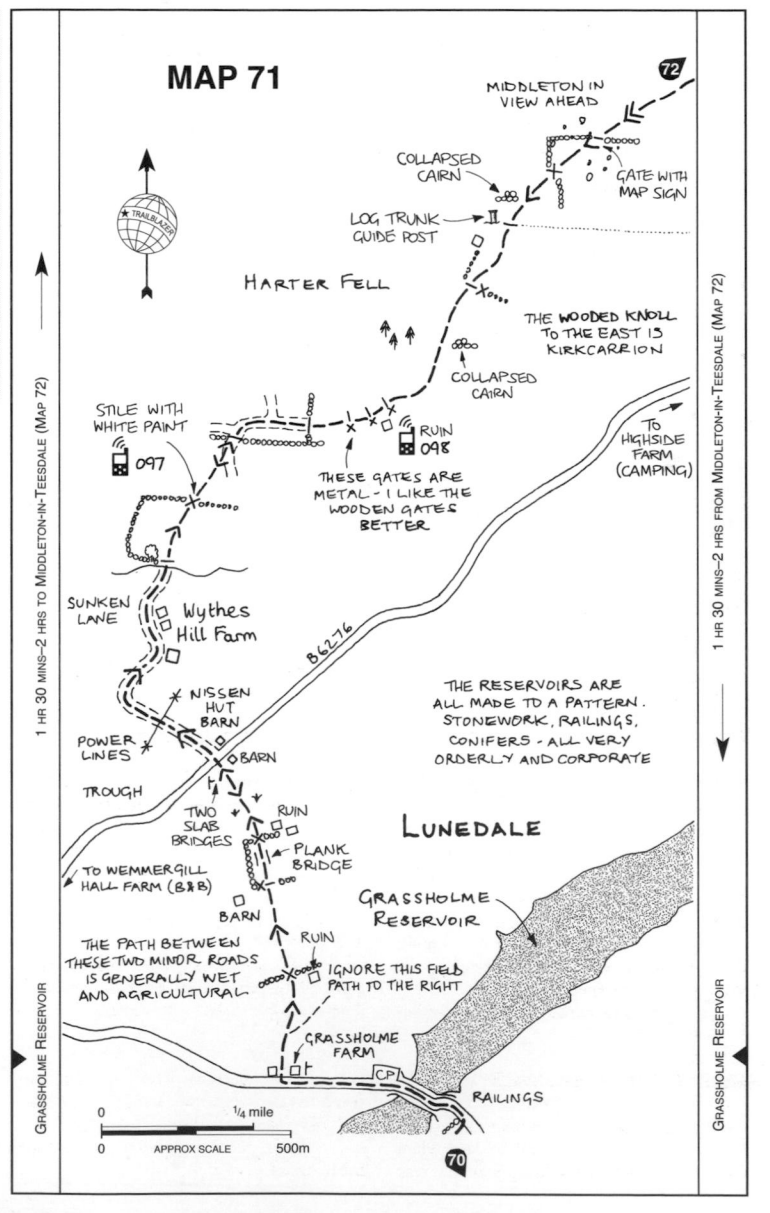

MAP 71

MIDDLETON IN VIEW AHEAD

72

COLLAPSED CAIRN

GATE WITH MAP SIGN

LOG TRUNK GUIDE POST

HARTER FELL

THE WOODED KNOLL TO THE EAST IS KIRKCARRION

COLLAPSED CAIRN

STILE WITH WHITE PAINT

097

RUIN 098

THESE GATES ARE METAL – I LIKE THE WOODEN GATES BETTER

TO HIGHSIDE FARM (CAMPING)

SUNKEN LANE

Wythes Hill Farm

B6276

NISSEN HUT BARN

POWER LINES

BARN

TROUGH

TWO SLAB BRIDGES

RUIN

PLANK BRIDGE

THE RESERVOIRS ARE ALL MADE TO A PATTERN. STONEWORK, RAILINGS, CONIFERS – ALL VERY ORDERLY AND CORPORATE

LUNEDALE

TO WEMMERGILL HALL FARM (B&B)

BARN

GRASSHOLME RESERVOIR

THE PATH BETWEEN THESE TWO MINOR ROADS IS GENERALLY WET AND AGRICULTURAL

RUIN

IGNORE THIS FIELD PATH TO THE RIGHT

GRASSHOLME FARM

CP

RAILINGS

0   ¼ mile

0   APPROX SCALE   500m

70

1 HR 30 MINS–2 HRS TO MIDDLETON-IN-TEESDALE (MAP 72)

1 HR 30 MINS–2 HRS FROM MIDDLETON-IN-TEESDALE (MAP 72)

GRASSHOLME RESERVOIR

GRASSHOLME RESERVOIR

ROUTE GUIDE AND MAPS

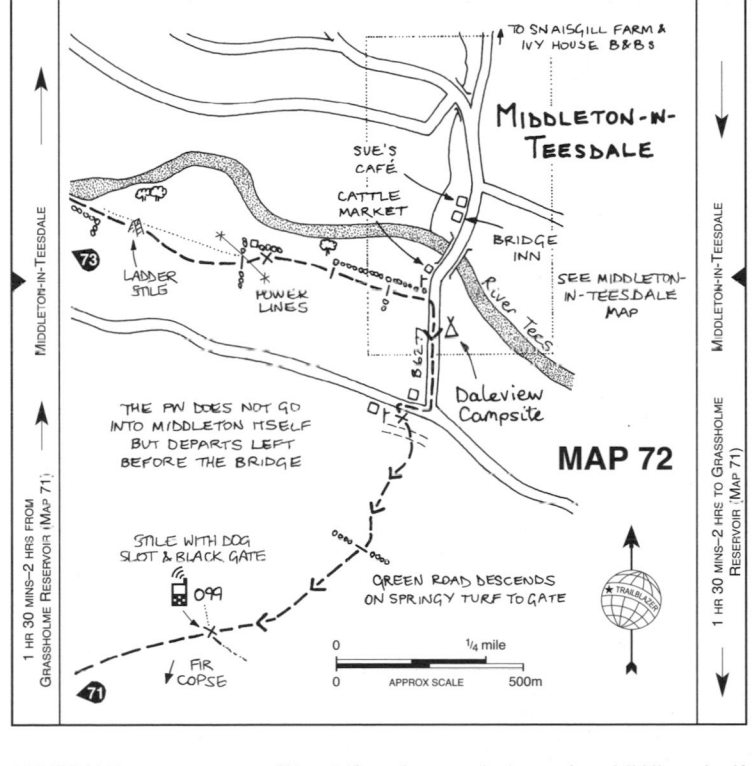

TO SNAISGILL FARM & IVY HOUSE B&Bs

MIDDLETON-IN-TEESDALE

SUE'S CAFÉ

CATTLE MARKET

BRIDGE INN

SEE MIDDLETON-IN-TEESDALE MAP

River Tees

MIDDLETON-IN-TEESDALE

MIDDLETON-IN-TEESDALE

73

LADDER STILE

POWER LINES

B6277

Daleview Campsite

MAP 72

THE PW DOES NOT GO INTO MIDDLETON ITSELF BUT DEPARTS LEFT BEFORE THE BRIDGE

1 HR 30 MINS–2 HRS FROM GRASSHOLME RESERVOIR (MAP 71)

1 HR 30 MINS–2 HRS TO GRASSHOLME RESERVOIR (MAP 71)

STILE WITH DOG SLOT & BLACK GATE

099

GREEN ROAD DESCENDS ON SPRINGY TURF TO GATE

TRAILBLAZER

FIR COPSE

0   1/4 mile

0   APPROX SCALE   500m

71

LUNEDALE   **[Map 71]**
Among the scattered homesteads of
Lunedale is *Wemmergill Hall Farm* (off
Map 71; ☎ 01833-640379, 🖳 www.wem
mergill-farm.co.uk; 1T or F/1D), 1½ miles
to the west of the trail along the B6276,
with great views over Selset Reservoir and,
at £40 (£25 single occupancy), it is among
the cheapest places for en suite B&B on the
Way. An evening meal costs £15.

Two miles (3km) in the other direction

(ie a stone's thrown from Middleton itself
by road) is the **campsite** at *Highside Farm*
(off Map 71; ☎ 01833-640135, 🖳 www
.highsidefarm.co.uk), Bow Bank. Pitching
at the small site costs £7.50 with showers
and they can do you a breakfast in the
morning if booked in advance. Open April
to September.

Alston Road Garage No 73 **bus** service
calls here if prebooked; see public transport
map and table, pp42-6 for details.

MIDDLETON-IN-TEESDALE
               [Map 72a, p176]
On the banks of the River Tees, this small
town thrived during the 19th century when
the now defunct lead-mining industry was

in its heyday. It's mostly laid out along one
street, with handsome architecture interspersed with a few quirky buildings.

See box p24 for details of the carnival
held here in July.

Services

The **tourist information centre** (☎ 01833-641001, 🖳 tic@middletonplus.myzen.co.uk), 10 Market Place, is open daily from 10am to 1pm and sells some interesting publications on the North Pennines.

For groceries try either the Co-op **supermarket** (daily 8am-10pm), or R&L Armitage **off-licence and general store**.

There is also a **pharmacy**, a **post office** and Winter's **gear shop**, which stocks most camping fuels as well as boots and general walking kit. The Barclays Bank here has a **cash machine**. Early closing day for the town is Wednesday.

Transport

The nearest **train** station is Darlington, 25 miles (40km) away. To get there take Arriva's No 95/96 **bus** to Barnard Castle and change there for the No 75/96 service to Darlington. Alternatively, for a **taxi** try the Middleton-based Alston Rd Garage (☎ 01833-640213). Alston Road also offers a bus service (No 73) to Langdon Beck and other villages in the area. See public transport map and table, pp42-6.

Where to stay

Unless they stage the next G8 summit here there is plenty of choice in town. The most convenient campsite is *Daleview Caravan Park and Camp Site* (☎ 01833-640233, 🖳 www.daleviewcaravanpark.co.uk; Mar-Oct) which you pass on your way in to town. They charge £4 per person including a shower and there's a bar which also does food (Sat and Sun 12-2pm, daily 7-9pm).

In the summer months *Kingsway Adventure Centre* (☎ 01833-640881, 🖳 www.kingswaycentre.co.uk) is full of school groups but at other times it will take individuals; it has 35 beds in bunkhouse/hostel accommodation and charges £10 bed only, or £24 full board. They also have 2T for £14 per person **B&B**; **camping** here costs £4 per person. Booking is essential.

Don't be put off by the grand appearance of *Grove Lodge* (☎ 01833-640798, 🖳 www.grovelodgeteesdale.co.uk; 2T/1D or T) just outside the town and with great views back to Kirkcarrion and Harter Fell; they

Middleton-in-Teesdale MAP 72a

Where to stay
1 Grove Lodge
2 Kingsway Adventure Centre
3 Brunswick House
4 Belvedere House
5 Daleview Caravan Park

welcome walkers as long as you don't shake yourself off in the hallway like a wet dog. En suite rooms, a cut above the rest, cost £45 single occupancy or £74 for a double/twin. There's a cottage (3 single beds) below the house for dog owners or larger groups.

They have a washing machine and drying room and can provide evening meals (from an á la carte menu with dishes costing from £6.50) or just a humble packed lunch (£3.25).

Brunswick House (☎ 01833-640393, 🖳 www.brunswickhouse.net; 2T/3D) is more central and their en suite rooms cost £58 (£37 for single occupancy). They also do as good an evening meal (at 7.30pm) as anywhere else in town and have a bar and can provide a packed lunch. Next door is ***Belvedere House*** (☎ 01833-640884, 🖳 www.thecoachhouse.net; 1T/2D all en suite) where an en suite for two sharing costs just £42 (single occupancy £25).

Where to eat

Closest to the Way, *The Bridge Inn* (☎ 01833-640283) is open for food daily 12-2.30pm and 6-9pm. However, at the time of writing, the pub was on the market so its future was uncertain. Almost next door is *The Conduit* (☎ 01833-640717, open Mon/Tue & Thur-Sat 9am-5pm, Sun 10am-5pm, to 4pm in winter, closed Wed) where you can get an all-day breakfast for around £5; they also serve lasagne, meat pies, home-made cakes and panini. Food is available as takeaway or eat in. Up the road, opposite the TIC, is a **fish and chips** shop.

MIDDLETON-IN-TEESDALE TO DUFTON   MAPS 72-83

Route overview

A thought-provoking 21 miles (**32km, 8-10hrs**) it may well be, back over the Pennines to Dufton, but if fitness, weather and daylight are all combined in a serendipitous trinity, you're in for one of the best days between Edale and Kirk Yetholm. A gradual climb with barely a thigh-burning ascent nor a knee-popping ending, the wilderness evolves steadily as you trace the River Tees close to its source. Then, as you cross the watershed, the walk draws to an end with one of the Seven Wonders of the Pennine Way.

The riverside walk out of Middleton starts off in a fairly tame, dog-on-a-lead fashion with tedious stiles and vision-hampering woodland, but as you continue upstream the spectacular effect of the river manifests itself as it cascades over unyielding dolerite sills to create the waterfalls of **Low Force** (Map 75) soon followed by the mesmerizing powerhouse of High Force.

High Force (see box p181) may be on the souvenir spoon and tea towel circuit (at least from the PW side of the river you don't have to pay a £1 to see it), but beyond the wild fell country of the North Pennines takes the path to a new dimension. Soon you cross the Tees at **Cronkley Bridge** (Map 77) where your day can end among the scattered, whitewashed communities of **Forest-in-Teesdale** or **Langdon Beck**. But who can resist recrossing the Tees and heading into the wilds of Upper Teesdale as it takes on the character of an upland Scottish burn. As the valley envelopes you, at times you'll find yourself squeezed almost into the river itself as a trio of ankle-twisting rockfalls edge you awkwardly towards the running waters.

With those hurdles behind you, round a corner and you come face-to-face with the splendidly named **Cauldron Snout** (Map 78) churning down a series of jumbled rocks. Scrambling up alongside, the roar of the foaming torrent drowns out all other sounds. Now beneath the dam wall of **Cow Green Reservoir** which feeds the Snout, the wilderness is temporarily muted as you scoot along the access road to the isolated farmstead of **Birkdale** (Map 79; see box p186). But once through the farmyard you're out on the open moors again,

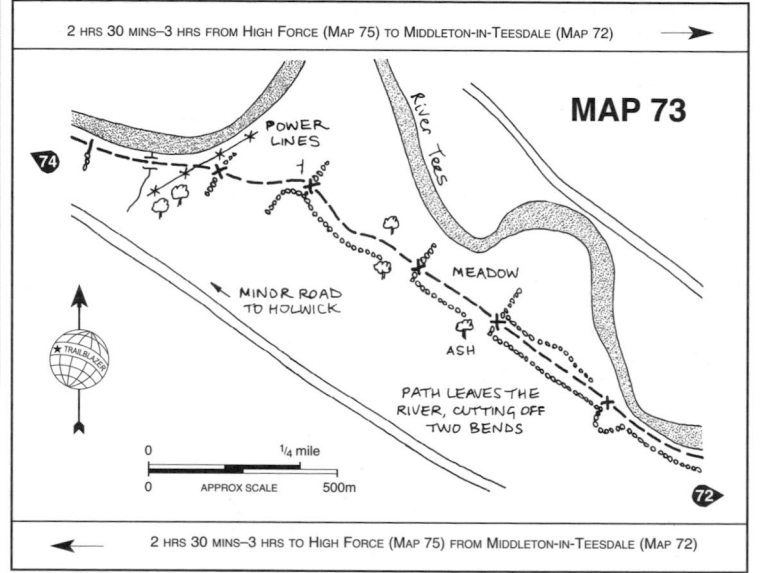

MAP 73

POWER LINES

River Tees

74

MINOR ROAD TO HOLWICK

TRAILBLAZER

MEADOW

ASH

PATH LEAVES THE RIVER, CUTTING OFF TWO BENDS

0   ¼ mile

0   APPROX SCALE   500m

72

crossing **Grain Beck** and facing the only mildly noteworthy climb of the day to a crest alongside Rasp Hill and its long abandoned mine workings.

Ahead of you **Maize Beck** (Maps 79 & 80) and its low-shelved cascades (waterfalls) glisten in the late afternoon sun and after a few soggy placements you join the stream and reach the **footbridge** raised tellingly high above the beck (GPS waypoint 105/505, see p259; not on all maps and *not* the one referred to on the wooden signs at Cow Green and below High Cup Nick). Before the **new bridge** the Pennine Way crossed the stream hereabouts on stepping stones to follow the direct and well-marked path on the south side which leads straight to the rim of High Cup. For details on the now obsolete 'flood route' which stays north of the beck see p186. Whichever way you approach it (the southern route being far more dramatic), it's no exaggeration to proclaim that the colossal glacier-carved abyss of **High Cup** (Map 81) is a spectacular climax to a brilliant day. If the wind gusting up the valley is not too bad, sit back a while and take it all in; the remaining four miles along miners' tracks are straightforward, following the north rim of the valley with the silvery thread of High Cup Gill far below. It all ends at the tidy village of **Dufton** (Map 83), a quintessential English hamlet with the inviting Stag Inn facing the hostel across the village green; one of the more delightful places to end a Pennine day.

Route-finding trouble spots

With clear paths, farms tracks as well as water courses large and small running alongside you throughout this stage, it's hard to lose track of the path, even in

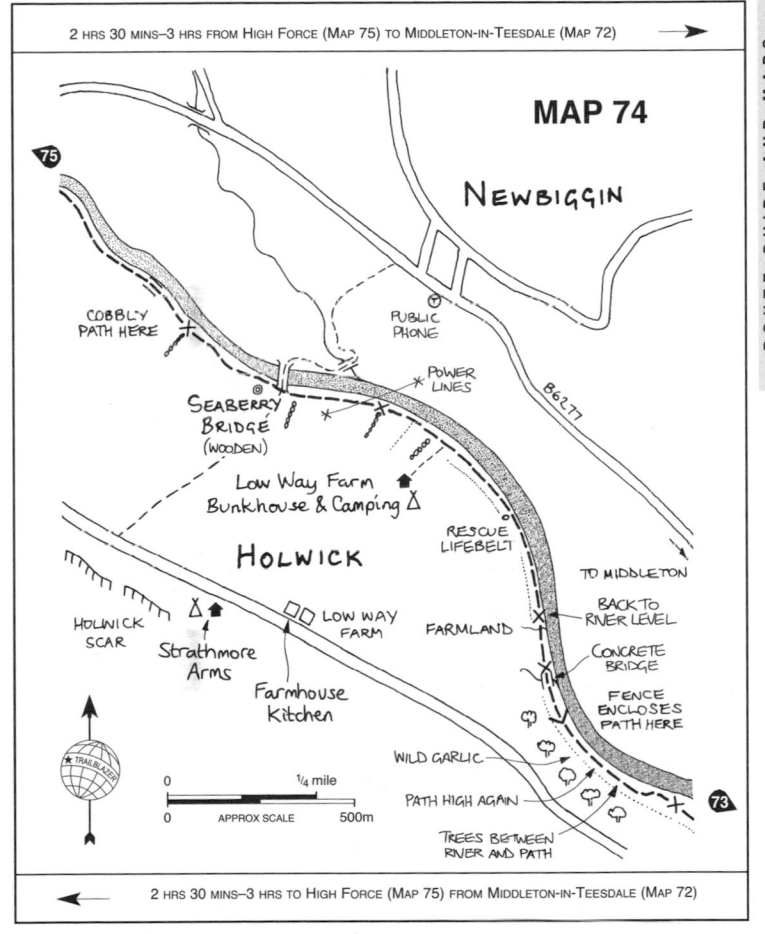

2 HRS 30 MINS–3 HRS FROM HIGH FORCE (MAP 75) TO MIDDLETON-IN-TEESDALE (MAP 72) →

MAP 74

NEWBIGGIN

COBBLY PATH HERE

PUBLIC PHONE

POWER LINES

B6277

SEABERRY BRIDGE (WOODEN)

Low Way Farm Bunkhouse & Camping △

RESCUE LIFEBELT

HOLWICK

TO MIDDLETON

HOLWICK SCAR

△ Strathmore Arms

LOW WAY FARM

FARMLAND

BACK TO RIVER LEVEL

CONCRETE BRIDGE

Farmhouse Kitchen

FENCE ENCLOSES PATH HERE

WILD GARLIC

PATH HIGH AGAIN

TREES BETWEEN RIVER AND PATH

73

0   1/4 mile
0   APPROX SCALE   500m

2 HRS 30 MINS–3 HRS TO HIGH FORCE (MAP 75) FROM MIDDLETON-IN-TEESDALE (MAP 72)

poor visibility. The exception would be going against the grain and taking the old 'flood escape route' via Maize Beck Gorge (see p186) mentioned above. In misty or very wet conditions it's just not worth it.

HOLWICK   **[Map 74]**
Low Way Farm (☎ 01833-640506) offers basic **camping** for £3, **bunkhouse** accommodation sleeping 28 in two barns for £6.50, and breakfast (£5.35) at the *Farmhouse Kitchen* next door. Booking in advance is recommended. There is a sign from the trail

and the barns are only about 200 metres off the route.

Alston Road Garage's No 73 **bus** service will call here if prebooked; see public transport map and table, pp42-6.

Just over half a mile from the Way is the *Strathmore Arms* (☎ 01833-640362, 🖳

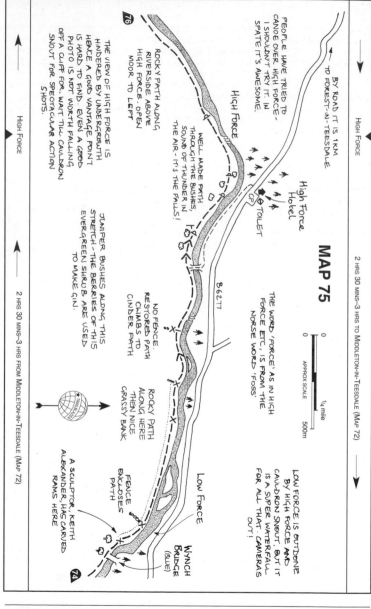

MAP 75

2 HRS 30 MINS–3 HRS TO MIDDLETON-IN-TEESDALE (MAP 72)

2 HRS 30 MINS–3 HRS FROM MIDDLETON-IN-TEESDALE (MAP 72)

HIGH FORCE

HIGH FORCE

BY ROAD IT IS 1KM TO FOREST-IN-TEESDALE

PEOPLE HAVE TRIED TO CANOE OVER HIGH FORCE – I SHOULDN'T TRY IT. IN SPATE IT'S AWESOME.

76

ROCKY PATH ALONG RIVERSIDE ABOVE HIGH FORCE. OPEN MOOR TO LEFT.

THE VIEW OF HIGH FORCE IS HINDERED BY UNDERGROWTH HENCE A GOOD VANTAGE POINT IS HARD TO FIND. EVEN A GOOD PHOTO IS NOT WORTH FALLING OFF A CLIFF FOR. WAIT TILL CAULDRON SNOUT FOR SPECTACULAR ACTION SHOTS.

HIGH FORCE

High Force Hotel

CP

TOILET

WELL MADE PATH THROUGH THE BUSHES, SOUND OF THUNDER IN THE AIR – IT'S THE FALLS!

B6277

THE WORD 'FORCE' AS IN HIGH FORCE ETC. IS FROM THE NORSE WORD 'FOSS'.

LOW FORCE IS OUTDONE BY HIGH FORCE AND CAULDRON SNOUT, BUT IT IS A SUPER WATERFALL FOR ALL THAT. CAMERAS OUT!

0   APPROX SCALE   ¼ mile

0   500m

NO FENCE. RESTORED PATH CLIMBS TO CINDER PATH

JUNIPER BUSHES ALONG THIS STRETCH – THE BERRIES OF THIS EVERGREEN SHRUB ARE USED TO MAKE GIN.

ROCKY PATH ALONG HERE THEN NICE GRASSY BANK

LOW FORCE

FENCE ENCLOSES PATH

A SCULPTOR, KEITH ALEXANDER, HAS CARVED RAMS HERE

TRUE NORTH

WYNCH BRIDGE (BLUE)

74

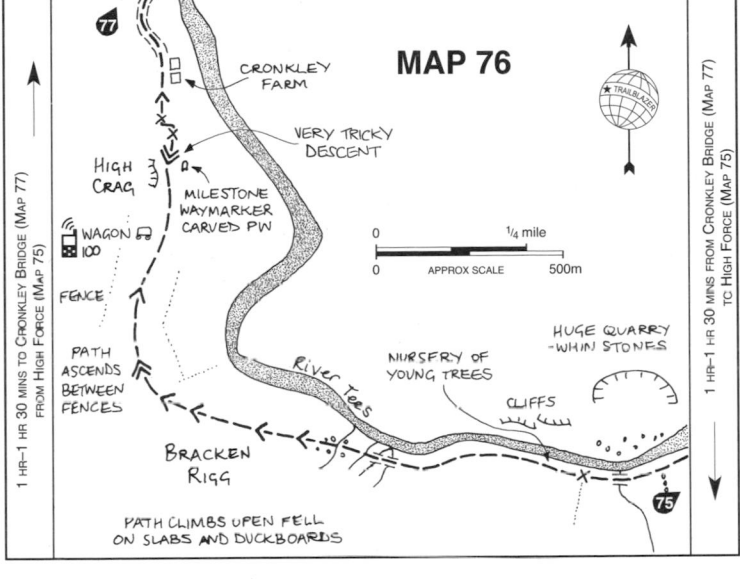

MAP 76

CRONKLEY FARM

VERY TRICKY DESCENT

HIGH CRAG

MILESTONE WAYMARKER CARVED PW

WAGON 100

FENCE

PATH ASCENDS BETWEEN FENCES

HUGE QUARRY - WHIN STONES

NURSERY OF YOUNG TREES

River Tees

CLIFFS

BRACKEN RIGG

PATH CLIMBS OPEN FELL ON SLABS AND DUCKBOARDS

★ TRAILBLAZER

0   ¼ mile

0   500m
APPROX SCALE

Left margin: 1 HR–1 HR 30 MINS TO CRONKLEY BRIDGE (MAP 77) FROM HIGH FORCE (MAP 75)

Right margin: 1 HR–1 HR 30 MINS FROM CRONKLEY BRIDGE (MAP 77) TC HIGH FORCE (MAP 75)

www.strathmorearms.co.uk; 2D/1T en suite) a pub with rooms from £50 (single occupancy costs £40). **Campers** can use the nearby field free of charge. Food (bar food and specials) is served Wed-Sat 12-3pm and 6-9pm; in winter 6-9pm only. The pub itself closes during the day except at the weekends.

❑ **High Force**   **[See Map 75]**

High Force is so big it has to claim some distinction over others. The highest? The biggest? These seem to belong elsewhere so what they say is it's the highest unbroken fall of water in England. The drop is 21 metres (70ft). It's certainly impressive, especially after rain when the water appears the colour of tea, tinged with the peat from the moors.

WA Poucher, the celebrated photographer and writer of a series of guides during the 1960s and '70s, said that it is a difficult subject to photograph well, facing north-east, hence having the wrong light conditions for effective photography. Its other problem, at least from the Pennine Way side of the river, is access for a good view. There are places where you can scramble through the undergrowth and cling on to the cliff edge but few where you can wield the camera effectively.

People have done some strange things here. Some have gone off the top, ending their lives in the torrent. Two boaters were stopped at the last minute from attempting to kayak off the top and a visitor from abroad slipped on the flat shelf at the lip and though saving himself, catapulted the infant on his back over the edge to its doom. There is an odd fascination about raging water which seems to compel some people to get just that little bit too close.

ROUTE GUIDE AND MAPS

HIGH FORCE [Map 75, p180]

High Force Hotel (☎ 01833-622222, 🖳 www.highforcehotel.com; 2S/1T/3D, all en suite) charges £35 for a single and £75 for a twin or double. Bar meals are served daily 12-2.30pm & Mon-Sat 7-8.45pm in the summer, in the winter daily at lunch but Wed-Sat only in the evening. They also have their own ales though they are no longer brewed on the premises.

FOREST-IN-TEESDALE [off Map 77]

On reaching Cronkley Bridge the nearest place with accommodation is Forest-in-Teesdale, a scattered collection of houses along the B6277 with a **post office/shop** on the south side of the village.

Alston Road Garage's No 73 **bus** service extends here if prebooked; see public transport map and table, pp42-6.

The Dale (☎ 01833-622303; 1D or T/1F) is one of those stalwarts among Pennine Way B&Bs. Mrs Bonnett has catered for walkers for many years and knows how to please them with massive helpings of good food, comfortable beds and a coal fire to sit by. Mr Bonnett used to be the security guard at the High Force waterfall and has some tales to tell. B&B costs £20 per person and an evening meal £11 but they will take you to the pub if you prefer. They will also do a packed lunch for £4; all in all outstanding value for money. You can find them by first locating the school then turning right at the top of the lane.

LANGDON BECK [Map 77]

Langdon Beck Youth Hostel (☎ 01833-622228, bookings ☎ 0870-770 5910, 🖳 langdonbeck@yha.org.uk; March-Nov) will be the chosen destination for many walkers, but note that the 31-bed hostel gets booked up, particularly in the summer months, with groups doing their sustainable living courses for young people; walkers who booked weeks ahead will be rewarded by their forethought. Adults are charged £12, under 18s £9, and evening meals are available at 7pm.

Half a mile north of the youth hostel is *Langdon Beck Hotel* (☎ 01833-622267, 🖳 www.langdonbeckhotel.com; 2S/2D/3T). Two of the twin rooms are suite (£70 for two sharing), the rest (standard rooms) have a shared bathroom and are £65; the singles cost £35.

The pub has a great evening meal menu served daily 7-9pm including a 9oz Teesdale sirloin steak with a plateload of trimmings for £10.50 as well as a few veggie options for around £7. They also have specials such as shepherd's pie and steak pie. Food is available Mon-Sat 12-2.30pm (to 2pm in winter) and Sun 12-3pm (to 2.30pm in winter) when a Sunday lunch is also on the menu.

Alston Road Garages No 73 **bus** runs from Langdon Beck to Middleton-in-Teesdale (see public transport map and table, pp42-6).

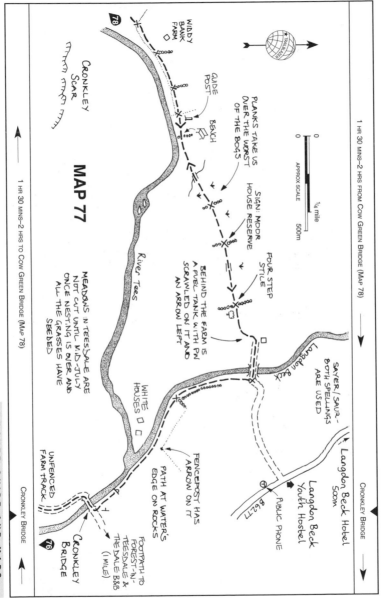

78

WIDDY
BANK
FARM

CRONKLEY
SCAR

GUIDE
POST

PLANKS TAKE US
OVER THE WORST
OF THE BOGS

BENCH

SIGN: MOOR
HOUSE RESERVE

MAP 77

0
APPROX SCALE

¼ mile

0   500m

River Tees

FOUR
STEP
STILE

BEHIND THE FARM IS
A FUEL TANK WITH PW
SCRAWLED ON IT AND
AN ARROW LEFT

SAYER/SAUR-
BOTH SPELLINGS
ARE USED

Langdon Beck

Langdon Beck Hotel
500m

Langdon Beck
Youth Hostel

PUBLIC PHONE

B6277

WHITE
HOUSES

MEADOWS N TEESDALE ARE
NOT CUT UNTIL MID-JULY
ONCE NESTING IS OVER AND
ALL THE GRASSES HAVE
SEEDED

FENCEPOST HAS
ARROW ON IT

PATH AT WATER'S
EDGE ON ROCKS

FOOTPATH TO
FOREST-IN-
TEESDALE &
THE DALE B&B
(1 MILE)

UNFENCED
FARM TRACK

CRONKLEY
BRIDGE

76

Map 77, Cronkley Scar 183

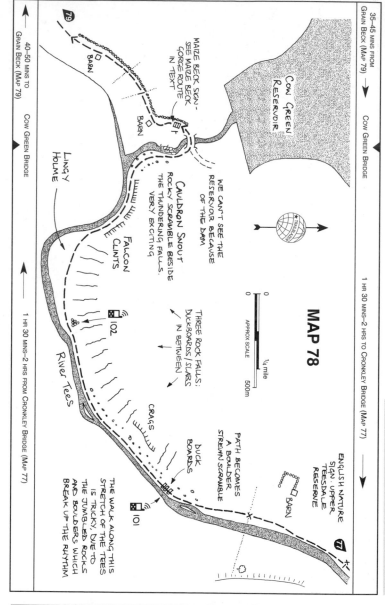

MAP 78

35-45 MINS FROM
GRAIN BECK (MAP 79) →

40-50 MINS TO
GRAIN BECK (MAP 79) →

COW GREEN BRIDGE

COW GREEN BRIDGE

1 HR 30 MINS-2 HRS TO CRONKLEY BRIDGE (MAP 77) →

1 HR 30 MINS-2 HRS FROM CRONKLEY BRIDGE (MAP 77) →

COW GREEN RESERVOIR

79

BARN

MAIZE BECK SIGN -
SEE MAIZE BECK
GORGE ROUTE
IN TEXT

BARN

WE CAN'T SEE THE
RESERVOIR BECAUSE
OF THE DAM

CAULDRON SNOUT
ROCKY SCRAMBLE BESIDE
THE THUNDERING FALLS.
VERY EXCITING

LINGY
HOLME

FALCON
CLINTS

THREE ROCK FALLS;
DUCKBOARDS / SLABS
IN BETWEEN

102

River Tees

CRAGS

DUCK
BOARDS

PATH BECOMES
A BOULDER
STREWN SCRAMBLE

BARN

ENGLISH NATURE
SIGN - UPPER
TEESDALE
RESERVE

77

101

THE WALK ALONG THIS
STRETCH OF THE TEES
IS TRICKY, DUE TO
THE JUMBLED ROCKS
AND BOULDERS WHICH
BREAK UP THE RHYTHM

0
¼ mile
APPROX SCALE
500m

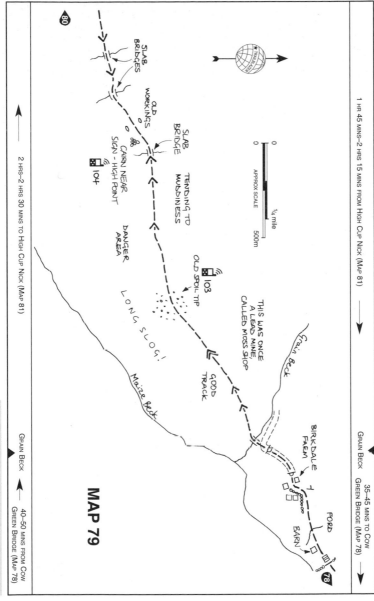

MAP 79

SLAB
BRIDGES

OLD
WORKINGS

SLAB
BRIDGE

CAIRN NEAR
SIGN - HIGH POINT

104

TENDING TO
MUDDINESS

103
OLD SPOIL TIP

DANGER
AREA

THIS WAS ONCE
A LEAD MINE,
CALLED MOSS SHOP

Grain Beck

LONG SLOG!

Maize Beck

GOOD
TRACK

BIRKDALE
FARM

FORD

BARN

APPROX SCALE

0
¼ mile
500m

0

GRAIN BECK   40–50 MINS FROM COW
GREEN BRIDGE (MAP 78)

ROUTE GUIDE AND MAPS

Map 79, Maize Beck 185

❑ Too Long a Winter

Even though these days a sealed road leads to it, walking past the front of Birkdale Farm (Map 79) you can't but help but be struck by the homestead's strikingly remote location. Said to be the highest occupied farmhouse in England, it makes Emily Bronte's Withins Height (see p103) look like a shed at the back of the garden.

In the 1970s the farmer whose family had long rented the property from Lord Barnard's extensive Raby Estate were the subject of a TV documentary. The show depicted three groups of local characters: Brian and Mary Bainbridge farming at Birkdale, a brief glimpse of a chauffeur-driven Mrs Field from Middleton, a preposterous caricature cut out of an Agatha Christie novel, and the soon-to-become famous Hannah Hauxwell (see box p172).

Brian Bainbridge who helped dig out the Cow Green Reservoir behind Cauldron Snout was followed as he and his wife returned to the empty homestead after several years' absence to give the place another go. He was filmed from a circling helicopter rounding sheep (or perhaps chasing them as they fled from the chopper) and staggering around the snowbound fells, staff in hand, hauling strays out of snow drifts. A decade earlier the disastrous winter of 1963 wiped out the then young farmer's entire flock and led him to eventually abandon Birkdale. He described that tragic year as just 'too long a winter' for the sheep and so gave the programme its title.

Among other characters, a smiling, ruddy-faced fellow herder George Haw, was asked about the attraction of life on the moors. 'Well I don't know, it's just a living that's all... I can't say there's any attraction to it, like'. Mary Bainbridge is mildly more upbeat to the same query 'I love the hills, the sheep, the loneliness'.

Too Long a Winter also set the 46-year-old daleswoman Hannah Hauxwell on her path to fame. Her story and presence are no less moving. Like a character out of a children's fairy tale, she is seen dragging her prize bull to market on a sleety winter's day; the outcome set to meet her financial needs for the coming year. Resigned but not necessarily devoted to a solitary life, she observes the wrong husband would not be worth having and is filmed at Mrs Field's annual harvest do tapping her feet in her giant-lapelled overcoat while all around her dance gaily. Like the Bainbridges (but not at all like the batty Mrs Field) Hauxwell's ingenuous innocence and ready acceptance of life's hardships set her apart and led to a staggering response from the viewing public; letters and food parcels came in from all over the country. Over the next twenty years other TV shows and books followed.

On her husband's death in 2006 Mary Bainbridge said 'He always thought the TV programme was a bit of a farce. Neither he nor I ever met Miss Hauxwell. I thought she was rather exploited.'

The video of Too Long a Winter is easily found on Amazon or eBay for a few pounds, along with what might be called the Hannah Hauxwell 'boxed set'. Tracing this prodigious output of 'Hannobilia' by director/producer Brian Cockcroft, ending in Hannah USA, you can't help feeling Mary Bainbridge may have had a point.

The Maize Beck Gorge route   [See Maps 80 and 81]

Wooden warning signs below Cow Green dam wall and at the walled enclosure above Dufton (see Maps 78 and 82) giving the grid ref '749270' refer to an **old footbridge** (GPS waypoint 509, see p259) once used to cross upper Maize Beck in times of flood when the former stepping stone route (now also bridged; GPS waypoint 105/505, see p259) was unsafe.

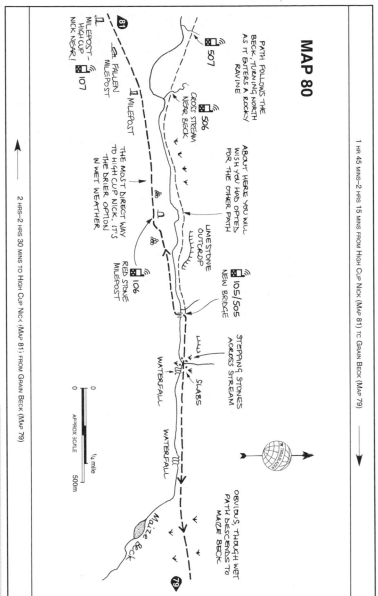

MAP 80

1 HR 45 MINS–2 HRS 15 MINS FROM HIGH CUP NICK (MAP 81) TO GRAIN BECK (MAP 79)

2 HRS–2 HRS 30 MINS TO HIGH CUP NICK (MAP 81) FROM GRAIN BECK (MAP 79)

PATH FOLLOWS THE
BECK, TURNING NORTH
AS IT ENTERS A ROCKY
RAVINE

507

506 CROSS STREAM
NEAR BECK

81

↿ MILEPOST

↿ FALLEN
MILEPOST

MILEPOST –
HIGH CUP
NICK NEAR!

107

ABOUT HERE YOU WILL
WISH YOU HAD OPTED
FOR THE OTHER PATH

THE MOST DIRECT WAY
TO HIGH CUP NICK. IT'S
THE DRIER OPTION
IN WET WEATHER.

LIMESTONE
OUTCROP

106 RED STONE
MILEPOST

105/505 NEW BRIDGE

STEPPING STONES
ACROSS STREAM

SLABS

WATERFALL

WATERFALL

OBVIOUS, THOUGH WET
PATH DESCENDS TO
MAIZE BECK

Maize Beck

79

APPROX SCALE
0   0
¼ mile   500m

With the newer bridge these signs are now obsolete and confusing, an irony compounded by the fact that were Maize Beck really in spate, this 'escape route' via the old footbridge would be so soggy you might as well take your chances on the stepping stones submerged in the torrent!

The regular southern route is preferable in all ways but to some the Gorge route will be a curiosity. Just don't expect a well-trodden track. The first two waypoints on the way identify a couple of stream crossings, from the second one (GPS waypoint 507, see p259) a thin trail leads directly to the crags, a couple of hundred metres downstream of the old bridge. Although you can usually easily ford the stream here, you'll have to walk up the narrowing gorge to find the bridge (and a signboard nearby) spanning an unusually tiered limestone chasm below. From the bridge milestones and the odd cairn lead southwest across an eroded limestone pavement to High Cup Nick (see box below).

❏ High Cup

Northbound walkers come upon the massive glaciated valley of High Cup (also known as High Cup Nick) quite suddenly and are always surprised by this incredible sight. It's no coincidence that it features on the cover of this edition as well as many other Pennine Way guidebooks. Suddenly the land drops away in front of you in a textbook U-shaped demonstration of the aftermath of glacial erosion. The sides are rimmed with strata of hard rock, basalt or dolerite, interspersed with jumbled scree and twinkling rivulets and from the head of the valley Maize Beck trickles down when it's not getting blown back in your face.

Strangely enough, none of the people who has seen fit to write about the Pennine Way has made much of it until recently. The curmudgeonly Wainwright hardly mentions it, others gloss over it and even JHB Peel in his invaluable book, *Along the Pennine Way*, loses the plot when it comes to describing High Cup Nick.

Perhaps words are not needed as even the most unimaginative are impressed by the sight. On a recent visit we met a guy who visited the valley head viewpoint regularly to paint it, photograph it and hoped one day to have his ashes scattered there.

DUFTON [Map 83, p191]

This quiet and attractive little village is a lovely place to stop after a great day's walking, whichever direction you're taking. Sadly the village shop is no more but there is an agricultural show here in August; see box p24 for details.

The Stag Inn (☎ 01768-351608, 🖳 www.thestagdufton.co.uk) has a nicely appointed self-catering cottage (1T/1D) next door but only for three nights' minimum (from £180); it is known for its substantial bar meals in the £8 range served Tue-Sun 12 noon to 2pm and daily 6.00 to 8.45pm (closed on Mondays Jan to March).

B&B for anything from one night or more is available a few doors along at *Hall Croft* (☎ 01768-352902, 🖳 r.walker@ leaseholdpartnerships.co.uk; 1T or D/2D) where two people sharing pay £50 and a single is £30; two of the rooms are en suite and the other has a private bathroom.

Coney Garth (☎ 01768-352582, 🖳 www.coneygarth.co.uk; 1T/1D or F) offers a warm welcome and costs £25 per person in the twin room and £30 for the double/ family room and has drying facilities on the Aga. Both rooms are en suite. They will do 'anything requested', including making up a tasty packed lunch. If you prefer you can opt for self-catering.

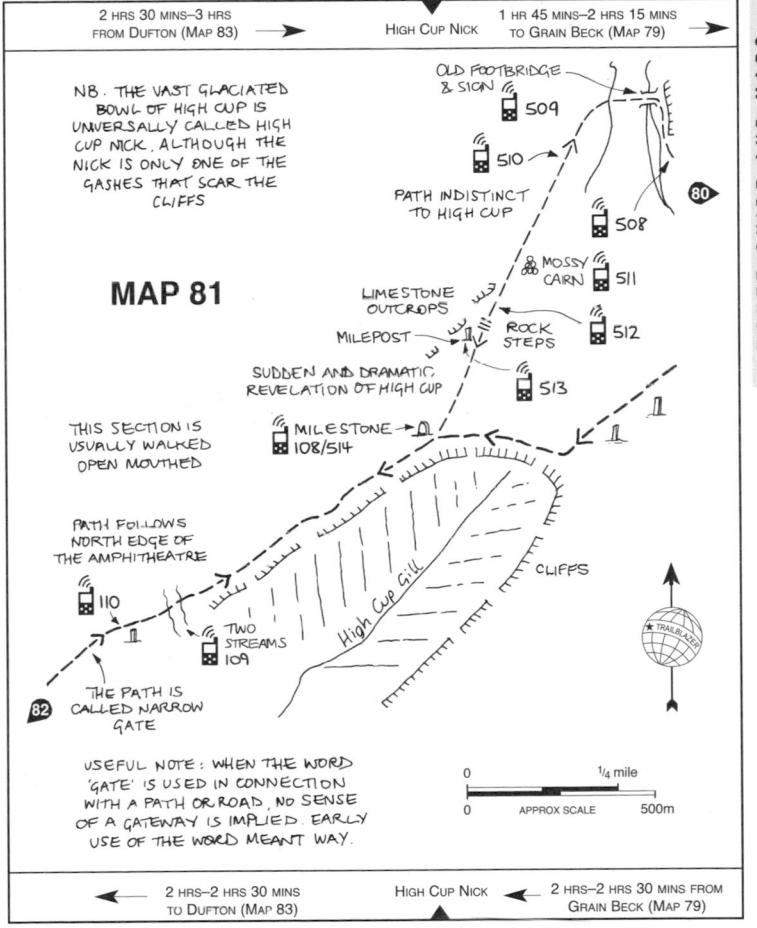

OLD FOOTBRIDGE & SIGN 509

NB. THE VAST GLACIATED BOWL OF HIGH CUP IS UNIVERSALLY CALLED HIGH CUP NICK, ALTHOUGH THE NICK IS ONLY ONE OF THE GASHES THAT SCAR THE CLIFFS

510

80

PATH INDISTINCT TO HIGH CUP   508

MOSSY CAIRN 511

MAP 81

LIMESTONE OUTCROPS

MILEPOST   ROCK STEPS 512

SUDDEN AND DRAMATIC REVELATION OF HIGH CUP 513

THIS SECTION IS USUALLY WALKED OPEN MOUTHED

MILESTONE 108/514

PATH FOLLOWS NORTH EDGE OF THE AMPHITHEATRE

CLIFFS

110

High Cup Gill

TWO STREAMS 109

82

THE PATH IS CALLED NARROW GATE

USEFUL NOTE: WHEN THE WORD 'GATE' IS USED IN CONNECTION WITH A PATH OR ROAD, NO SENSE OF A GATEWAY IS IMPLIED. EARLY USE OF THE WORD MEANT WAY.

0   1/4 mile
0   APPROX SCALE   500m

TRAILBLAZER

Dufton Youth Hostel (☎ 01629-592708, bookings ☎ 0870-770 5800, 🖳 dufton@yha.org.uk; mid-March to Oct) opposite the pub is one of the best on the Way; an evening meal is served at 7pm. Accommodation in the 34-bed hostel costs £14 for adults and £10 for under 18s.

Camping at *Grandie Caravan Park* (☎ 01768-351573) costs £5 per person and it's open March to January. They have

space for up to 20 tents. **Brow Farm** (☎ 01768-352865, 🖳 www.browfarm.com; 1S/1T/2D all en suite) offers en suite comfortable B&B for £29 per person. Also at this end of the village is **Ghyll View** (☎ 01768-351855; 1S/2T), a friendly place open Mar-Oct only, with B&B from £23 per person for non en suite rooms; guests have their own sitting room and dining room. (cont'd on p192)

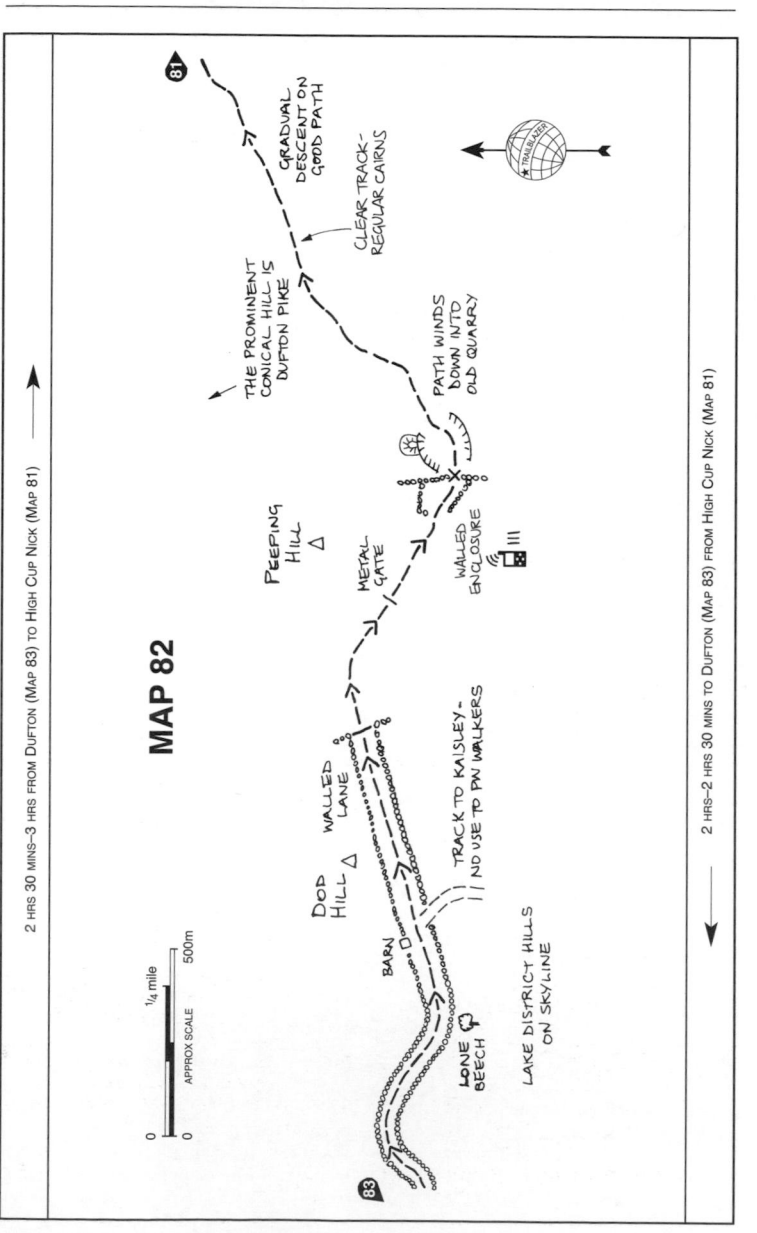

2 HRS 30 MINS–3 HRS FROM DUFTON (MAP 83) TO HIGH CUP NICK (MAP 81)

MAP 82

GRADUAL DESCENT ON GOOD PATH

CLEAR TRACK– REGULAR CAIRNS

THE PROMINENT CONICAL HILL IS DUFTON PIKE

PATH WINDS DOWN INTO OLD QUARRY

PEEPING HILL △

METAL GATE

WALLED ENCLOSURE

DOD HILL △

WALLED LANE

TRACK TO KAISLEY– NO USE TO PW WALKERS

BARN

LONE BEECH

LAKE DISTRICT HILLS ON SKYLINE

¼ mile
APPROX SCALE
0   500m

2 HRS–2 HRS 30 MINS TO DUFTON (MAP 83) FROM HIGH CUP NICK (MAP 81)

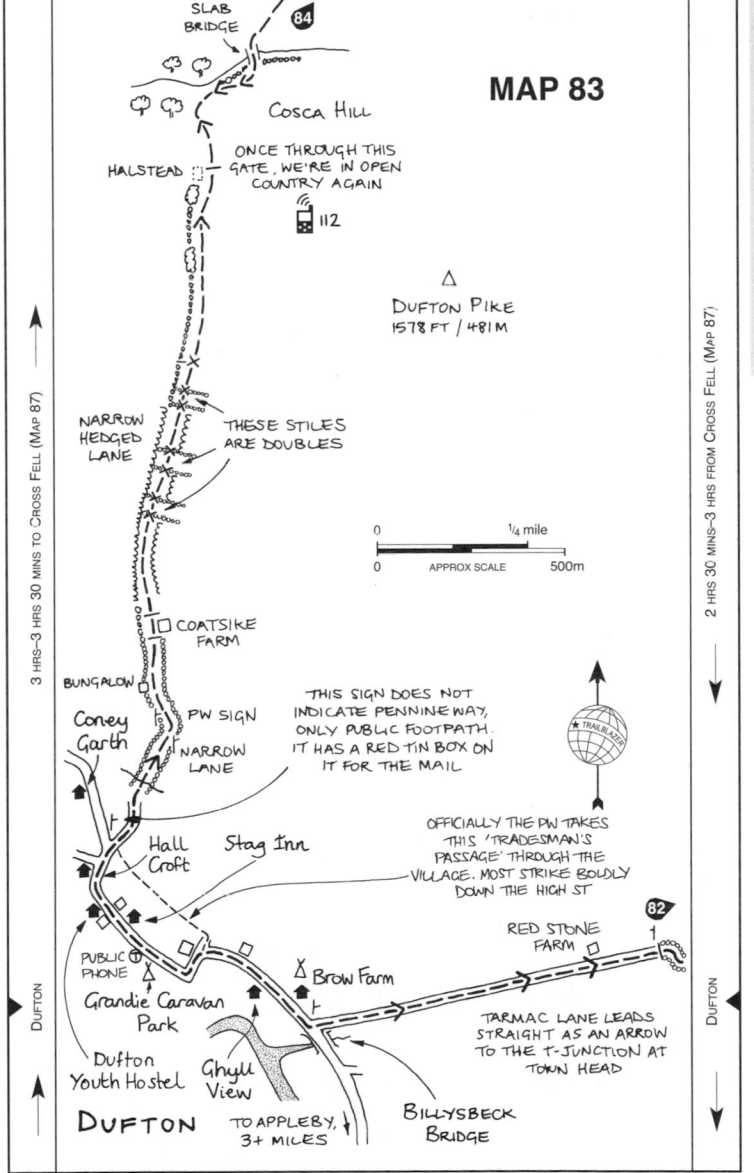

SLAB
BRIDGE

84

MAP 83

Cosca Hill

ONCE THROUGH THIS
GATE, WE'RE IN OPEN
COUNTRY AGAIN

HALSTEAD

112

△
DUFTON PIKE
1578 FT / 481 M

3 HRS–3 HRS 30 MINS TO CROSS FELL (MAP 87)

2 HRS 30 MINS–3 HRS FROM CROSS FELL (MAP 87)

NARROW
HEDGED
LANE

THESE STILES
ARE DOUBLES

0   ¼ mile

0   500m
APPROX SCALE

COATSIKE
FARM

BUNGALOW

THIS SIGN DOES NOT
INDICATE PENNINE WAY,
ONLY PUBLIC FOOTPATH.
IT HAS A RED TIN BOX ON
IT FOR THE MAIL

Coney
Garth

PW SIGN

NARROW
LANE

★ TRAILBLAZER

OFFICIALLY THE PW TAKES
THIS 'TRADESMAN'S
PASSAGE' THROUGH THE
VILLAGE. MOST STRIKE BOLDLY
DOWN THE HIGH ST

Hall
Croft

Stag Inn

82

RED STONE
FARM

PUBLIC
PHONE

△ Brow Farm

DUFTON

Grandie Caravan
Park

Dufton
Youth Hostel

Ghyll
View

TARMAC LANE LEADS
STRAIGHT AS AN ARROW
TO THE T-JUNCTION AT
TOWN HEAD

DUFTON

DUFTON

DUFTON

TO APPLEBY,
3+ MILES

BILLYSBECK
BRIDGE

(cont'd from p189) Robinson's operate a limited **bus** service (see public transport map and table, pp42-6) to Penrith and Appleby, the latter only three miles along the road (despite what the road sign near the campsite says).

Appleby is an attractive country town on the Carlisle–Leeds railway with banks, several pubs and bakery or two, all settled around a bend in the River Eden. If you're due for a day off, you could a lot worse than scheduling it around Dufton and Appleby.

DUFTON TO ALSTON   MAPS 83-94

Route overview

It won't have escaped your notice that the **21 miles (32km, 9-10hrs)** between Dufton to Alston include the climb over Cross Fell. At 893m (2930ft) it is the Pennine Way's highest point and, excluding the peaks in the immediate vicinity and The Cheviot (which is not directly on the Way), Cross Fell stands up by quite a margin too. Altogether this stage involves nearly 1100m of ascent. However, notwithstanding the possibility of losing the route in **bad visibility** (see below), it will most likely be the prolonged trudge **down the infamous 'Corpse Road' miners' track** on the far side of Cross Fell to Garrigill that will do you in, starting with pulverizing the soles of your feet.

You should also be acquainted with the fact that along the sixteen miles to Garrigill the only places for refreshment are mountain streams and the only shelter are rabbit-filled sink holes and **Greg's Hut** (see box p196) so go well prepared. Though by now your Pennine route-finding instincts should be well honed, in anything less than perfect weather, this is a section to take seriously. Nobody should set off without adequate protective clothing, supplies and at the very least, a compass. The GPS waypoints (see pp256-62) on this section are particularly prolific for a reason. To be caught out in a rain or even hailstorm in July or August is not at all unlikely and many a walker has struggled in to Greg's Hut in desperate straits, as the visitor's book testifies.

On the bright side, once you set your mind to it, the long haul up to the summit of Cross Fell is actually not so bad. It begins gently enough along farm lanes and byways skirting around **Dufton Fell** before a comparatively short and sharp haul up to **Knock Fell** (Map 85). Now at less than 100m below Cross Fell, the lion's share of the climbing is behind you, but it's unlikely to be that simple...

If you're lucky the surreal geodesic forms atop **Great Dun Fell** (Map 86; which you may have spotted from Dufton village green) will act as a beacon, but the chances are the weather may have begun to deteriorate. From Knock Fell once you gain the line of snow poles and slabs that lead to the radar-tracking station access road, navigation-wise you should be home free. From this point looking east you can see the back end of Cow Green Reservoir, the only obvious man-made feature in a grey-green vista of fells and dales.

The northbound descent to the windy col and climb onto **Little Dun Fell** can take the wind out of you, but now the views to both sides are potentially fantastic. Passing close by the source of the River Tees, the final haul onto the summit

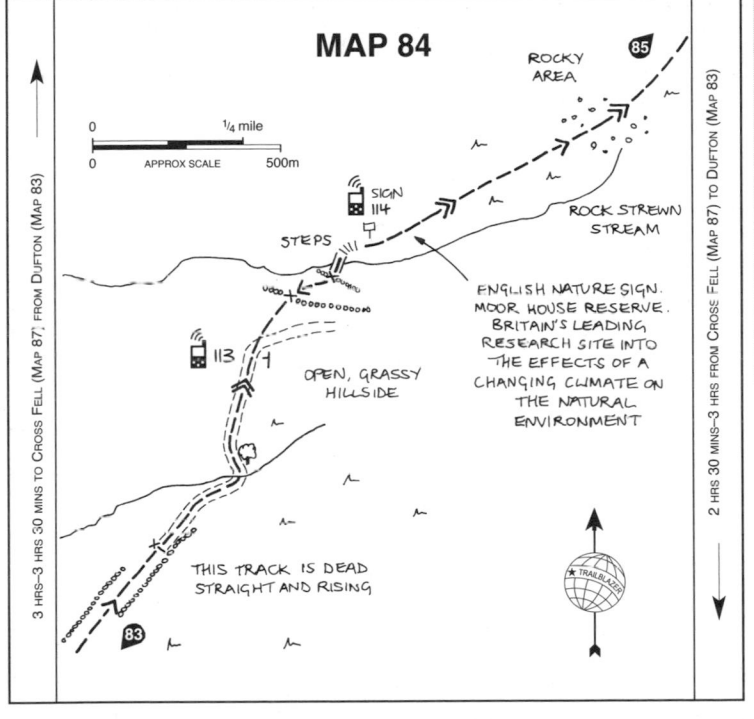

ROUTE GUIDE AND MAPS

MAP 84

ROCKY AREA

85

0   ¼ mile

0   APPROX SCALE   500m

SIGN
114

STEPS

ROCK STREWN STREAM

ENGLISH NATURE SIGN.
MOOR HOUSE RESERVE.
BRITAIN'S LEADING
RESEARCH SITE INTO
THE EFFECTS OF A
CHANGING CLIMATE ON
THE NATURAL
ENVIRONMENT

113

OPEN, GRASSY
HILLSIDE

THIS TRACK IS DEAD
STRAIGHT AND RISING

★ TRAILBLAZER

83

3 HRS–3 HRS 30 MINS TO CROSS FELL (MAP 87); FROM DUFTON (MAP 83)

2 HRS 30 MINS–3 HRS FROM CROSS FELL (MAP 87) TO DUFTON (MAP 83)

plateau and stone-cross shelter on **Cross Fell** (Map 87) is less severe; keeping track of the cairns will be the main priority in the mist.

The good news is, once off the summit plateau and securely installed on the miners' path leading past **Greg's Hut**, even the thickest pea souper with croutons and a side salad should not err you from the track that unwinds and undulates and unwinds some more like a stuck record for every inch of seven miles down to Garrigill. Corpse Road they call it, and you'll feel like one by the end of it. Over the years walkers have tried every trick in the book to save their soles from the purgatory of the rough, stony surface. But as with so many Pennine days, it all ends happily at the diminutive haven of **Garrigill** (Map 91). If you've missed the village shop the only alternative is a pint or two in the pub next door. Things could be worse.

Despite its limited accommodation options (something which you'll have become used to by now) Garrigill is actually a lovely place to end the tough hike over from Dufton and you may prefer to roll in the five miles to Alston with the 16½-mile hike to Greenhead on the Wall; it's flatter but less consistent. Those

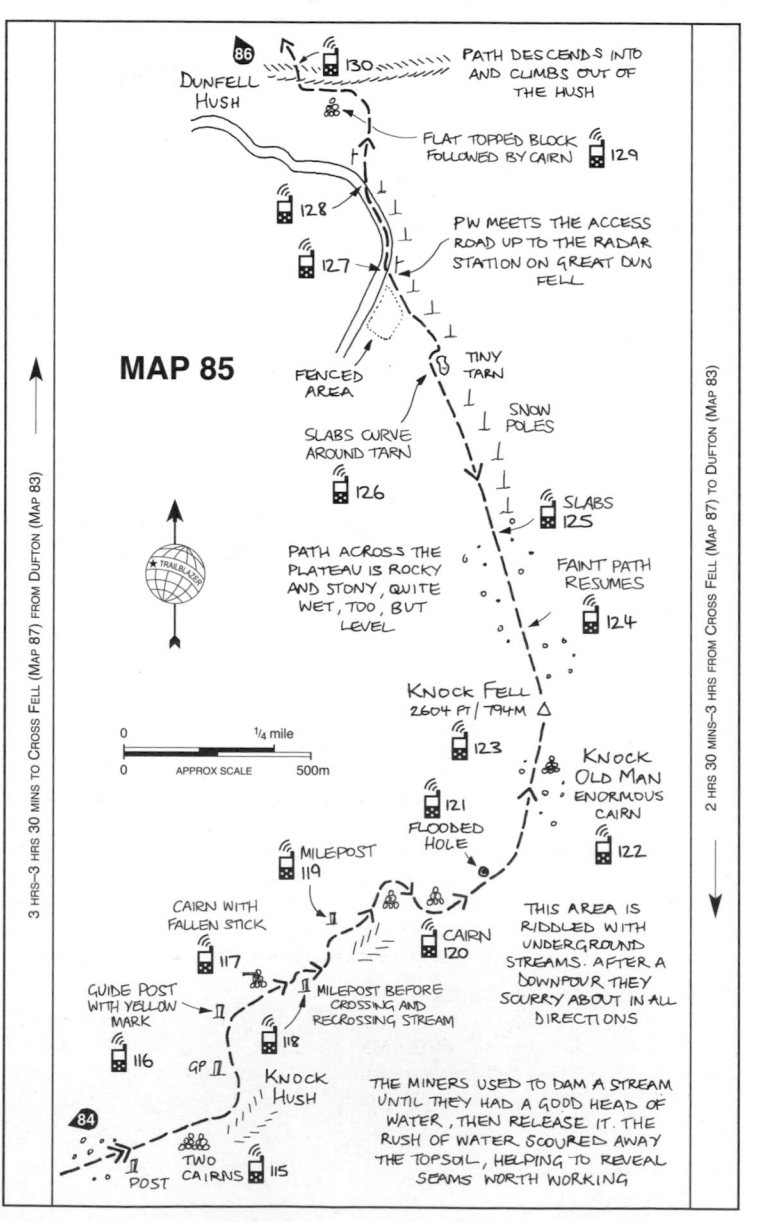

MAP 85

86 Dunfell Hush

130 PATH DESCENDS INTO AND CLIMBS OUT OF THE HUSH

FLAT TOPPED BLOCK FOLLOWED BY CAIRN 129

128

127 PW MEETS THE ACCESS ROAD UP TO THE RADAR STATION ON GREAT DUN FELL

FENCED AREA

TINY TARN

SNOW POLES

SLABS CURVE AROUND TARN

126

SLABS 125

PATH ACROSS THE PLATEAU IS ROCKY AND STONY, QUITE WET, TOO, BUT LEVEL

FAINT PATH RESUMES

124

★ TRAILBLAZER

0   ¼ mile
0   APPROX SCALE   500m

KNOCK FELL 2604 PT / 794M △

123

KNOCK OLD MAN ENORMOUS CAIRN

121 FLOODED HOLE

122

MILEPOST 119

CAIRN WITH FALLEN STICK

117

CAIRN 120

THIS AREA IS RIDDLED WITH UNDERGROUND STREAMS. AFTER A DOWNPOUR THEY SCURRY ABOUT IN ALL DIRECTIONS

GUIDE POST WITH YELLOW MARK

116   GP

MILEPOST BEFORE CROSSING AND RECROSSING STREAM

118

KNOCK HUSH

84

POST   TWO CAIRNS 115

THE MINERS USED TO DAM A STREAM UNTIL THEY HAD A GOOD HEAD OF WATER, THEN RELEASE IT. THE RUSH OF WATER SCOURED AWAY THE TOPSOIL, HELPING TO REVEAL SEAMS WORTH WORKING

3 HRS–3 HRS 30 MINS TO CROSS FELL (MAP 87) FROM DUFTON (MAP 83)

2 HRS 30 MINS–3 HRS FROM CROSS FELL (MAP 87) TO DUFTON (MAP 83)

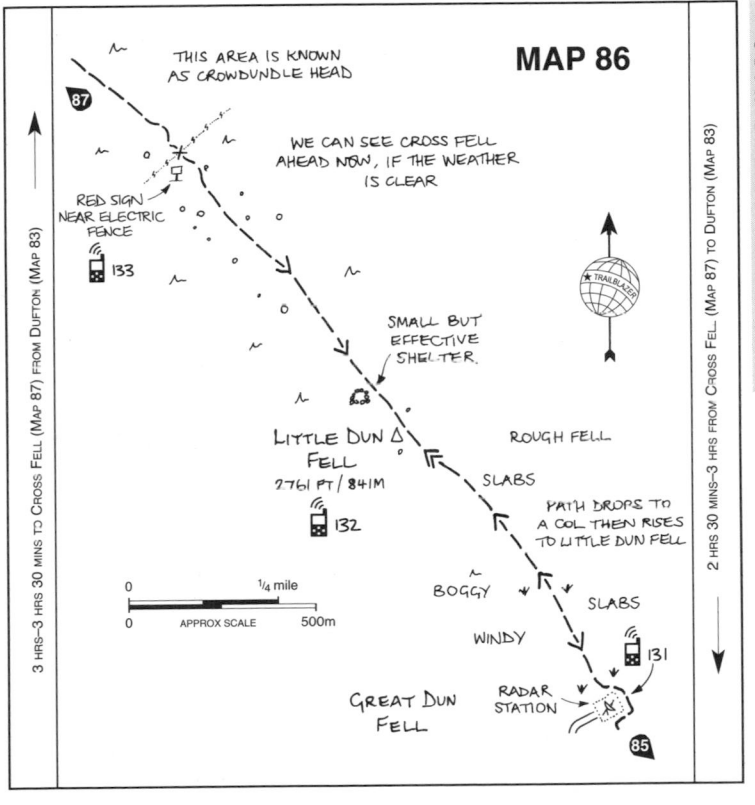

keen to power on to the dizzy heights of **Alston** (Map 93) beware, it's not the harmless riverside spindown that the map may suggest. Its latter half crumbles into a tedious negotiation of overgrown paths punctuated with numerous stiles, sprung gates and other walkers' traps that will most likely finish you off as you stagger past the cemetery into the market town and a well-earned break.

Route-finding trouble spots

In good weather the route poses no great problems; Cross Fell may not exactly match the razor-edged profile of the Matterhorn but the globes of the tracking station atop Great Dun Fell are very distinctive landmarks. Even then, the actual trail gets a bit thin on the flat plateau from Knock Fell towards the tracking station access road. *(cont'd on p199)*

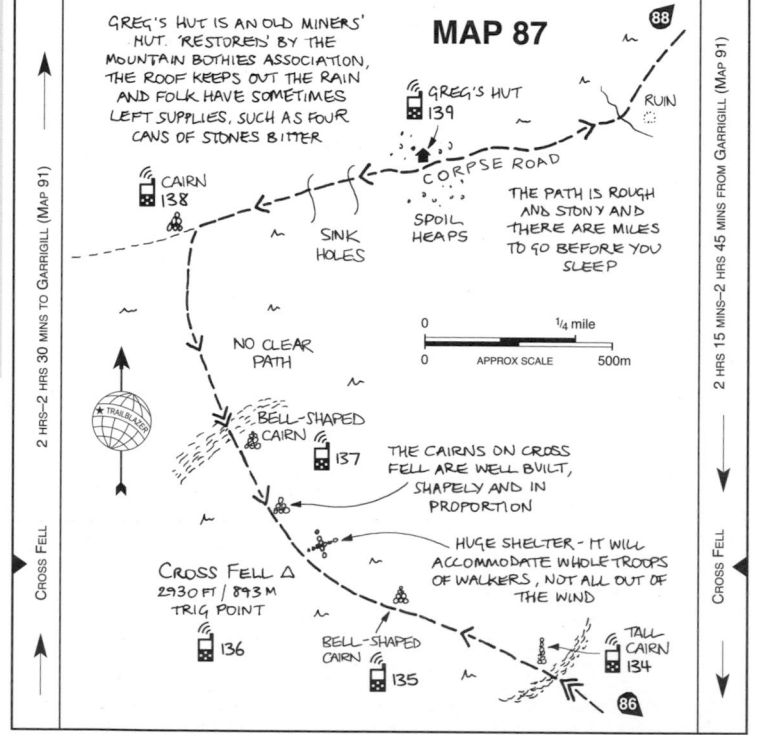

GREG'S HUT IS AN OLD MINERS' HUT. 'RESTORED' BY THE MOUNTAIN BOTHIES ASSOCIATION, THE ROOF KEEPS OUT THE RAIN AND FOLK HAVE SOMETIMES LEFT SUPPLIES, SUCH AS FOUR CANS OF STONES BITTER

MAP 87

88

RUIN

GREG'S HUT 139

CORPSE ROAD

CAIRN 138

SINK HOLES

SPOIL HEAPS

THE PATH IS ROUGH AND STONY AND THERE ARE MILES TO GO BEFORE YOU SLEEP

NO CLEAR PATH

0 — 1/4 mile
0 — APPROX SCALE — 500m

★ TRAILBLAZER

BELL-SHAPED CAIRN 137

THE CAIRNS ON CROSS FELL ARE WELL BUILT, SHAPELY AND IN PROPORTION

HUGE SHELTER - IT WILL ACCOMMODATE WHOLE TROOPS OF WALKERS, NOT ALL OUT OF THE WIND

CROSS FELL △ 2930 FT / 893 M TRIG POINT
136

BELL-SHAPED CAIRN 135

TALL CAIRN 134

86

2 HRS-2 HRS 30 MINS TO GARRIGILL (MAP 91)
CROSS FELL

2 HRS 15 MINS-2 HRS 45 MINS FROM GARRIGILL (MAP 91)
CROSS FELL

❏ Greg's Hut   [See Map 87]

Greg's Hut is a welcome and well-maintained bothy just over the summit of Cross Fell where walkers can take refuge or just pop in for a nose around. It holds a special place in the heart of many wayfarers. Originally it was used by lead miners whose tailing can be seen all around. They would stay here all week and walk home at the weekend. 'Greg' was actually John Gregory, a climber who died following an epic climbing accident in the Alps in 1968 in spite of the heroic efforts of his companion who held him on the rope and tended his injuries all night. Rescuers arrived too late.

Thanks to the efforts of the Mountain Bothies Association, the hut has been repaired and maintained. There are two rooms, the inner one has a raised sleeping platform with a stove, although fuel is scarce. Certainly you're unlikely to find any on the surrounding fell.

This is a classic mountain bothy, unique along the Pennine Way, and it's hard to drag yourself out of it in horrible conditions. The visitors' book could be published as it stands, telling a multitude of stories, most of them epics of embellishment or endurance.

ROUTE GUIDE AND MAPS

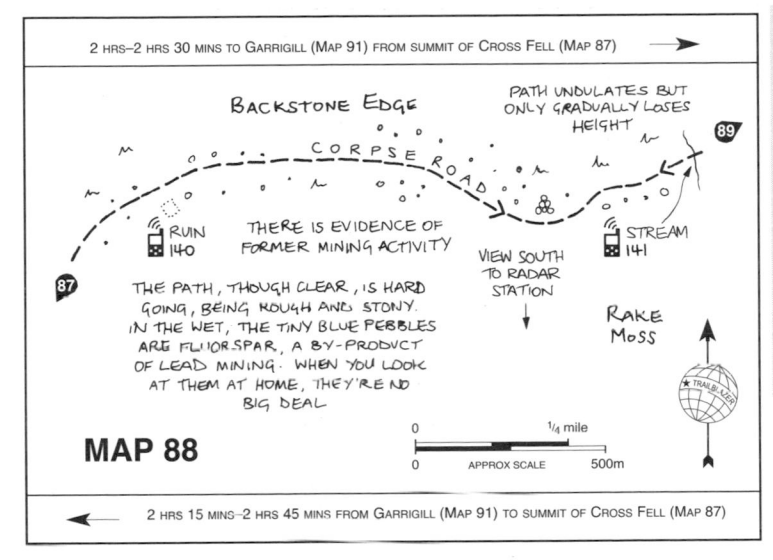

BACKSTONE EDGE

PATH UNDULATES BUT ONLY GRADUALLY LOSES HEIGHT

89

CORPSE ROAD

RUIN 140

THERE IS EVIDENCE OF FORMER MINING ACTIVITY

STREAM 141

87

THE PATH, THOUGH CLEAR, IS HARD GOING, BEING ROUGH AND STONY. IN THE WET, THE TINY BLUE PEBBLES ARE FLUORSPAR, A BY-PRODUCT OF LEAD MINING. WHEN YOU LOOK AT THEM AT HOME, THEY'RE NO BIG DEAL

VIEW SOUTH TO RADAR STATION
↓

RAKE MOSS

★ TRAILBLAZER

MAP 88

0   1/4 mile

0   APPROX SCALE   500m

❏ Lead mining in the Pennines

The history of digging in the earth for lead in the Pennine hills goes back to the Romans and probably earlier, evidence having been uncovered that Romans further exploited existing workings soon after they arrived.

The growth in the building of abbeys and castles increased the demand for lead for the roofs and stained-glass windows but it was not until the 19th century that mining assumed industrial proportions as the demand for lead increased.

The industry started to suffer when cheaper foreign sources threatened local production and by the early years of the 20th century mining was in decline. Today there is no lead mining in Britain although some of the old pits have been re-opened to exploit other minerals found there such as barytes and fluorspar. The ore, galena, also has a use in producing X-ray equipment.

The ruins evident around Alston and around Keld in Swaledale are a reminder of the extensive industry involved in lead mining at one time. Old spoil tips, ruined mine buildings and the occasional remains of a chimney are all that is left of this activity, now long discarded as uneconomic. Traces of bell pits are often to be seen as hollows in the ground. They used to sink a shaft to a certain level then widen the bottom of the hole until it was unsafe to go further. Everything dug out went to the surface in a bucket, firstly by hand and then by a winch, sometimes drawn up on a wheel by a horse walking in a circle. It was a primitive industry in the early days, reliant on the muscle power of the miners themselves. With the advent of engineering, ways were found to mechanize production and so multiply the output, increasing profits for the owners.

Around Middleton-in-Teesdale mining rights were held by the London Lead Mining Company, a Quaker concern, active from the latter part of the 1700s until early in the 1900s when they pulled out in the face of cheap imported ore from Europe.

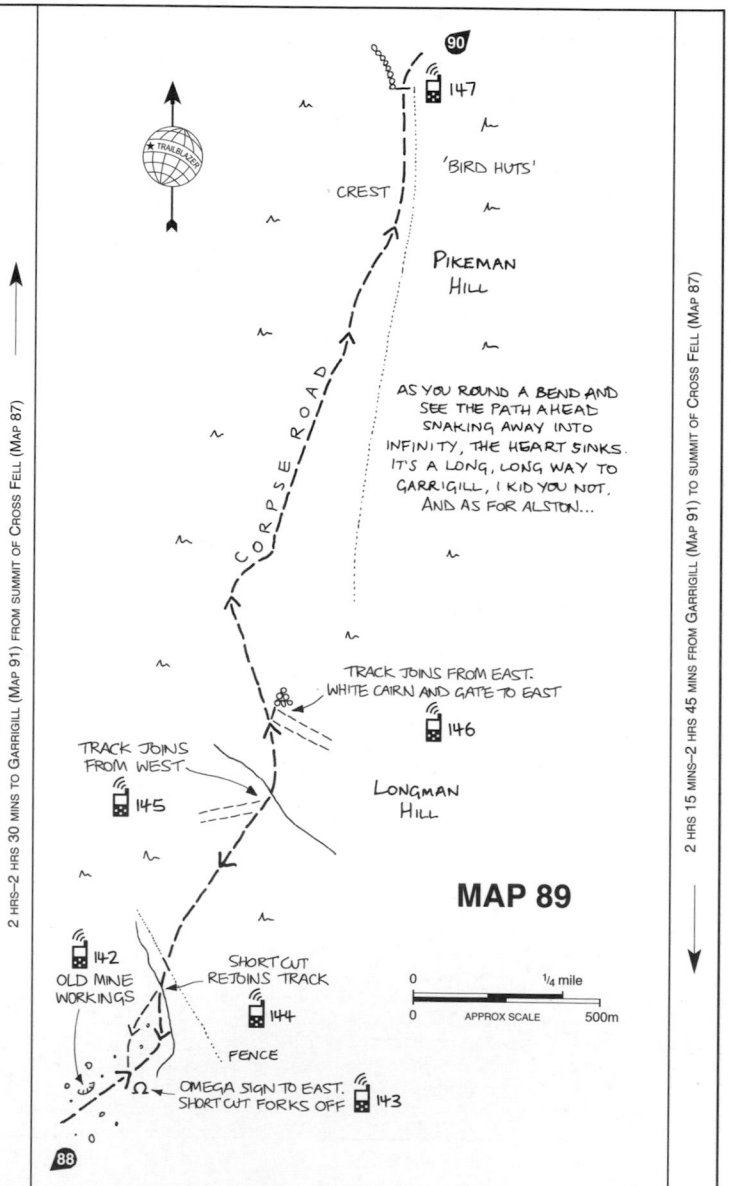

★ TRAILBLAZER

90 147

'BIRD HUTS'

CREST

PIKEMAN HILL

AS YOU ROUND A BEND AND
SEE THE PATH AHEAD
SNAKING AWAY INTO
INFINITY, THE HEART SINKS.
IT'S A LONG, LONG WAY TO
GARRIGILL, I KID YOU NOT.
AND AS FOR ALSTON...

CORPSE ROAD

TRACK JOINS FROM EAST.
WHITE CAIRN AND GATE TO EAST
146

TRACK JOINS
FROM WEST
145

LONGMAN
HILL

MAP 89

142
OLD MINE
WORKINGS

SHORT CUT
REJOINS TRACK
144

0   ¼ mile
0   APPROX SCALE   500m

FENCE

Ω   OMEGA SIGN TO EAST.   143
SHORT CUT FORKS OFF

88

2 HRS–2 HRS 30 MINS TO GARRIGILL (MAP 91) FROM SUMMIT OF CROSS FELL (MAP 87)

2 HRS 15 MINS–2 HRS 45 MINS FROM GARRIGILL (MAP 91) TO SUMMIT OF CROSS FELL (MAP 87)

(cont'd from p195) In poor visibility a surfeit of GPS waypoints are there if you want them; alternatively use a compass or the access road to get you up to Great Dun Fell's summit station. From there continue over the windy saddles to Cross Fell's flattened apex – oxygen is not needed.

Leaving the summit windshelters again there is no distinct path but several small cairns march north. Otherwise a mist-blinded northward stagger will lead you eventually down to the unmissable Corpse Road track, Greg's Hut nearby and eventually a footsore arrival in Garrigill.

As noted earlier, the overgrown fields after you bridge the South Tyne on the way to Alston can also confound you, even if the river on your left is a guide.

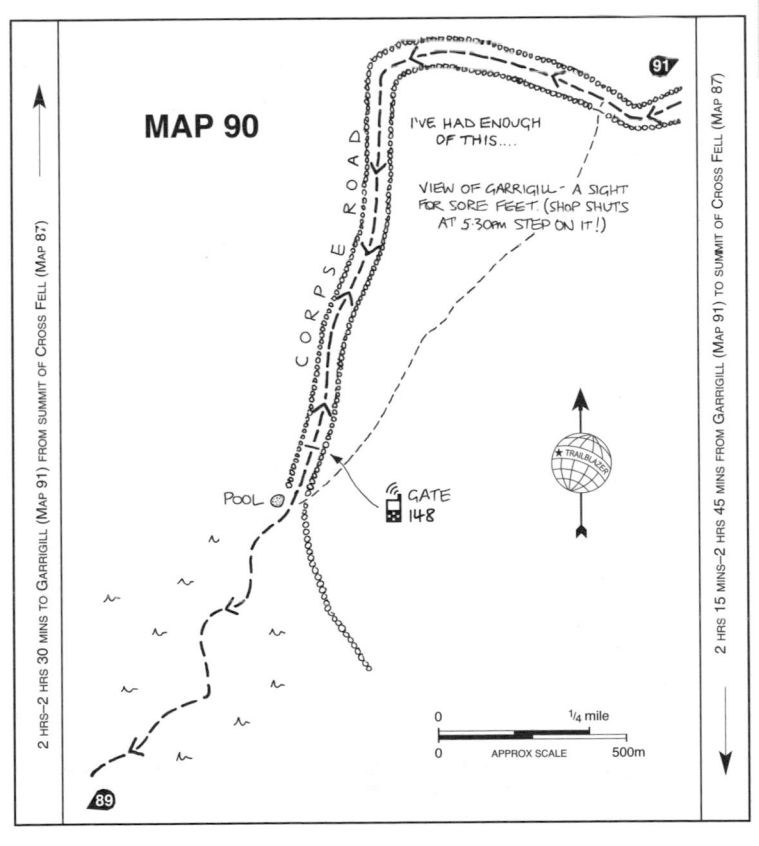

ROUTE GUIDE AND MAPS

MAP 90

C O R P S E   R O A D

I'VE HAD ENOUGH OF THIS....

VIEW OF GARRIGILL - A SIGHT FOR SORE FEET. (SHOP SHUTS AT 5·30PM STEP ON IT!)

POOL

GATE 148

TRAILBLAZER

0 .... ¼ mile
0 .... APPROX SCALE 500m

91

89

2 HRS 15 MINS–2 HRS 45 MINS FROM GARRIGILL (MAP 91) TO SUMMIT OF CROSS FELL (MAP 87)

2 HRS–2 HRS 30 MINS TO GARRIGILL (MAP 91) FROM SUMMIT OF CROSS FELL (MAP 87)

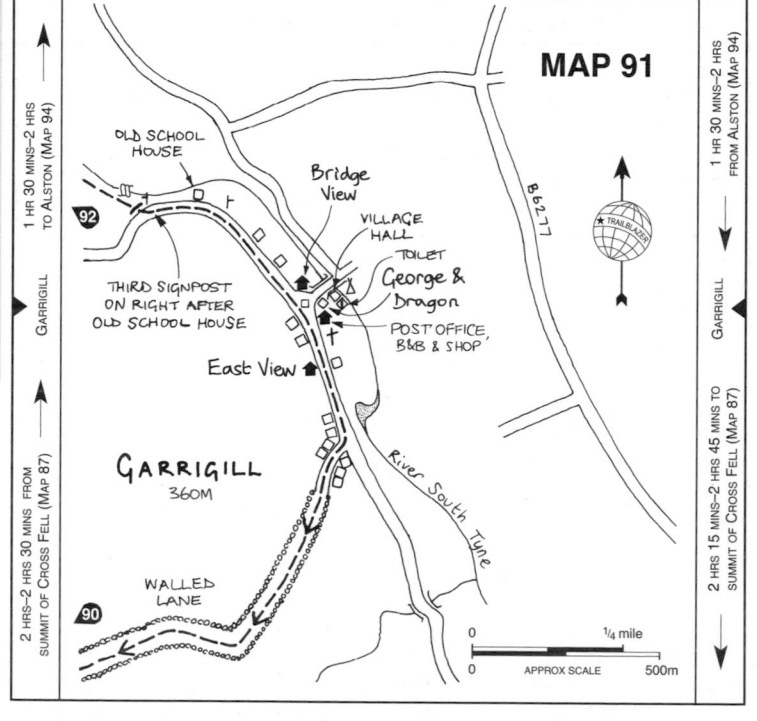

MAP 91

1 HR 30 MINS–2 HRS TO ALSTON (MAP 94)

1 HR 30 MINS–2 HRS FROM ALSTON (MAP 94)

GARRIGILL

GARRIGILL

2 HRS–2 HRS 30 MINS FROM SUMMIT OF CROSS FELL (MAP 87)

2 HRS 15 MINS–2 HRS 45 MINS TO SUMMIT OF CROSS FELL (MAP 87)

OLD SCHOOL HOUSE

92

THIRD SIGNPOST ON RIGHT AFTER OLD SCHOOL HOUSE

Bridge View

VILLAGE HALL

TOILET

George & Dragon

POST OFFICE, B&B & SHOP

East View

GARRIGILL
360M

River South Tyne

WALLED LANE

90

B6277

★ TRAILBLAZER

0   ¼ mile

0   APPROX SCALE   500m

GARRIGILL   [Map 91]

Garrigill's **post office** (Mon-Sat 9am-5.30pm, to 12.30pm on Tue, Sun 8-11.30am) transacts the usual business and includes a shop as well as selling **hot drinks**. It's also home to *Garrigill Post Office Guesthouse* (☎ 01434-381257, 🖳 www.garrigill-guesthouse.co.uk; 2S/1D/2T, £25/pp). It's clean and comfortable but don't expect the rooms in this 300-year-old building to be palatial.

Also on the village green is *Bridge View B&B* (☎ 01434-382448, 🖳 www .bridgeview.org.uk; 1F private bathroom) where the room costs £24 per person and a packed lunch is £4. At the time of writing the owner was planning to offer a foot-massage service but this would only be possible for walkers without any open blisters.

Nearby you'll also find *East View* (☎ 01434-381561, 🖳 www.eastview-garrigill.co.uk; 1D or T/1D) with rooms from £25 per person.

If you want to **camp** at Garrigill, you can pitch up behind the village hall. Check at the pub first and leave a donation before you leave.

Next to the post office *The George and Dragon* (☎ 01434-381293, 🖳 www.garrigill-pub.co.uk) has provided a recharge for many a weary walker with a menu that changes daily and features freshly cooked seasonal food; try the Sicilian Fresh Tuna Casserole with pasta for under a tenner if that is on the menu.

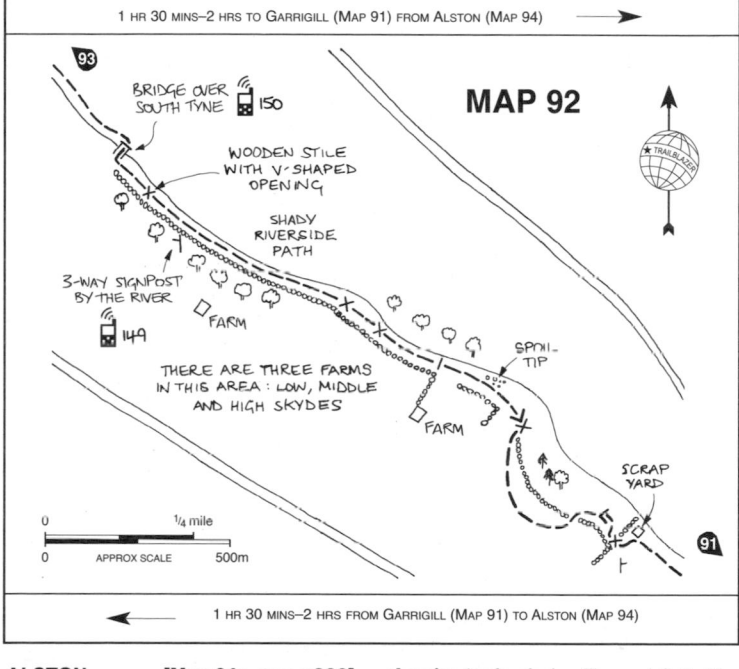

1 HR 30 MINS–2 HRS TO GARRIGILL (MAP 91) FROM ALSTON (MAP 94)

BRIDGE OVER SOUTH TYNE 150

MAP 92

WOODEN STILE WITH V-SHAPED OPENING

SHADY RIVERSIDE PATH

3-WAY SIGNPOST BY THE RIVER 149

FARM

THERE ARE THREE FARMS IN THIS AREA: LOW, MIDDLE AND HIGH SKYDES

SPOIL TIP

FARM

SCRAP YARD

0 ¼ mile
0 APPROX SCALE 500m

91

1 HR 30 MINS–2 HRS FROM GARRIGILL (MAP 91) TO ALSTON (MAP 94)

ALSTON [Map 94a, see p203]

Alston is England's highest market town and its steep cobbled streets and 18th-century buildings give it a bit of character. It does, however, have a faint air of decline about it compared to other like-sized towns along the Way, although this could be an unfair impression following two days of remote hiking.

Services

The **tourist information centre** (☎ 01434-382244, 🖳 www.visiteden.co.uk), in the Town Hall on Front St, is open Apr-Oct Mon-Sat 10am-5pm, Sun 10am-4pm, Nov-Mar Mon-Sat 10am-3pm.

Alston Wholefoods sells fair-trade chocolate, interesting cheeses (eg Northumberland Nettle, Swaledale Ewe) and environmentally friendly goods. There's also a **Co-op** (Mon-Sat 8am-8pm, Sun 9am-5pm), two **butchers** and a

chemist (early closing Tue and Sat). The branches of HSBC and Barclays here have **cash machines**; there is also a **post office**.

Transport

If you want to break the walk here you can get a **bus** to Hexham and catch a **train** on the Newcastle to Carlisle line. Between them Stagecoach, Robinson's and Wright Brothers operate buses to Carlisle, Penrith, Hexham and Nenthead (see public transport map and table, pp42-6).

For a **taxi** try Hendersons (☎ 01434-381204) or Alston Taxis (☎ 01434-381386).

South Tyneside Railway (☎ 01434-381696, 🖳 www.strps.org.uk) operates trains from Alston to Stonehaugh (2¼ miles) on 'Northern England's highest narrow-gauge railway'. Trains run daily in holiday periods from March to October and at weekends at other times. *(cont'd on p204)*

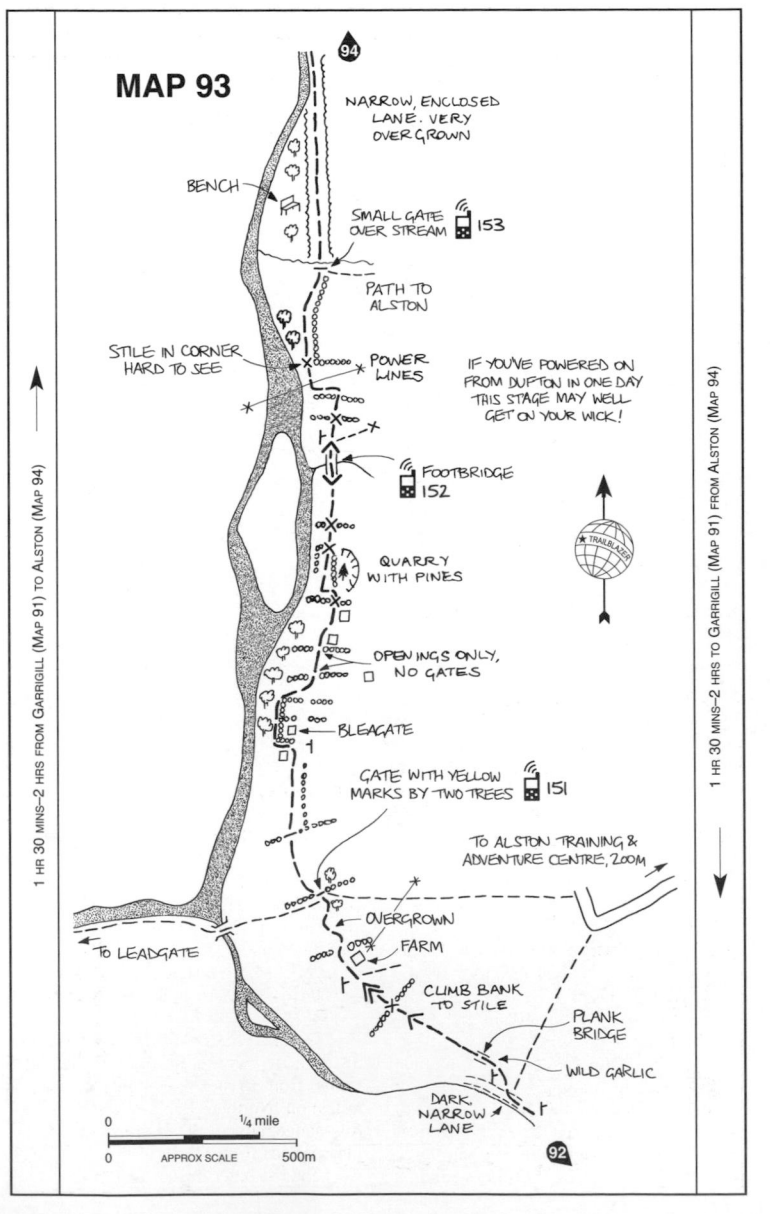

MAP 93

94

NARROW, ENCLOSED LANE. VERY OVERGROWN

BENCH

SMALL GATE OVER STREAM 153

PATH TO ALSTON

STILE IN CORNER HARD TO SEE

POWER LINES

IF YOU'VE POWERED ON FROM DUFTON IN ONE DAY THIS STAGE MAY WELL GET ON YOUR WICK!

FOOTBRIDGE 152

QUARRY WITH PINES

OPENINGS ONLY, NO GATES

BLEAGATE

GATE WITH YELLOW MARKS BY TWO TREES 151

TO ALSTON TRAINING & ADVENTURE CENTRE, 200M

TO LEADGATE

OVERGROWN

FARM

CLIMB BANK TO STILE

PLANK BRIDGE

WILD GARLIC

DARK NARROW LANE

TRAILBLAZER

1 HR 30 MINS–2 HRS FROM GARRIGILL (MAP 91) TO ALSTON (MAP 94)

1 HR 30 MINS–2 HRS TO GARRIGILL (MAP 91) FROM ALSTON (MAP 94)

0   ¼ mile

0   APPROX SCALE   500m

92

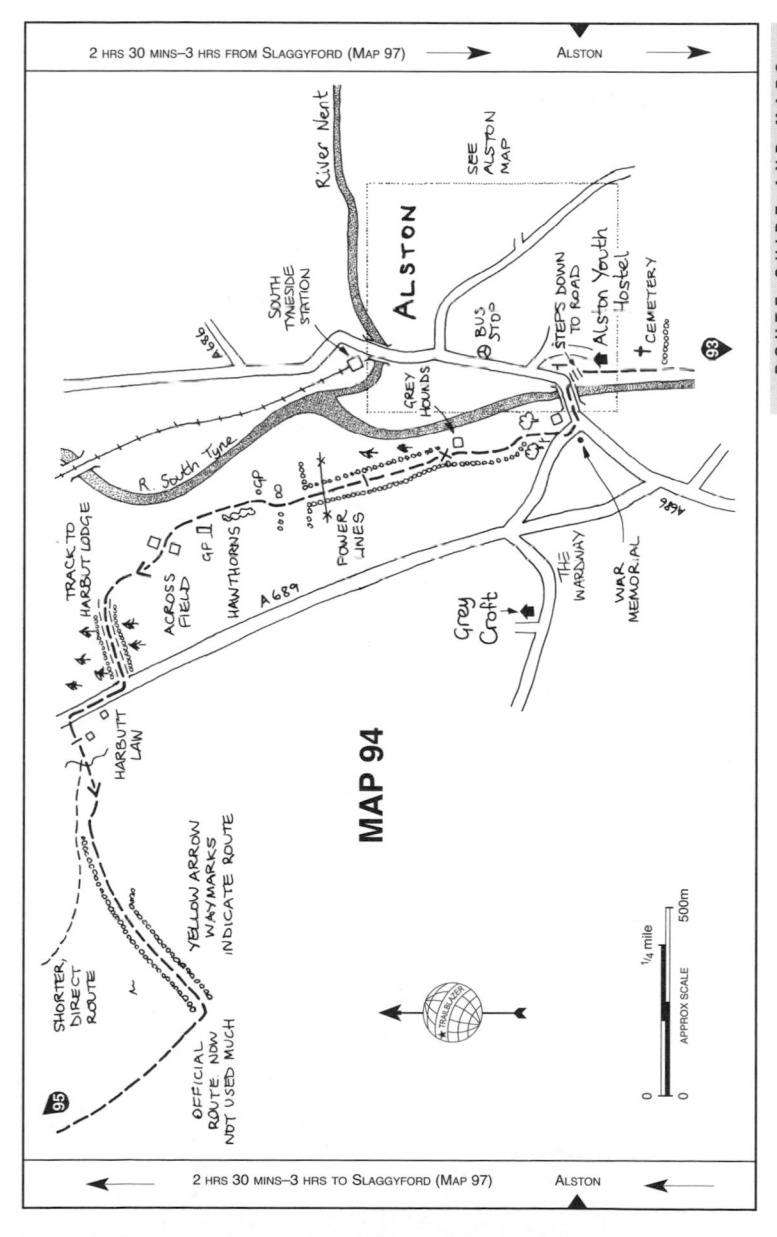

2 HRS 30 MINS–3 HRS FROM SLAGGYFORD (MAP 97) → ALSTON →

93

River Nent

SEE ALSTON MAP

ALSTON

SOUTH TYNESIDE STATION

A686

BUS STOP

STEPS DOWN TO ROAD

Alston Youth Hostel

† CEMETERY

GREY HOUNDS

R South Tyne

GP

POWER LINES

GP

HAWTHORNS

ACROSS FIELD

A689

TRACK TO HARBUT LODGE

A686

THE WARDWAY

Grey Croft

WAR MEMORIAL

HARBUTT LAW

MAP 94

YELLOW ARROW WAYMARKS INDICATE ROUTE

SHORTER, DIRECT ROUTE

OFFICIAL ROUTE NOW NOT USED MUCH

95

TRAILBLAZER

APPROX SCALE

¼ mile

500m

0

0

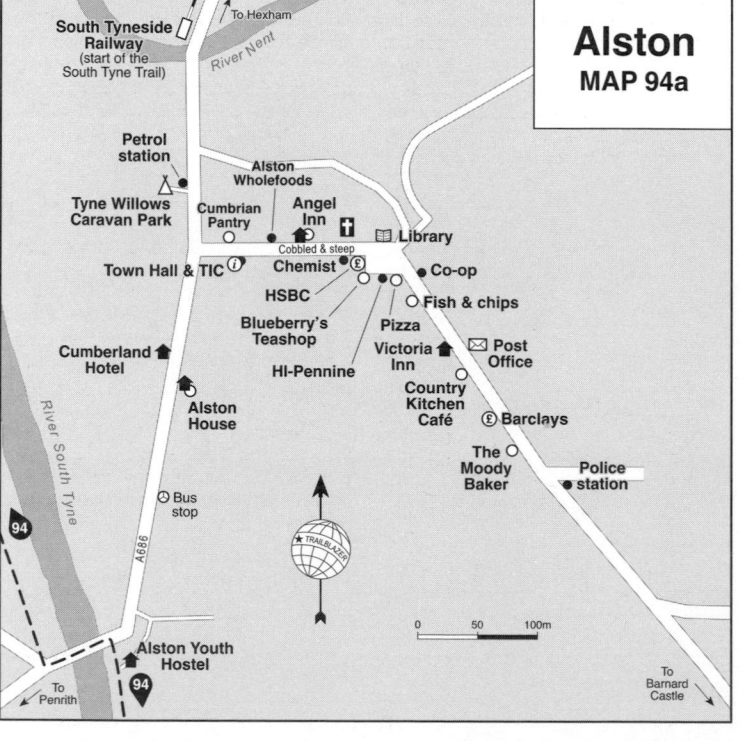

Alston
MAP 94a

South Tyneside Railway (start of the South Tyne Trail)

To Hexham

River Nent

Petrol station

Alston Wholefoods

Tyne Willows Caravan Park

Cumbrian Pantry

Angel Inn

Library

Cobbled & steep

Town Hall & TIC

Chemist

Co-op

HSBC

Fish & chips

Blueberry's Teashop

Pizza

Cumberland Hotel

Victoria Inn

Post Office

HI-Pennine

Alston House

Country Kitchen Café

Barclays

River South Tyne

The Moody Baker

Police station

Bus stop

A686

TRAILBLAZER

0   50   100m

Alston Youth Hostel

To Penrith

94

To Barnard Castle

(cont'd from p201) Steam locomotives are used on some services; see the website or phone them for details. Volunteers are hoping to restore the line from Stonehaugh to Slaggyford – the line originally went to Hexham.

Where to stay
Alston Training and Adventure Centre (☎ 01434-381886, 🖳 www.alstontraining .co.uk; off Map 93), not far off the Pennine Way, offers **camping** (£4 per person), **bunkhouse** accommodation (40+ beds; £12, or £17 with breakfast), evening meals (£6) and packed lunches (£3). It's best to book both accommodation and food in advance. If it's not packed out it may be a better bet than what's available in Alston.

Alternatively, if already in Alston, make your way past lots of derelict cars behind the Texaco garage to *Tyne Willows Caravan Park* (☎ 01434-382515). It costs £5 to **camp** on the bit of grass allocated for tents and the ablution block is like something out of a Tarkowsky movie.

Alston Youth Hostel (☎ 01629-529708, bookings ☎ 0870-770 5668, 🖳 alston@yha.org.uk, open Apr-Oct) overlooks the South Tyne; it offers an evening meal and has 30 beds for £11.95 (£9 for under 18s).

There are several pubs, some past their prime; you may find traditional B&Bs a better bet. Pubs with rooms include *The Victoria Inn* (☎ 01434-381194; 4S/2T/2F, some en suite) which charges £44 for two but may not be your first choice. *The Angel Inn* (☎ 01434-381363; 1S/1T/2D) down the hill also does B&B, non en suite, for £16.50, and is used to walkers. *Cumberland Hotel* (☎ 01434-381875, 🖳 www.alstoncumberlandhotel .co.uk; 2D/3F all en suite) is a better bet offering a double or twin from £60 and £35 for single occupancy. One of the family rooms has three single beds.

Alston House (☎ 01434-382200, 🖳 www.alstonhouse.co.uk; 6D, T or F, all en suite) is the pick of the crop in town, licensed, and with B&B costing £60 for two sharing or £45 for single occupancy plus a great **restaurant** (see House Café).

Out of town (see Map 94) the award-winning *Grey Croft* (☎ 01434-381383, 🖳 www.greycroftalston.co.uk; 1D/1T both en suite), Middle Park, The Raise, is a favourite among walkers and with the rooms being redecorated at the time of writing this should continue; B&B is £58 for two sharing, single occupancy costs £39.

Where to eat
Not all the pubs do great food; try either *The Angel Inn* (see above; food served Mon-Thur 12-2pm & 6-9pm and all day Fri-Sun), or the *House Café* (Tue-Fri 10am-4pm & 6-9pm, Sat 10am-5pm, 6-9pm, Sun 10am-8.30pm), at Alston House, with day-time snacks and salads for under £5 as well as evening meals. *Cumberland Hotel* (see column opposite) serves food Mon-Sat 12-9pm, Sun 12-2pm & 6-9pm.

Blueberry's Tea Shop (☎ 01434-381928) serves lunches and an all-day breakfast daily from 9am to 5pm. In addition to the *fish and chip shop*, *Country Kitchen Café* also serves fish and chips, and nearby *The Moody Baker* (☎ 01434-382003; Mon-Fri 8am-4pm Sat 8am-3.30pm) co-operative has an excellent range of home-made food, to take away, focusing on local produce and organic ingredients where possible.

Cumbrian Pantry (☎ 01434-381406; 9am-4pm Tue-Thur, to 5pm Fri-Sun) prepares meals to be eaten in as well as food, such as sandwiches and cakes, to be eaten in or taken away.

ALSTON TO GREENHEAD   MAPS 94-102

Route overview
Some days along the Pennine Way are classics, others are less memorable and today's **17-mile (27km, 7¹/₂-9¹/₂hrs)** walk from Alston to Greenhead falls into the latter category but fear not, there are only one or two like it and this is the last. It's also a sad day because around you the true Pennine chain comes to an end as you schlep along the South Tyne Valley. What hills continue on the far side of the Wall are really part of the Southern Uplands massif: England's sturdy backbone probes gently into Scotland's quivering belly.

No matter, the first objective is **Slaggyford** (Map 97), a name that suggests a glum colliery or worse, but which in reality is a residential village with no services bar a public telephone and a B&B. Here you join the course of a former railway now known as the **South Tyne Trail** which at one point is left for a mile or so in a pedantic struggle through fields and people's backyards before passing in and out of the viaduct at Burnstones.

The **Maiden Way** (Map 98), a former Roman Road is now underfoot as you leave the valley and march more or less due north over marsh and marsh grass. You then descend to the more arable muck of the **Hartley Burn floodplain** (Map 99) before heading up again via a couple of farmyards onto the misery that dares call itself **Blenkinsopp Common** (Map 100), the crossing of which seems like an expedition over a country abandoned by man and beast. The '-sopp' suffix is a clue for once on the moor the path becomes indistinct or not worth following until you crest **Black Hill**, not unlike its sodden cousin in the northern Peak District all those miles ago, but without the blessings of a slab causeway.

You come upon a row of huge pylons and all that remains now is to cross the A69 (Map 102) without getting run over – no thoughtful footbridge or underpass here. The village of Greenhead is in sight, arrived at by gingerly circumnavigating its golf course and dropping steeply into the dispersed hamlet. If the day is still young and your spirit untramelled, get a feed in Greenhead Hotel and consider powering on a few miles to Burnhead or Once Brewed. After tomorrow's thigh-stretching stage you may be glad you did.

Was it just us or is this stage a navigational headache at times? You're about to find out so read the **Route-finding trouble spots** carefully.

Alston to Greenhead: route-finding trouble spots

This stage is not helped by waymarking that at times verges on the extra sensory. The Way from Alston to Harbut Law (Map 94) on the A689 is easy enough but here ensues a sometimes discreetly signed arc back to the road at Castle Nook Farm (Map 95). Onwards to Slaggyford is merely the usual steeplechase of farm walls and fences until you pass under the *correct* viaduct near Lintley Farm (Map 96) to rejoin the South Tyne river and the road to Slaggyford.

Joining the South Tyne Trail ('STT') along a former railway, watch out for a sign (if there is one) as the Pennine Way shoots off just after the bridge over Knar Burn (Map 97). It leads to the collection of houses known as Merry Knowe. Those in the 'merry know' may prefer to simply stick to the STT until it reaches Burnstones and slither down the left bank on the north end of the viaduct (as most clearly do) to join up with the Maiden Way section. This too is not blindingly obvious until you make it to the A689 and over Hartley Burn (Map 99).

The next trick is projecting yourself accurately at Ulpham Farm (Map 100); a compass may be handy. And it will be again after you leave the magic bus in Greenriggs' yard. Once on the moor the Way supposedly turns west to join and follow a fence line north, but unless global warming has dried the land since this was written, looking west you wouldn't want to go there, even if they did sign it clearly. Instead tip-toe your way across the higher morass on a bearing of 300° or so to meet the point where the fence intercepts the more visible wall leading to Wain Rigg. Once crossed, the route down to the A69 and from there to Greenhead is less complicated, or at least near enough the end to be muddled (and muddied) through.

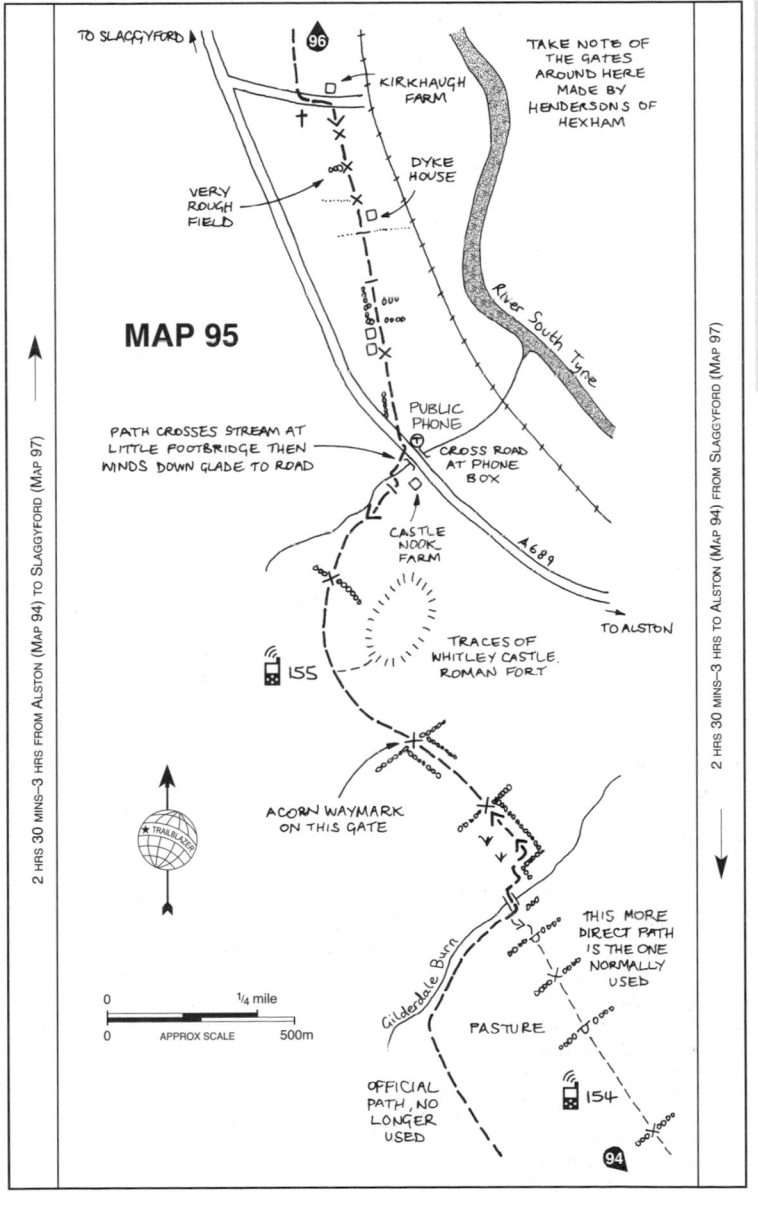

TO SLAGGYFORD

96

KIRKHAUGH FARM

TAKE NOTE OF THE GATES AROUND HERE MADE BY HENDERSONS OF HEXHAM

DYKE HOUSE

VERY ROUGH FIELD

MAP 95

River South Tyne

PUBLIC PHONE

PATH CROSSES STREAM AT LITTLE FOOTBRIDGE THEN WINDS DOWN GLADE TO ROAD

CROSS ROAD AT PHONE BOX

CASTLE NOOK FARM

A689

TO ALSTON

TRACES OF WHITLEY CASTLE ROMAN FORT

155

ACORN WAYMARK ON THIS GATE

THIS MORE DIRECT PATH IS THE ONE NORMALLY USED

Gilderdale Burn

PASTURE

154

★ TRAILBLAZER

0   ¼ mile
0   APPROX SCALE   500m

OFFICIAL PATH, NO LONGER USED

94

2 HRS 30 MINS–3 HRS FROM ALSTON (MAP 94) TO SLAGGYFORD (MAP 97)

2 HRS 30 MINS–3 HRS TO ALSTON (MAP 94) FROM SLAGGYFORD (MAP 97)

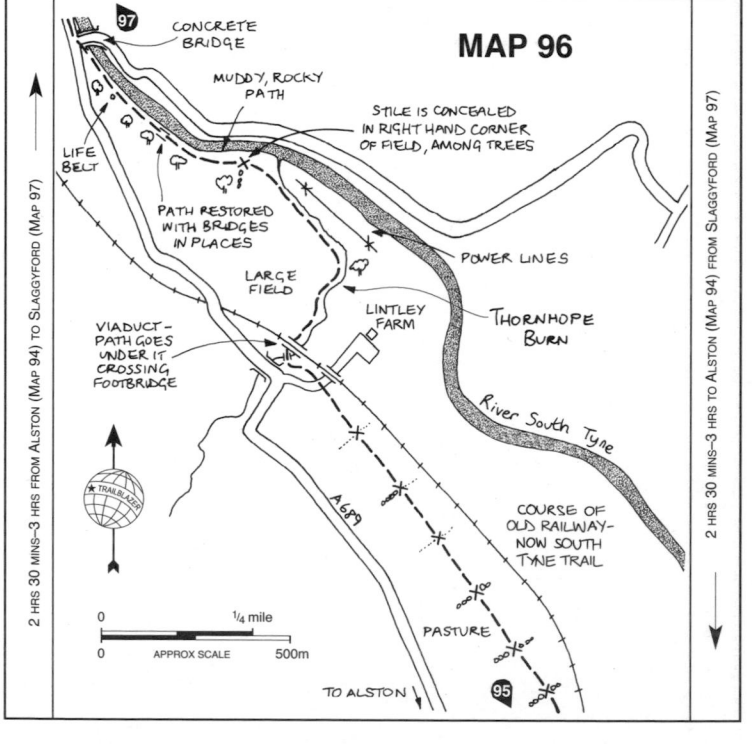

MAP 96

CONCRETE BRIDGE

MUDDY, ROCKY PATH

STILE IS CONCEALED IN RIGHT HAND CORNER OF FIELD, AMONG TREES

LIFE BELT

PATH RESTORED WITH BRIDGES IN PLACES

POWER LINES

LARGE FIELD

LINTLEY FARM

THORNHOPE BURN

VIADUCT – PATH GOES UNDER IT CROSSING FOOTBRIDGE

River South Tyne

TRAILBLAZER

A689

COURSE OF OLD RAILWAY – NOW SOUTH TYNE TRAIL

0   ¼ mile

0   APPROX SCALE   500m

PASTURE

TO ALSTON

2 HRS 30 MINS–3 HRS FROM ALSTON (MAP 94) TO SLAGGYFORD (MAP 97)

2 HRS 30 MINS–3 HRS TO ALSTON (MAP 94) FROM SLAGGYFORD (MAP 97)

SLAGGYFORD   [Map 97]

If you're having a hard day or are on your own schedule, Slaggyford is only six miles from Alston.

Right in the village, *Yew Tree Chapel* (☎ 01434-382525 🖳 www.yewtreechapel .co.uk; 2D or T/1T all en suite) has been spectacularly converted into an unusual B&B with two sharing paying from £60

KNARSDALE   [Map 97]

A mile down the road you can **camp** at *Stonehall Farm* (☎ 01434-381349). At £4 it's basic, there's an outside toilet and a water tap, but the pub, the Kirkstyle Inn, is just 50 metres down the road. Just before the pub is *Stonecroft* (☎ 01434-382995; 2T en suite) where **B&B** costs £30/pp and a packed lunch costs from £3. Pennine

and single occupancy from £35. Packed lunches (£5) and evening meals (£15) are also available for anyone without transport if booked in advance; baptisms are by special appointment. It's well worth a visit – even if you don't plan to stay as they sometimes do cups of tea and home-made biscuits for passers by, though all guests are given a cup of tea and biscuits on arrival.

Wayfarers are always looking for an excuse to stop at the *Kirkstyle Inn* (☎ 01434-381559; food served Wed-Mon 12-2pm, & Mon, Wed-Sat 6-9pm). From the choice of beers to the tasty bar menu and the atmosphere this place has everything walkers go for and is the sort of hostelry you'll be hallucinating about when you're halfway between Byrness and Kirk Yetholm.

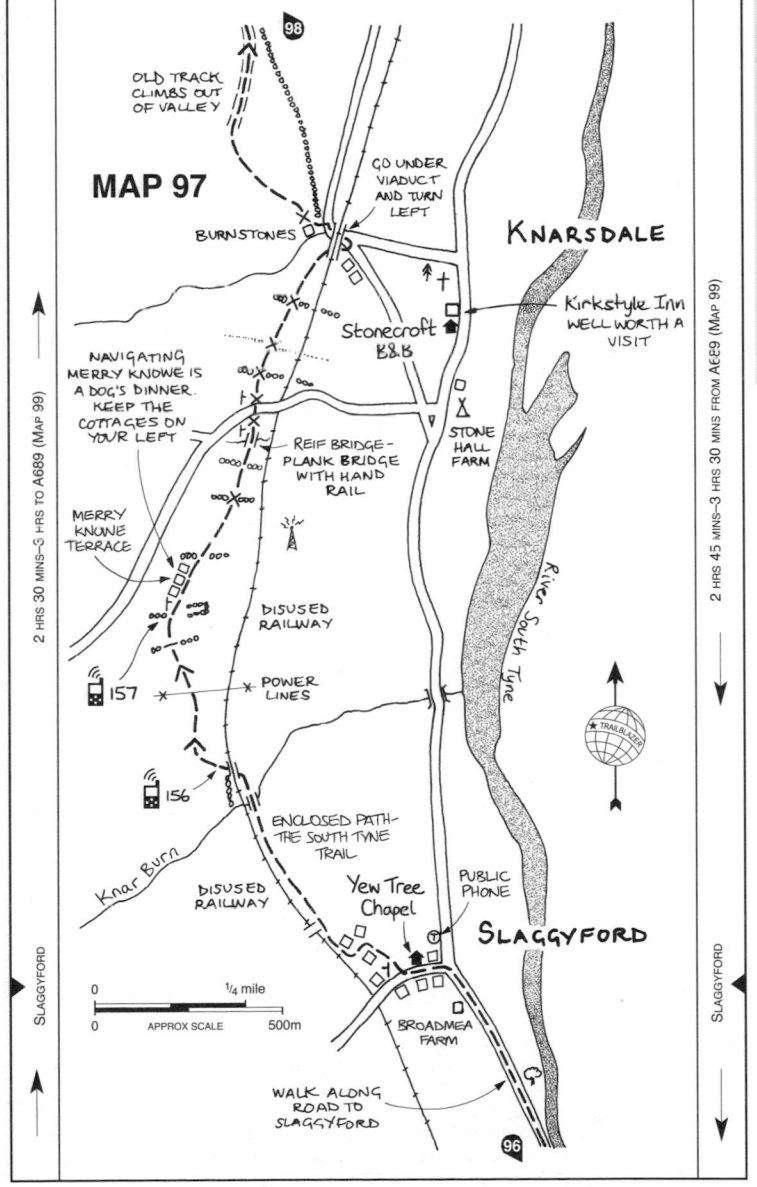

MAP 97

OLD TRACK CLIMBS OUT OF VALLEY

98

GO UNDER VIADUCT AND TURN LEFT

BURNSTONES

KNARSDALE

Kirkstyle Inn WELL WORTH A VISIT

Stonecroft B&B

NAVIGATING MERRY KNOWE IS A DOG'S DINNER. KEEP THE COTTAGES ON YOUR LEFT

REIF BRIDGE – PLANK BRIDGE WITH HAND RAIL

STONE HALL FARM

MERRY KNOWE TERRACE

DISUSED RAILWAY

157

POWER LINES

156

ENCLOSED PATH – THE SOUTH TYNE TRAIL

Knar Burn

DISUSED RAILWAY

Yew Tree Chapel

PUBLIC PHONE

SLAGGYFORD

BROADMEA FARM

WALK ALONG ROAD TO SLAGGYFORD

96

River South Tyne

★ TRAILBLAZER

0   ¼ mile

0   APPROX SCALE   500m

2 HRS 30 MINS–3 HRS TO A689 (MAP 99)

2 HRS 45 MINS–3 HRS 30 MINS FROM A689 (MAP 99)

SLAGGYFORD

SLAGGYFORD

ROUTE GUIDE AND MAPS

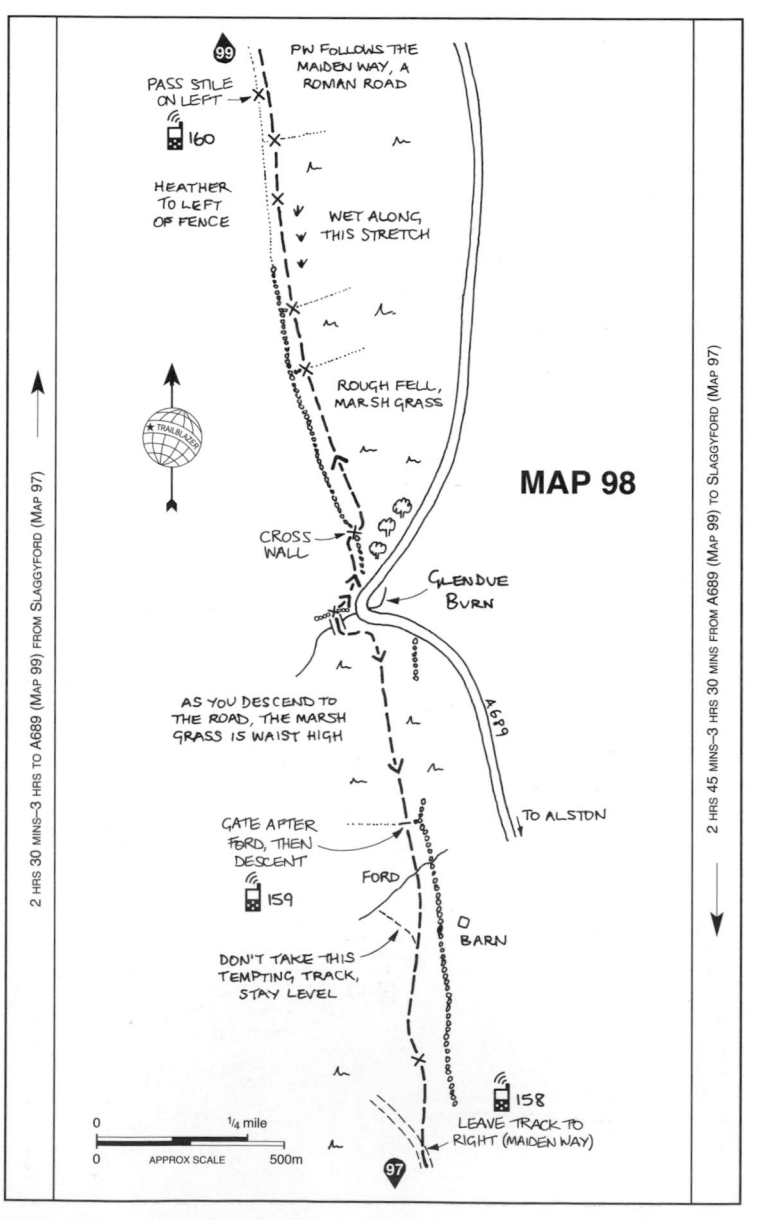

MAP 98

2 HRS 30 MINS–3 HRS TO A689 (MAP 99) FROM SLAGGYFORD (MAP 97)

2 HRS 45 MINS–3 HRS 30 MINS FROM A689 (MAP 99) TO SLAGGYFORD (MAP 97)

99

PW FOLLOWS THE
MAIDEN WAY, A
ROMAN ROAD

PASS STILE
ON LEFT

160

HEATHER
TO LEFT
OF FENCE

WET ALONG
THIS STRETCH

ROUGH FELL,
MARSH GRASS

★ TRAILBLAZER

CROSS
WALL

GLENDUE
BURN

A689

AS YOU DESCEND TO
THE ROAD, THE MARSH
GRASS IS WAIST HIGH

TO ALSTON

GATE AFTER
FORD, THEN
DESCENT

159

FORD

BARN

DON'T TAKE THIS
TEMPTING TRACK,
STAY LEVEL

0   1/4 mile
0   APPROX SCALE   500m

158
LEAVE TRACK TO
RIGHT (MAIDEN WAY)

97

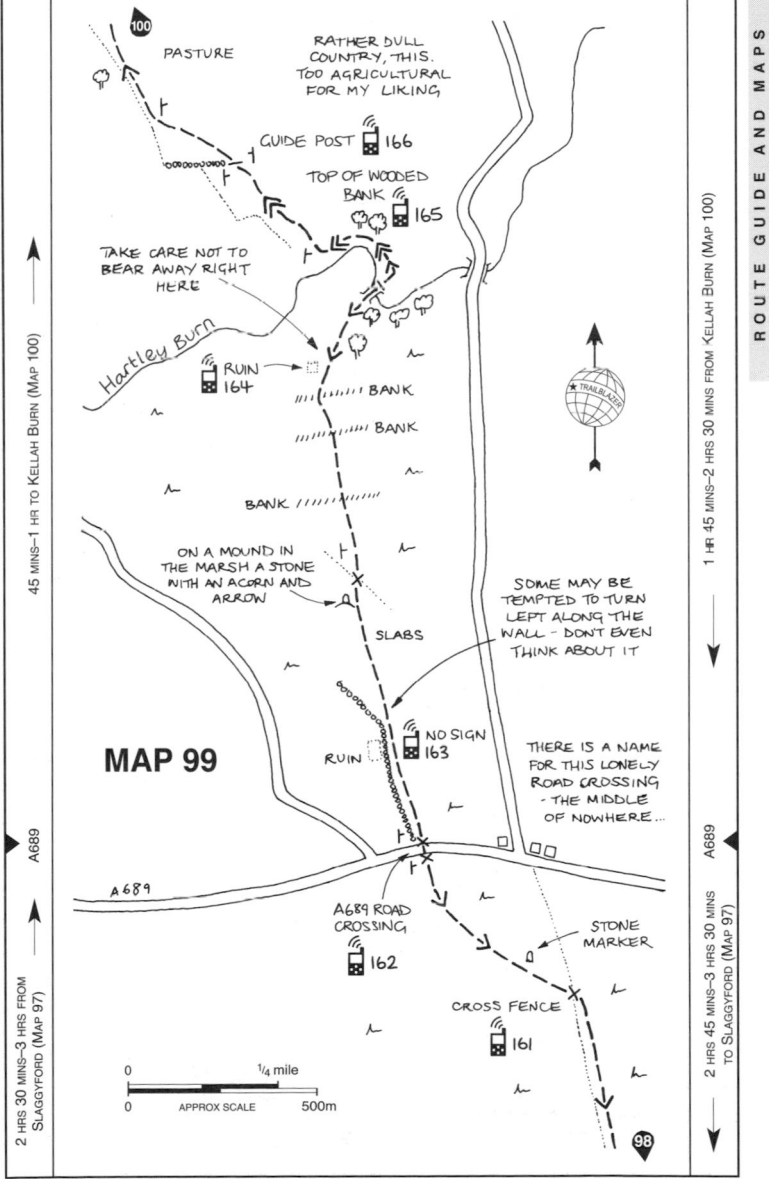

PASTURE

RATHER DULL
COUNTRY, THIS.
TOO AGRICULTURAL
FOR MY LIKING

GUIDE POST 166

TOP OF WOODED
BANK 165

TAKE CARE NOT TO
BEAR AWAY RIGHT
HERE

Hartley Burn

RUIN
164

BANK

BANK

BANK

ON A MOUND IN
THE MARSH A STONE
WITH AN ACORN AND
ARROW

SLABS

SOME MAY BE
TEMPTED TO TURN
LEFT ALONG THE
WALL - DON'T EVEN
THINK ABOUT IT

NO SIGN
163

RUIN

THERE IS A NAME
FOR THIS LONELY
ROAD CROSSING
- THE MIDDLE
OF NOWHERE ...

MAP 99

A689

A689

A689 ROAD
CROSSING
162

STONE
MARKER

CROSS FENCE
161

0   ¼ mile

0   APPROX SCALE   500m

45 MINS–1 HR TO KELLAH BURN (MAP 100)

2 HRS 30 MINS–3 HRS FROM
SLAGGYFORD (MAP 97)

1 HR 45 MINS–2 HRS 30 MINS FROM KELLAH BURN (MAP 100)

2 HRS 45 MINS–3 HRS 30 MINS
TO SLAGGYFORD (MAP 97)

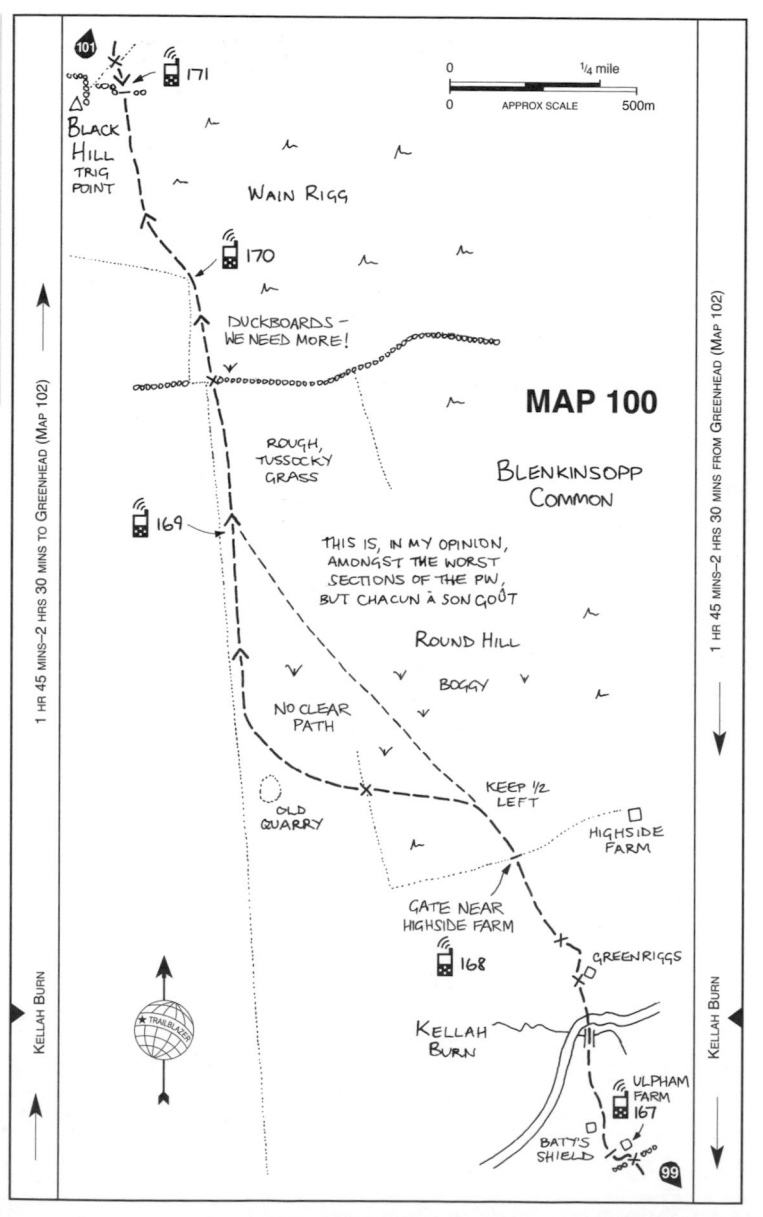

MAP 100

1 HR 45 MINS–2 HRS 30 MINS TO GREENHEAD (MAP 102)

1 HR 45 MINS–2 HRS 30 MINS FROM GREENHEAD (MAP 102)

KELLAH BURN

KELLAH BURN

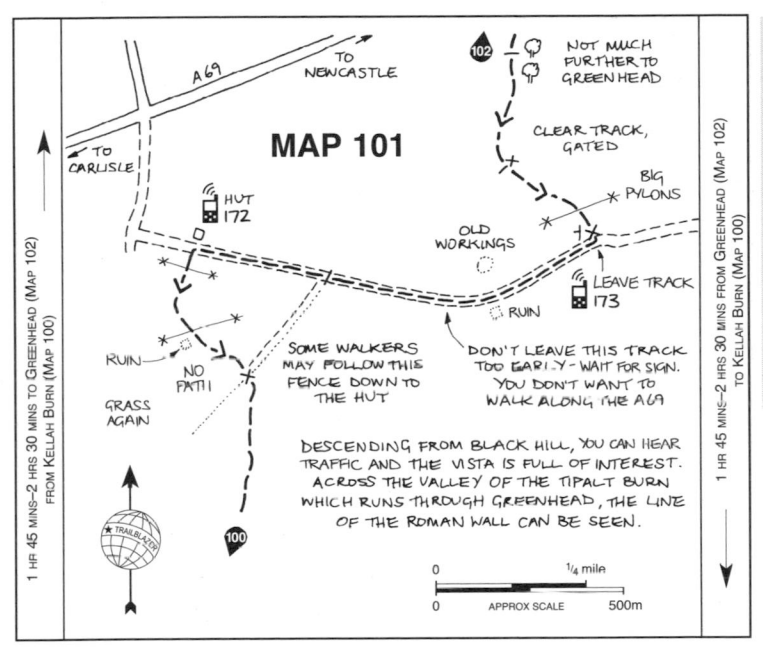

MAP 101

A69

TO NEWCASTLE

TO CARLISLE

102 — NOT MUCH FURTHER TO GREENHEAD

CLEAR TRACK, GATED

BIG PYLONS

HUT 172

OLD WORKINGS

LEAVE TRACK 173

RUIN

RUIN

NO PATH

SOME WALKERS MAY FOLLOW THIS FENCE DOWN TO THE HUT

DON'T LEAVE THIS TRACK TOO EARLY - WAIT FOR SIGN. YOU DON'T WANT TO WALK ALONG THE A69

GRASS AGAIN

DESCENDING FROM BLACK HILL, YOU CAN HEAR TRAFFIC AND THE VISTA IS FULL OF INTEREST. ACROSS THE VALLEY OF THE TIPALT BURN WHICH RUNS THROUGH GREENHEAD, THE LINE OF THE ROMAN WALL CAN BE SEEN.

★ TRAILBLAZER

100

0   ¼ mile

0   APPROX SCALE   500m

1 HR 45 MINS–2 HRS 30 MINS TO GREENHEAD (MAP 102)
FROM KELLAH BURN (MAP 100)

1 HR 45 MINS–2 HRS 30 MINS FROM GREENHEAD (MAP 102)
TO KELLAH BURN (MAP 100)

ROUTE GUIDE AND MAPS

GREENHEAD [Map 102]

Having arrived in the rather dispersed hamlet of Greenhead, you can take solace from the fact that you're very near **Britain's geographical centre**; a point equidistant from all shores. Not a lot of people know that.

Transport

The line for the Newcastle to Carlisle railway runs through Greenhead but services no longer stop here. If this alarms you inconsolably Arriva operates hourly **buses** to Haltwhistle **railway** station, only 3 miles (5km) away. Greenhead is also a stop on the Hadrian's Wall bus route (AD122 and No 185) to Once Brewed, Hexham, Newcastle and Carlisle (see public transport map and table, pp42-6).

Where to stay and eat

Right in the centre, *Roam-n-Rest Caravan Park* (☎ 01697-747213) knows a cunning pun when it sees one and is a tidy site which charges **campers** £4 per tent. It's open Apr-Oct.

A converted Methodist chapel houses the 40-bed *Greenhead Youth Hostel* (☎ 0870-770 5842, 🖳 dougsandragreenh@ btconnect.com; Feb-Oct; 40 beds), now owned by the hotel over the road, where beds cost £13 (£9.50 under 18s) and evening meals are available.

Nearby *Four Wynds Guest House* (☎ 01697-747972, 🖳 www.four-wynds-guest-house.co.uk) changed hands in 2007 and the new owners are building new rooms all of which will be en suite with a shower; they are also building a bathroom for anyone who prefers to have a bath. They expect to charge £28 per person and hope to be open by June 2008 but check the website.

The much-improved *Greenhead Hotel* (☎ 01697-747411, 🖳 www.greenhead-hotel.co.uk; 3D/1T all en suite), in the middle of town, offers B&B in spacious rooms for £65 for two sharing and around £40 for single occupancy; there is room in two of the doubles for an extra bed. It's your only bet for a **feed in the evening** but that too is much improved thanks to the new enthusiastic owners. Food is served Mar-Sep daily noon-8.30pm, Oct-Mar daily noon-3pm, 5.30-8.30pm.

Back on the Way, half a mile north of the village, *Holmhead Guest House* (☎ 01697-747402, 🖳 www.holmhead.com; 2T/2D all en suite) was on the market in 2007 but still should be a multiple accommodation complex for Wall-bound wayfarers. The pleasant walk there crosses a river, follows a track along the bank, through sheep fields and thence to the homestead.

If she's still there Pauline, who works as a local archaeological and historical guide, will be able to answer most of your questions as she serves up an exceptional evening meal (B&B guests only; £25) or a no less impressive breakfast. There's a drying room and if the rates (£66-70 for two sharing, £43 for single occupancy) are too steep they also have an 8-berth **camping barn** (£12 plus £3 for a sleeping bag) and if you're nearly skint you can **camp** for £5.

There's a kitchenette in the camping barn and Pauline will sell basic ingredients (such as milk or bread) to anyone in the camping barn.

❏ Thirlwall Castle

Thirlwall Castle was built in the 14th century by the powerful like-named family for protection and defence against border raiders. At that time the castle must have represented an impregnable stronghold to men armed only with spear and sword but by the 17th century these lawless times had passed and the Thirlwall family moved to more comfortable quarters in Hexham.

As a reminder of a time when the Borders were the scene of raids and struggles, Thirlwall serves a purpose but we have more absorbing antiquities than this to investigate. Ahead lies The Wall! But see p216 if you want a cup of tea before heading off.

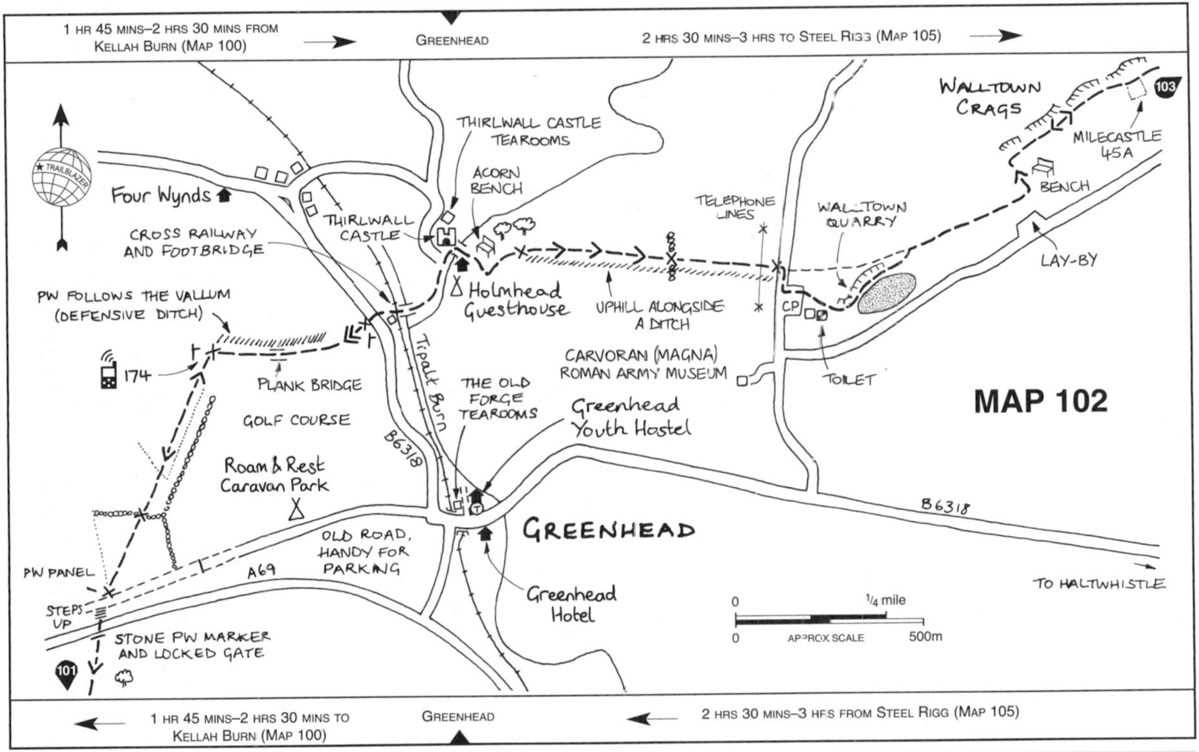
1 HR 45 MINS–2 HRS 30 MINS FROM KELLAH BURN (MAP 100)
GREENHEAD
2 HRS 30 MINS–3 HRS TO STEEL RIGG (MAP 105)
TRAILBLAZER
Four Wynds
CROSS RAILWAY AND FOOTBRIDGE
THIRLWALL CASTLE
THIRLWALL CASTLE TEAROOMS
ACORN BENCH
Holmhead Guesthouse
UPHILL ALONGSIDE A DITCH
TELEPHONE LINES
WALLTOWN QUARRY
WALLTOWN CRAGS
MILECASTLE 45A
BENCH
LAY-BY
CP
TOILET
PW FOLLOWS THE VALLUM (DEFENSIVE DITCH)
174
PLANK BRIDGE
GOLF COURSE
Tipalt Burn
B6318
THE OLD FORGE TEAROOMS
Greenhead Youth Hostel
CARVORAN (MAGNA) ROMAN ARMY MUSEUM
MAP 102
Roam & Rest Caravan Park
OLD ROAD, HANDY FOR PARKING
A69
GREENHEAD
Greenhead Hotel
B6318
TO HALTWHISTLE
0
1/4 mile
0
APPROX SCALE
500m
PW PANEL
STEPS UP
STONE PW MARKER AND LOCKED GATE
101
103
1 HR 45 MINS–2 HRS 30 MINS TO KELLAH BURN (MAP 100)
GREENHEAD
2 HRS 30 MINS–3 HRS FROM STEEL RIGG (MAP 105)

The *Old Forge Tea Rooms* (☎ 07921-864113; Mon-Wed and Fri-Sat 10am-5pm and Sun 11am-4.30pm; Nov to March or Easter Fri, Sat, Mon 10am-4.30pm, Sun 11am-4pm) serves snacks on home-made bread and an all-day breakfast.

Alternatively try *Thirlwall Castle Tearooms* (☎ 016977-47271; Thur-Mon 9.30am-5pm) which offers soup, bacon and sausage buns, toasties, scones and also does afternoon teas. The owner will open on a Wednesday if booked in advance.

GREENHEAD TO BELLINGHAM   MAPS 102-112

Route overview

Gird your loins for this is a tough one, a **22-mile (33km, 9-10½hrs)** stage that feels every yard of it thanks to over 900 galling metres of ascent; nearly as much as Day 1. You remember Day 1 don't you?

Greenhead is left behind via the rather inflated if not bouncy ruin of Thirlwall Castle and at **Walltown Crags** you join **Hadrian's Wall** itself. As you follow the best-preserved part of the wall for eight miles it is the frequent **climbs and drops**, many stepped, which will account for the day's exertions. Indeed you may prefer to break this stage (or lengthen the previous day) by staying in or around **Once Brewed** (Map 105).

The walk along the wall is now rather popular and for the first time since Malham you may feel a bit crowded by day-walking 'civilians'. If so, raise your eyes to the horizon and the views of the ramparts following the Whin Sill, swooping and soaring past the quacking wildfowl in **Crag Lough**.

Soon enough you reach **Rapishaw Gap** (Map 106) and forsake the Wall-walking throng, north towards sunless forests and some fine walking. Revisionists and environmentalists condemn the post-war boom in plantation monoculture which anyway now seems to have had its day thanks to foreign imports. The trails which pass through them too are dismissed though today at least, your transit through **Wark Forest** (Map 107) generally avoids the main gravel drives for more agreeable and shady trails which never overstay their welcome. Haughton Common is a sunlit interlude and when you emerge from the forest ahead of **Stonehaugh** (off Map 109) the now not so distant Cheviots can be seen to the far north.

Here ensues a pleasant mixture of pasture, farmland and quiet lanes until a radio mast indicates one more climb, **Shitlington Crag** (Map 111). Thereafter it's downhill all the way, the penultimate mile along the annoyingly busy B6320 until it bridges the North Tyne and leads you into town along the riverbank. This is actually a great day, overseen by the knowledge that journey's end is nigh. **Bellingham** awaits. Nobody gives up here.

Route-finding trouble spots

In short: there are none. The initial section along the Wall follows as fine a landmark as you could wish for, and once you head into the badlands of the former cattle-thieving barbarians things do not deteriorate. Indeed this feels like one of

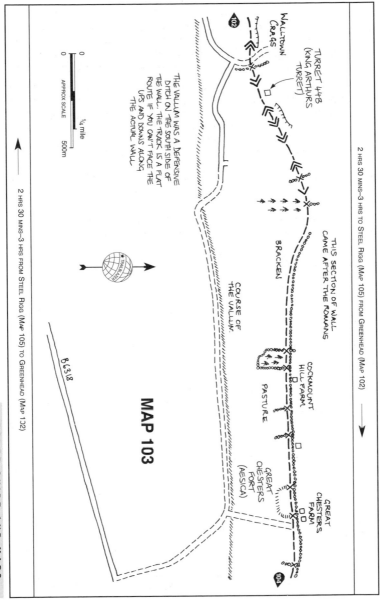

2 HRS 30 MINS–3 HRS TO STEEL RIGG (MAP 105) FROM GREENHEAD (MAP 102) →

WALLTOWN CRAGS

TURRET 44B (KING ARTHUR'S TURRET)

THIS SECTION OF WALL CAME AFTER THE ROMANS

BRACKEN

COURSE OF THE VALLUM

COCKMOUNT HILL FARM

PASTURE

GREAT CHESTERS FORT (AESICA)

GREAT CHESTERS FARM

THE VALLUM WAS A DEFENSIVE DITCH ON THE SOUTH SIDE OF THE WALL. THE TRACK IS A FLAT ROUTE IF YOU CAN'T FACE THE UPS AND DOWNS ALONG THE ACTUAL WALL.

0   APPROX SCALE   ¼ mile
0   500m

B6318

MAP 103

← 2 HRS 30 MINS–3 HRS FROM STEEL RIGG (MAP 105) TO GREENHEAD (MAP 102)

the best-marked stages on the entire Pennine Way; an example for which Northumberland National Park should be praised.

BURNHEAD [Map 104]

Right on the Pennine Way so you may well walk into it, you'll get a warm welcome at *Burnhead* (☎ 01434-320841, 🖳 www .burnheadbedandbreakfast.co.uk; 2T en suite) and they charge £30 per person (the single room costs £35); packed lunches are available on request.

Milecastle Inn (☎ 01434-321372, 🖳 www.milecastle-inn.co.uk) on Military Road is just 10 minutes walk away for an evening meal (food is served Easter to end Oct daily 12-9pm; 12-3pm & 6-9pm the rest of the year).

❏ Hadrian's Wall

The Roman Emperor Hadrian first conceived the project after visiting Britain in AD122 and finding out for himself the extent of the difficulty faced by the occupying army in northern Britain. It was impossible to hold any kind of control over the lawless tribes in the area that is now called Scotland so, as the Chinese had done nearly 400 years earlier, it was decided to build a defensive wall. The line of the wall, drawn from the Solway to the Tyne, followed the fault-line of the Whin Sill, an 'escarpment' of resistant dolerite which acted as a natural east–west barrier.

The Wall ran for approximately 80 Roman miles (73 modern miles or 117km) and had turrets or milecastles every (Roman) mile and larger forts at intervals along its length. The forts would have had a garrison of 500 cavalry or 1000 foot soldiers, and milecastles were manned by 50 men. The Wall was made of stone and turf and would have been five metres high and with a defensive ditch, the vallum, set between two mounds of earth, running the length of the southern side. Behind that ran a road to supply and provision the troops manning the wall.

The construction of the Wall was supervised by the Imperial Legate, Aulus Platorius Nepos, and construction took ten years. It remained in use for 200 years but as the Romans withdrew it fell into disuse and gradually the stones were plundered to build farmsteads and roads. Thirlwall Castle is among the many local buildings with stones from the Roman Wall.

Today English Heritage, the National Trust and the National Park authorities preserve and protect what remains of the wall, keeping it tidy and providing the information that we need to help us imagine what it was all for. It's well-worth visiting **Housesteads Fort** (off Map 106; ☎ 01434-344363, open daily 10am-6pm Apr-Sep and 10am-4pm Oct-Mar; adult £4.10), just before the Way heads north. You'll be pleased to know the communal latrines are particularly well preserved.

The information we have about the history of the Wall is fragmentary and circumstantial, historians having disputed for centuries over the finer details. What is certain is that the Wall is an extraordinary example of military might whilst demonstrating perhaps the futility of human endeavour. How can you hold back the tide of human expansion by anything so transient as a wall? Impressive, inspiring, unique, yes, but ultimately a failure. When we turn our back on it and head north into Wark Forest, the sight of the Whin Sill is like a breaking wave. The Wall blends into the landscape. The northern tribes had only to wait.

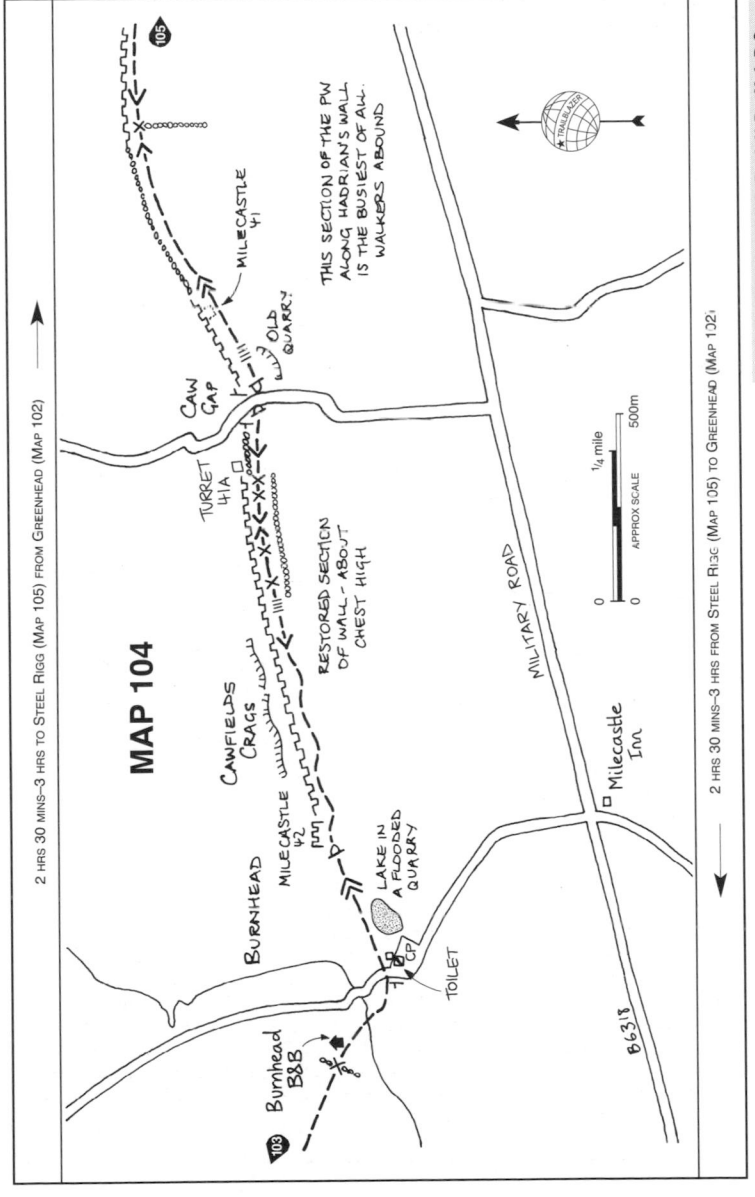

MAP 104

2 HRS 30 MINS–3 HRS TO STEEL RIGG (MAP 105) FROM GREENHEAD (MAP 102)

2 HRS 30 MINS–3 HRS FROM STEEL RIGG (MAP 105) TO GREENHEAD (MAP 102)

THIS SECTION OF THE PW ALONG HADRIAN'S WALL IS THE BUSIEST OF ALL WALKERS ABOUND.

MILECASTLE 41

OLD QUARRY

CAW GAP

TURRET 41A

RESTORED SECTION OF WALL – ABOUT CHEST HIGH

CAWFIELDS CRAGS

BURNHEAD

MILECASTLE 42

LAKE IN A FLOODED QUARRY

CP

TOILET

MILITARY ROAD

Milecastle Inn

B6318

Burnhead B&B

¼ mile   500m
APPROX SCALE

TRAILBLAZER

ONCE BREWED [Map 105]

Not really a village, Once Brewed is about half a mile south of the Way on the B6318, better known for nearly two millennia as the 'Military Road'.

Doubtless the origins of the name torment your curiosity. The Twice Brewed Inn, a staging post between Carlisle and Newcastle, gained its name around 1710 when General Wade found the local ale so weak he advised that it be brewed again. When the hostel was opened in the 1930s, the YHA's pithsome patron, Lady Trevelyan, remarked that she hoped her cup of tea would be brewed once, not twice like the General's ale and so the name was born.

See box p24 for details of the Roman Wall show held here in June.

Services

The Northumberland National Park Visitor Centre acts as a **tourist information centre** (TIC; ☎ 01434-344396, open 9.30am-5pm mid-March to Oct, to 5.30pm in July and August, Sat/Sun 10am-3pm Nov to mid-March) is the focal point with its own café. Visit ☐ www.hadrians-wall.org for the whole story on the area, including more regional accommodation.

Internet access is available at The Twice Brewed Inn (see column opposite).

Transport

The Hadrian's Wall **Bus** Service (designated route 'AD122' in honour of the Wall's inauguration by the Emperor Hadrian) stops outside the TIC throughout the season. Many of these buses also stop at the **railway station** at Haltwhistle on the Carlisle–Newcastle line with frequent trains coming and going throughout the day. The No 185 and No 681 also stop here. For further information see the public transport map and table, pp42-6).

For a **taxi**, call Sprouls Taxis (☎ 01434-321064 or ☎ 07712-321064) or Turnbulls (☎ 01434-320105).

Where to stay and eat

The obvious choice for **campers** is *Winshields Farm* (☎ 01434-344243, ☐ www.winshields.co.uk; open Apr to Nov) right by the main road, where the charge is £5 per person. They also have a **bunkhouse** sleeping nine for £6 per person. Everyone can use the shower/toilet facilities and a cooked breakfast can be provided as well as packed lunches. There is also a shop on site selling food essentials.

Once Brewed Youth Hostel (☎ 01434-344360, bookings ☎ 0870-770 5980, ☐ oncebrewed@yha.org.uk; open all year) is a purpose-built hostel with 77 beds, mostly in four-bedded rooms. You can book an evening meal and beds cost £14 (£10 for under 18s).

Other accommodation in the area includes the superior *Vallum Lodge* (☎ 01434-344248, ☐ www.vallum-lodge.co .uk; 3T/2D/1F all en suite) charging £66 for two and £50 for single occupancy.

Between the youth hostel and Vallum Lodge is *The Twice Brewed Inn* (☎ 01434-344534, ☐ www.twicebrewedinn.co.uk; 2S/3D & 3T en suite/3D & 3T) with a single for £28, basic doubles/twins from £48 and en suites from £60. The pub here serves food daily from 11am to 8.30pm (to 9pm Fri & Sat) in summer and daily 12-8pm (to 8.30pm Fri & Sat) in winter with some good vegetarian options and has broadband **internet** (£1 for 30 mins).

Another great spot is *Saughy Rigg Farm* (off Map 105; ☎ 01434-344120, ☐ www.saughyrigg.co.uk; 2S/3D/4T/2F en suite) charges £35 for a single; rates for two sharing are from £55 to £65. A four-course evening meal costs £17 (check out the mouthwatering menu on their website). The pleasingly isolated farm is about half a mile north of Hadrian's Wall along the road from the Steel Rigg car park.

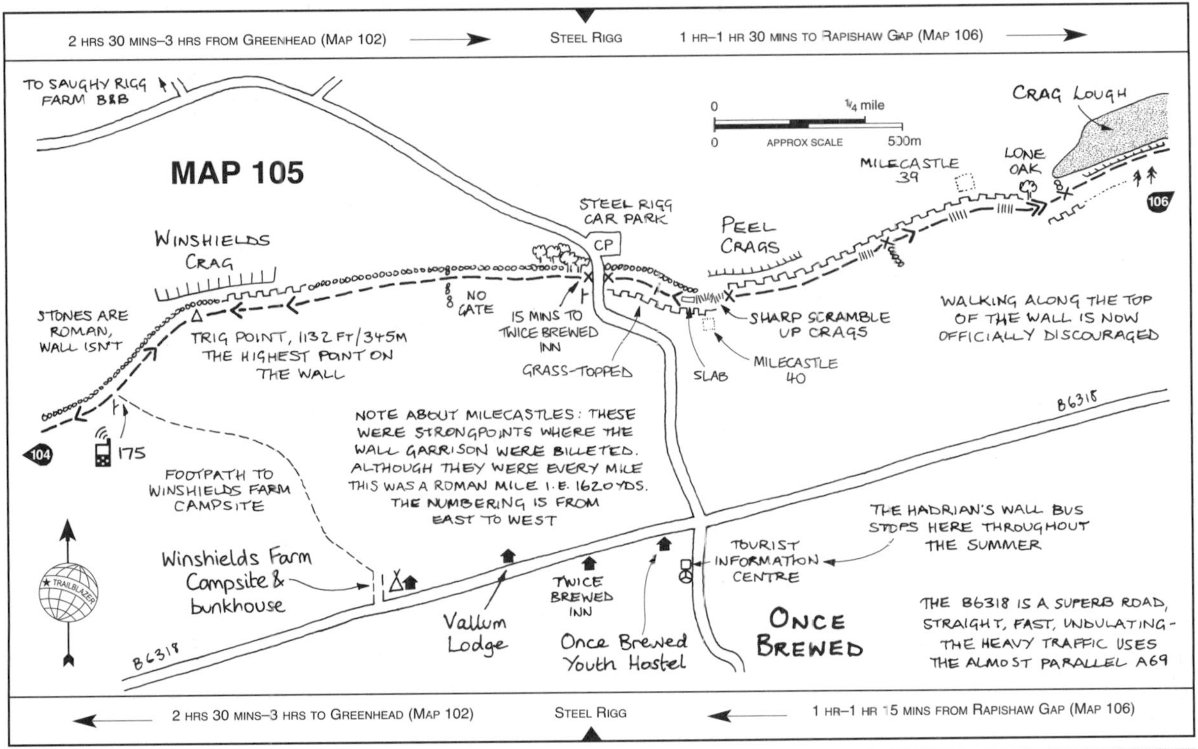
2 HRS 30 MINS–3 HRS FROM GREENHEAD (MAP 102)
STEEL RIGG
1 HR–1 HR 30 MINS TO RAPISHAW GAP (MAP 106)
TO SAUGHY RIGG FARM B&B
MAP 105
0 ¼ mile
0 APPROX SCALE 500m
CRAG LOUGH
LONE OAK
MILECASTLE 39
106
STEEL RIGG CAR PARK
CP
WINSHIELDS CRAG
PEEL CRAGS
STONES ARE ROMAN, WALL ISN'T
TRIG POINT, 1132 FT/345M THE HIGHEST POINT ON THE WALL
NO GATE
15 MINS TO TWICE BREWED INN
GRASS-TOPPED
SLAB
SHARP SCRAMBLE UP CRAGS
MILECASTLE 40
WALKING ALONG THE TOP OF THE WALL IS NOW OFFICIALLY DISCOURAGED
B6318
104
175
NOTE ABOUT MILECASTLES: THESE WERE STRONGPOINTS WHERE THE WALL GARRISON WERE BILLETED. ALTHOUGH THEY WERE EVERY MILE THIS WAS A ROMAN MILE I.E. 1620 YDS. THE NUMBERING IS FROM EAST TO WEST
FOOTPATH TO WINSHIELDS FARM CAMPSITE
THE HADRIAN'S WALL BUS STOPS HERE THROUGHOUT THE SUMMER
TOURIST INFORMATION CENTRE
Winshields Farm Campsite & bunkhouse
TWICE BREWED INN
TRAILBLAZER
Vallum Lodge
Once Brewed Youth Hostel
ONCE BREWED
THE B6318 IS A SUPERB ROAD, STRAIGHT, FAST, UNDULATING - THE HEAVY TRAFFIC USES THE ALMOST PARALLEL A69
B6318
2 HRS 30 MINS–3 HRS TO GREENHEAD (MAP 102)
STEEL RIGG
1 HR–1 HR 15 MINS FROM RAPISHAW GAP (MAP 106)

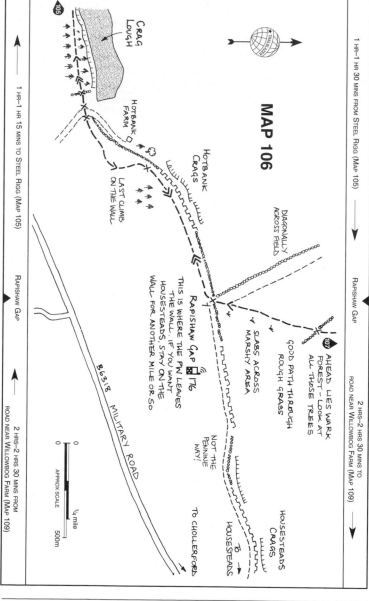

MAP 106

CRAG LOUGH

1 HR-1 HR 30 MINS FROM STEEL RIGG (MAP 105)

RAPISHAW GAP

2 HRS-2 HRS 30 MINS TO ROAD NEAR WILLOWBOG FARM (MAP 109)

HOTBANK FARM

HOTBANK CRAGS

LAST CLIMB ON THE WALL

1 HR-1 HR 15 MINS TO STEEL RIGG (MAP 105)

RAPISHAW GAP

2 HRS-2 HRS 30 MINS FROM ROAD NEAR WILLOWBOG FARM (MAP 109)

DIAGONALLY ACROSS FIELD

AHEAD LIES WARK FOREST – LOOK AT ALL THOSE TREES

107

GOOD PATH THROUGH ROUGH GRASS

SLABS ACROSS MARSHY AREA

Rapishaw Gap 176

THIS IS WHERE THE PW LEAVES THE WALL. IF YOU WANT HOUSESTEADS, STAY ON THE WALL FOR ANOTHER MILE OR SO

NOT THE PENNINE WAY!

HOUSESTEADS CRAGS

TO HOUSESTEADS

TO CHOLLERFORD

B6318 MILITARY ROAD

APPROX SCALE

0   ¼ mile

0   500m

222 Greenhead to Bellingham

ROUTE GUIDE AND MAPS

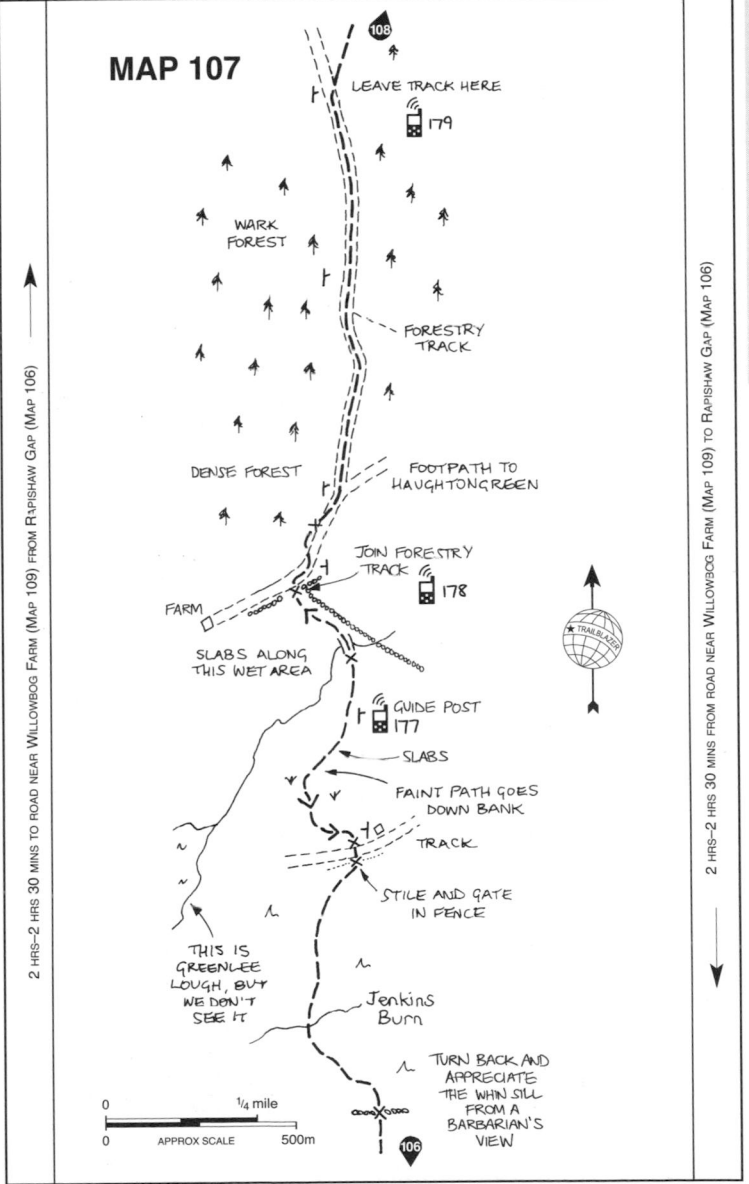

MAP 107

108

LEAVE TRACK HERE

179

WARK FOREST

FORESTRY TRACK

DENSE FOREST

FOOTPATH TO HAUGHTONGREEN

JOIN FORESTRY TRACK

178

FARM

SLABS ALONG THIS WET AREA

GUIDE POST 177

SLABS

FAINT PATH GOES DOWN BANK

TRACK

STILE AND GATE IN FENCE

THIS IS GREENLEE LOUGH, BUT WE DON'T SEE IT

Jenkins Burn

TURN BACK AND APPRECIATE THE WHIN SILL FROM A BARBARIAN'S VIEW

106

TRAILBLAZER

2 HRS–2 HRS 30 MINS TO ROAD NEAR WILLOWBOG FARM (MAP 109) FROM RAPISHAW GAP (MAP 106)

2 HRS–2 HRS 30 MINS FROM ROAD NEAR WILLOWBOG FARM (MAP 109) TO RAPISHAW GAP (MAP 106)

0   ¼ mile

0   APPROX SCALE   500m

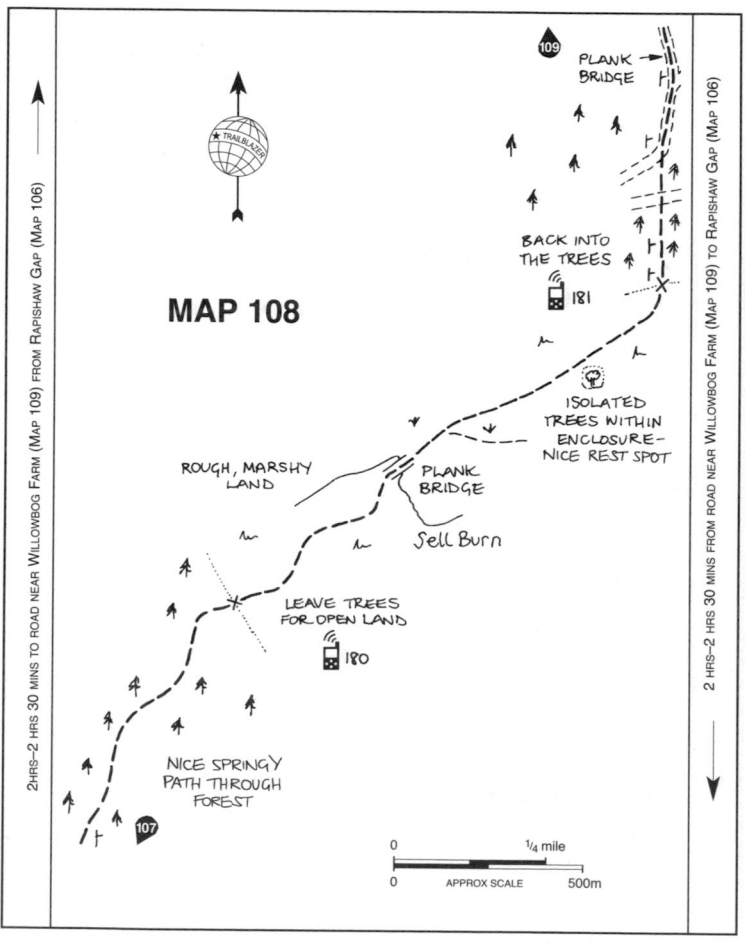

ROUTE GUIDE AND MAPS

2HRS–2 HRS 30 MINS TO ROAD NEAR WILLOWBOG FARM (MAP 109) FROM RAPISHAW GAP (MAP 106)

2 HRS–2 HRS 30 MINS FROM ROAD NEAR WILLOWBOG FARM (MAP 109) TO RAPISHAW GAP (MAP 106)

MAP 108

109
PLANK BRIDGE

BACK INTO THE TREES
181

ISOLATED TREES WITHIN ENCLOSURE – NICE REST SPOT

ROUGH, MARSHY LAND
PLANK BRIDGE
Sell Burn

LEAVE TREES FOR OPEN LAND
180

NICE SPRINGY PATH THROUGH FOREST
107

0 ...... ¼ mile
0 ...... APPROX SCALE 500m

STONEHAUGH   **[off Map 109]**
Aside from licking dew off the grass, there are hardly any opportunities for refreshments on the route today except at the forestry outpost of Stonehaugh, eight miles from Bellingham, where, if you feel that you simply cannot walk any further, you could head for the Forestry Commission's

Stonehaugh Camp Site (☎ 01434-230798). The site, which charges £4 per tent plus £4 per person, is open from April to October. It's a mile off the route and there are no shops for five miles although they can provide provisions and a packed lunch if you call ahead though they may request a deposit.

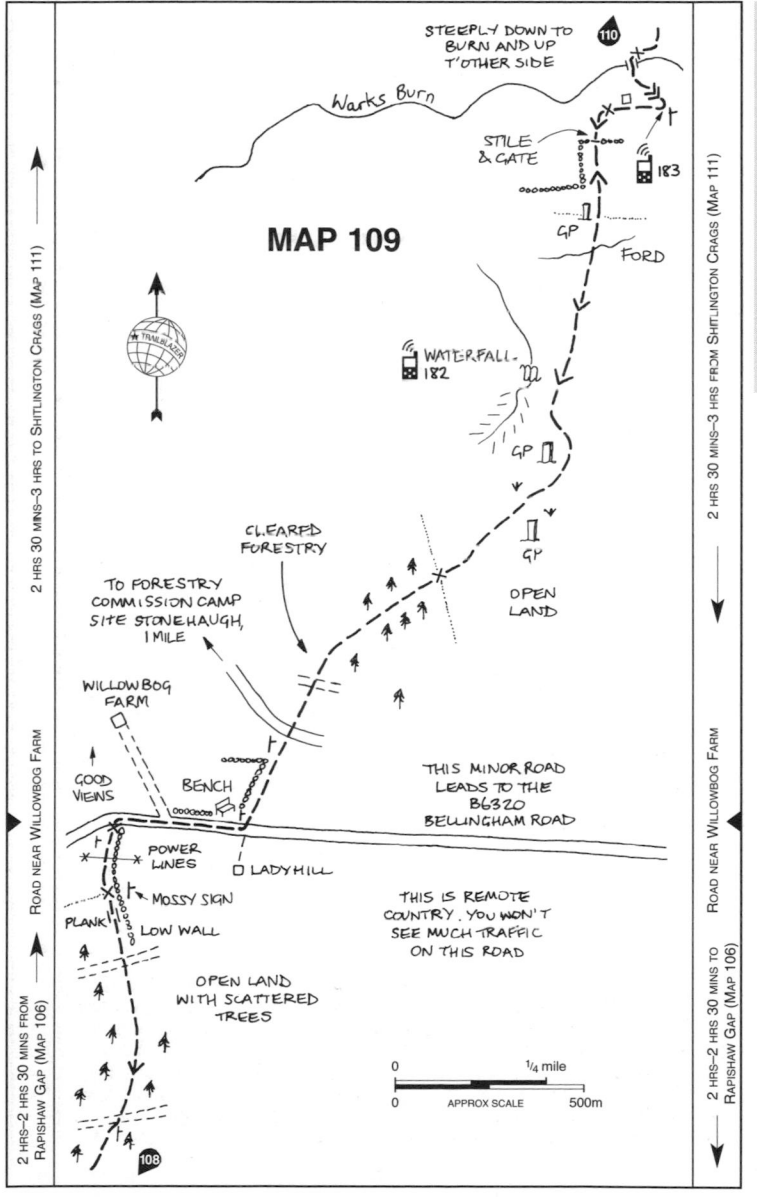

MAP 109

STEEPLY DOWN TO
BURN AND UP
T'OTHER SIDE

110

Warks Burn

STILE
& GATE

183

GP

FORD

WATERFALL
182

GP

CLEARED
FORESTRY

GP

OPEN
LAND

TO FORESTRY
COMMISSION CAMP
SITE STONEHAUGH,
1 MILE

WILLOWBOG
FARM

GOOD
VIEWS

BENCH

THIS MINOR ROAD
LEADS TO THE
B6320
BELLINGHAM ROAD

POWER
LINES

LADYHILL

MOSSY SIGN

PLANK

LOW WALL

THIS IS REMOTE
COUNTRY. YOU WON'T
SEE MUCH TRAFFIC
ON THIS ROAD

OPEN LAND
WITH SCATTERED
TREES

0   ¼ mile

0   APPROX SCALE   500m

108

2 HRS 30 MINS–3 HRS TO SHITLINGTON CRAGS (MAP 111)

2 HRS 30 MINS–3 HRS FROM SHITLINGTON CRAGS (MAP 111)

ROAD NEAR WILLOWBOG FARM

ROAD NEAR WILLOWBOG FARM

2 HRS–2 HRS 30 MINS FROM RAPISHAW GAP (MAP 106)

2 HRS–2 HRS 30 MINS TO RAPISHAW GAP (MAP 106)

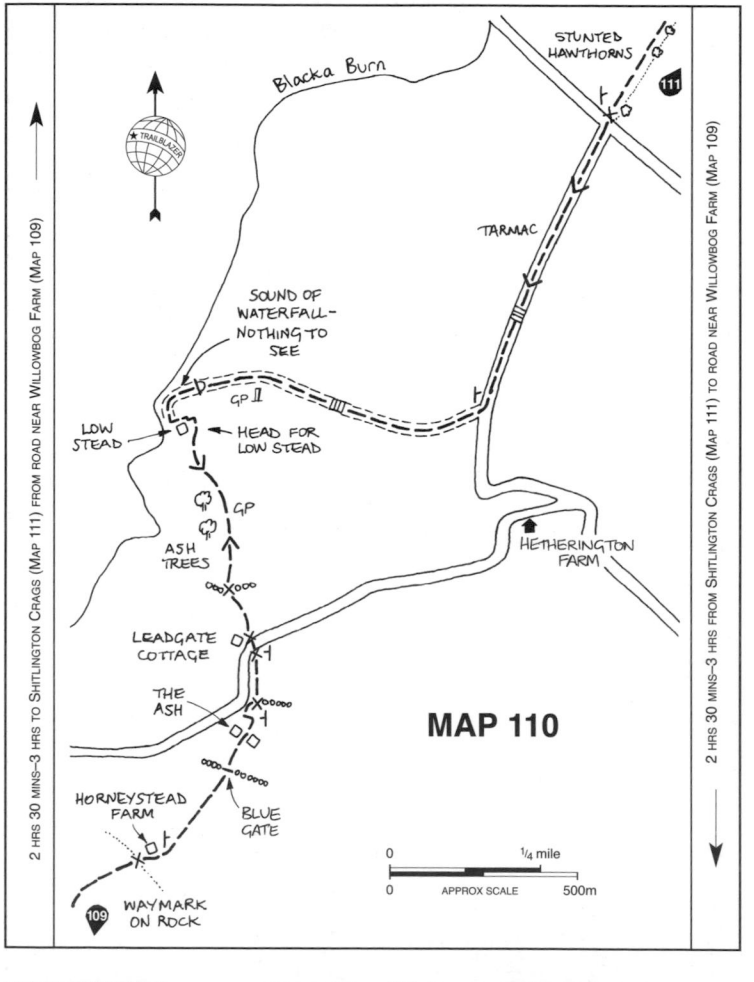

MAP 110

HETHERINGTON [Map 110]

Two miles further on *Hetherington Farm* (☎ 01434-230260; 2D/1T) just a few hundred metres from the Way welcomes walkers and offers very comfortable B&B with a double en suite with a four-poster bed for £70 for two sharing (£40 single occupancy), the other double, also en suite, at £60 or £35 single occupancy, and a standard twin for £52 or £30 single. The owner will take you to the pub in the evening for a meal.

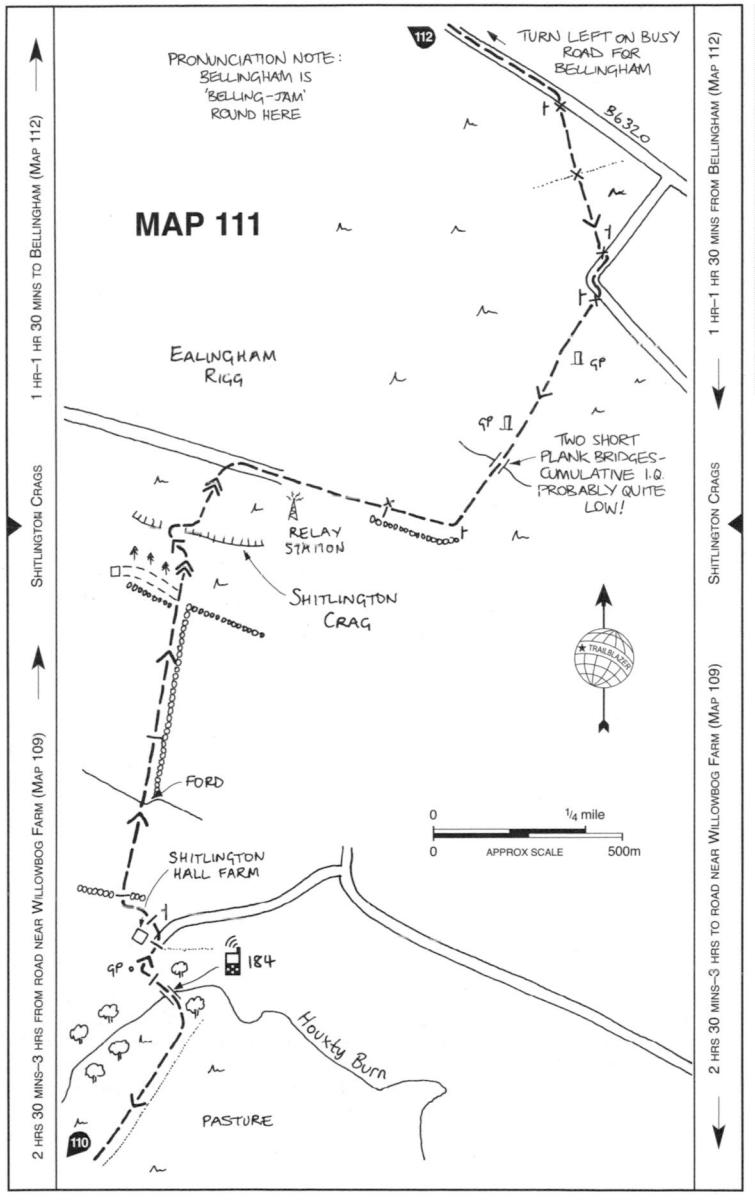

MAP 111

PRONUNCIATION NOTE:
BELLINGHAM IS
'BELLING-JAM'
ROUND HERE

TURN LEFT ON BUSY ROAD FOR BELLINGHAM

B6320

EALINGHAM RIGG

RELAY STATION

SHITLINGTON CRAG

TWO SHORT PLANK BRIDGES - CUMULATIVE I.Q. PROBABLY QUITE LOW!

gp

gp

FORD

SHITLINGTON HALL FARM

gp

184

Houxty Burn

PASTURE

TRAILBLAZER

0   1/4 mile
0   APPROX SCALE   500m

1 HR-1 HR 30 MINS TO BELLINGHAM (MAP 112)

SHITLINGTON CRAGS

2 HRS 30 MINS-3 HRS FROM ROAD NEAR WILLOWBOG FARM (MAP 109)

1 HR-1 HR 30 MINS FROM BELLINGHAM (MAP 112)

SHITLINGTON CRAGS

2 HRS 30 MINS-3 HRS TO ROAD NEAR WILLOWBOG FARM (MAP 109)

ROUTE GUIDE AND MAPS

BELLINGHAM [Map 112a]

This old market town on the North Tyne is the last place on the Pennine Way offering most things you may need. Note Bellingham is pronounced Belling-jam.

See box p24 for details of the show held here in August.

Services

Besides the **tourist information centre** (☎ 01434-220616, 🖳 bellinghamtic@btconnect.com; Easter to late May & Oct Mon-Sat 9.30am-1pm, 2-5pm, late May to end Sep Mon-Sat 9.30am-1pm, 2-5.30pm, Easter to end Sep Sun 1-5pm, Nov-Easter Mon-Fri 1-4pm), there's a **post office**, **chemist**, **bakery** and a couple of **supermarkets** (Mon-Sat 8am-10pm, Sun 10am-10pm). Coleman fuel and gas canisters are sold at Bellingham Country Stores.

Barclays has a **cash machine** but the Lloyds TSB branch doesn't.

Transport

Bellingham is a stop on **bus** services run by Snaiths, Tyne Valley Coaches and the Royal Mail Postbus (see public transport map and table, pp42-6). For a **taxi** call Howard Snaith Coaches ☎ 01830-520609 or Bellingham Taxis ☎ 01434-220570.

Where to stay

Before the bridge on your way to town you'll pass *Bellingham Brown Rigg Camping and Caravan Club* (☎ 01434-220175; Easter to Oct) which charges £5.65 plus £6.60 per person.

Closer to the town centre *Demesne Farm Campsite and Bunkhouse* (☎ 01434-220258, 🖳 www.demesnefarmcampsite.co.uk) has camping for £4.50 and its 15-bed self-catering **bunkhouse** (£15.95/£11.95) was affiliated to the YHA in 2007, effectively becoming the Bellingham YH. It has a well-equipped kitchen and a sitting area.

Lynn View (☎ 01434-220344; 1T/2D; open Mar-Nov) offer B&B for only £44 for two sharing and £24 for single occupancy.

Crofters End (☎ 01434-220034; 1S/1T or F) is another friendly place where standard rooms cost £25 per person; they are open Easter to Oct and are right on the

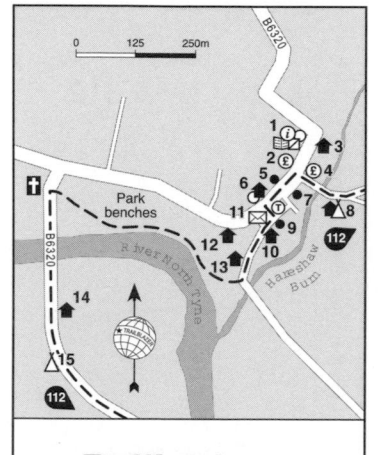

Bellingham
MAP 112a

Where to stay and eat
1 Fountain Cottage Tea Rooms
3 Lynn View
6 Cheviot Hotel
8 Demesne Farm Campsite & YHA bunkhouse
10 The Rose & Crown
12 The Black Bull
13 Lyndale GH
14 Crofters End
15 Brown Rigg Camping Park

Other
1 TIC, library & toilet
2 Barclays
4 LloydsTSB
5 Chemist
7 Bellingham Country Stores
9 Co-op
11 Post Office

Pennine Way. *Lyndale Guest House* (☎ 01434-220361, 🖳 www.lyndaleguesthouse.co.uk; 1D/1T/1F) is a bright and friendly place charging £30 per person. The family room is actually a 'unit' – a double and a single room with a bathroom in between.

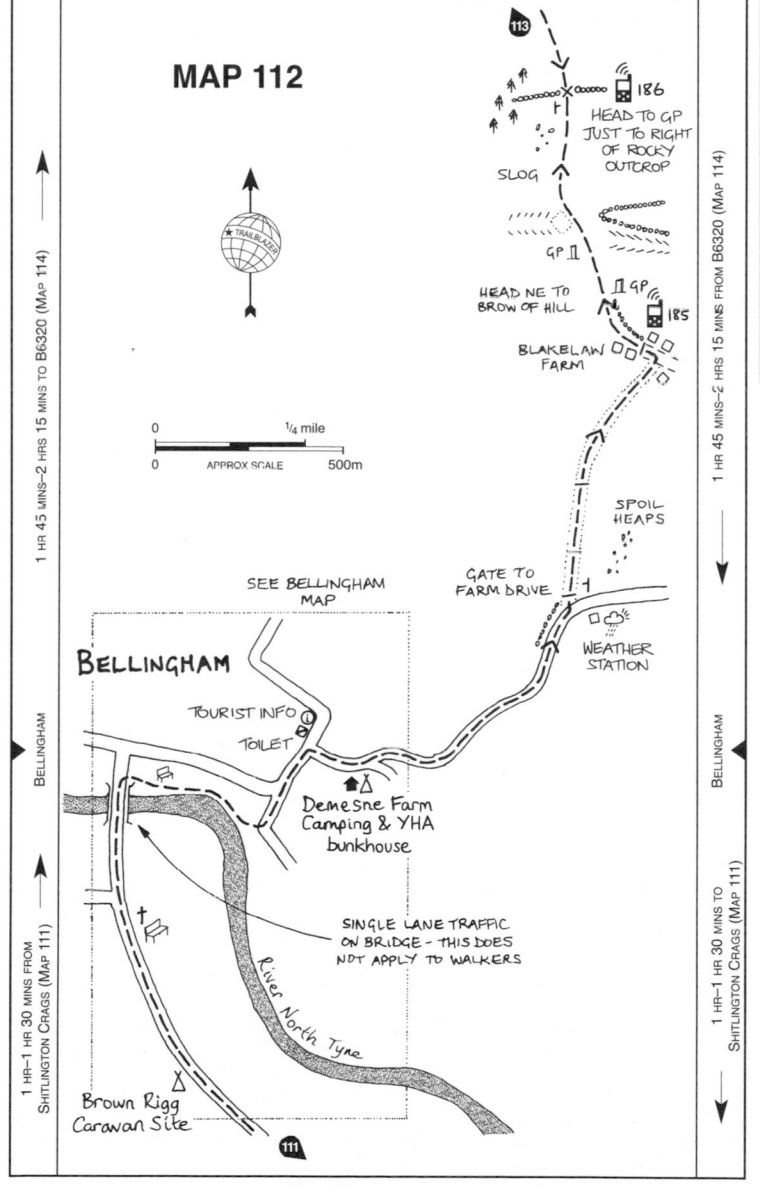

MAP 112

TRAILBLAZER

0 — 1/4 mile
APPROX SCALE
0 — 500m

113

186
HEAD TO GP
JUST TO RIGHT
OF ROCKY
OUTCROP

SLOG

GP

GP
HEAD NE TO
BROW OF HILL

185

BLAKELAW
FARM

SPOIL
HEAPS

GATE TO
FARM DRIVE

SEE BELLINGHAM
MAP

BELLINGHAM

WEATHER
STATION

TOURIST INFO
TOILET

Demesne Farm
Camping & YHA
bunkhouse

SINGLE LANE TRAFFIC
ON BRIDGE – THIS DOES
NOT APPLY TO WALKERS

River North Tyne

Brown Rigg
Caravan Site

111

1 HR 45 MINS–2 HRS 15 MINS TO B6320 (MAP 114)

1 HR 45 MINS–2 HRS 15 MINS FROM B6320 (MAP 114)

BELLINGHAM

BELLINGHAM

1 HR–1 HR 30 MINS FROM
SHITLINGTON CRAGS (MAP 111)

1 HR–1 HR 30 MINS TO
SHITLINGTON CRAGS (MAP 111)

Of the pubs *The Cheviot Hotel* (☎ 01434-220696, 🖥 www.thecheviothotel.co .uk; 1S/3T/2D/1F all en suite) is the best choice at £56 for two sharing or £32 for the single.

Where to eat

Fountain Cottage Tea Rooms (Tue-Sun 10am-5pm summer), by the tourist information centre, does light lunches and teas. *The*

Cheviot Hotel (see left) is the best of the pubs, with favourites such as steak and ale pie (£6.25) or fish & chips (takeaway for £3.10) and a carvery on Sunday; food is served Mon-Sat 12-2pm, Sun 12.30-2.30pm & daily 7-9pm takeaways available till 10pm. *The Black Bull* (open evenings only) and *Rose and Crown* also do pub grub.

Besides the tearoom and the pubs your only option is a snack from the **bakery**.

BELLINGHAM TO BYRNESS   MAPS 112-120

Route overview

It's only **15 miles (24km, 7¼-9hrs)** from Bellingham to the lonesome frontier outpost of Byrness, a place of minimal services and interest other than as the penultimate overnight stop on the Pennine Way.

The good news is that this stage is, in local vernacular 'a dolly', an easy and occasionally thrilling section and just what a personal trainer would recommend prior to your upcoming trans-Cheviot marathon.

Once you've climbed out of the North Tyne valley onto the moors it's an enjoyable day too, far from noisy roads as you meander through knee-deep heather over **Deer Play** (Map 114), **Whitley Pike** (Map 115) and around **Padon Hill's** (Map 116) distinctive cairn.

At this point a short, steep and sodden ascent alonside **Redesdale Forest** leads to a interminable slalom of irksome bog- and puddle-dodging between the plantation's northern edge and a fence. You'll need to be nimble-footed if you want to keep your feet dry.

When this ends at a **Forestry Commission sign** (Map 117) welcoming Pennine Way walkers the fun, such as it's been, ends. From here on you're trudging up and down, a little left, a little right along a forestry road that you're warned is used by logging machinery. A spell to magic up a temporary mountain bike could come in handy.

Soon the A68 comes into both earshot and view and you converge with it near **Blakehope Burn** car park (Map 119). Here the last mile or so to **Byrness** is a pleasant walk through woodland and along the **River Rede**, a gentle end to a thankfully undemanding if soggy-bottomed day. Just as well for tomorrow requires heroic commitment.

Route-finding trouble spots

In very bad visibility the route may get a little thin as it branches around a bog below Callerhues Crag on the way to Hareshaw House. Soon after, at the B6320 you must make sure you set off at the right bearing, NNW, to lock on to the line of guide posts leading to Deer Play hill then down and up again to Whitley Pike.

The descent from here to the minor road crossing, Padon Hill, Brownrigg Head and all that follows is staightforward if irritating with extremes of unavoidable peat mush and mindless forestry roads.

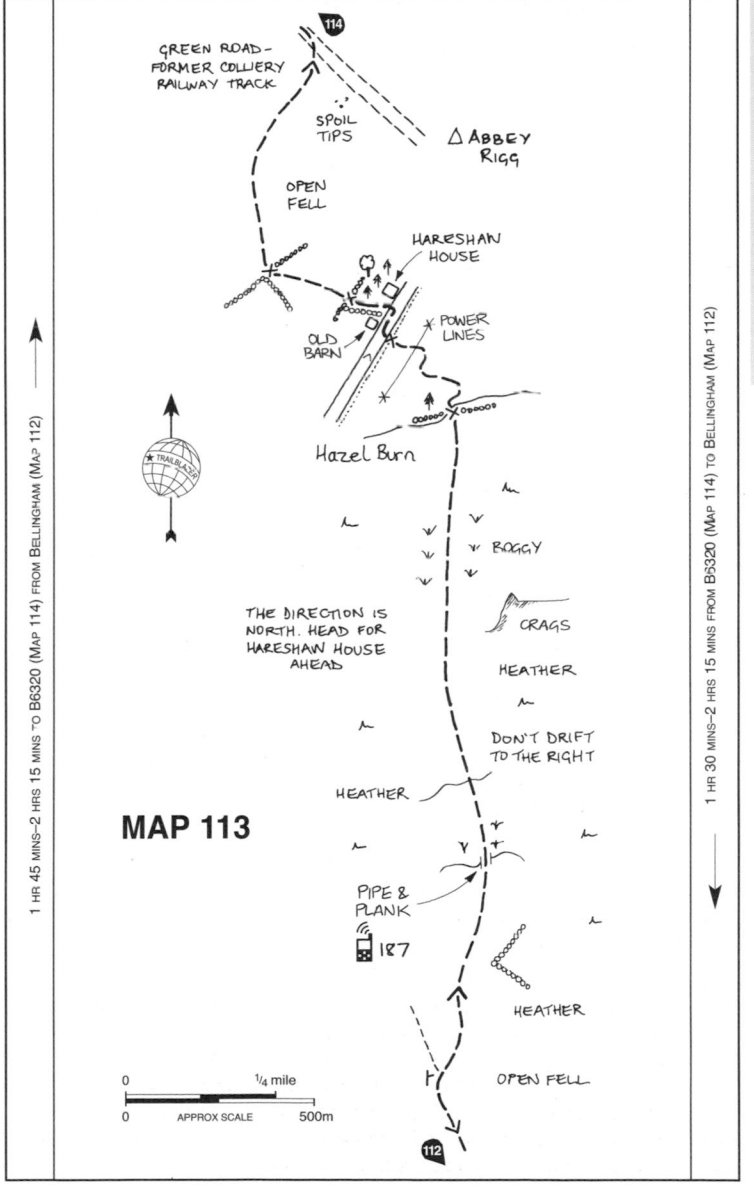

ROUTE GUIDE AND MAPS

GREEN ROAD –
FORMER COLLIERY
RAILWAY TRACK

114

SPOIL
TIPS

△ ABBEY
RIGG

OPEN
FELL

HARESHAW
HOUSE

OLD
BARN

POWER
LINES

TRAIL BLAZER

Hazel Burn

BOGGY

THE DIRECTION IS
NORTH. HEAD FOR
HARESHAW HOUSE
AHEAD

CRAGS

HEATHER

DON'T DRIFT
TO THE RIGHT

HEATHER

MAP 113

PIPE &
PLANK

187

HEATHER

HEATHER

OPEN FELL

0   ¼ mile

0   APPROX SCALE   500m

112

1 HR 45 MINS–2 HRS 15 MINS TO B6320 (MAP 114) FROM BELLINGHAM (MAP 112)

1 HR 30 MINS–2 HRS 15 MINS FROM B6320 (MAP 114) TO BELLINGHAM (MAP 112)

ROUTE GUIDE AND MAPS

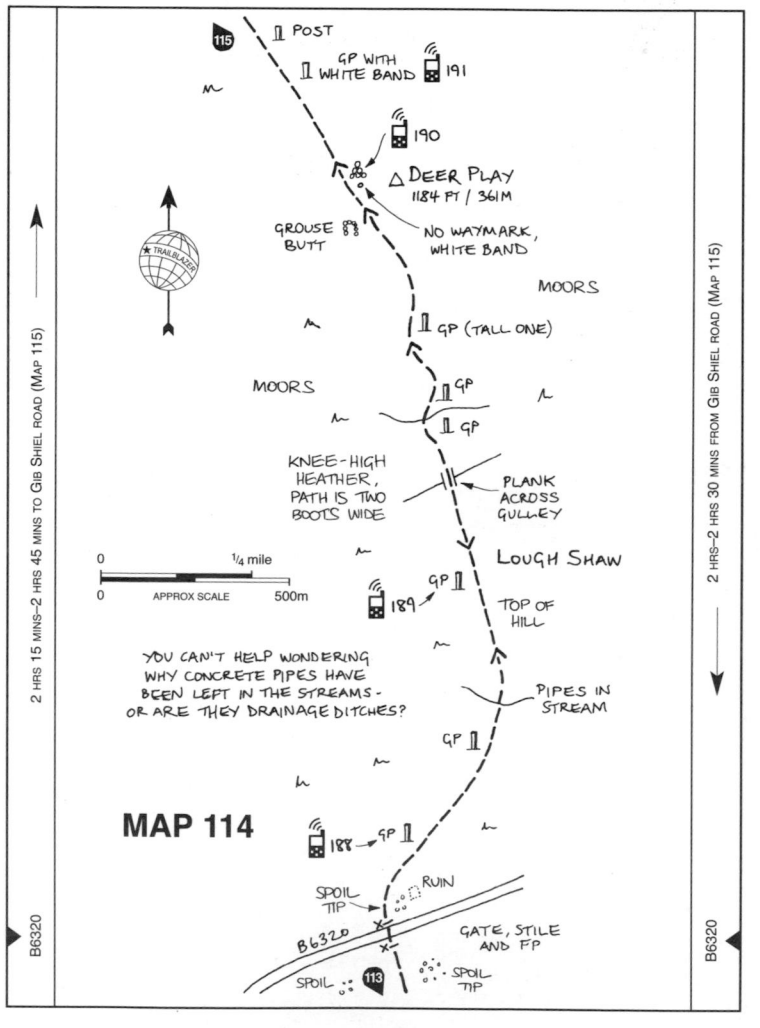

2 HRS 15 MINS–2 HRS 45 MINS TO GIB SHIEL ROAD (MAP 115)

2 HRS–2 HRS 30 MINS FROM GIB SHIEL ROAD (MAP 115)

POST

GP WITH WHITE BAND   191

190

△ DEER PLAY
1184 FT / 361M

GROUSE BUTT

NO WAYMARK, WHITE BAND

MOORS

GP (TALL ONE)

MOORS

GP

GP

KNEE-HIGH HEATHER, PATH IS TWO BOOTS WIDE

PLANK ACROSS GULLEY

LOUGH SHAW

GP

189   GP

TOP OF HILL

YOU CAN'T HELP WONDERING WHY CONCRETE PIPES HAVE BEEN LEFT IN THE STREAMS – OR ARE THEY DRAINAGE DITCHES?

PIPES IN STREAM

GP

MAP 114

188   GP

SPOIL TIP

RUIN

B6320

GATE, STILE AND FP

SPOIL

SPOIL TIP

★ TRAILBLAZER

¼ mile

0

APPROX SCALE   500m

B6320

B6320

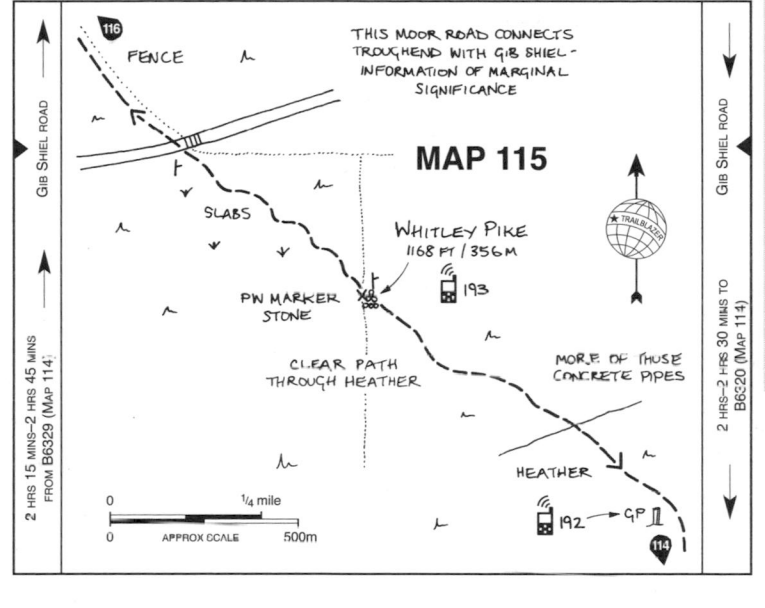

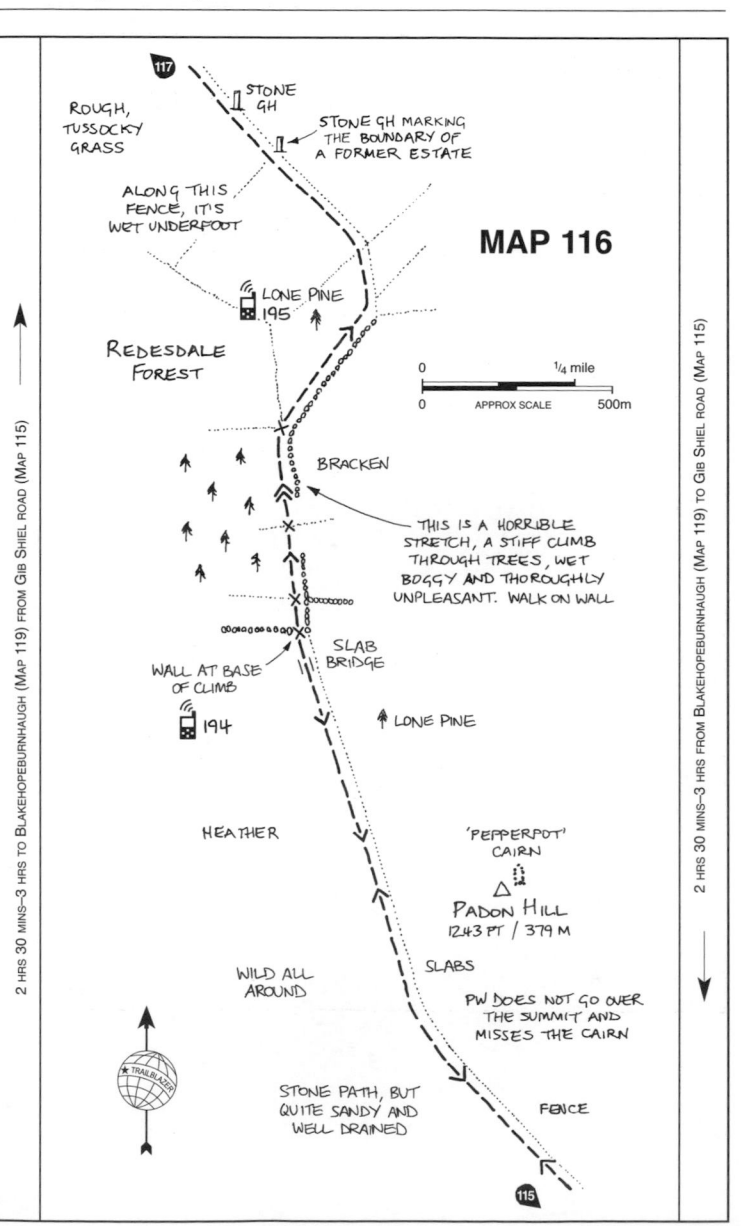

MAP 116

117

STONE GH

STONE GH MARKING
THE BOUNDARY OF
A FORMER ESTATE

ROUGH,
TUSSOCKY
GRASS

ALONG THIS
FENCE, IT'S
WET UNDERFOOT

LONE PINE
195

REDESDALE
FOREST

0   1/4 mile

0   500m
APPROX SCALE

BRACKEN

THIS IS A HORRIBLE
STRETCH, A STIFF CLIMB
THROUGH TREES, WET
BOGGY AND THOROUGHLY
UNPLEASANT. WALK ON WALL

SLAB
BRIDGE

WALL AT BASE
OF CLIMB

194

LONE PINE

HEATHER

'PEPPERPOT'
CAIRN

△
PADON HILL
1243 PT / 379 M

WILD ALL
AROUND

SLABS

PW DOES NOT GO OVER
THE SUMMIT AND
MISSES THE CAIRN

STONE PATH, BUT
QUITE SANDY AND
WELL DRAINED

FENCE

115

TRAILBLAZER

2 HRS 30 MINS–3 HRS TO BLAKEHOPEBURNHAUGH (MAP 119) FROM GIB SHIEL ROAD (MAP 115)

2 HRS 30 MINS–3 HRS FROM BLAKEHOPEBURNHAUGH (MAP 119) TO GIB SHIEL ROAD (MAP 115)

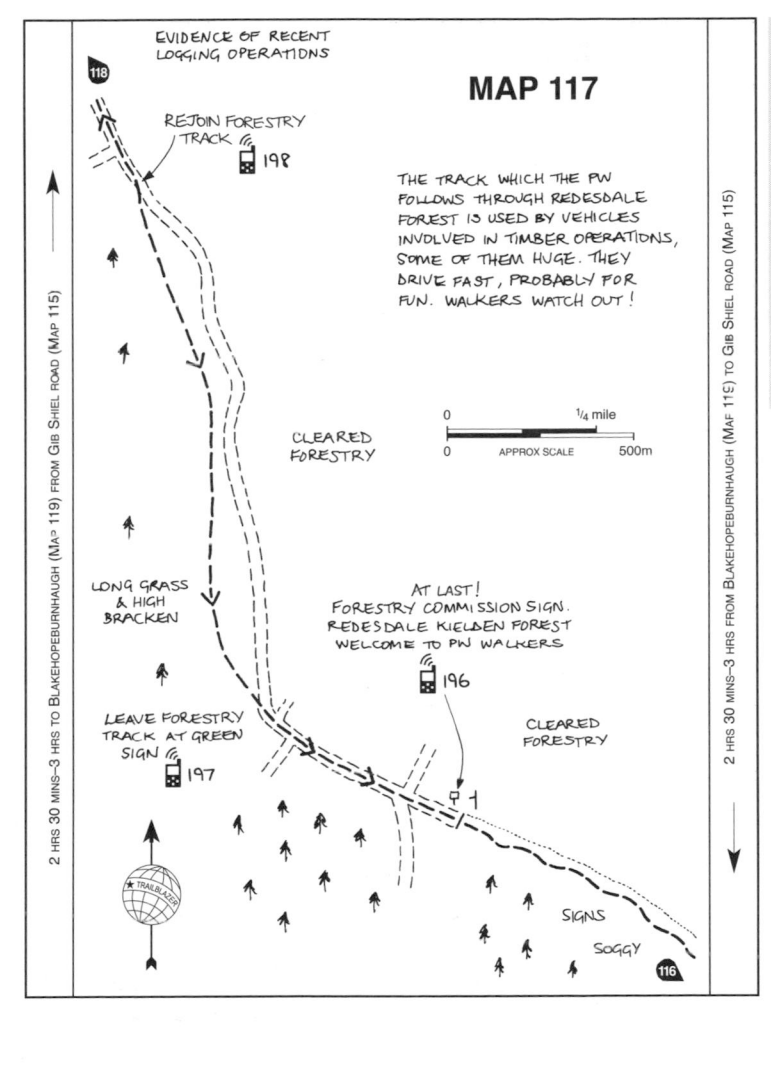

EVIDENCE OF RECENT LOGGING OPERATIONS

118

MAP 117

REJOIN FORESTRY TRACK 198

THE TRACK WHICH THE PW FOLLOWS THROUGH REDESDALE FOREST IS USED BY VEHICLES INVOLVED IN TIMBER OPERATIONS, SOME OF THEM HUGE. THEY DRIVE FAST, PROBABLY FOR FUN. WALKERS WATCH OUT!

CLEARED FORESTRY

0   1/4 mile
0   APPROX SCALE   500m

LONG GRASS & HIGH BRACKEN

AT LAST! FORESTRY COMMISSION SIGN. REDESDALE KIELDEN FOREST WELCOME TO PW WALKERS 196

CLEARED FORESTRY

LEAVE FORESTRY TRACK AT GREEN SIGN 197

★ TRAILBLAZER

SIGNS

SOGGY

116

2 HRS 30 MINS–3 HRS TO BLAKEHOPEBURNHAUGH (MAP 119) FROM GIB SHIEL ROAD (MAP 115)

2 HRS 30 MINS–3 HRS FROM BLAKEHOPEBURNHAUGH (MAP 119) TO GIB SHIEL ROAD (MAP 115)

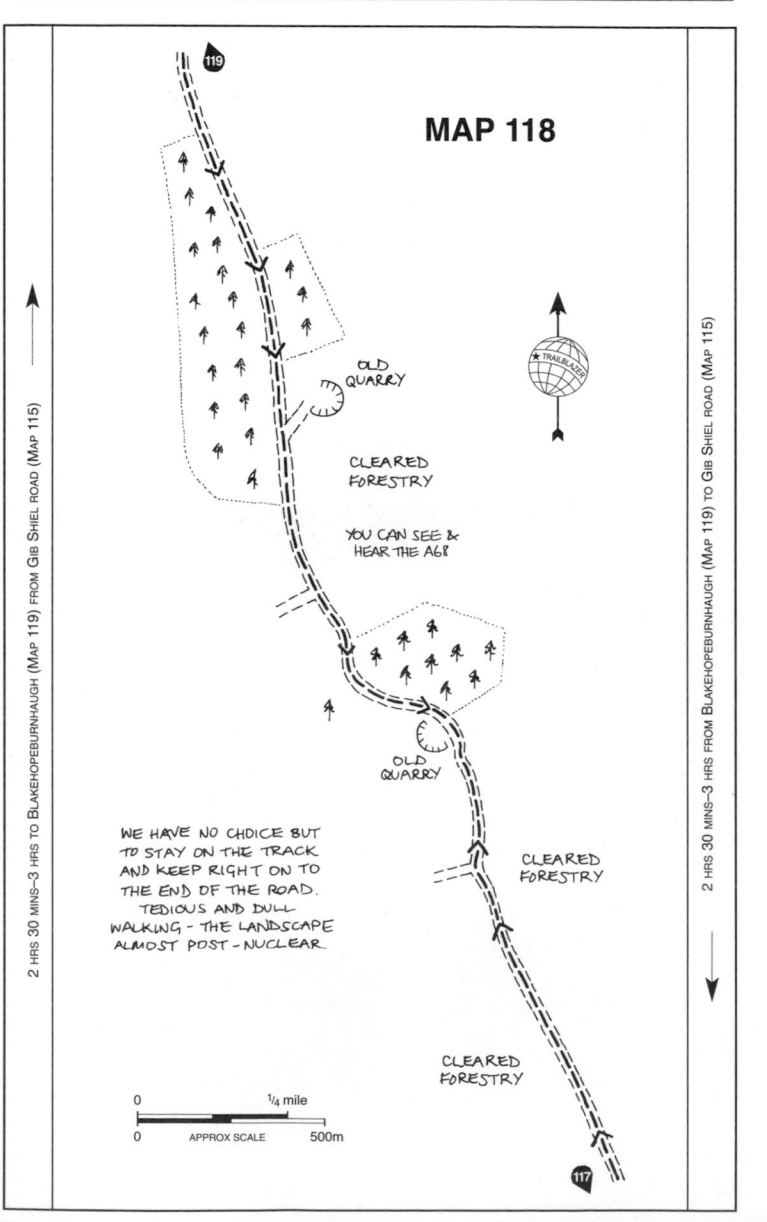

MAP 118

119

OLD QUARRY

CLEARED FORESTRY

YOU CAN SEE & HEAR THE A68

OLD QUARRY

CLEARED FORESTRY

WE HAVE NO CHOICE BUT TO STAY ON THE TRACK AND KEEP RIGHT ON TO THE END OF THE ROAD. TEDIOUS AND DULL WALKING - THE LANDSCAPE ALMOST POST - NUCLEAR.

CLEARED FORESTRY

117

0   ¼ mile

0   APPROX SCALE   500m

2 HRS 30 MINS–3 HRS TO BLAKEHOPEBURNHAUGH (MAP 119) FROM GIB SHIEL ROAD (MAP 115)

2 HRS 30 MINS–3 HRS FROM BLAKEHOPEBURNHAUGH (MAP 119) TO GIB SHIEL ROAD (MAP 115)

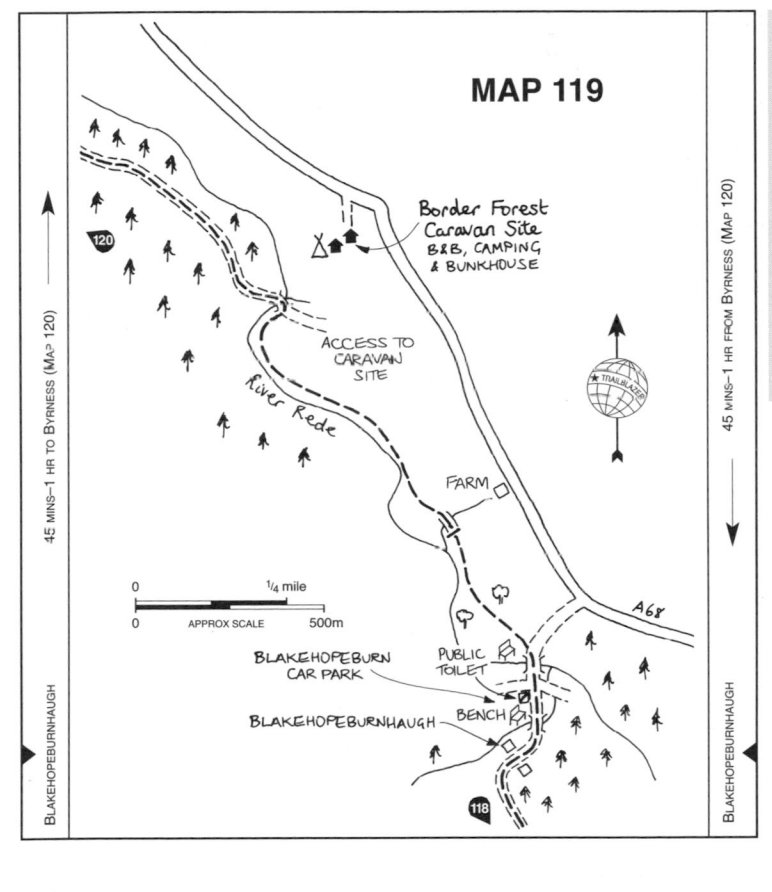

MAP 119

Border Forest
Caravan Site
B&B, CAMPING
& BUNKHOUSE

120

ACCESS TO
CARAVAN
SITE

River Rede

★ TRAILBLAZER

FARM

A68

0   ¼ mile

0   APPROX SCALE   500m

BLAKEHOPEBURN
CAR PARK

PUBLIC
TOILET

BLAKEHOPEBURNHAUGH

BENCH

118

45 MINS–1 HR TO BYRNESS (MAP 120)

45 MINS–1 HR FROM BYRNESS (MAP 120)

BLAKEHOPEBURNHAUGH

BLAKEHOPEBURNHAUGH

BYRNESS [Map 120]

These days this collection of buildings strung out along the A68 offers **barely enough** to fortify you for the final hurdle, so arrive prepared.

The Byrness (☎ 01830-520231, 🖳 www.thepennineway.co.uk/thebyrness; 1D en suite/2T) is a former hotel offering B&B for £30 per person and evening meals from £12.50.

Forest View Walkers' Accommodation (Byrness YH; ☎ 01830-520425, 🖳 joycetaylor1703@hotmail.co.uk; open all day, all year; 20 beds) came back from the brink in 2006 and has recently modernized rooms (2, 3 or 4 beds) in two converted forestry cottages for £15 (£13 for under

18s) as well as evening meals; it's also licensed. You'll pass round the back of *Border Forest Caravan Park* (see Map 119; ☎ 01830-520259, 🖳 www.borderforest.com) with **camping** for £6 and two plain, en suite **motel-type rooms** for £40 a go and sleeping up to three people but with no breakfast). Closed November to February.

With no pub, the only place for a feed is the less than stellar *café* in the petrol station (daily 8am-5pm; shop closes 6pm) which sells fast food.

Both Snaiths and Munro's operate **bus** services here and Byrness is also a stop on National Express's No 383 service (see the public transport map and table, pp42-6).

BYRNESS TO KIRK YETHOLM   MAPS 120-135

Route overview

Of all the challenges met so far these **27 miles (43km, 10-13hrs)**, across the Cheviot massif, will be the most demanding. It's as if every stage has been a preparation for today and your mental preparation must be right. You can do it. Keep telling yourself that. The proud fraternity of Penninites has done it before you and there is no reason why you should not take your place among them.

Few walkers normally tackle 27 miles in a single day, but this is the Last Day so you can risk a burnout. Rude stone shelters on some summits and the two refuge huts (see below) are the only protection if things turn nasty.

For those who decide to make **two days** of it, you'll enjoy it even more. Wild camping offers the freedom of the hills but it might be necessary to drop down off the exposed plateau. Alternatively you could spend the night in one of the two identical **refuge huts** (Map 125 and Map 131) with room for up to six on the floor. There's no water at either although notes tell you where to look.

At around Mile 15 a crossroads just after Windy Gyle offers a 1½ mile (2km) descent to Uswayford B&B (see p244) or, in the other direction a little further to Cocklawfoot road end, nine miles from Kirk Yetholm where Valleydene B&B (see p252) will pick you up.

Extensive and maybe even excessive **slabbing** helps make the single day's effort all the more achievable, primarily as rhythm-maintaining tram rails. Although you gain height while still half asleep, the ascent to **Windy Gyle** (Map 127), followed by the intermittently slabbed climb to the **Auchope Cairn duckboard promenade** (Map 130) may take the wind out of you, even if at this point you have broken the back of the day. The final significant climb up **The Schil** (Map 131) will be enough though; altogether a day's total of **over 1600m** or a vertical mile.

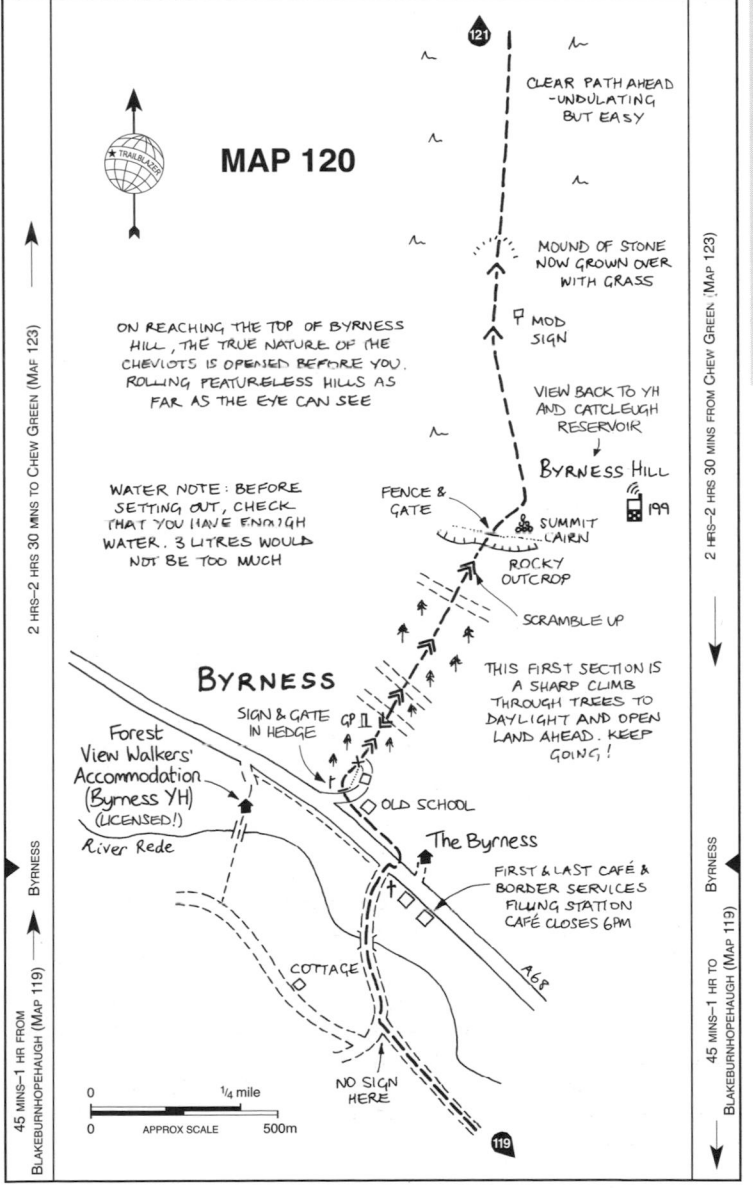

MAP 120

🌐 TRAILBLAZER

2 HRS–2 HRS 30 MINS TO CHEW GREEN (MAP 123)

CLEAR PATH AHEAD —UNDULATING BUT EASY

MOUND OF STONE NOW GROWN OVER WITH GRASS

⚑ MOD SIGN

2 HRS–2 HRS 30 MINS FROM CHEW GREEN (MAP 123)

ON REACHING THE TOP OF BYRNESS HILL, THE TRUE NATURE OF THE CHEVIOTS IS OPENED BEFORE YOU. ROLLING FEATURELESS HILLS AS FAR AS THE EYE CAN SEE

VIEW BACK TO YH AND CATCLEUGH RESERVOIR

BYRNESS HILL

WATER NOTE: BEFORE SETTING OUT, CHECK THAT YOU HAVE ENOUGH WATER. 3 LITRES WOULD NOT BE TOO MUCH

FENCE & GATE

SUMMIT CAIRN

📱 199

ROCKY OUTCROP

SCRAMBLE UP

BYRNESS

THIS FIRST SECTION IS A SHARP CLIMB THROUGH TREES TO DAYLIGHT AND OPEN LAND AHEAD. KEEP GOING!

SIGN & GATE IN HEDGE

CP Ⅱ

Forest View Walkers' Accommodation (Byrness YH) (LICENSED!)

OLD SCHOOL

The Byrness

River Rede

FIRST & LAST CAFÉ & BORDER SERVICES FILLING STATION CAFÉ CLOSES 6PM

A68

COTTAGE

NO SIGN HERE

0   ¼ mile

0   APPROX SCALE   500m

ROUTE GUIDE AND MAPS

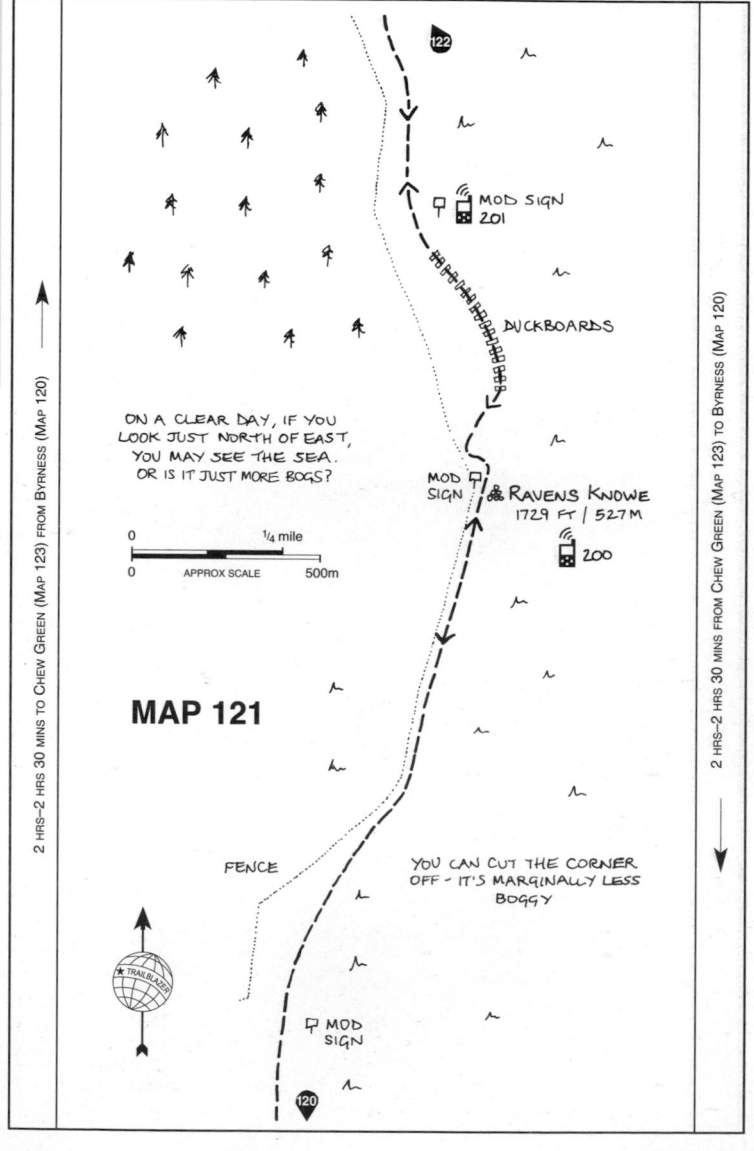

2 HRS–2 HRS 30 MINS TO CHEW GREEN (MAP 123) FROM BYRNESS (MAP 120)

2 HRS–2 HRS 30 MINS FROM CHEW GREEN (MAP 123) TO BYRNESS (MAP 120)

122

MOD SIGN
201

DUCKBOARDS

ON A CLEAR DAY, IF YOU
LOOK JUST NORTH OF EAST,
YOU MAY SEE THE SEA.
OR IS IT JUST MORE BOGS?

MOD
SIGN

RAVENS KNOWE
1729 FT / 527 M

200

0   ¼ mile
0   APPROX SCALE   500m

MAP 121

FENCE

YOU CAN CUT THE CORNER
OFF – IT'S MARGINALLY LESS
BOGGY

★ TRAILBLAZER

MOD
SIGN

120

(Opposite): One of the busiest sections of the Pennine Way is the short part following Hadrian's Wall (see p218). (Photo © Chris Scott).

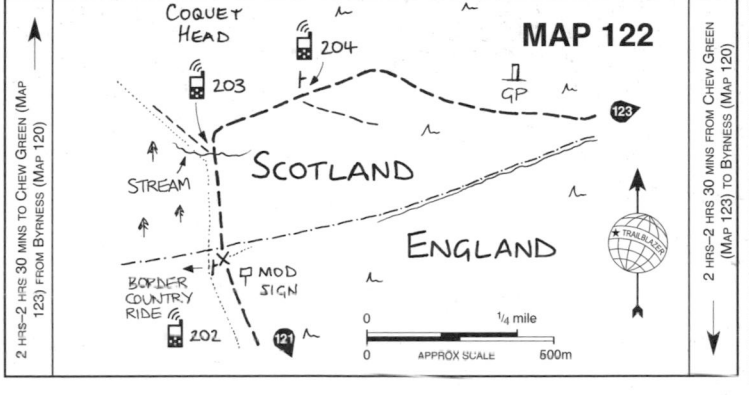

As for the so-called low-level or high-level finale; both diverge for about 1½ miles (2.7km) though the former takes just ninety minutes, the latter a little longer. If weather, energy and daylight are all on your side it's well worth the effort to watch your last Pennine sunset from the heights of **White Law** (Map 133) or thereabouts before spilling down over moorland and pasture to a bridge a mile by road from town.

At last you pull back your shoulders and pick up your dragging feet. There's no point in looking beaten. The villagers in **Kirk Yetholm** (Map 135) don't care one way or the other, but you have your pride. It's over, your walk. At the Border Hotel don't expect curiosity, sympathy or admiration, just their book to sign if you ask. You read there the comments of fellow lengthsmen and women, mostly nonchalant or triumphant, some philosophical. Add yours if you like as you celebrate with a beer, the traditional end to what you'll probably now agree is still Britain's most challenging long-distance trail.

Route-finding trouble spots

Once the fenceline slabs set in after Lambs Hill there's very little to err you from the path. Up to that point waymarking and paths are reasonably clear. From Auchope Cairn the knee-popping decent to the second hut is well trodden, as is the trail round and up to The Schil and down to the ladder style leading to the **high or low route** split both of which roll unambiguously down to Kirk Yetholm.

All in all, even in poor visibility this very long day is made much easier by good waymarking and orientation aids (aka 'slabs and fence lines'). All you have to do is last the distance.

(Opposite) Top: There are two refuge huts (see p238) to break the demanding 27-mile final stage of the walk. **Bottom**: Kirk Yetholm and the Border Hotel (see p253) mark the end of the Pennine Way. Sign the book and sink a pint to celebrate. (Photos © Chris Scott).

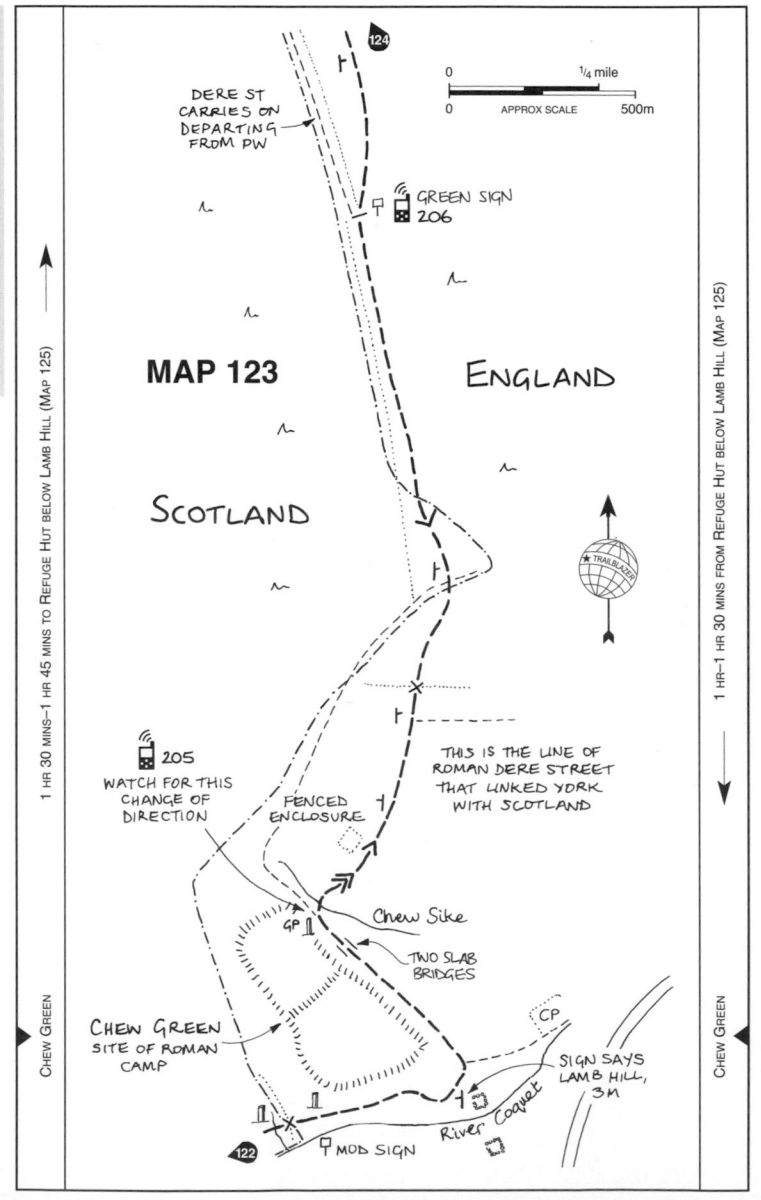

ROUTE GUIDE AND MAPS

1 HR 30 MINS–1 HR 45 MINS TO REFUGE HUT BELOW LAMB HILL (MAP 125)

1 HR–1 HR 30 MINS FROM REFUGE HUT BELOW LAMB HILL (MAP 125)

CHEW GREEN

CHEW GREEN

124

DERE ST
CARRIES ON
DEPARTING
FROM PW

GREEN SIGN
206

MAP 123

ENGLAND

SCOTLAND

★ TRAILBLAZER

205
WATCH FOR THIS
CHANGE OF
DIRECTION

FENCED
ENCLOSURE

THIS IS THE LINE OF
ROMAN DERE STREET
THAT LINKED YORK
WITH SCOTLAND

GP

Chew Sike

TWO SLAB
BRIDGES

CHEW GREEN
SITE OF ROMAN
CAMP

CP

SIGN SAYS
LAMB HILL,
3M

River Coquet

122

MOD SIGN

0   ¼ mile
0   APPROX SCALE   500m

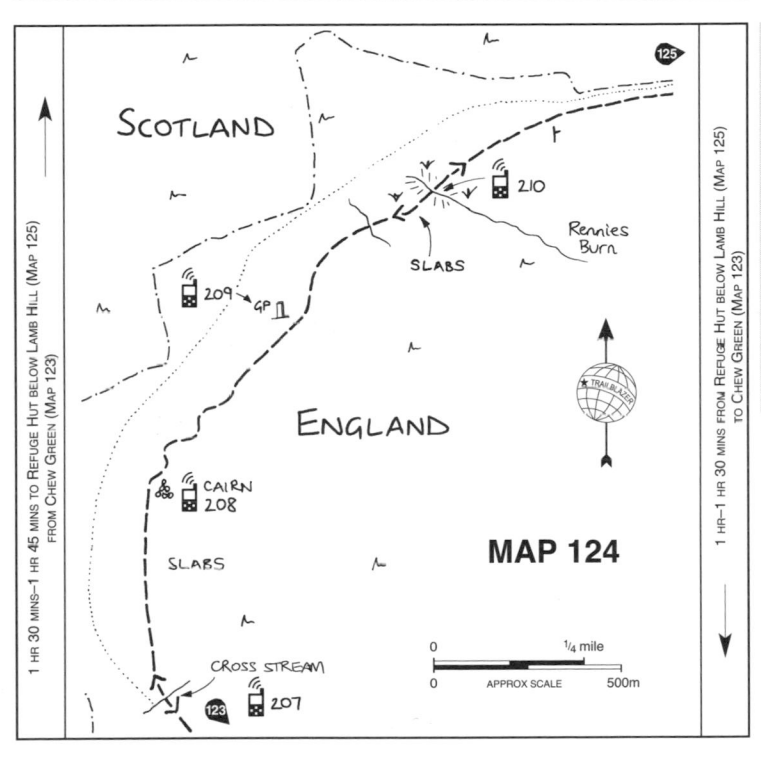

ROUTE GUIDE AND MAPS

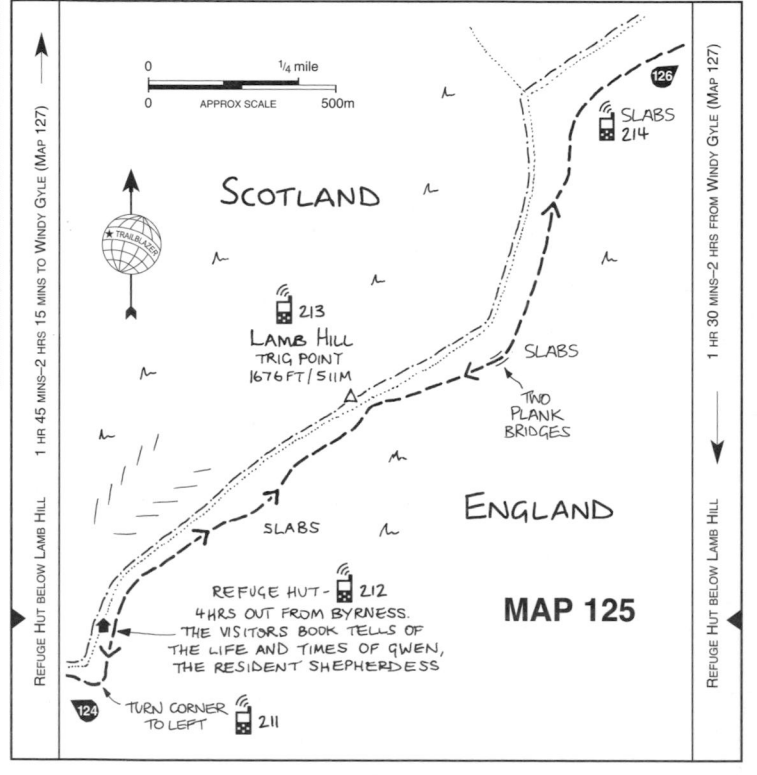

1 HR 45 MINS–2 HRS 15 MINS TO WINDY GYLE (MAP 127)

1 HR 30 MINS–2 HRS FROM WINDY GYLE (MAP 127)

REFUGE HUT BELOW LAMB HILL

REFUGE HUT BELOW LAMB HILL

0 ¼ mile
0 APPROX SCALE 500m

SCOTLAND

★ TRAILBLAZER

126

SLABS 214

213

LAMB HILL
TRIG POINT
1676FT/511M

SLABS

TWO
PLANK
BRIDGES

SLABS

ENGLAND

MAP 125

REFUGE HUT- 212
4 HRS OUT FROM BYRNESS.
THE VISITORS BOOK TELLS OF
THE LIFE AND TIMES OF GWEN,
THE RESIDENT SHEPHERDESS

124 TURN CORNER
TO LEFT 211

USWAYFORD **[off Map 128, p246]**
Uswayford Farm (☎ 01669-650237;
1T/1D/1F) is 1½ miles off the trail; the only
B&B between Byrness and Kirk Yetholm.
Turning up here on spec would be a bit of a
gamble so call ahead. B&B costs £30 per
person or £40 with an evening meal; there
is nowhere else to eat. To reach it take the
footpath signed 'Uswayford' one mile
north-east of Russell's Cairn.

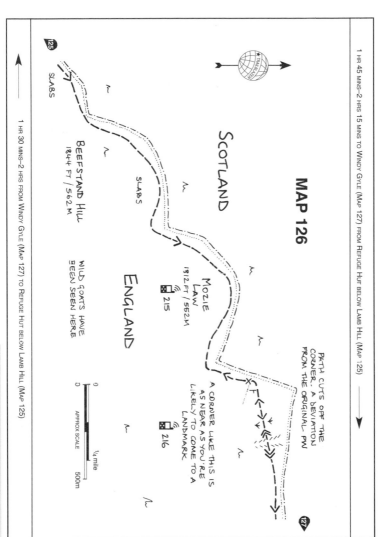

1 HR 45 MINS–2 HRS 15 MINS TO WINDY GYLE (MAP 127) FROM REFUGE HUT BELOW LAMB HILL (MAP 125)

1 HR 30 MINS–2 HRS FROM WINDY GYLE (MAP 127) TO REFUGE HUT BELOW LAMB HILL (MAP 125)

MAP 126

SCOTLAND

ENGLAND

125

SLABS

SLABS

BEEFSTAND HILL
1844 FT / 562 M

MOZIE LAW
1812 FT / 562 M
215

216

WILD GOATS HAVE BEEN SEEN HERE

PATH CUTS OFF THE CORNER. A DEVIATION FROM THE ORIGINAL PW

A CORNER LIKE THIS IS AS NEAR AS YOU'RE LIKELY TO COME TO A LANDMARK.

127

APPROX SCALE

0 — ¼ mile

0 — 500m

TIME BLOCK

ROUTE GUIDE AND MAPS

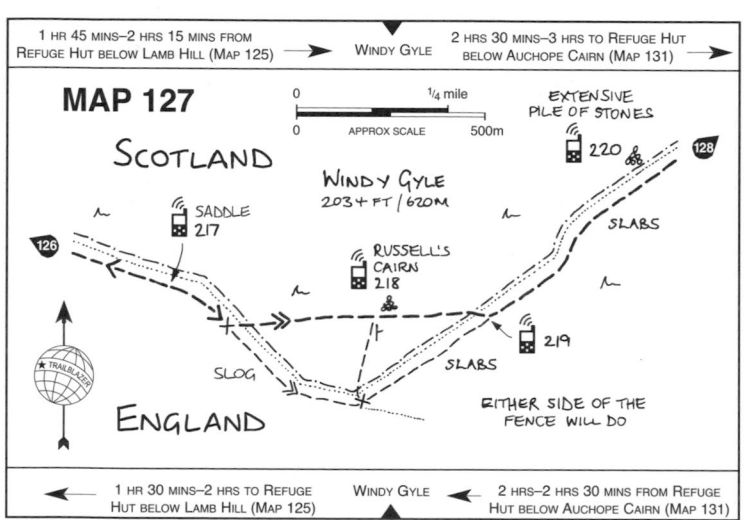

1 HR 45 MINS–2 HRS 15 MINS FROM REFUGE HUT BELOW LAMB HILL (MAP 125) → WINDY GYLE 2 HRS 30 MINS–3 HRS TO REFUGE HUT BELOW AUCHOPE CAIRN (MAP 131) →

MAP 127

0   1/4 mile
0   APPROX SCALE   500m

SCOTLAND

EXTENSIVE PILE OF STONES

220

128

SADDLE 217

WINDY GYLE 2034 FT / 620M

SLABS

126

RUSSELL'S CAIRN 218

219

SLOG

SLABS

ENGLAND

EITHER SIDE OF THE FENCE WILL DO

1 HR 30 MINS–2 HRS TO REFUGE HUT BELOW LAMB HILL (MAP 125) ← WINDY GYLE ← 2 HRS–2 HRS 30 MINS FROM REFUGE HUT BELOW AUCHOPE CAIRN (MAP 131)

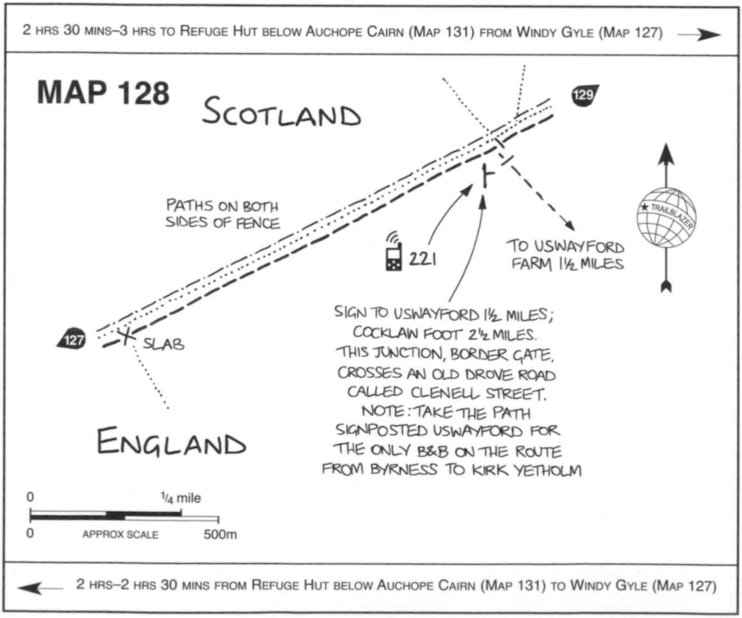

2 HRS 30 MINS–3 HRS TO REFUGE HUT BELOW AUCHOPE CAIRN (MAP 131) FROM WINDY GYLE (MAP 127) →

MAP 128   SCOTLAND

129

PATHS ON BOTH SIDES OF FENCE

221

TO USWAYFORD FARM 1½ MILES

127

SLAB

SIGN TO USWAYFORD 1½ MILES; COCKLAW FOOT 2½ MILES. THIS JUNCTION, BORDER GATE, CROSSES AN OLD DROVE ROAD CALLED CLENELL STREET. NOTE: TAKE THE PATH SIGNPOSTED USWAYFORD FOR THE ONLY B&B ON THE ROUTE FROM BYRNESS TO KIRK YETHOLM

ENGLAND

0   1/4 mile
0   APPROX SCALE   500m

← 2 HRS–2 HRS 30 MINS FROM REFUGE HUT BELOW AUCHOPE CAIRN (MAP 131) TO WINDY GYLE (MAP 127)

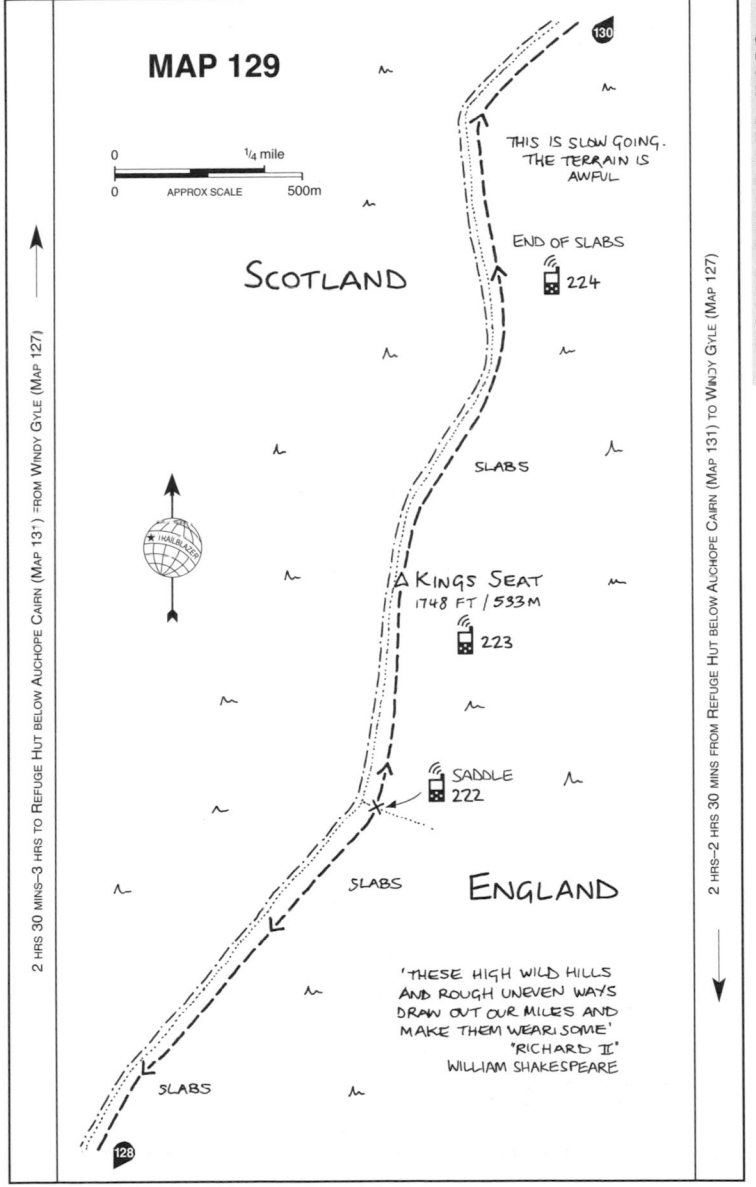

MAP 129

0   1/4 mile

0   APPROX SCALE   500m

SCOTLAND

130

THIS IS SLOW GOING. THE TERRAIN IS AWFUL

END OF SLABS
224

SLABS

★ TRAILBLAZER

KINGS SEAT
1748 FT / 533M
223

SADDLE
222

SLABS

ENGLAND

'THESE HIGH WILD HILLS AND ROUGH UNEVEN WAYS DRAW OUT OUR MILES AND MAKE THEM WEARISOME' "RICHARD II" WILLIAM SHAKESPEARE

SLABS

128

2 HRS 30 MINS–3 HRS TO REFUGE HUT BELOW AUCHOPE CAIRN (MAP 131) FROM WINDY GYLE (MAP 127)

2 HRS–2 HRS 30 MINS FROM REFUGE HUT BELOW AUCHOPE CAIRN (MAP 131) TO WINDY GYLE (MAP 127)

ROUTE GUIDE AND MAPS

ROUTE GUIDE AND MAPS

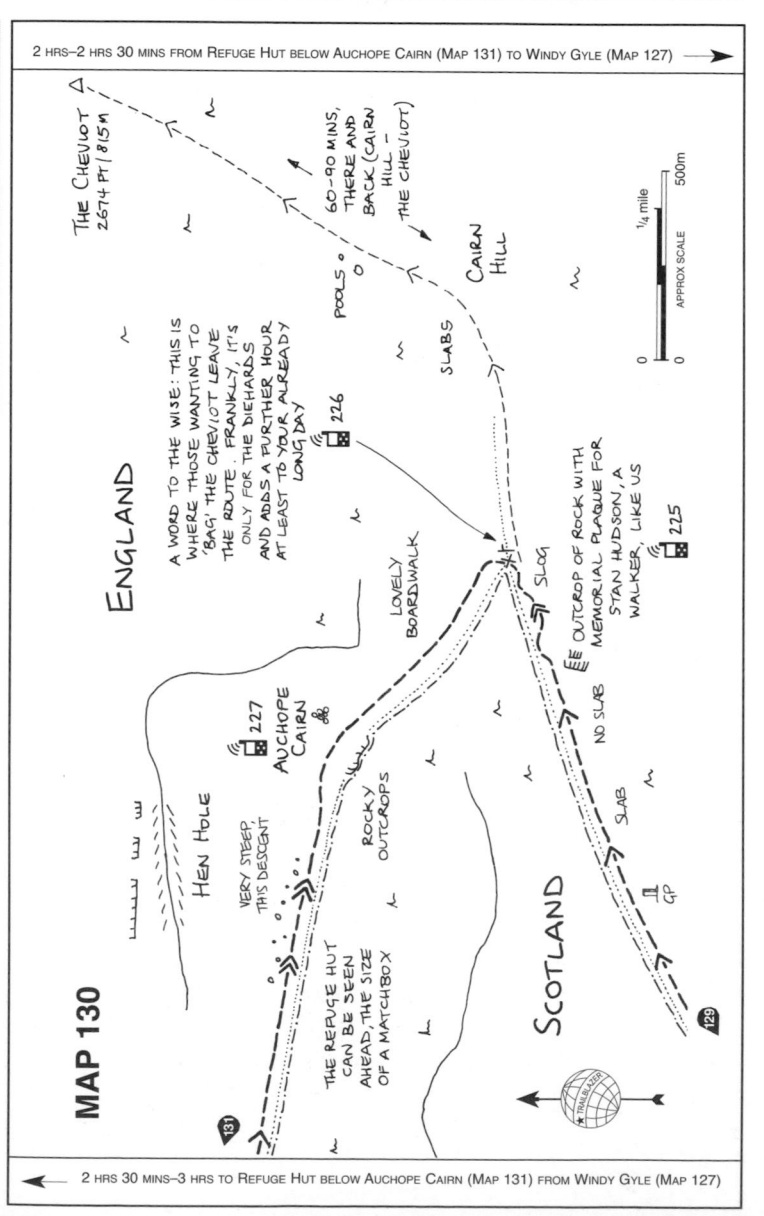

2 HRS–2 HRS 30 MINS FROM REFUGE HUT BELOW AUCHOPE CAIRN (MAP 131) TO WINDY GYLE (MAP 127) →

THE CHEVIOT 2674 PT 1 815 M

60–90 MINS, THERE AND BACK (CAIRN HILL – THE CHEVIOT)

CAIRN HILL

POOLS

SLABS

¼ mile   500m

APPROX SCALE

0   0

A WORD TO THE WISE: THIS IS WHERE THOSE WANTING TO 'BAG' THE CHEVIOT LEAVE THE ROUTE. FRANKLY, IT'S ONLY FOR THE DIEHARDS AND ADDS A FURTHER HOUR AT LEAST TO YOUR ALREADY LONG DAY

ENGLAND

226

225

OUTCROP OF ROCK WITH MEMORIAL PLAQUE FOR STAN HUDSON, A WALKER, LIKE US

LOVELY BOARDWALK

SLABS

SLAB

NO SLAB

SLAB

227

AUCHOPE CAIRN

ROCKY OUTCROPS

VERY STEEP, THIS DESCENT

HEN HOLE

SCOTLAND

GP

THE REFUGE HUT CAN BE SEEN AHEAD, THE SIZE OF A MATCHBOX

MAP 130

131

129

← 2 HRS 30 MINS–3 HRS TO REFUGE HUT BELOW AUCHOPE CAIRN (MAP 131) FROM WINDY GYLE (MAP 127)

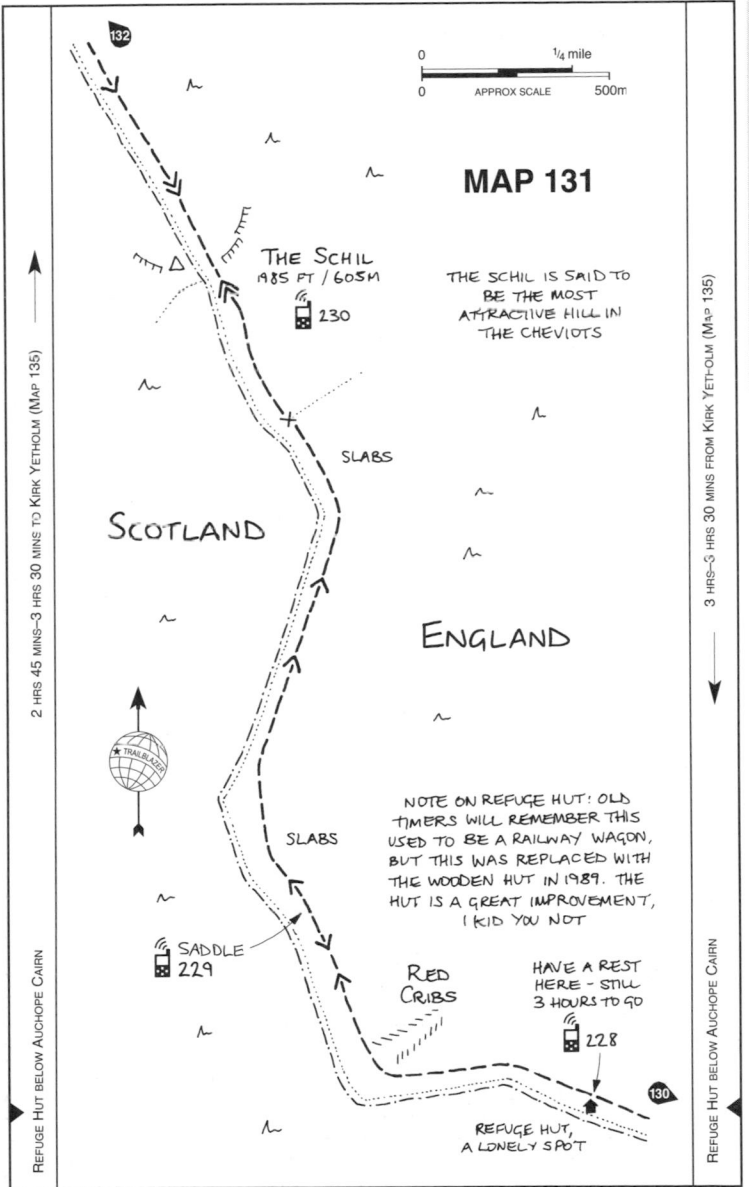

132

0   ¼ mile
0   APPROX SCALE   500m

MAP 131

THE SCHIL
1985 FT / 605M
230

THE SCHIL IS SAID TO
BE THE MOST
ATTRACTIVE HILL IN
THE CHEVIOTS

SLABS

SCOTLAND

ENGLAND

★ TRAILBLAZER

SLABS

NOTE ON REFUGE HUT: OLD
TIMERS WILL REMEMBER THIS
USED TO BE A RAILWAY WAGON,
BUT THIS WAS REPLACED WITH
THE WOODEN HUT IN 1989. THE
HUT IS A GREAT IMPROVEMENT,
I KID YOU NOT

SADDLE
229

RED
CRIBS

HAVE A REST
HERE - STILL
3 HOURS TO GO
228

130

REFUGE HUT,
A LONELY SPOT

2 HRS 45 MINS—3 HRS 30 MINS TO KIRK YETHOLM (MAP 135)

3 HRS—3 HRS 30 MINS FROM KIRK YETHOLM (MAP 135)

REFUGE HUT BELOW AUCHOPE CAIRN

REFUGE HUT BELOW AUCHOPE CAIRN

ROUTE GUIDE AND MAPS

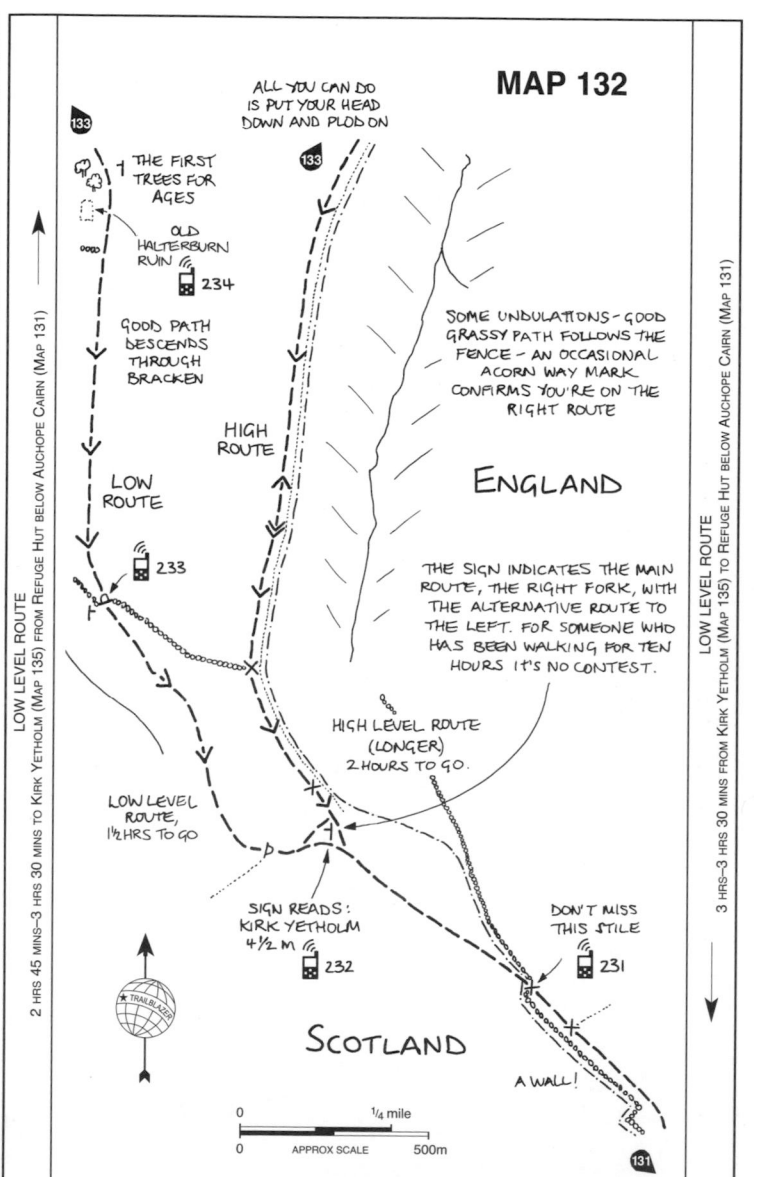

MAP 132

ALL YOU CAN DO
IS PUT YOUR HEAD
DOWN AND PLOD ON

133

THE FIRST
TREES FOR
AGES

OLD
HALTERBURN
RUIN 234

GOOD PATH
DESCENDS
THROUGH
BRACKEN

HIGH
ROUTE

LOW
ROUTE

233

SOME UNDULATIONS - GOOD
GRASSY PATH FOLLOWS THE
FENCE - AN OCCASIONAL
ACORN WAY MARK
CONFIRMS YOU'RE ON THE
RIGHT ROUTE

ENGLAND

THE SIGN INDICATES THE MAIN
ROUTE, THE RIGHT FORK, WITH
THE ALTERNATIVE ROUTE TO
THE LEFT. FOR SOMEONE WHO
HAS BEEN WALKING FOR TEN
HOURS IT's NO CONTEST.

HIGH LEVEL ROUTE
(LONGER)
2 HOURS TO GO.

LOW LEVEL
ROUTE,
1½ HRS TO GO

SIGN READS:
KIRK YETHOLM
4½ M 232

DON'T MISS
THIS STILE
231

SCOTLAND

A WALL!

131

0   ¼ mile

0   APPROX SCALE   500m

★ TRAILBLAZER

LOW LEVEL ROUTE
2 HRS 45 MINS–3 HRS 30 MINS TO KIRK YETHOLM (MAP 135) FROM REFUGE HUT BELOW AUCHOPE CAIRN (MAP 131)

LOW LEVEL ROUTE
3 HRS–3 HRS 30 MINS FROM KIRK YETHOLM (MAP 135) TO REFUGE HUT BELOW AUCHOPE CAIRN (MAP 131)

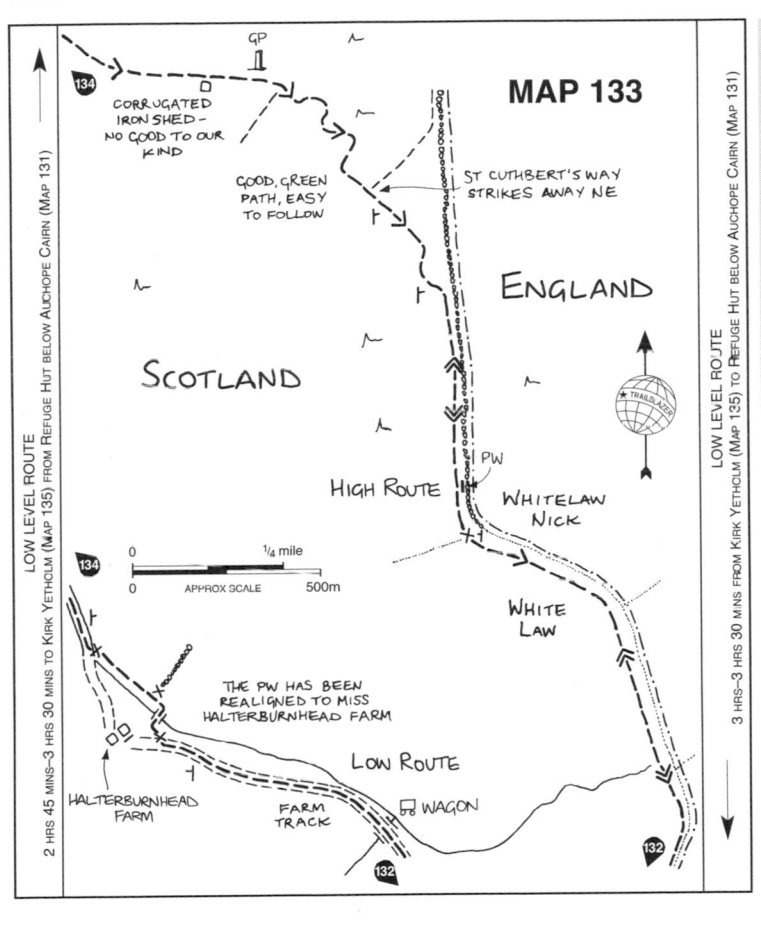

MAP 133

GP

134

CORRUGATED
IRON SHED –
NO GOOD TO OUR
KIND

GOOD, GREEN
PATH, EASY
TO FOLLOW

ST CUTHBERT'S WAY
STRIKES AWAY NE

ENGLAND

SCOTLAND

HIGH ROUTE

PW

WHITELAW
NICK

WHITE
LAW

★ TRAILBLAZER

0   1/4 mile

134

0   500m
APPROX SCALE

THE PW HAS BEEN
REALIGNED TO MISS
HALTERBURNHEAD FARM

LOW ROUTE

WAGON

HALTERBURNHEAD
FARM

FARM
TRACK

132

132

LOW LEVEL ROUTE
2 HRS 45 MINS–3 HRS 30 MINS TO KIRK YETHOLM (MAP 135) FROM REFUGE HUT BELOW AUCHOPE CAIRN (MAP 131)

LOW LEVEL ROUTE
3 HRS–3 HRS 30 MINS FROM KIRK YETHOLM (MAP 135) TO REFUGE HUT BELOW AUCHOPE CAIRN (MAP 131)

ROUTE GUIDE AND MAPS

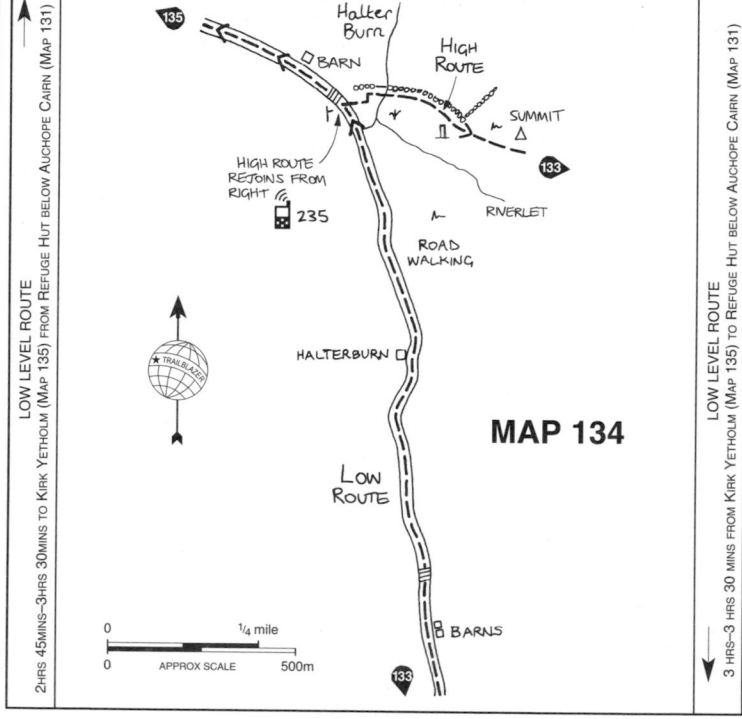

LOW LEVEL ROUTE
2HRS 45MINS–3HRS 30MINS TO KIRK YETHOLM (MAP 135) FROM REFUGE HUT BELOW AUCHOPE CAIRN (MAP 131)

LOW LEVEL ROUTE
3 HRS–3 HRS 30 MINS FROM KIRK YETHOLM (MAP 135) TO REFUGE HUT BELOW AUCHOPE CAIRN (MAP 131)

Halter Burn
HIGH ROUTE
BARN
SUMMIT
HIGH ROUTE REJOINS FROM RIGHT
235
RIVERLET
ROAD WALKING
HALTERBURN
MAP 134
LOW ROUTE
★ TRAILBLAZER
0   ¼ mile
0   APPROX SCALE   500m
BARNS
133
133
135

KIRK YETHOLM   [Map 135]

It's probably fair to say that only a fraction of the people who have heard of this pleasant little village would have done so if the Pennine Way did not end here. As it is, it offers a perfect and well-appointed spin down to your big walk.

See box p24 for details of Yetholm Festival week held in June.

Transport

Munro's operates regular **bus** services to Kelso (20-35 minutes) from where you can catch the service to Berwick-upon-Tweed or Newcastle; both are on the mainline rail network to London or Edinburgh and also on National Express coach routes. And for the very last time we repeat: 'see public transport map and table, pp42-6'.

For a **taxi** call Peter Hogg taxis on ☎ 01835-863039 or ☎ 01835-863755.

Places to stay and eat

On your way in you pass *Valleydene* (☎ 01573-420286; 2T/2D/1F), a friendly establishment which charges £25 per person for two sharing an en suite room, £22 in a standard room and single occupancy from £25. Dogs are welcome. They offer a very useful service of picking you up at Cocklawfoot halfway along the leg from Byrness (see Map 128, p246) and dropping you back there the next morning for £15 for a one-night stay and £5 for a two-night stay.

In the centre of the village is *Mill House* (☎ 01573-420604, 🖥 www.mill houseyetholm.co.uk; 1T/1D/1F) a comfortable place with internet access in every room, a drying room for walking gear and a hot tub for guests' use. B&B costs from £30/pp.

Recovered (literally) from a fire in 2006 *The Border Hotel* (☎ 01573-420237, 🖳 www.theborderhotel.com; 1D/3D or T/1D or F, all en suite) has a characterful bar where the big book of 'Pennine Lengthspersons' awaits your contribution. B&B costs £45 per person (from £45 for single occupancy). The **menu** here offers a knee-weakening range of dishes to help pile back the calories burned up during the haul over from Byrness. Food is served daily 12-2pm and 6-9pm (to 8.30pm in winter).

Round the corner *Kirk Yetholm Youth Hostel* (☎ 01573-420639, bookings ☎ 0870-155 3255, 🖳 reservations@syha.org

.uk; open Apr-Sep) costs £12.50 (£9.50 for under 18s) has 21 beds as well as washing and drying facilities.

Cross Keys B&B (☎ 01573-420727, 🖳 www.crosskeyshousekirkyetholm.co.uk; 2D or T) charges £40 for single occupancy and £58 for a double room.

TOWN YETHOLM [Map 135]

It could be one more mile too many but in **Town Yetholm** you'll find a **shop** (Mon-Sat 7am-12.30pm, 1.30-5pm, closed Wed afternoon, Sun 9am-12 noon) and a **post office** (closed afternoons, Wed and Sat). There's also the *Plough Hotel* (☎ 01573-420215; 3D/2T, some en suite) where B&B costs £35 for single occupancy and £60 for two sharing.

ROUTE GUIDE AND MAPS

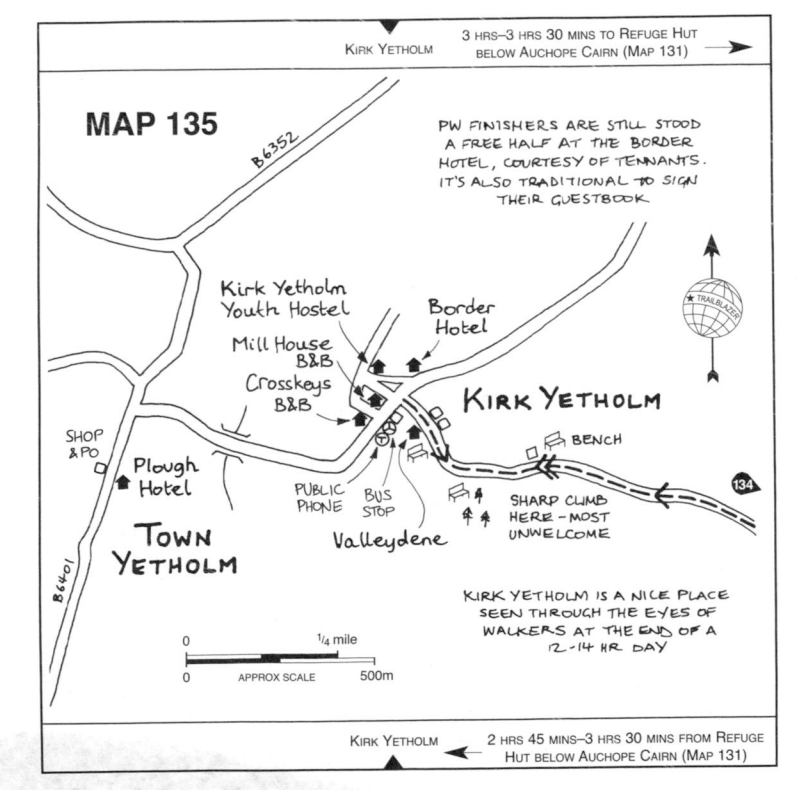

❏ St Cuthbert's Way and other continuations

In the unlikely event that you want to extend your walk, **St Cuthbert's Way** is a long-distance trail that runs from Kirk Yetholm to Holy Island on the Northumberland coast. It passes via Wooler and arrives, somewhat dishevelled, at Lindisfarne on the east coast where the castle, reached via a causeway, would round off your adventure in great style.

If you still just can't stop walking there's also a link to the **Southern Upland Way** and with a certain amount of ingenuity to the **West Highland Way** and from there on to the **Great Glen Way**. It's therefore possible to walk from Derbyshire to Inverness, a great challenge for anyone with the stamina and the time.

The pastime of walking the long-distance trails grows on you. Getting back to normal life is hard. You're likely to find that everyday cares are less important now that you've communed with curlews and breathed the wind on Windy Gyle. One of the attractions of walking is the tangible sense of being out of the everyday world yet bonded to a community with different values from the common herd:

We are Pilgrims, Master; we shall go
Always a little further: it may be
Beyond that last blue mountain barred with snow,
Across that angry or that glimmering sea.

So it is that the Trailblazer marketing department feels compelled to alert you to the full range of its **British Walking Guides** series listed on p270. For you my friend, the walking is *not* over.

Trail map key

Pennine Way	Water	B&B/guesthouse/ youth hostel
Other path	Cleft/small valley	Campsite
4 x 4 track	Crags	Building
Tarmac road	Stream	Signpost
Steps	River	Church/religious site
Slope/ Steep slope	Bog or marsh	Public toilet
Stile and fence	Hedge	Public telephone
Gate and fence	Trees/woodland	Bus stop
Cattle grid	Rough grassland	CP Car park
Bridge	Trig point	GPS marker
Stone wall	GP Guide post	88 Map continuation

Town plan key

Where to stay	Tourist Information	Bus stop
Where to eat	Library/bookstore	Public telephone
Campsite	Internet	Public toilet
Post office	Museum/gallery	Rail line & station
Bank/ATM	Church/cathedral	Park
	Bus station	Other

APPENDIX – GPS WAYPOINTS

Each GPS waypoint below was taken on the route at the reference number marked on the map as below. This list of GPS waypoints is also available in downloadable form from the Trailblazer website – www.trailblazer-guides.com/books/pennineway/GPS.

Edale

MAP NO	REF	GPS WAYPOINT		DESCRIPTION
Map 3	001	53° 22.514'	01° 52.925'	Sign: to Edale Head; keep left
Map 3	002	53° 22.821'	01° 52.959'	Kinder Low summit
Map 4	003	53° 23.820'	01° 52.587'	Kinder Downfall
Map 4	004	53° 24.464'	01° 54.279'	Snake Path junction
Map 7	005	53° 27.679'	01° 51.588'	Bleaklow Head summit
Map 7	006	53° 27.955'	01° 51.801'	Milestone by fence
Map 8	007	53° 28.515'	01° 54.359'	Fence above Reaps Farm

Crowden

MAP NO	REF	GPS WAYPOINT		DESCRIPTION
Map 10	008	53° 31.409'	01° 54.785'	Cross stream joining Crowden Great Brook
Map 11	009	53° 31.718'	01° 54.280'	Slabs start on Meadowgrain Clough
Map 12	010	53° 32.332'	01° 53.144'	Black Hill summit
Map 12	011	53° 33.038'	01° 52.659'	Wooden shelter
Map 15	012	53° 34.747'	01° 57.494'	Last gate before Standedge Cutting
Map 15	013	53° 34.890'	01° 57.640'	Milestone before Standedge Cutting

Standedge

MAP NO	REF	GPS WAYPOINT		DESCRIPTION
Map 15	014	53° 35.371'	01° 58.958'	Millstone Edge trig point
Map 16	015	53° 35.862'	01° 59.683'	Oldham Way split, turn right
Map 17	016	53° 36.908'	02° 00.943'	White Hill summit trig point
Map 18	017	53° 38.475'	02° 02.460'	Shelter of sorts
Map 18	018	53° 38.635'	02° 02.615'	Blackstone Edge trig point
Map 18	019	53° 39.008'	02° 02.506'	Aiggin Stone, turn left
Map 18	020	53° 38.968'	02° 02.876'	Drainage ditch, turn right
Map 20	021	53° 41.687'	02° 03.358'	Slabs start after Warland reservoir
Map 20	022	53° 42.676'	02° 02.530'	Withen's Gate; Calderdale Way path to left

Hebden

MAP NO	REF	GPS WAYPOINT		DESCRIPTION
Map 22	023	53° 44.337'	02° 02.790'	Sign to Badger Farm after Calder ascent

Colden

MAP NO	REF	GPS WAYPOINT		DESCRIPTION
Map 23	024	53° 45.516'	02° 03.070'	Pennine Way path goes away from the wall after Mt Pleasant Fm
Map 24	025	53° 45.831'	02° 03.398'	Junction with path to Clough Hole Bridge near arched barn
Map 24	026	53° 46.389'	02° 04.894'	Pennine Way meets Pennine Bridleway. Turn right to Gorple reservoirs
Map 26	027	53° 48.002'	02° 02.817'	Leave Walshaw reservoirs, up to Top Withins
Map 27	028	53° 48.963'	02° 01.592'	Junction with Japanese Ga... Withins ruins

Ponden

MAP NO	REF	GPS WAYPOINT		DESCRIPTION
Map 29	029	53° 50.789'	02° 01.885'	Old Bess Hill
Map 29	030	53° 51.212'	02° 02.349'	High point with trig point t...

Ponden (cont'd)

MAP NO	REF	GPS WAYPOINT		DESCRIPTION
Map 29	031	53° 51.470'	02° 02.544'	Stone shelter
Map 31	032	53° 52.241'	02° 02.649'	Wooden door to garden with trees and hut
Map 31	033	53° 52.334'	02° 02.548'	Ladder stile; change direction

Ickornshaw

Map 31	034	53° 53.154'	02° 03.182'	Spring after terraced houses
Map 32	035	53° 55.111'	02° 03.871'	Cross road (Bench #5)
Map 32	036	53° 55.216'	02° 04.355'	Wall ends, two plank bridges
Map 33	037	53° 55.275'	02° 04.852'	Broken 'Penninc Way' slab
Map 33	038	53° 55.278'	02° 05.030'	Pinhaw Beacon summit trig point
Map 33	039	53° 55.430'	02° 05.973'	Turn left off road
Map 33	040	53° 55.883'	02° 07.244'	Stile under pylon near Brown House Farm

Thornton

Map 36	041	53° 58.233'	02° 07.316'	Concrete tank, slight ascent
Map 36	042	53° 58.436'	02° 07.035'	Post on Scaleber Hill

Gargrave

Map 37	043	53° 59.466'	02° 06.920'	Leave lane right into field
Map 38	044	54° 00.166'	02° 07.606'	Pennine Way sign by four walls in field corner
Map 38	045	54° 00.410'	02° 07.703'	Fallen sign near wall
Map 38	046	54° 00.562'	02° 07.825'	Second post coming off Eshton Moor

Malham

Map 41	047	54° 04.395'	02° 09.408'	Top of Malham Cove, turn north
Map 42	048	54° 05.041'	02° 10.073'	Signpost to Malham
Map 42	049	54° 05.124'	02° 09.828'	Post with blue flash
Map 43	050	54° 07.066'	02° 10.612'	Meet and cross road, fallen Guidepost sign
Map 44	051	54° 07.530'	02° 11.339'	Crucial sign, head right
Map 44	052	54° 08.609'	02° 12.095'	Fountains Fell cairn
Map 45	053	54° 08.604'	02° 13.029'	Meet wall coming down Fountains Fell
Map 46	054	54° 09.037'	02° 15.043'	Bracken Bottom turn off; base of Pen-y-ghent climb
Map 46	055	54° 09.361'	02° 14.835'	Pen-y-ghent summit
Map 46	056	54° 09.794'	02° 14.952'	First left turn on descent
Map 47	057	54° 09.840'	02° 16.276'	Left turn near Hull Pot
Map 48	058	54° 08.906'	02° 17.357'	Bench #6 by Horton

Horton

Map 49	059	54° 10.316'	02° 17.446'	Jackdaw Hole (trees)
Map 49	060	54° 11.405'	02° 17.189'	Turn west, up hill to viaduct view
Map 50	061	54° 11.780'	02° 18.204'	Ruin
Map 50	062	54° 13.169'	02° 18.242'	Meet Cam End Road, turn north-east
Map 52	063	54° 14.413'	02° 16.420'	Join tarmac
Map 53	064	54° 14.757'	02° 15.673'	Leave tarmac for West Cam Road above Snaizeholme
Map 54	065	54° 16.638'	02° 14.461'	Leave West Cam Road to right
Map 54	066	54° 16.980'	02° 13.957'	First of three cairns along faint path
	067	54° 17.386'	02° 13.612'	Half gate, path bends right
	068	54° 17.500'	02° 13.297'	Gate with stile before Gaudy House Farm

Hawes

MAP NO	REF	GPS WAYPOINT		DESCRIPTION
Map 57	069	54°19.453'	02°13.123'	Walled lane ends
Map 57	070	54°20.050'	02°14.068'	Sheepfold by gate
Map 58	071	54°20.514'	02°14.390'	Duckboards between cairns
Map 58	072	54°20.687'	02°14.507'	Slabs start
Map 58	073	54°21.351'	02°14.465'	Cairn after ascent
Map 59	074	54°22.257'	02°13.969'	Great Shunner Fell summit
Map 59	075	54°22.617'	02°13.531'	Handsome cairn
Map 59	076	54°22.915'	02°13.091'	Wooden bridge
Map 60	077	54°22.878'	02°11.463'	Join walled lane down to Thwaite

Thwaite

Map 61	078	54°22.867'	02°09.571'	Wall above meadow; rough ascent follows
Map 61	079	54°22.935'	02°09.135'	Kisdon House

Keld

Map 62	080	54°24.665'	02°09.945'	Fence on open fell
Map 63	081	54°25.880'	02°10.446'	Pole with no sign
Map 63	082	54°26.343'	02°10.107'	Cairn
Map 64	083	54°26.585'	02°09.949'	Guidepost near Tan Hill

Tan Hill Inn

Map 65	084	54°27.968'	02°08.150'	Guidepost opposite sheepfold
Map 65	085	54°28.091'	02°07.827'	Big cairn
Map 65	086	54°28.534'	02°06.285'	Guidepost before bridge
Map 67	087	54°29.739'	02°03.673'	Gate before Trough Heads Farm
Map 67	088	54°30.182'	02°03.924'	Gate in wall

Bowes alternative route – OS only

Map 67	787	NY	96035 11223	Gate before Trough Heads Farm
Map 67	788	NY	96298 12584	Coarse gravel track joins farm track
Map 67a	789	NY	96915 12823	Gate after East Mellwaters Farm
Map 67a	790	NY	98198 13085	Leave road after Lady Myres Farm

Bowes

Map 67b	791	NY	97800 14935	Leave road for Stoney Keld short cut
Map 67b	792	NY	97559 15064	Gate near Stoney Keld spring
Map 67b	793	NY	96791 15536	Bridge behind Levy Pool Farm
Map 67b	794	NY	96681 16085	Hazelgill Beck
Map 67b	795	NY	96709 16355	Triangular stone
Map 67b	796	NY	96695 16423	Pennine Way crosses track; new wall
Map 67c	797	NY	96754 16709	Cross Hare Sike
Map 67c	798	NY	96557 17230	Gate before Goldsborough crag
Map 67c	799	NY	96016 17512	Hop across stream
Map 67c	800	NY	95491 17639	South of Goldsborough crag
Map 67c	801	NY	94826 17962	Meet Baldersdale Road
Map 69	802	NY	94158 18134	Tiny gate/stile
Map 69	803	NY	93376 18192	Two routes rejoin in Baldersdale

Cross A66

Map 68	089	54°30.779'	02°04.150'	Guidepost by ford at wall corner
Map 68	090	54°31.098'	02°04.176'	Cairn
Map 68	091	54°31.182'	02°04.303'	Hill top cairn – Ravock Castle
Map 68	092	54°31.587'	02°04.600'	Guidepost before you drop to fo'

Cross A66 (cont'd)

MAP NO	REF	GPS WAYPOINT		DESCRIPTION
Map 69	093	54°32.412'	02°05.363'	Two fallen stone posts by gate
Map 69	094	54°32.716'	02°05.499'	Post
Map 69	095	54°33.224'	02°05.951'	Path joins road

Baldersdale

Map 70	096	54°34.727'	02°06.527'	Rail sleeper Guidepost
Map 71	097	54°36.152'	02°07.152'	Stile with white paint
Map 71	098	54°36.297'	02°06.826'	Ruined barn
Map 72	099	54°36.832'	02°05.451'	Stile with dog slot by black gate

Middleton-in-Teesdale

Map 76	100	54°38.921'	02°12.722'	Rail wagon near hill top

Langdon Beck

Map 78	101	54°39.048'	02°15.757'	First rockfall; start of duckboards
Map 78	102	54°38.868'	02°16.361'	Cairn after second rockfall
Map 79	103	54°38.447'	02°18.943'	Old spoil tip
Map 79	104	54°38.304'	02°20.068'	Cairn near sign – high point
Map 80	105	54°38.158'	02°21.723'	New bridge at Maize Beck

Maize Beck alternative route – OS only

Map 80	505	NY	76633	26884	New bridge at Maize Beck
Map 80	506	NY	76132	26877	Cross stream near beck
Map 80	507	NY	75313	26918	Hop across stream, path re-appears
Map 81	508	NY	74924	26942	Path reaches lower gorge
Map 81	509	NY	74898	27101	Old footbridge and sign
Map 81	510	NY	74742	27008	Between two mileposts
Map 81	511	NY	74615	26873	Mossy cairn
Map 81	512	NY	74519	26646	Eroded limestone pavement
Map 81	513	NY	74436	26440	Milepost – close to High Cup Nick
Map 81	514	NY	74422	26305	Alternative route meets main route at milepost

Map 80	106	54°38.088'	02°22.249'	Red stone milepost
Map 80	107	54°37.912'	02°23.333'	Milepost, High Cup Nick near...
Map 81	108	54°37.834'	02°23.772'	Alternative route meets main route at milepost
Map 81	109	54°37.629'	02°24.497'	Cross two streams
Map 81	110	54°37.592'	02°24.648'	Milepost with another below
Map 82	111	54°37.168'	02°25.822'	Walled enclosure – easy track down

Dufton

Map 83	112	54°38.260'	02°28.702'	Halstead (derelict) out on open land
Map 84	113	54°38.911'	02°28.072'	Path leaves track to left and contours hill at signpost
Map 84	114	54°39.088'	02°27.833'	Sign
Map 85	115	54°39.244'	02°27.433'	Two cairns close together
Map 85	116	54°39.314'	02°27.204'	Guidepost with yellow mark
Map 85	117	54°39.431'	02°26.831'	Cairn with fallen stick
Map 85	118	54°39.649'	02°26.602'	Milepost before crossing and recrossing stream
Map 85	119	54°39.736'	02°26.402'	Milepost
Map 85	120	54°39.800'	02°26.337'	Cairn before hairpins
Map 85	121	54°39.843'	02°26.243'	Flooded hole
Map 85	122	54°39.901'	02°26.029'	Knock Old Man cairn

Dufton (cont'd)

MAP NO	REF	GPS WAYPOINT		DESCRIPTION
Map 85	123	54°39.987'	02°25.912'	Knock Fell summit
Map 85	124	54°40.110'	02°25.927'	Faint path resumes
Map 85	125	54°40.171'	02°26.005'	Pass west of slabs
Map 85	126	54°40.368'	02°26.128'	Slabs curve around tarn
Map 85	127	54°40.620'	02°26.293'	Join tracking station access road
Map 85	128	54°40.718'	02°26.395'	Leave access road
Map 85	129	54°40.825'	02°26.639'	Flat topped block followed by cairn before Dun Fell Hush
Map 85	130	54°40.859'	02°26.765'	North edge of Dunfell Hush
Map 86	131	54°41.057'	02°26.900'	Just east of Great Dun Fell Radar station
Map 86	132	54°41.466'	02°27.500'	Little Dun Fell summit
Map 86	133	54°41.845'	02°28.071'	Red sign near electric fence!
Map 87	134	54°42.061'	02°28.506'	Tall cairn on edge of summit plateau
Map 87	135	54°42.156'	02°28.818'	Bell-shaped cairn
Map 87	136	54°42.183'	02°29.088'	Cross Fell summit
Map 87	137	54°42.282'	02°29.142'	Another shapely cairn before steep drop
Map 87	138	54°42.654'	02°29.427'	Path from Cross Fell meets Corpse Rd at cairn
Map 87	139	54°42.770'	02°28.789'	Greg's Hut
Map 88	140	54°43.045'	02°28.035'	Very ruined ruin
Map 88	141	54°43.037'	02°26.852'	Stream
Map 89	142	54°43.061'	02°26.725'	Old mine workings
Map 89	143	54°43.113'	02°26.547'	Omega sign to east – short cut the track
Map 89	144	54°43.290'	02°26.340'	Short cut rejoins track
Map 89	145	54°43.526'	02°26.124'	A track joins from west
Map 89	146	54°43.633'	02°26.064'	A track joins from east; white cairn/gate to east
Map 89	147	54°44.528'	02°25.768'	Path leaves wall near 'bird huts'
Map 90	148	54°45.085'	02°25.163'	Gate at walled lane down to Garrigill

Garrigill

Map 92	149	54°46.678'	02°25.408'	Three-way signpost by river
Map 92	150	54°46.812'	02°25.712'	Bridge over South Tyne
Map 93	151	54°47.097'	02°26.234'	Gate with yellow marks by two trees
Map 93	152	54°47.854'	02°26.369'	Footbridge
Map 93	153	54°48.196'	02°26.400'	Small gate over stream meets path to Alston

Alston

Map 95	154	54°49.225'	2°27.727'	Take direct route to Gilderdale Burn crossing
Map 95	155	54°49.795'	2°28.634'	Approaching Whitley Castle
Map 97	156	54°52.271'	2°30.722'	Leave South Tyne Trail at sliding gate, head up hill
Map 97	157	54°52.425'	2°30.794'	Merry Knowe terrace
Map 98	158	54°53.244'	2°30.636'	Leave track to right (Maiden Way)
Map 98	159	54°53.497'	2°30.556'	Gate after ford, then descent
Map 98	160	54°54.952'	2°31.098'	Pass stile on left
Map 99	161	54°55.101'	2°31.195'	Second stile, cross and head past stone marker
Map 99	162	54°55.238'	2°31.509'	A689 road crossing
Map 99	163	54°55.435'	2°31.601'	Head for stone on mound
Map 99	164	54°55.935'	2°31.814'	Ruin

Alston (cont'd)

MAP NO	REF	GPS WAYPOINT		DESCRIPTION
Map 99	165	54°56.144'	2°31.655'	Top of the wooded bank
Map 99	166	54°56.234'	2°31.923'	Guidepost
Map 100	167	54°56.391'	2°32.271'	Ulpham Farm barn with red doors
Map 100	168	54°56.897'	2°32.513'	Gate near Highside Farm
Map 100	169	54°57.332'	2°33.267'	Point on wall and Pennine Way
Map 100	170	54°57.629'	2°33.332'	Corner of wall on left
Map 100	171	54°57.938'	2°33.512'	Gate east of Black Hill summit
Map 101	172	54°58.179'	2°33.649'	After pylons, join track near hut
Map 101	173	54°58.395'	2°33.613'	Leave track to left
Map 102	174	54°58.345'	2°32.683'	Turn right, go along edge of golf course

Greenhead

Map 105	175	55°00.151'	2°24.367'	Path south-east to Winshields Farm
Map 106	176	55°00.705'	2°20.555'	Rapishaw Gap; leave Wall, north-north-east
Map 107	177	55°01.557'	2°20.622'	Guidepost after slabs
Map 107	178	55°01.875'	2°20.679'	Join Forestry track, turn right
Map 107	179	55°02.468'	2°20.563'	Leave Forestry track to right
Map 108	180	55°02.893'	2°20.149'	Leave trees for open land
Map 108	181	55°03.378'	2°19.094'	Back into the forest
Map 109	182	55°04.880'	2°17.807'	Waterfall
Map 109	183	55°05.239'	2°17.592'	Turn left downhill to river
Map 111	184	55°06.741'	2°16.060'	Near Houxty Burn

Bellingham

Map 112	185	55°09.349'	2°14.456'	Guidepost
Map 112	186	55°09.591'	2°14.529'	Cross wall after stiff ascent
Map 113	187	55°10.068'	2°14.492'	Pipe and plank
Map 114	188	55°11.476'	2°14.879'	Guidepost after crossing B6320
Map 114	189	55°11.892'	2°14.716'	Guidepost after Lough Shaw summit
Map 114	190	55°12.381'	2°14.950'	West of Deer Play summit
Map 114	191	55°12.506'	2°15.176'	Guidepost with white band
Map 115	192	55°12.630'	2°15.257'	Guidepost
Map 115	193	55°12.905'	2°16.088'	Whitley Pike
Map 116	194	55°14.118'	2°17.523'	Wall at base of climb
Map 116	195	55°14.573'	2°17.319'	Lone pine after forest climb
Map 117	196	55°15.251'	2°18.998'	Forestry Commission sign, track starts
Map 117	197	55°15.673'	2°19.087'	Leave track to left for parallel path
Map 117	198	55°16.013'	2°19.296'	Rejoin forestry track

Byrness

Map 120	199	55°19.389'	2°21.429'	Byrness Hill summit
Map 121	200	55°20.966'	2°20.797'	Ravens Knowe
Map 121	201	55°21.496'	2°21.074'	Ministry of Defence (MoD) sign
Map 122	202	55°21.581'	2°21.142'	'Border Country Ride' on left
Map 122	203	55°21.943'	2°21.164'	After stream, turn right
Map 122	204	55°22.031'	2°20.936'	Guidepost. Fork left down to Chew Green
Map 123	205	55°22.346'	2°20.127'	Turn right along Dere St, away from Chew Green
Map 123	206	55°23.326'	2°20.017'	Green sign as you leave Dere Street
Map 124	207	55°23.677'	2°20.070'	Cross stream
Map 124	208	55°23.944'	2°19.976'	Cairn

Byrness (cont'd)

MAP NO	REF	GPS WAYPOINT		DESCRIPTION
Map 124	209	55°24.130'	2°19.753'	Guidepost
Map 124	210	55°24.319'	2°19.441'	Gully (Rennies Burn)
Map 125	211	55°24.401'	2°18.700'	Turn corner to left
Map 125	212	55°24.573'	2°18.560'	First refuge hut
Map 125	213	55°24.807'	2°17.952'	Lamb Hill summit
Map 125	214	55°25.219'	2°17.536'	Turn right, slabs
Map 126	215	55°25.720'	2°16.232'	Mozie Law summit
Map 126	216	55°25.712'	2°15.644'	Turn left towards sign
Map 127	217	55°25.891'	2°14.266'	Saddle. Steeply up to Windy Gyle
Map 127	218	55°25.821'	2°13.700'	Windy Gyle summit (Russell's Cairn)
Map 127	219	55°25.923'	2°13.269'	Rejoin wall
Map 127	220	55°26.004'	2°13.156'	Extensive pile of stones
Map 128	221	55°26.281'	2°12.203'	Sign for Uswayford Farm B&B
Map 129	222	55°26.726'	2°11.580'	Saddle
Map 129	223	55°26.988'	2°11.483'	Kings Seat
Map 129	224	55°27.631'	2°11.194'	Slabs end
Map 130	225	55°28.002'	2°10.154'	Outcrop with memorial plaque
Map 130	226	55°28.071'	2°09.900'	Ahead for The Cheviot, left for Auchope Cairn
Map 130	227	55°28.340'	2°10.349'	Auchope Cairn
Map 131	228	55°28.509'	2°11.670'	Second refuge hut
Map 131	229	55°29.022'	2°12.215'	Saddle
Map 131	230	55°29.675'	2°12.374'	The Schil summit
Map 132	231	55°30.196'	2°12.943'	Stile not to be missed
Map 132	232	55°30.308'	2°13.357'	High and Low routes diverge
Map 132	233	55°30.748'	2°14.115'	Saddle, wall, Guidepost
Map 132	234	55°31.232'	2°14.065'	Old Halterburn ruin. Tree
Map 134	235	55°32.546'	2°15.252'	High route rejoins from right

INDEX

Page references in bold type refer to maps

access 66-8
accidents 68
accommodation 13-18, 72, *see also place name*
accommodation, booking in advance 13
agricultural shows 24
Aiggin Stone 92, **95**
Airton 26, 117, 125, **127**
Alston 26-7, 195, 201, **203**, **204**, 204-5
annual events 24
Appleby 192
areas of outstanding natural beauty (AONBs) 60
ATMs 26
Auchope Cairn 238, **248**

B&Bs 16, 21, 27, 30
Backpackers Club 37, 38
baggage-forwarding services 20, 64
Baldersdale 26-7, 163, **171**, 172
bank holidays 17
banks 20
Barber Booth 74
bed and breakfasts 16, 21, 27, 30
Bellingham 24, 26-7, 228, **228**, **229**, 230
birds 51-6
birdwatching 37
Birkdale 177, **185**, 186
black grouse 53, 156
Black Hill (nr Crowden) 86, **87**
Black Hill (Greenhead) 206, **212**
Blackshaw Head 26-7, 92, 102
Blackstone Edge 92, 94, **95**
Blakehope Burn 230, **237**
Bleaklow Head 76, **81**
Blenkinsopp Common 206, **212**
blisters 35, 69
bogs 48
bookings 13-18
books 37
boots 34
Bowes 24, 26-7, 165, **167**
Bowes variant route 163, **167-9**
Brontës of Haworth 112
budgeting 21
bunkhouses 15, 21, 29
Burnhead 26-7, 218, **219**
bus services 44-6

business hours 17
Byrness 26-7, 238, **239**

cafés 27
Calder Valley 99, **100**
Cam End 141, **143**
Campaign to Protect Rural England (CPRE) 61
camping 21
camping barns 15, 29
camping gear 36, 38
camping supplies 19
camping, wild 14, 28
campsites 14, 27, 28
cash machines 26
Cauldron Snout 177, **184**
cell phones 17, 36
Chew Green Roman camp **242**
climate 23
clothing 35
Clough Edge 76, **82**
coach services 41, 45
Colden 26-7, 103, **104**, 107
Coldwell Hill 92, **97**
compass 36
conservation 58-62
cooking gear 14, 19
Corpse Road miners' track 192, **196-9**
Countryside Code 66-7
Cow Green Reservoir 177
Cowling 26-7, 115, **116**
Crag Lough 216, **221**, **222**
Cronkley Bridge 177, **183**
Cross Fell 193, **196**
Crowden 26-7, 76, **83**, 84
curlew 54

day walks 31
daylight hours 23
Deer Play 230, **232**
DEFRA 60
dehydration 70
Dere St Roman road **242**
Devil's Dyke 76
dialects 38
difficulty 9
Diggle 26-7, 90
Dodd Fell 141, **146**

dogs, walking with 24
Douk Ghyll Scar **139**
driving 41
Dufton 24, 26-7, 178, 188-9, **191**, 192
Dufton Fell 192
duration 12

Earby 26-7, **120**, 121
East Marton 26-7, 117, 121, **122**
economic impact 63-4
Edale 24, 26-7, 72-4, **73**
Edale Cross 74
emergency services 68
emergency signal 68
English Heritage 60
environmental impact 64-6
equipment 33-9
erosion 65
Eshton Moor 117, **126**
exposure 69

fairs, country 24
fell running 140
festivals 24
field barns 153
first-aid kit 35
flora and fauna 47-62
flowers, wild 37, 47
food shops 27
footwear 34
forecast, weather 69
forests 49-51
Forest-in-Teesdale 26-7, 177, 182
Forestry Commission 50, 60
Fountains Fell 131, **134**, 138
fungi 49

Gargrave 24, 26-7, 117, 123, **124**, 125, **125**
Garrigill 26-7, 193, **200**
God's Bridge 163, **166**
Google Earth 39
GPS 10-12
GPS waypoints 256-262
gradients 10
Grain Beck 178, **185**
Graining Water 103, **105**
grasses 47-9
Great Dun Fell 192, **195**
Great Shunner Fell 151
Greenhead 26-7, 214, **215**, 216
Greg's Hut 192, 196, **196**

Grindsbrook Clough 76
group walking tours 20
grouse shooting 67
guesthouses 18

Hadfield 26-7, 84
Hadrian's Wall **215**, **217**, 218, **219**, **221**, **222**
Hannah's Meadow 172, **173**
Hardraw 24, 26-7, 151, 152, **152**
Harter Fell 163, **174**
Hartley Burn 205, **211**
hats 35
Hauxwell, Hannah 172, 186
Hawes 24, 26-7, 141, 147, 149-51, **148**, **149**
Haworth 26-7, 103, 110-13, **111**
headwear 35
heat exhaustion 70
heatstroke 70
heather 49
Hebden Bridge 24, 26-7, 92, 99-102, **101**
Heptonstall Moor 103
Hetherington 26-7, 226, **226**
High Cup 178, **187**, 188
High Force 26-7, 177, **180**, 181, 182
highlights 31-2
history 9
holidays, school 17
Holwick 26-7, 179, **179**
Horton-in-Ribblesdale 26-7, 131, 138, **139**, 140
hostels 15, 21, 27, 29
hotels 18
Housesteads Fort 218
hyperthermia 70
hypothermia 69

Ickornshaw 26-7, 115, **116**
Ickornshaw Moor 103
information
  further sources 37
  National Parks 37
  walkers' associations 37
inns 18
insurance, travel/medical 17
itineraries 25-8

Jack Bridge **104**, 107
Jackdaw Hill 140, **142**
Jacob's Ladder 74, **77**

Keld 26-7, 151, 158, **159**
KFC 161
Kidhow Gate 141, **146**
Kinder Downfall 74, **78**
Kinder Edges 74
Kinder Low 74, **77**
Kinder Scout **75**, 76, **77**
Kirk Yetholm 26-7, 241, 252-3, **253**
Kirkby Malham 26-7, 117, **127**, 128
Kisdon Hill 151, **159**
Knarsdale 26-7, 208, **209**
Knock Fell 192, **194**

Laddow Rocks 84, **85**
lambing 67
Langdon Beck 26-7, 177, 182, **183**
lapwing 55
lead mining 197
Ling Gill 141, **143**
Little Dun Fell 192, **195**
local businesses 63
Local Nature Reserves (LNRs) 60-1
local transport 41, 44-6
Long Distance Walkers' Association 38
Longendale Valley 76
Lothersdale 26-7, 117, **118**
Low Force 177, **180**
Lumbutts **97**
Lunedale 26-7, **174**, 175

Maiden Way 205, **210**
Maize Beck 178, **185**, **187**
Maize Beck Gorge route 186, **187**, 188, **189**
Malham 24, 26-7, 117, 128, **129**, 130-1, **130**
Malham Cove **129**, 131
mammals 56-8
Mankinholes 26-7, 92, 94, **97**, 99
map keys 255
map, public transport 42
map scale 71
maps 38, 39, 71
Middleton-in-Teesdale 24, 26-7, 175-7, **175**, **176**
Mill Hill 74
Millstone Edge **91**, 92
minimum impact walking 63-8
mobile phones 17, 36
money 19
Muker 26-7, 158
Mytholm **100**, 103

National Nature Reserves (NNRs) 60-1
national parks 59, 60
  information 37
national trails 60
National Trust 61
Natural England 59, 60
Nether Booth 74
Northumberland National Park 60

Once Brewed 26-7, 216, 220, **221**
opening hours 17
orchids 48
owls 56

packhorse roads 141
Padfield 26-7, 84
Padon Hill 230, **234**
Peak District National Park 60
peat 79
Pen-y-ghent 131, **136**, 140
Pinhaw Beacon 117, 119
poles, walking 36
Ponden 26-7, 103, 108, **109**
post offices 20, 26-7
poste restante 20
public transport
  maps 42-3
  services 44-6
pubs 17, 18, 19, 27

Race Yate 163, **171**
rail services 40-1, 46
rainfall, average 23
Ramblers Association 37, 38
Rapishaw Gap 216, **222**
Ravock Castle 163, **170**
Redesdale Forest 230, **234**
Redmires 92, **95**
refuge huts 238
rehydration 70
reptiles 58
restaurants 27
Ribble Way **137**
Right to Roam 66-8
River Rede 230, **237**
Rottenstone Hill 141, **147**
route finding 10
Royal Society for the Protection of Birds (RSPB) 61, 62
rucksacks 33

safety, outdoor 68-70
satellite images 39
Scaleber Hill 117
Schil, The 238, **249**
seasons 22, 65
self-guided holidays 20
Shitlington Crag 216, 227
shops, food 27
Sites of Special Scientific Interest (SSSIs) 61, 172
slabs 9, 238
Slaggyford 26-7, 205, 208, **209**
sleeping bags 36
Sleightholme Moor 163, **164**
Snaizeholme Valley **146**
Snake Pass 76, 80
socks 34
South Tyne Trail 205, 206
Special Areas of Conservation (SACs) 61
St Cuthbert's Way 254
Stanbury 26-7, 108, **109**, 110
Standedge 26-7, 89-90, **91**
Standedge Cutting 89, **91**
Stephenson, Tom 9
stone slabs 9, 238
Stonehaugh 26-7, 216, 224
Stonesdale Moor 151, **160**
Stoodley Pike 92, **98**, 99
sunburn 70
Swaledale 24, 151

Tan Hill **162**
Tan Hill Inn 26-7, 151, 161, **162**
telephone, mobile 17
temperatures, average 23
Thirlwall Castle 214, **215**
Thornton-in-Craven 24, 26-7, 117, **120**, 121
Three Peaks Challenge 24, 140
Thwaite 26-7, 151, **157**, 158
Time, British Summer (BST) 17
time needed 12
toiletries 35
toilet paper, disposal 65
Top Withins **108**
Torside 26-7, **83**, 84
tourist information centres 26, 37
tours, guided 20
Town Yetholm 26-7, 253, **253**
town/village facilities 26-7
trail information 37
trail maps 71

trail map key 255
transport, local 41, 44-6
transport, national 40
travel insurance 17
trees 49-51
Twice Brewed 24

Upper Booth 26-7, 74, **75**, 80
Uswayford 26-7, 244

village and town facilities 26-7

walkers' associations 37
walkers' organizations 37
walking companies 20
walking poles 36
walking season 22-3
walking times 71
walking tours 20
Walltown Crags **215**, 216, **217**
Walshaw Dean reservoirs 103, **106**, **107**
Wark Forest 216, **223**
water filters 19
water, drinking 18-19
waypoints 256-62
waypoints online 11
weather forecast 69
websites 37
weekend walks 32
Wensleydale Creamery 149, **149**
Wessenden Head 86, **87**
whistle 36, 68
White Law 241, **251**
Whitley Pike 230, **233**
Widdop **106**, 107
wild camping 14, 28
wild flowers 37, 47-9
wildlife 37, 56-8, 65
Wildlife Trusts, The 61
Windy Gyle 238, 246
Winshields Crag **221**
Withams Moor 163
Withen's Gate 92, **97**
Withens Height 103, **108**
Woodland Trust 61
woodlands 48, 49, 50, 51
Wytham Moor 163, **166**

Yetholm 24
YHA hostels 16
Yorkshire Dales National Park 60
youth hostels 16

Himalaya by Bike – a route & planning guide
Laura Stone 336pp, 28 colour & 50 B&W photos, 60 maps
ISBN 978 1 905864 04 1, *1st edn*, £14.99, – **due mid 2008**
An all-in-one guide for Himalayan cycle-touring. Covers the Himalayan regions of Pakistan, Tibet, India, Nepal and Sikkim with detailed km-by-km guides to main routes including the Karakoram Highway and the Friendship Highway. Plus town and city guides.

Adventure Motorcycling Handbook – a route & planning guide *Chris Scott, 5th edn*, 288pp, 28 colour & 100 B&W photos
ISBN 978 1 873756 80 5, £12.99
Every red-blooded motor-cyclist dreams of making the Big Trip – this book shows you how. Top ten overland machines, choosing a destination, bike preparation, documentation and shipping, route outlines. Plus – ten first-hand accounts of epic biking adventures worldwide.
'The first thing we did was buy the Adventure Motorcycling Handbook*.'*
Ewan McGregor, *The Long Way Round*

Adventure Cycle-Touring Handbook – a route & planning guide *Stephen Lord*, 320pp, 28 colour & 100 B&W photos
ISBN 978 1 873756 89 8, *1st edition*, £13.99
Now guide for anyone planning (or dreaming) about taking a bicycle on a long-distance adventure. This comprehensive manual will make that dream a reality whether it's cycling in Tibet or pedalling from Patagonia to Alaska. Part 1 covers Practicalities; Part 2 includes Route outlines; and Part 3 has Tales from the Saddle.'*The definitive guide to how, where, why and what to do on a cycle expedition*' *Adventure Travel*

Tibet Overland – a route & planning guide *Kym McConnell*
1st edition, 224pp, 16pp colour maps
ISBN 978 1 873756 41 6, £12.99
Featuring 16pp of full colour mapping based on satellite photographs, this is a guide for mountain bikers and other road users in Tibet. Includes detailed information on over 9000km of overland routes across the world's highest and largest plateau. Includes Lhasa–Kathmandu route and the route to Everest North Base Camp. '*... a wealth of advice...*' *HH The Dalai Lama*

Sahara Overland – a route & planning guide *Chris Scott*
2nd edition, 640 pages, 24 colour & 170 B&W photos
ISBN 978 1 873756 76 8 Hardback £19.99
Fully-updated 2nd edition covers all aspects Saharan, from acquiring documentation to vehicle choice and preparation; from descriptions of the prehistoric art sites of the Libyan Fezzan to the ancient caravan cities of southern Mauritania. How to 'read' sand surfaces, using GPS – it's all here along with detailed off-road itineraries covering 26,000kms in nine countries. '*THE essential desert companion for anyone planning a Saharan trip on either two wheels or four.*' *Trailbike Magazine*

Trans-Siberian Handbook *Bryn Thomas*
7th edition, 448pp, 60 maps, 40 colour photos
ISBN 978 1 873756 94 2, £13.99
First edition short-listed for the **Thomas Cook Guidebook Awards**. New seventh edition of the most popular guide to the world's longest rail journey. How to arrange a trip, plus a km-by-km guide to the routes. Updated and expanded to include extra information on travelling independently in Russia. New mapping. '*The best guidebook is Bryn Thomas's "Trans-Siberian Handbook"*' *The Independent*

TREKKING GUIDES

Europe
Corsica Trekking – GR20
Dolomites Trekking – AV1 & AV2
Scottish Highlands – The Hillwalking Guide
Tour de Mont Blanc
Trekking in the Pyrenees
Walker's Haute Route: Mt Blanc to Matterhorn

Africa
Kilimanjaro

South America
Inca Trail, Cusco & Machu Picchu

Australasia
New Zealand – The Great Walks

Asia
Trekking in the Annapurna Region
Trekking in the Everest Region
Trekking in Ladakh
Nepal Mountaineering Guide

The Walkers' Haute Route – Mt Blanc to the Matterhorn
Alexander Stewart 224pp, 60 maps, 30 colour photos
ISBN 978-1-905864-08-9, £11.99   **due mid 2008**
From Mont Blanc to the Matterhorn, Chamonix to Zermatt, the 180km walkers' Haute Route traverses one of the finest stretches of the Pennine Alps – the range between Valais in Switzerland and Piedmont and Aosta Valley in Italy. Includes Chamonix and Zermatt guides.

Tour du Mont Blanc   *Jim Manthorpe*
1st edition, 224pp, 60 maps, 30 colour photos
ISBN 978-1-905864-12-6, £11.99   **due mid 2008**
At 4807m (15,771ft), Mont Blanc is the highest mountain in western Europe, and one of the most famous mountains in the world. The trail (105 miles, 168km) that circumnavigates the massif, passing through France, Italy and Switzerland, is the most popular long distance walk in Europe. Includes Chamonix and Courmayeur guides.

Scottish Highlands – The Hillwalking Guide
1st edition, Jim Manthorpe   312pp, 86 maps, 40 photos
ISBN 978-1-873756-84-3, £11.99
This guide covers 60 day-hikes in the following areas: ● Loch Lomond, the Trossachs and Southern Highlands ● Glen Coe and Ben Nevis ● Central Highlands ● Cairngorms and Eastern Highlands ● Western Highlands ● North-West Highlands ● The Far North ● The Islands. Plus: 3- to 4-day hikes linking some regions.

New Zealand – The Great Walks   *Alexander Stewart*
1st edition, 272pp, 60 maps, 40 colour photos
ISBN 978-1-873756-78-2, £11.99
New Zealand is a wilderness paradise of incredibly beautiful land-scapes. There is no better way to experience it than on one of the nine designated Great Walks, the country's premier walking tracks which provide outstanding hiking opportunities for people at all levels of fitness. Also includes detailed guides to Auckland, Wellington, National Park Village, Taumaranui, Nelson, Queenstown, Te Anau and Oban.

Kilimanjaro: the trekking guide to Africa's highest mountain
Henry Stedman, 2nd edition, 320pp, 40 maps, 30 photos
ISBN 978-1-873756-97-1, £11.99
At 19,340ft the world's tallest freestanding mountain, Kilimanjaro is one of the most popular destinations for hikers visiting Africa. It's possible to walk up to the summit: no technical skills are necessary. Includes town guides to Nairobi and Dar-Es-Salaam, excursions in the region and a detailed colour guide to flora and fauna. **Includes Mount Meru.**   *'Stedman's wonderfully down-to-earth, practical guide to the mountain'. **Longitude Books***

Corsica Trekking – GR20 *David Abram*
1st edition, 208pp, 32 maps, 30 colour photos
ISBN 978-1-873756-98-0, £11.99
Slicing diagonally across Corsica's jagged spine, the legendary red-and-white waymarks of the GR20 guide trekkers across a succession of snow-streaked passes, Alpine meadows, massive boulder fields and pristine forests of pine and oak – often within sight of the sea. Physically demanding from start to finish, it's a superlative 170km, two-week trek. Includes guides to gateway towns: Ajaccio, Bastia, Calvi, Corte and Porte-Vecchio. *'Indispensible'. The Independent 'Excellent guide'. The Sunday Times*

Trekking in the Pyrenees *Douglas Streatfeild-James*
3rd edition, 320pp, 97 maps, 60 colour photos
ISBN 978-1-873756-82-9, £11.99
All the main trails along the France-Spain border including the GR10 (France) coast to coast trek and the GR11 (Spain) from Roncesvalles to Andorra, plus many shorter routes. 90 route maps include walking times and places to stay. *'Readily accessible, well-written'. John Cleare*

Dolomites Trekking Alta Via 1 & Alta Via 2 *Henry Stedman*
2nd edn, 192pp, 52 trail maps, 7 town plans, 38 colour photos
ISBN 978-1-873756-83-6, £11.99
AV1 (9-13 days) & AV2 (10-16 days) are the most popular long-distance hikes in the Dolomites. Numerous shorter walks also included. Places to stay, walking times and points of interest, plus detailed guides to Cortina and six other towns.

The Inca Trail, Cusco & Machu Picchu *Richard Danbury*
3rd edition 320pp, 65 maps, 35 colour photos
ISBN 978-1-873756-86-7, £11.99
The **Inca Trail** from Cusco to Machu Picchu is South America's most popular trek. Practical guide including detailed trail maps, plans of Inca sites, plus guides to Cusco and Machu Picchu. This expanded third edition includes new guides to the **Santa Teresa Trek** and the **Choquequirao Trek** as well as the **Vilcabamba Trail**. *'Danbury's research is thorough... you need this one'. The Sunday Times*

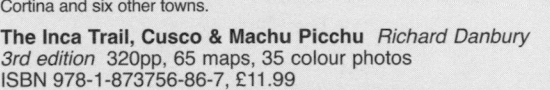

Trekking in Ladakh *Charlie Loram*
3rd edition, 288pp, 75 maps, 24 colour photos
ISBN 978-1-873756-75-1, £12.99
Fully revised and extended 3rd edition of Charlie Loram's practical guide. Includes 75 detailed walking maps, guides to Leh, Manali and Delhi plus information on getting to Ladakh. *'Extensive...and well researched'. Climber Magazine 'Were it not for this book we might still be blundering about...' The Independent on Sunday*

Trekking in the Annapurna Region *Bryn Thomas*
4th edition, 288pp, 55 maps, 28 colour photos
ISBN 978-1-873756-68-3, £11.99
Fully revised guide to the most popular walking region in the Himalaya. Includes route guides, Kathmandu and Pokhara city guides and getting to Nepal. *'Good guides read like a novel and have you packing in no time. Two from Trailblazer Publications which fall into this category are* 'Trekking in the Annapurna Region' *and* 'Silk Route by Rail' *'. Today*

TRAILBLAZER'S LONG-DISTANCE PATH (LDP) WALKING GUIDES

We've applied to destinations which are closer to home Trailblazer's proven formula for publishing definitive route guides for adventurous travellers. Britain's network of long-distance trails enables the walker to explore some of the finest landscapes in the country's best walking areas and they are an obvious starting point for this series. These are guides that are user-friendly, practical, informative and environmentally sensitive.

● **Unique mapping features**
In many walking guidebooks the reader has to read a route description then try to relate it to the map. Our guides are much easier to use because walking directions, tricky junctions, places to stay and eat, points of interest and walking times are all written onto the maps themselves in the places to which they apply. With their uncluttered clarity, these are not general-purpose maps but fully edited maps **drawn by walkers for walkers**.

● **Largest-scale walking maps**
At a scale of just under 1:20,000 (8cm or 3⅛ inches to one mile) the maps in these guides are bigger than even the most detailed British walking maps currently available in the shops.

● **Not just a trail guide – includes where to stay, where to eat and public transport** Our guidebooks are a complete guide, not just a trail guide. They include: what to see, where to stay (pubs, hotels, B&Bs, campsites, bunkhouses, hostels), where to eat. There is detailed public transport information for all access points to each trail so there are itineraries for all walkers, both for hiking the route in its entirety and for day walks.

West Highland Way *Charlie Loram* ISBN 978-1-905864-13-3, £9.99
3rd edition, 192pp, 53 maps, 10 town plans, 40 colour photos

Pennine Way *Keith Carter & Chris Scott* ISBN 978-1-905864-02-7, £11.99
2nd edition, 272pp, 135 maps & town plans, 40 colour photos

Coast to Coast *Henry Stedman* ISBN 978-1-905864-09-6, £9.99
3rd edition, 240pp, 109 maps & town plans, 40 colour photos

Pembrokeshire Coast Path *Jim Manthorpe* ISBN 978-1-905864-03-4, £9.99
2nd edition, 208pp, 96 maps & town plans, 40 colour photos

Offa's Dyke Path *Keith Carter* ISBN 978-1-905864-06-5, £9.99
2nd edition, 208pp, 88 maps & town plans, 40 colour photos

South Downs Way *Jim Manthorpe* ISBN 978-1-873756-95-9, £9.99
2nd edition, 192pp, 60 maps & town plans, 40 colour photos

Hadrian's Wall Path *Henry Stedman* ISBN 978-1-905864-14-0, £9.99
2nd edition, 192pp, 60 maps & town plans, 40 colour photos

North Downs Way *John Curtin* ISBN 978-1-873756-96-6, £9.99
1st edition, 192pp, 60 maps & town plans, 40 colour photos

The Ridgeway *Nick Hill* ISBN 978-1-873756-88-1, £9.99
1st edition, 192pp, 53 maps & town plans, 40 colour photos

Cornwall Coast Path *Edith Schofield* ISBN 978-1-873756-93-5, £9.99
2nd edition, 224pp, 112 maps & town plans, 40 colour photos

'The same attention to detail that distinguishes its other guides has been brought to bear here'. **The Sunday Times**

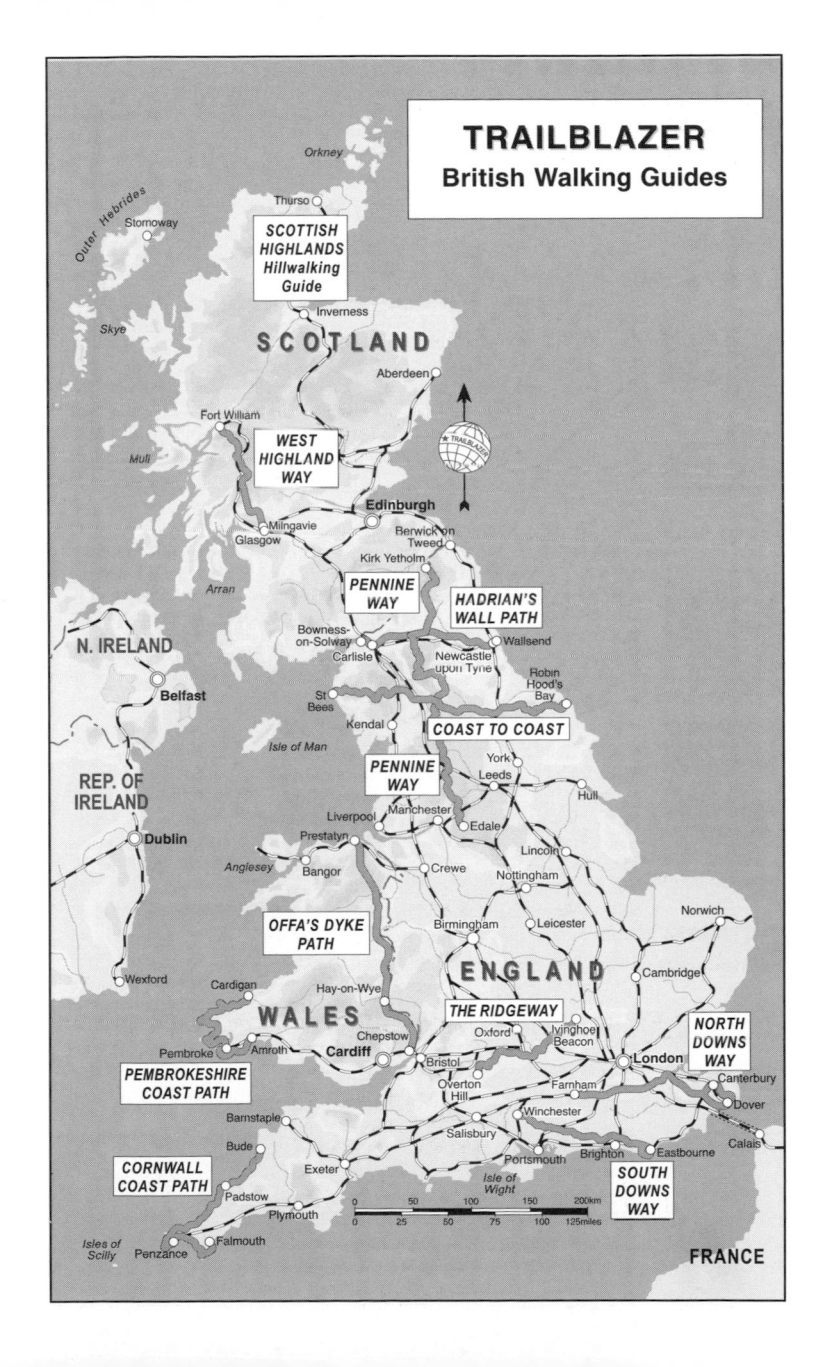

TRAILBLAZER
British Walking Guides

Orkney

Thurso

Outer Hebrides

Stornoway

SCOTTISH
HIGHLANDS
Hillwalking
Guide

Skye

Inverness

SCOTLAND

Aberdeen

TRAILBLAZER

Muli

Fort William

WEST
HIGHLAND
WAY

Milngavie
Glasgow

Edinburgh

Berwick on
Tweed

Arran

Kirk Yetholm

PENNINE
WAY

HADRIAN'S
WALL PATH

N. IRELAND

Bowness-
on-Solway

Carlisle

Wallsend

Newcastle
upon Tyne

Belfast

St
Bees

Robin
Hood's
Bay

COAST TO COAST

Kendal

REP. OF
IRELAND

Isle of Man

PENNINE
WAY

York

Leeds

Hull

Liverpool

Manchester

Dublin

Prestatyn

Edale

Anglesey

Bangor

Crewe

Lincoln

Nottingham

Norwich

OFFA'S DYKE
PATH

Birmingham

Leicester

ENGLAND

Cambridge

Wexford

Cardigan

Hay-on-Wye

WALES

THE RIDGEWAY

NORTH
DOWNS
WAY

Pembroke

Amroth

Chepstow

Cardiff

Bristol

Oxford

Ivinghoe
Beacon

London

Canterbury

PEMBROKESHIRE
COAST PATH

Overton
Hill

Farnham

Dover

Barnstaple

Winchester

Calais

Bude

Salisbury

Brighton

Eastbourne

CORNWALL
COAST PATH

Exeter

Portsmouth

SOUTH
DOWNS
WAY

Padstow

Plymouth

Isle of
Wight

Isles
of Scilly

Penzance

Falmouth

0   50   100   150   200km
0   25   50   75   100   125miles

FRANCE

TRAILBLAZER GUIDES – TITLE LIST

Adventure Cycle-Touring Handbook	1st edn out now
Adventure Motorcycling Handbook	5th edn out now
Australia by Rail	5th edn out now
Azerbaijan	3rd edn out now
The Blues Highway – New Orleans to Chicago	2nd edn out now
China Rail Handbook	1st edn late 2008
Coast to Coast (British Walking Guide)	3rd edn out now
Cornwall Coast Path (British Walking Guide)	2nd edn out now
Corsica Trekking – GR20	1st edn out now
Dolomites Trekking – AV1 & AV2	2nd edn out now
Inca Trail, Cusco & Machu Picchu	3rd edn out now
Indian Rail Handbook	1st edn mid 2008
Hadrian's Wall Walk (British Walking Guide)	2nd edn mid 2008
Himalaya by Bike – a route and planning guide	1st edn mid 2008
Japan by Rail	2nd edn out now
Kilimanjaro – the trekking guide (includes Mt Meru)	2nd edn out now
Mediterranean Handbook	1st edn out now
Nepal Mountaineering Guide	1st edn late 2008
New Zealand – The Great Walks	1st edn out now
North Downs Way (British Walking Guide)	1st edn out now
Norway's Arctic Highway	1st edn out now
Offa's Dyke Path (British Walking Guide)	2nd edn out now
Overlanders' Handbook – worldwide driving guide	1st edn early 2009
Pembrokeshire Coast Path (British Walking Guide)	2nd edn out now
Pennine Way (British Walking Guide)	2nd edn out now
The Ridgeway (British Walking Guide)	1st edn out now
Siberian BAM Guide – rail, rivers & road	2nd edn out now
The Silk Roads – a route and planning guide	2nd edn out now
Sahara Overland – a route and planning guide	2nd edn out now
Sahara Abenteuerhandbuch (German edition)	1st edn out now
Scottish Highlands – The Hillwalking Guide	1st edn out now
South Downs Way (British Walking Guide)	2nd edn out now
South-East Asia – The Graphic Guide	1st edn out now
Tibet Overland – mountain biking & jeep touring	1st edn out now
Tour du Mont Blanc	1st edn mid 2008
Trans-Canada Rail Guide	4th edn out now
Trans-Siberian Handbook	7th edn out now
Trekking in the Annapurna Region	4th edn out now
Trekking in the Everest Region	5th edn late 2008
Trekking in Ladakh	3rd edn out now
Trekking in the Pyrenees	3rd edn out now
The Walkers' Haute Route – Mont Blanc to Matterhorn	1st edn mid 2008
West Highland Way (British Walking Guide)	3rd edn mid 2008

www.trailblazer-guides.com